Medicine
and
Health
1988

GROLIER INCORPORATED, DANBURY, CONNECTICUT

Jean Paradise, *Group Editorial Director*
Robert Famighetti, *Executive Editor*
Zelda Haber, *Design Director*

EDITORIAL STAFF

John P. Elliott, *Senior Editor*
Jacqueline Laks Gorman, *Senior Editor*
Richard Hantula, *Senior Editor*
William A. McGeveran, Jr., *Senior Editor*

Terrence Adolph, *Associate Editor*
Michael Feist, *Associate Editor*
Anne L. Galperin, *Assistant Editor*
Ingrid Strauch, *Editorial Assistant*
Kay Blake, *Clerical Assistant*

Bryan H. Bunch, *Adjunct Editor*
Inez Salinger Glucksman, *Adjunct Editor*
AEIOU Inc., *Indexing*

ART/PRODUCTION STAFF

Joan Gampert, *Associate Design Director*
Marvin Friedman, *Senior Designer*
Marc Sferrazza, *Designer*
Adrienne Weiss, *Designer*
Joyce Deyo, *Photo Editor*
Margaret McRae, *Photo Editor*
Marcia Rackow, *Photo Editor*
Mynette Green, *Assistant Production Supervisor*
Valerie James, *Clerical Assistant*

Medicine and Health is not intended as a substitute for the medical advice of physicians. Readers should regularly consult a physician in matters relating to their health and particularly regarding symptoms that may require diagnosis or medical attention.

PUBLISHED BY GROLIER INCORPORATED 1988
This annual is also published as *Health & Medical Horizons 1988*.

Copyright © 1988 by Macmillan Educational Company
a division of Macmillan, Inc.

ISBN 0-7172-8203-1

Library of Congress Catalog Card Number 82-645223

Grolier Incorporated offers a varied selection of both adult and children's book racks. For details on ordering, please write:
Grolier Incorporated, Sherman Turnpike, Danbury, CT 06816, Attn: Premium Department.

Manufactured in the United States of America

For Your Health

Knowledge about the best ways to prevent and combat disease is growing constantly. This book will keep you up-to-date on the new advances and on what you can do to help yourself and your family stay healthy.

Page 16

Page 28

Page 102

FEATURE ARTICLES

Contents Continues

SPOTLIGHT ON HEALTH

A series of concise reports on practical health topics.

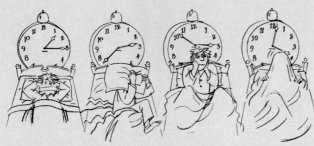

Health and Medical News

Learning to Relax

═══════════*Mark Deitch*═══════════

"Relax."

It's probably the commonest bit of everyday advice.

"Just relax." "Take it easy." "Go with the flow." "Be cool."

Easier said than done. As most of us know from harsh experience, simply telling an uptight person to simmer down rarely accomplishes that end. In fact, it usually serves only to turn up the heat. True relaxation is hard to come by, perhaps harder than ever these days. For evidence, check out the bookstore shelves lined with self-help guides promising to teach you how to slow down and save your life. Or witness the proliferation of stress-management clinics and consultants, many with high-powered corporate client lists.

How is it that relaxation has become so precious a commodity that we need paid experts (and hucksters) to show the way? If relaxation is now valued as a state of grace, the best route to an answer may lie in examining its infernal opposite—stress.

Broadly defined, stress is any change in the environment that causes the body to adapt. Just about every departure from the normal routine—whether it's trying

In a meditation class, students seek inner peace through concentration.

5

out a new route to work or contracting a rare tropical disease—qualifies as a stressor, or source of stress. The emotional content of a stressor is less significant than the fact of change itself; thus, an ostensibly happy event, like the birth of a child, can prove to be as stressful as a tragedy, like the death of a loved one.

When most people talk about "stress," they're probably referring to its psychological and emotional effects. For stress researchers, however, the term also encompasses physical illness, injury, exercise, changes in climate, and other palpable impingements of the environment on the body.

Fight or Flight

Until very recently, the central dogma of stress re-search was that *all* stress reactions, physical and psychological, were rooted in a single, archetypal "fight-or-flight" response. This approach was pioneered in the 1930's by the Austrian endocrinologist Hans Selye and has dominated popular and professional discussions of stress ever since. In Selye's view, the body has one central mechanism for arousal and self-protection when confronted by environmental challenge. This primordial mechanism has lost most of its applicability in modern times, however, and the thwarting of the instinct has led to the epidemic of stress-related disorders we see today.

To illustrate the fight-or-flight response, Selye and his followers typically employ a primal scenario with two leading characters: a caveman and a saber-toothed tiger. While making his way down to the watering hole one antediluvian day, the caveman is surprised by the hungry tiger. Instantaneously, the caveman's biochemistry goes on red alert. The hypothalamus, a control center located deep within the brain, sends out an SOS to the pituitary gland, which in turn releases the hormonal messenger adrenocorticotropin (ACTH). ACTH races down to the adrenals, two roughly pyramid-shaped glands atop the kidneys that pour out the potent "stress hormones" epinephrine (adrenaline) and glucocorticoids. At the same time, the neurons of the central nervous system increase production of norepinephrine, a chemical that contributes to physical and psychological arousal.

Mark Deitch is a medical writer and editor.

The sudden jolt of neural and hormonal activity causes the caveman's heart and lungs to work faster and harder; his metabolism goes into overdrive, with fats and sugar pouring into the bloodstream for extra energy; blood flow increases to the major muscles and decreases to the abdominal organs. Several subtler changes are also under way. The chemical components of the body's blood-clotting mechanism increase in number, as do the natural opiate-like painkillers (called endorphins and enkephalins) circulating in the blood, while immune system activity is suppressed.

In much less time than it has taken to tell, the caveman's body is prepared for extraordinary action, such as breaking off a nearby branch to belt the charging tiger and then—or instead—dashing to the first available shelter. This, in its purest form, is the fight-or-flight response. The problem, in Selye's theory, is that modern Western men and women, unlike our more environmentally adapted ancestors, have no direct outlet for this elaborate physiological buildup that occurs each time we encounter challenge or change. The contemporary urban office worker, for example, while not menaced by saber-toothed tigers, does have to contend with an unremitting stream of smaller stressors: traffic jams or overcrowded buses and subways; surly or unhelpful sales clerks; broken bank machines; blank-faced subordinates, unreasonable deadlines, and unsympathetic superiors. The arousal mechanism is always "on," but it has no place to go, since clobbering a colleague with the "in" box and running up the nearest tree is not considered appropriate behavior.

Something eventually has to give, and when it does, the individual's weakest genetic link is likely to go first. For some people, prolonged stress can cause depression or a host of other psychological disorders. In others, it may produce headaches, backaches, skin problems, sexual dysfunction, incontinence, or digestive complaints. Many experts believe long-term stress contributes directly to high blood pressure and heart disease. There is also suggestive evidence that stress weakens the immune system, hence increasing vulnerability to infectious disease, and may even play a role in cancer.

The most recent research findings have modified some of Selye's conclusions. Rather than a single systemic response to every environmental challenge, it now appears that different stressors—and

Even an ostensibly happy event like a wedding can be a source of stress.

sometimes different intensities of the same stressors—will produce different physiological adaptations. In other words, running a marathon and taking a bar exam are both highly stressful events, but they won't necessarily produce the same pattern of hormonal changes and other chemical events within the body. Furthermore, psychologists studying the mental and behavioral aspects of stress now believe that individual personality traits—your psychic "hardiness," or ability to cope successfully with stress—are more important than the actual environmental challenges in determining the long-term effects of stress on health.

What this means is that your hormones are not necessarily at the complete mercy of your environment. A stress-resistant individual may, in fact, be able to cope with a major life event, like losing a job, more effectively than a less "hardy" personality deals with a relatively minor hassle, like a traffic ticket. The difference between the two appears to lie not so much in the intensity of their respective reactions as in the duration. Whereas a psychologically hardy individual tends to reach a peak of arousal quickly and then calm down equally fast, the more stress-prone type builds to a high level of response and stays there for extended stretches of time.

Psychologists are not, however, in complete agreement as to which personality traits confer "hardiness." Most attempts at definition rely on such soft-edged qualities as "optimism," "joy," and "positive outlook on the worth of one's work." Also unclear are whether hardiness is inborn or can be learned and whether its real relationship to relative good health is one of cause or effect.

Hearts and Minds

Probably the best-known connection between personality and health is the proposed link between "Type A" behavior and heart disease. Almost 30 years ago, two Stanford University cardiologists, Meyer Friedman and Ray Rosenman, first published their observations that hostile, impatient, fiercely competitive people, whom Friedman and Rosenman termed Type A's, were more likely to suffer heart attacks than their more laid-back, easygoing counterparts, the Type B's. As defined by Friedman and Rosenman, the Type A is a relentlessly driven person, and one of the things that drives him (most

Tensions On and Off the Job

Although all jobs create some stress, few are as pressured as that of a stock trader (left, the American Stock Exchange). On the other hand, not having a job causes strain of another kind (below, lines at an unemployment office). Even getting to and from the job is often stressful (right, rush hour on the San Francisco-Oakland Bay Bridge).

Type A's are men) hardest is the clock. He has a short attention span and shorter fuse: having to wait for anything sends him into a fury. He is always doing at least two things at once and is probably simultaneously planning several more. His speech is a series of rapid, angry bursts, and he interrupts others constantly. The Type A is so competitive that he cannot bear to lose even to a child; he is a particular menace on the highway, where every other driver is viewed as a blood rival.

Almost everyone has at least a little bit of Type A in him or her, which may come out at work or in other stressful circumstances. The true Type A, however, behaves this way all the time: he is no more likely to let up on vacation than he is at the office.

The constant high levels of stress hormones that course through the bloodstream of Type A's are believed to affect the heart in several ways. First of all, the stressed heart works harder, which may ultimately lead to high blood pressure and amplification of any arrhythmia, or irregularity in the heartbeat. Animal studies suggest that chronic stress encourages the development of atherosclerosis, the hardening and narrowing of the arteries that is central to heart disease. Stress also seems to stimulate the body's blood-clotting mechanism, and it's now believed that up to 90 percent of heart attacks are precipitated by clots that lodge in the arteries that feed the heart. In addition, Type A's often tend to be heavy smokers and coffee drinkers, and both cigarette smoke and excessive caffeine can harm the heart.

For these reasons, the American Heart Association in 1981 added Type A behavior to its list of independent risk factors for heart disease. Further support for the Type A hypothesis came in 1984 with the publication of a federally funded study, led by Dr. Friedman, that found that heart attack victims who had been trained to modify their Type A responses survived longer, on average, than those who had not. By this time, the term "Type A" had moved from medical shorthand to popular buzz-phrase. Several large corporations, whose high offices, needless to say, were populated largely by hard-driving Type A's, took the stress connection so seriously that they hired stress management consultants and set up behavior modification clinics to save the hearts of their top executives. (Such programs usually consist of training in some form of relaxation or meditation technique, along with group counseling sessions.) Type A modification also began to be integrated into rehabilitation programs for people recovering from heart attacks or bypass surgery.

Many cardiologists, however, remain unconvinced by the Type A hypothesis, and recent research seems to have strengthened the grounds for skepticism. The heaviest blow was landed by Dr. Robert Case and coworkers at St. Luke's-Roosevelt Hospital Center in New York, who in 1985 published a study of 516 heart attack victims that showed no correlation between personality type and length of survival. Other researchers have since weighed in with studies suggesting that Friedman and Rosenman's definition of Type A behavior is too wide-ranging and that more specific traits, such as hostility or cynicism, may be the true culprits in causing heart disease. Still other reports have targeted grief and loneliness as the crucial psychosocial risk factors.

While most experts today would agree that *some* kind of connection exists between stress and heart disease, the jury remains out on what exactly that link may be, how significant it is, and, most important, what to do about it. Meyer Friedman, a self-professed former Type A, with triple-bypass surgery scars to show for it, continues to insist that changing behavior can save lives. In his book *Treating Type A Behavior—and Your Heart*, he advises readers to schedule personal relaxation time into every working day, make a conscious effort to do only one thing at a time, refrain from interrupting others, practice smiling at strangers, and force themselves to apologize at least twice each day, even if no particular offense has been committed.

On the other hand, Ray Rosenman, Friedman's former collaborator and co-formulator of the Type A hypothesis, now expresses reservations about the practicality of altering unhealthy behaviors, at least as a population-wide goal. With sufficient motivation and exceptional persistence, some people can effect lasting personality changes, Rosenman agrees. But he says it's highly unlikely that the short-term, intensive (and highly expensive) stress management programs favored by many corporations and wealthy individuals will accomplish such goals. Rosenman and others are now looking into more widely applicable approaches to stress reduction, such as beta-blocker drugs, which shield the heart from the stimulatory action of certain hormones.

A New Mind-Body Problem

While the Type A debate continues to simmer, a new and potentially wider-reaching mind-body controversy has emerged. The storm center is the fledgling field of psychoneuroimmunology, which focuses on the effects of mind and mood on the immune system. Although research in this area has so far been even less conclusive than that conducted on behavior and the heart, psychoneuroimmunology holds the tantalizing promise of demonstrating scientifically what so many people intuitively suspect: that our thoughts and emotions can be major influences on our resistance to infection and, perhaps, cancer.

The human body, scientists have long believed, has two complex and separate intelligence-gathering systems that enable it to adapt to the external environment. One is the central nervous system, with its billions of brain cells and trillions of interconnecting synapses, whose task is sorting, storing, and orchestrating responses to sensory stimuli. The other is the immune system, also designed to recognize, remember, and react to incoming information, which in this case takes the form of antigens, or foreign microorganisms and other particles that enter the body.

Recent research indicates that these two systems may not be so separate after all. In fact, they can and do communicate with one another via several different chemical pathways, including some of the hormones and other messengers involved in the stress response. The implication is that psychological factors, such as how well or poorly one copes with stress, may have a direct bearing on how one's immune system responds to disease.

For any infectious disease, be it the common cold or AIDS, the effectiveness of individual immune responses varies widely—which means, in essence, that some people get sick faster and more severely than others. Some of this variance is attributable to preexisting medical conditions, but among basically healthy people, there's no reliable method for anticipating resistance to illness. One of the key pursuits of psychoneuroimmunology research is the attempt to pinpoint personality traits that could help to predict susceptibility to disease.

Thus far, most of the results fall into the "promising, but needs more study" category. For example, in one study of dental students, personality profiles derived from questionnaire responses accurately predicted who would come down with the most colds during an academically stressful year. Similar successes were achieved in predicting mononucleosis infections in a group of West Point cadets. Rheumatoid arthritis is not an infectious disease in the classical sense, but it does involve a perverse overreaction of the immune system; at the Harrington Arthritis Research Center in Phoenix, women patients who recorded the highest scores on a test that measured everyday life stresses also demonstrated changes in white blood-cell levels that have been linked to rheumatoid flare-ups. Other studies suggest that severely stressed individuals have reduced activity of natural killer cells, which are believed to protect the body from cancer. (Various studies have shown that physical stress can promote tumor development in animals.)

At the Third International Conference on AIDS, held in Washington, D.C., last June, University of California researchers described a study in which psychological factors, such as optimism, social support, and involvement in self-care, were

compared with specific immune functions in five AIDS patients. Although this study group was very small, the results showed not only better immune function but noticeably prolonged survival among those with the best attitudes.

Compelling as these preliminary studies may be, skeptics voice concern that advocates of psychoneuroimmunology tend to overemphasize the intangibles of personality while giving short shrift to the material culprit, disease. At worst, a "blame the patient" mentality may ensue. This attitude is suggested, however inadvertently, by various popular books of recent vintage that exhort readers to laugh, relax, think positively, or otherwise enlist their "mind power" as a means of boosting immunity and beating chronic disease. From advice like this, it's cruelly easy to conclude that those who do succumb to devastating illness are themselves at fault for failing to laugh hard enough or think the right thoughts.

In fact, this kind of thinking is so common that studies that do not bear out such simplistic

Using biofeedback monitoring, a person can learn to relax by regulating muscular or mental processes.

conclusions are often poorly received. Barrie Cassileth, a University of Pennsylvania psychologist, took personality profiles of 359 patients in an advanced stage of cancer and found, upon follow-up, that mental outlook had nothing at all to do with their ultimate survival. After publishing this report in 1985, she was deluged by angry responses from the public and health professionals, who objected not to the methodology or execution of the study but to the results. Apparently many people did not want to learn that in the battle with cancer, a good state of mind is just not enough.

Coping Strategies

The big questions about the role of stress in heart disease, infection, and cancer remain unanswered, but that doens't mean you can't or shouldn't do something about managing the stress in your life. And while learning to cope with stress won't guarantee good health or longevity, it can certainly enhance your enjoyment of living.

Following are brief rundowns of ten common stress-reduction or relaxation techniques, arranged in alphabetical order. Though each method has its diehard advocates, there's nothing intrinsically superior about any one approach and actually considerable overlap among them. The common thread may be the conviction that mind and body are inseparable and interactive, and that regular, productive interludes from the pressures of everyday life can be restorative to both.

Biofeedback. All our muscular and mental activities leave measurable evidence, whether in the form of body temperature changes, blood pressure fluctuations, or patterns of electrochemical current.

Tensions within a family can often be alleviated by counseling, as at this psychiatric hospital in Pennsylvania.

Biofeedback provides a means of monitoring the trace of a given activity and marking (usually with an auditory tone) a desirable level or state. With this information, or "feedback," you may learn to regulate physical or mental processes you thought were beyond your control. If, for example, you have chronic back problems caused by stress-induced muscle spasms, biofeedback equipment can be hooked up via electrical leads to the problem area of your back, and the system programmed to beep when the muscles are fully relaxed. You can then experiment with different postures or mental states until you can set off the beep at will. Ideally, you will eventually be able to relax your muscles without access to the machine. Biofeedback techniques have also been applied, with some experimental success, to supposedly involuntary body functions, such as regulating blood pressure. For more information and referrals, contact the neurology or behavioral medicine departments of your nearest university medical center, or the Biofeedback Society of America, 10200 West 44th Ave., Suite 304, Wheat Ridge, Colo. 80033, (303) 422-8436.

Counseling. Unburdening oneself to a sanctioned confessor, whether priest or psychoanalyst, is a time-honored means of easing psychic distress. The aim of traditional, "insight-oriented" psychoanalysis is to root out the deep causes of stress and unhappiness, which may reside in one's early family experiences. This process is long, demanding, and often expensive—which is why several shorter-term alternative approaches have emerged. These "results-oriented" techniques emphasize practical and immediate ways of dealing with stress-producing situations. The most popular of these methods are *behavioral* and *cognitive* therapies; the following simple examples may help explain the differences between the two. Let's say there's a person at work with whom you frequently quarrel, after which you go away feeling frustrated and angry and with a nagging sense of self-doubt. A basic behavioral approach might be to alter your responses to this person, perhaps taking a deep breath or mentally counting to ten before making any angry rejoinder. In this way, you avoid escalating the argument to the point where you feel self-defeated, and at the same time you deny him or her the satisfaction of having once again goaded you past tolerance. In a cognitive aproach, you might try to rewrite your mental "script" for these

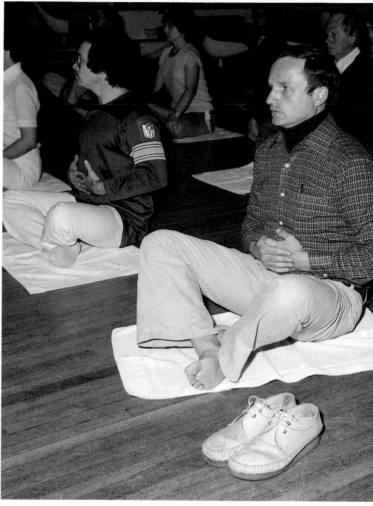

In yoga classes, relaxation comes through breathing exercises and slow, prolonged muscular extensions.

encounters, telling yourself that you are a reasonable, responsible, and competent individual and that your antagonist's assaults, however annoying, cannot disrupt your fundamental soundness. With this positive perspective, you may then be able to deal with the person more effectively.

Exercise. Physical conditioning (running, walking, dancing, weight-lifting, etc.) has a somewhat ambiguous relationship with stress. On the one hand, exertion is itself a stressor, and overdoing it can worsen your mental and physical troubles. On the other hand, a multitude of exercisers swear by its stress-busting and mood-boosting properties, even though the science behind these effects isn't clear. Perhaps, some researchers

13

suggest, exercise may be more valuable in preventing stress disorders than in relieving them. Well-conditioned muscles are less likely to stiffen and spasm than underused ones; by the same token, a well-trained heart (also a muscle) may not respond as violently to a sudden buildup of stress hormones. As for exercising the blues away: the much-reported mood lift may be the result of improved blood flow to the brain, or possibly it's the break from the daily routine, rather than the actual workout, that acts as tonic to the spirit. Another proposed explanation is the release of endorphins, or natural opiates, that accompanies prolonged exercise (endorphins may be responsible for the "runner's high" that endurance athletes often experience). The full range of endorphins' actions is not known, however, and some researchers have linked high levels of these chemicals to increased risk for heart disease.

Hypnosis. In clinical applications, the hypnotist (usually a psychiatrist or psychologist) induces the subject to enter a trance state of deep relaxation and focused attention. In this state, the subject may be unusually open to suggestion, which takes the form of an individualized coping strategy (such as repeating a phrase or concentrating on an image or feeling that the person associates with relaxation).

For undetermined reasons, many people seem to accept and internalize a therapeutic message better under hypnosis than if it were simply presented in normal conversation. After an initial session, or series of sessions, with a hypnotherapist, most subjects can be taught to hypnotize themselves, which enables them to focus in on the selected strategy whenever it is needed. For more information and referrals, contact the American Society of Clinical Hypnosis, 2250 East Devon Avenue, Suite 336, Des Plaines, Ill. 60018.

Imagery. This technique combines elements of hypnosis and meditation. It can be practiced alone or with a trained guide who directs the flow of your thoughts. In essence, you learn to counteract stress by conjuring to mind images of peace and beauty, such as a walk in the woods or a sunset on the beach. The deeper you go into the image, the more sensory systems are brought into play, so that with practice you may not only see the sunset, but also feel the sand underfoot, smell the surf, and taste the salty spray on your lips. Once you have mastered the ability to block stress with soothing images, you may go on to visualizing potentially stressful situations in advance and imagining ways in which you can control and turn them to your advantage.

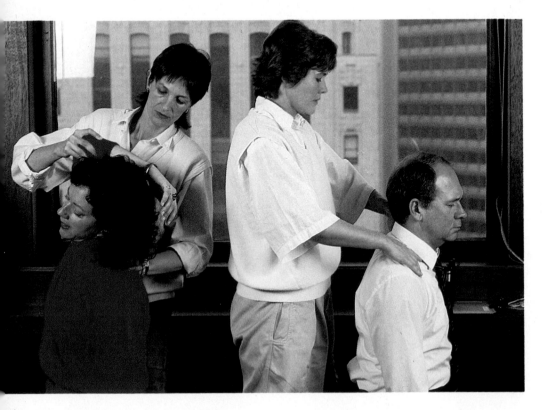

Clients of Corporate Stress-busters, a San Francisco massage business, have their kinks rubbed out right in their offices.

Massage. Despite a reputation unfairly tainted by association with sleazy sex parlors, massage can be a legitimate therapy that in the hands of a skilled practitioner approaches an art form. Proponents claim that massage not only eases muscle tension but also improves circulation and releases toxic chemical buildups in the tissues. The two dominant techniques are Swedish massage, which involves rubbing, stroking, and kneading the skin and muscles; and the Shiatsu, which focuses on various "pressure points" and "meridiens" on the body that purportedly conduct vital energy. Some practitioners claim profound psychological, as well as physical, benefits: repressed emotions, they contend, may be locked into muscular patterns of tension and pain. Through the masseur's or masseuse's ministrations, the physical release of tension may also bring about a psychic catharsis. For more information and referrals, contact the American Massage Therapy Association, 1130 West North Shore, Chicago, Ill. 60626, (312) 761-AMTA. This organization has more than 5,000 registered members practicing in all 50 states and in Canada (primarily Ontario and British Columbia).

Meditation. Commonly associated with Eastern religions and philosophies, meditation as a relaxation technique can be practiced without knowledge or endorsement of any specific beliefs. The essence of meditation, at least from a Western self-help standpoint, is to sit quietly in a relaxed posture, close your eyes, and concentrate your thoughts on a single word, image, or physical function, like breathing. Eventually, the mind will be cleared of all conflicting thoughts, and a deep sense of peace and well-being may result. Through meditation, Hindu and Buddhist masters have reportedly learned to control such autonomic functions as heart rate, blood pressure, and body temperature; laboratory studies, however, have so far failed to discern any measurable difference between the effects of meditation and those of simply doing nothing. Probably the best popular introduction to secular, therapeutic meditation is *The Relaxation Response* and subsequent books by Dr. Herbert Benson.

Progressive relaxation. This technique is based on the principle that the best way to relax a muscle is to tense it first. Ideally, it is performed while lying down in a quiet room with no time pressures, but in a pinch you can practice it sitting at your desk or on a train or bus. Start by closing your eyes, breathing deeply, and letting your mind wander for a minute or two. Then concentrate on tensing, holding, and finally relaxing the various muscle groups of your body, working from head down to toes, one group at a time. Inhale with each muscle contraction, and exhale as the tension is released. Once you become adept at this technique, you can run through all the muscle groups in just a few minutes, and the effect may be something like a wave of relaxation coursing through the body.

Scanning. The preparation for scanning is almost identical to that for progressive relaxation: lying quietly with eyes closed, breathing easily, and letting the mind go. The essential difference is that no deliberate physical activity is involved. Instead, you focus mentally on each muscle group or body part in turn, "scan" the area for any sign of tension or discomfort, and then concentrate on releasing the stress with a slowly exhaled breath. According to scanning advocates, this technique promotes body awareness and a greater sense of control over your own characteristic stress reactions.

Yoga. Like meditation, yoga is part of a larger philosophical system but can be usefully employed in a translated and stripped-down form. As such, it consists of breathing exercises and a wide variety of physical postures ("asanas") that require mental concentration and slow, prolonged muscular extensions. The central lessons of yoga are self-attunement and self-control; peripheral benefits may include improved posture, flexibility, circulation, and breathing. Beginning yoga classes are offered at many Y's and community centers, as well as at specialized schools. If possible, visit a few different classes until you find an instructor that you like and feel comfortable with. The books of Richard Hittleman, especially *Introduction to Yoga*, and the television show *Lilias, Yoga, and You* may also prove useful for novices. □

SUGGESTIONS FOR FURTHER READING

BENSON, HERBERT, and MIRIAM Z. KLIPPER. *The Relaxation Response.* New York, Avon, 1976.
CHARLESWORTH, EDWARD, and RONALD NATHAN. *Stress Management.* New York, Ballantine Books, 1985.
FRIEDMAN, MEYER, and DIANE ULMER. *Treating Type A Behavior—and Your Heart*, New York, Ballantine Books, 1985.

Sears Tower
Cinderella
Mississippi
plural
man
men
Supermen
dix
une
six

Do You Have A Gifted Child?

James H. Borland, Ph.D.

Seth, a four-year-old, has a passion for mathematics. To amuse himself while his preschool classmates struggle with the numbers from one to ten, Seth does long division in his head and solves problems involving positive and negative integers and fractions. He recently devised a "metric time system" in which hours have 100 minutes and minutes 100 seconds. When given the time of day in conventional time, Seth can make a conversion to "metric time" nearly instantaneously.

Andrea, a high school junior, approaches her schoolwork dutifully but with little enthusiasm. Although most of Andrea's teachers feel that she could do better in school, none has suggested that she would ever be a brilliant student. Recently, however, under the tutelage of her English teacher, Andrea has discovered that she has a love, and quite an aptitude, for writing. Over the last few months, she has written a novel and two volumes of poetry at home (often at the expense of her homework), and she published one of her poems in a junior literary magazine.

Fourteen-year-old Maria is a dedicated student who is consistently at the head of her class. Her work is neat, carefully prepared, and always submitted on time. Polite and attentive in class, Maria is understandably a favorite with her teachers. "My best student in years," gushes one teacher. "I wish I had 25 more like her." Her teachers' only concern is her relentless perfectionism. "She has to learn that an A minus is not the end of the world," sighs her science teacher.

Jonathan, also 14 years old, is Maria's polar opposite. Rude, abrasive, sometimes openly hostile, he is a constant irritant to his teachers on those days he deigns to attend class. Apparently unconcerned about grades, Jonathan brags that he is failing all of his courses "without even trying." Although Jonathan's IQ is over 150, his teachers are unimpressed. "He must have cheated on the test," claims one teacher.

The four students described above may appear to be quite different from one another, but they have one thing in common—they have all been identified by their schools as gifted. Although the term typically evokes the image of a puny, spectacled bookworm, gifted children are a remarkably diverse lot. They may be star pupils like Maria or disaffected rebels like Jonathan, prodigies like Seth or late bloomers like Andrea. This diversity, while in many respects a useful antidote to the common stereotype, also creates considerable confusion. And no issue is more confusing than the most basic one of all, the one summed up in the question "What is a gifted child?"

Diverse Definitions

It sometimes seems that there are as many definitions of the gifted child as there are gifted children. While this reflects a healthy ferment of ideas in the field of the education of the gifted, it also creates some practical problems. For example, a child who is identified as gifted in school A may not be deemed gifted if he or she transfers to school B, simply because the new school district employs a different definition of giftedness. This is understandably difficult for children and their parents to understand. However, if we take a look

James H. Borland is director of graduate programs in the education of the gifted and early childhood special education at Teachers College, Columbia University.

at some of the issues surrounding the notion of giftedness in children, it becomes easy to see why there is so much confusion.

One of the greatest difficulties stems from the fact that giftedness is a value-laden concept. This means, among other things, that what was "gifted" in years past may not be "gifted" today. The poet Ovid, for example, wrote that Julius Caesar was possessed of "genius divine" because he could "wage a war unsuited to his boyish years." While in ancient Rome that quality would mark a child as gifted, today such a trait is more likely to land a child in a correctional facility. Moreover, an ability useful in our society, such as a facility with computers, would be useless in an aboriginal culture. Giftedness is thus a matter of where, as well as when, one is born. Even within our contemporary culture, different people value different traits and abilities. Some argue that the ability to achieve at the highest levels in school is exemplary of giftedness. Others content that high grades and test scores reflect only an ability to "play the school game" well and have nothing to do with real-world productivity, which for them is the true hallmark of giftedness.

To complicate matters further, different educators use different rationales to justify and to guide programs for the gifted in the schools. Underlying each of these rationales is a different conception of giftedness. Essentially, there are two major schools of thought. The first of these might be called the "national resources" school. Advocates of this approach view gifted children as a largely untapped,

Famous Prodigies

Among those whose extraordinary gifts were evident at an early age were the literary Brontë sisters (from left to right, Anne, Emily, and Charlotte) and the musical genius Wolfgang Amadeus Mozart (shown at the harpsichord with his father and sister).

potentially valuable resource that should be identified and developed for the national good. Central to this rationale is the belief that giftedness is best reflected in adult productivity. The school's task thus becomes one of identifying those children who are most likely to become gifted (that is, productive) adults and helping them on their way to success. This is the thinking that informed the push for programs for the gifted in the United States during the post-Sputnik panic of the late 1950's and early 1960's.

An alternative to this approach is the "special educational" model, whose advocates view the gifted as exceptional children for whom the regular core curriculum is inappropriate or insufficient and a differentiated curriculum is needed. Central to this approach is the belief that each child, whether gifted, "average," or disabled in some way, has a right to an appropriate education. The school's task, therefore, is to identify children who are not receiving the education they deserve and to modify their course of study so that it matches their abilities or potential. The focus of this approach is the need of the individual child in the classroom

today, not the need of society at some point far in the future.

One can see, therefore, that schools have quite a bit of latitude when it comes to deciding what kind of students will be singled out for special instruction in programs for the gifted. This latitude is in no way restricted by the definitions proposed by the authorities in the field. For example, one of the most frequently quoted definitions of giftedness was advanced by psychologist Paul Witty in the 1950's.

According to Witty, the gifted are those "whose performance, in a potentially valuable line of human activity, is consistently remarkable." This definition is difficult to dispute, but it raises as many questions as it answers. For example, how do we define "potentially valuable" areas of activity? And what constitutes "consistently remarkable" performance, especially when children are involved?

The federal government offers some, but not sufficient, guidance in this area. In 1971, in a report to Congress entitled *Education of the Gifted and Talented*, the U.S. Office of Education proposed a definition that listed no fewer than six aptitude and performance areas in which children could be gifted:

1. General intellectual ability
2. Specific academic aptitude
3. Creative or productive thinking
4. Leadership ability
5. Visual and performing arts
6. Psychomotor ability

In reality, most school districts view the first two of these areas as most worthy of attention in special programs. But this still leaves quite a bit of room for choice. For example, the percentage of students identified as gifted can range anywhere from 1 percent of the student population to 20 percent or more. Moreover, if a school chooses to base its definition of giftedness on achievement in academic subjects, there is still the question of *which* academic areas should be the focus.

The upshot of all of this is that students are identified as gifted and placed into special programs for a variety of reasons and as the result of a number of practices and procedures. As a rough generalization, however, it is probably safe to state that the students most commonly identified as gifted are the 3 to 5 percent of the student body in a given school or school district that demonstrates the greatest academic achievement or intellectual aptitude. Unless otherwise indicated, this is the group to which the phrase "gifted child" refers in this article.

Identifying Without Labeling

Given the difficulties that schools experience just trying to define the gifted child, one could logically assume that identifying gifted children, that is, selecting them for special programs, is equally difficult. In fact, if anything, identification is an even more problematic undertaking.

The technical problem of identifying children for

Identification: The Sooner the Better

The earlier the age at which children can be identified as gifted, the sooner they can begin to receive an appropriate education. At left, a preschooler taking an IQ test makes up a story using props. At right, a teacher works on an individual basis with young students.

placement in programs for the gifted is complicated by the desirability of the label "gifted child." While it is not true, as is generally assumed, that all parents think their child is gifted, there are usually enough parents who want their children to have the benefits, real or imagined, of placement into a program for the gifted to make the task of identification a trying one for school personnel.

In general, the identification problem becomes less intractable for educators if it is seen as a matter of placement, not labeling.

If schools view the process of identifying the gifted as one of separating the "truly gifted" children from the "merely average," the task is daunting if not impossible. Trying to identify the gifted in this manner presupposes the possibility of being able to determine, with unerring accuracy, who deserves (or in the future will deserve) the label "gifted" and who does (or will) not. In fact, this is a distasteful notion to many, implying the existence of an elite group, "the gifted," that is readily distinguishable from the rest of us.

If, however, school personnel view identification as a process of placing children into a program that is right for them, the process is less intimidating. In fact, one can select certain children and not others for a program for the gifted and still concur

with the agreeable notion that all children are in some manner gifted (but only some of these gifted children need *this* particular program). One can also recognize and correct mistakes in identification if they are looked at as simply placements that did not work out. If, however, identification is seen as labeling, correcting one's mistakes becomes a matter of changing a child's status in life and deciding that he or she is no longer, or never really was, gifted.

A related issue is the age at which children should be identified. In one sense, the earlier the better. The sooner a child can be recognized as exceptional, the sooner that child can receive an appropriate education. Unfortunately, the younger a child is, the more difficult it becomes to use reliable identification procedures. For example, aptitude tests, which usually play a role in identification, are much less valid and reliable with younger children.

This does not mean that early identification is not practicable or that one cannot have faith in placement decisions made when children are quite young. The Hollingworth Preschool at Teachers College, Columbia University, for example, screens candidates as young as 2½ years of age for its three-year-old program. Although no pretense is made of being able to identify "gifted three-year-olds," the selection process employed at this preschool

Separate schools and classes for the gifted have been called "full-time solutions to full-time problems." Here, in a math class at the Nueva Learning Center in Hillsborough, Calif., a school for gifted children, students proceed at their own speed.

consistently results in the selection of children who are able to benefit from the enriched offerings that constitute its curriculum. The key to the preschool's success in identifying precocious children is its reliance on a case-study method that utilizes a variety of sources of information about applicants, including tests, parent questionnaires, and direct observation of the children.

The actual process of identifying children for programs for the gifted varies considerably from school to school. There are some programs in which admission is contingent upon a score on a single test, such as an IQ test. Although this practice is more prevalent than many educators would like to admit, it is difficult to defend. No single measure is capable of revealing enough information about a student to make such an important placement decision, nor is any single measure sufficiently reliable to stand on its own. Moreover, tests reflect differently on various groups within a pluralistic society, and reliance on tests alone will inevitably result in underrepresentation of students from minority cultures.

Easier to defend is the practice of gathering information from a variety of sources for use in making placement decisions. Among the sources of information are aptitude tests such as IQ tests (individually administered ones are more reliable than group tests); achievement tests (which measure learning in specific subject or skill areas); and tests of specific cognitive factors (such as spatial ability or deductive reasoning). Although they were popular a few years ago, so-called creativity tests are used much less frequently today because of serious doubts about whether they really measure something that could plausibly be identified as human creativity.

In addition to tests, ratings and recommendations can also be very useful. The most popular are teacher rating scales, which ask teachers to indicate the presence or absence and the frequency of certain behaviors thought to reflect giftedness. Useful but less popular are parent referrals, on which parents supply information about their children (these are particularly appropriate with very young children and surprisingly accurate), and peer ratings, on which children supply information about other children. Sometimes, especially with older children, self-nomination is employed as well. Finally, particularly in programs for children gifted in the arts, examples of students' work (such as works of art, performances, writing) are judged by artists or other professionals.

Whatever tests or other methods are used, it is important that there be multiple sources of information and that the data gathered be interpreted carefully and sensitively. Many schools go to considerable trouble to collect information from a variety of sources and then lose this wealth of information by using a matrix or a formula to combine the scores and ratings into a single composite "giftedness index." Better by far is the practice of treating each candidate as an individual, using a case-study approach. A committee of educators should look at each child's file and decide on the child's placement as a matter of educational judgment, and provisions should be built into the process for reevaluating placements (and perhaps removing children from the program if it is in their interest) at a later date.

Grouping: A Spectrum of Alternatives

Gifted children can be grouped for instruction in a variety of ways, ranging from complete segregation in homogeneous groups to full-time integration into heterogeneous classes. Probably the most frequent setting in which gifted children find themselves is the regular heterogeneous classroom. In some schools there is not even the pretense of a program for the gifted; other districts claim that differentiation of the curriculum takes place in the regular classroom. However, the realities of a regular heterogeneous classroom are such that teachers are already taxed beyond reason just dealing with the basic curriculum and the range of abilities among their children. To expect these teachers to make additional curricular differentiations for the gifted is unrealistic at best, cynical at worst.

An arrangement that represents a compromise of sorts between heterogeneous and completely homogeneous grouping is the part-time "pull-out" program. In this format, which is the most popular one in current use, gifted children spend most of their time in the regular classroom, but they are taken out of this setting periodically to receive special instruction with their gifted peers. The time spent in the "gifted program" varies considerably from school to school (from five mornings per week to 20 minutes per week in this writer's experience). However, if the program is to have an impact on the students' educational progress, at least one-half day per week should be spent in the special class, and a full day is preferable by far.

Pull-out programs, for all their popularity, have serious drawbacks that schools ought to consider before adopting this format. First, they are expensive, requiring additional teachers and rooms while leaving empty desks in the regular classroom. Second, they fragment the program of gifted students, taking them away from the regular classroom from time to time, often to the annoyance of the classroom teacher. Third, they create the perception that the program for the gifted is an addition to, not an integral part of, the children's curricula. Fourth, they lend themselves to activities that are often trivial at best, since the teacher of the gifted is asked to teach something apart from the regular curriculum but is given little, if any, guidance about what this "something" should be.

Most important, however, is the problem highlighted by a recent national study in the United States of programs for the gifted, published in a book entitled *Educating Able Learners*. In the words of the authors of this study, the pull-out program is "a part-time solution to a full-time problem." That is, a school district realizes that the regular classroom is wrong for its gifted students, creates a special program that is thought to be right for them, and then decides that they should spend the majority of their time in the wrong classroom. Moreover, the authors of the report found that only 65 percent of the pull-out programs and 48 percent of the resource rooms (a variation of pull-out programs) nationwide met the minimal criteria required to be judged "substantial."

At the other end of the grouping continuum are special schools and self-contained classes for the gifted. These can take many forms, but they all have in common the fact that gifted students receive all of their instruction with their ability peers. Although there is a widespread conception that ability grouping is harmful to students, especially students who are not gifted, the research does not bear this out. Instead, there is evidence that grouping children by ability not only fosters greater school achievement but more positive self-concepts

Students at Hunter High School, a school for the gifted in New York City, plan a trip with their adviser. The opportunity for independent study and research is an important element of a curriculum for the gifted, who can be considered producers as well as consumers of knowledge.

and better attitudes toward school as well. Self-contained classes and special schools are clearly, to borrow the words of the recent nationwide study, "full-time solutions to full-time problems."

A Defensible Curriculum

The goal of special education for the gifted is a defensible differentiated curriculum—learning activities that are different from those experienced by other students and can be justified in light of the students' exceptional characteristics. What does this entail? It is difficult to specify absolutely, but some desirable elements of a defensible differentiated curriculum are the following:

An emphasis on higher-level thinking processes. While a student can for the most part master the basic curriculum simply by memorizing presented material, most educators realize that there are

other, higher-level thinking processes needed for advanced problem solving. Programs for the gifted have been in the vanguard of the movement to introduce critical thinking, creative thinking, and other thinking skills into the classroom. In fact, some programs for the gifted, especially pull-out programs, focus on these skills exclusively, and this narrow focus can become a problem. Too often, the "curriculum" of such programs consists of "creativity kits," instruction in "the" creative problem-solving method, and other activities of questionable value. Higher-level thinking is desirable, even essential, in programs for the gifted, but it must be taught and learned in the context of appropriate content.

Exposure to challenging, meaningful content. It is important that gifted students be exposed to topics, issues, and problems that are challenging and important and that they acquire a significant body of knowledge. Exposure to our intellectual and cultural heritage and the essentials of a sound liberal arts education are indispensable facets of a strong program for the gifted.

Opportunities for small-group or independent study. While hardly the panacea that some have made it out to be, the opportunity to work independently on projects of their own choosing should be available to gifted students. If, as Abraham J. Tannenbaum asserts, the gifted are producers, not merely consumers, of knowledge, gifted students should have the chance at least to emulate producers of knowledge in different fields by engaging in various types of research.

Opportunities for students to work at an appropriate pace and level. The one-grade-per-year, kindergarten-at-age-five lockstep, although an administrative convenience, does not constitute the best educational plan for all students. This is particularly true for the gifted and raises the issue of acceleration, a variety of provisions whereby students meet educational requirements at an earlier age or a faster pace than is typical. Among the forms that acceleration can take are early admission (to kindergarten or college), grade skipping, earning advanced standing in high school or college through special courses and examinations, ungraded schools, and special progress programs (for example, covering three years' worth of work in two calendar years).

There are two incontrovertible facts about educational acceleration. The first of these is that the vast majority of parents, teachers, and administrators believes that acceleration is harmful to students socially, emotionally, or in some other way. The second fact is that there is no evidence in any of the research on acceleration to indicate that its effects are anything but positive for the gifted. It is unlikely that any other practice in the education of the gifted has been demonstrated so unequivocally to be of value for students, and it is unlikely that any other practice is greeted by practitioners with such wariness.

Myths die hard, and administrative arrangements cemented by over a century of use are difficult to change. Nevertheless, we should not let folklore, anecdotal reasoning, or administrative convenience prevent gifted students (or any other students) from progressing at an educational pace that is right for them. If an analysis of a gifted student's needs indicates that he or she would benefit from acceleration, there is no legitimate reason to deny the student the opportunity for the more appropriate education that acceleration would provide.

Sources of Stress

The common stereotype of the gifted child not only paints a picture of a physically underdeveloped egghead but also suggests that such a child is socially isolated and probably somewhat unbalanced emotionally as well. Fortunately, the latter part of this stereotype is as untrue as the former.

Gifted children as a group are no less gregarious and no less popular than their age peers. In fact, there is some research to show that intellectually gifted students are usually quite adept socially, that they are frequently found in positions of leadership, and that they have the same interest in games and sports as do other children. This is not to say that gifted children do not differ socially from other children. The research tells us that they are more likely than other children to seek out older playmates or friends. And, perhaps paradoxically,

Achievement tests are one source of information about a child's capabilities.

although the gifted can hold their own quite well in social situations, they also tend to need more time alone.

With respect to emotional development, there is no reason to believe that gifted children differ significantly from other children. Giftedness does not predispose one to eccentric behavior or inevitable neurosis or psychosis. In fact, once again the research that is available suggests that intellectually gifted children might enjoy a slight edge in this respect, having a lower incidence of behavioral and emotional disorders.

Although giftedness is often thought of only in terms of academic ability, it can also find expression in music.

Nevertheless, there are certain sources of stress that are the common lot of gifted children. Most children deal with these stresses quite well; a small number do not. But whether they cause serious trouble or are taken in stride, the following are some pressures and problems with which gifted children often must contend.

Being different. Gifted children are different from other children by definition, and, especially for adolescents and preadolescents, being different is often seen as something to be avoided. Most gifted children are able to accept the fact of their special abilities and to realize that everybody is different in some way, but some will do everything they can to appear to be like other children, including, in some cases, not excelling in school. Constant reminders from parents and teachers that one is gifted are often unappreciated; quiet encouragement to do one's best to develop one's potential is usually more effective. Programs in which children are grouped homogeneously serve to minimize apparent differences in school ability and to eliminate the sometimes embarrassing routine of conspicuously leaving the regular classroom to go to the part-time pull-out program.

Being bored. Gifted children are often bored in school. It is far from stimulating to sit through day after day of instruction designed to teach something one already knows, and some children react by making sarcastic comments to teachers and peers or acting out. The problem here, when it is a problem, is caused by the situation, not the child. Again, the answer is a special program and a curriculum that serves an educational, not an anesthetic, function.

Being a perfectionist. Some gifted children have great difficulty accepting anything less than perfection from themselves. For these children, an A minus or a 98 will not do; such marks may even connote failure. Such attitudes toward oneself generally result from the internalization of the attitudes or perceived wishes of others, especially parents. Parents who constantly harp on their child's giftedness may be unintentionally sending the message that the child is "good" only when achieving at the highest level. Perfectionism is a hindrance to accomplishment and development; it interferes with the risk-taking that is essential to creativity and effective problem-solving. It also removes most of the joy from learning, and this is one of the worst things that can happen to a gifted child.

Being too aware. Gifted children can develop a cognitive awareness of things they are not ready to deal with emotionally. This is especially true of precocious preschoolers. At an early age, these children can learn, among other things, that people die and do not return, that people sometimes hurt those whom they love, and that truly horrible things happen in this world. This knowledge is difficult enough for adults to deal with; for young children it can create serious difficulties. While it is impossible, and probably unwise, to shield children from the realities of the modern world, it is important to be sensitive to what the children are learning from their environment and the mass media. Talking, comforting, and reassurance are needed, as is the ability to know what the child needs to know when a question is asked about a sensitive or troubling issue. Sometimes the appropriate answer to the question "Where did I come from?" is "Cleveland," not a detailed explanation of human procreation.

Being too busy. Gifted children are often interested in and adept at doing many things. Their interests and enthusiasms often propel them into elective classes in school, various extracurricular activities, one or more sports, religious classes and activities, and multiple hobbies. This diverse routine can result in a well-rounded child, but it can also result in exhaustion. For some gifted children, their interests and abilities are truly an embarrassment of riches. They sometimes need help in deciding what they can comfortably accomplish in their busy week and what must go by the wayside.

Avoiding a Tragic Waste

In an ideal world, special education for the gifted or for any other group would not be needed. Each child would be treated as an individual and would receive precisely the education that he or she required.

Given the world that we inhabit, however, and given the schools that we have, those children we call gifted will not reach their potential without special education of some form.

People often ask, "If these kids are so 'gifted,' why can't they learn on their own? Why do they need special classes?" Leaving aside the point that we do not expect any children to "learn on their own," one can best answer this question by quoting from the U.S. Office of Education's report, *Education of the Gifted and Talented:*

> Contrary to widespread belief, these students cannot ordinarily excel without assistance. . . . Gifted students who have had the advantage of special programs have shown remarkable improvements in self-understanding and in ability to relate well to others, as well as in improved academic and creative performance. . . .
>
> Gifted and talented youth are a unique population, differing markedly from their age peers in abilities, talents, interests, and psychological maturity. They are . . . possibly the most neglected of all groups with special educational needs. . . . The resultant waste is tragic.

SOURCES OF FURTHER INFORMATION

American Association for Gifted Children, c/o Project SENG, School of Professional Psychology, Wright State University, Dayton, Ohio 45435.

Center for the Advancement of Academically Talented Youth, Johns Hopkins University, 2933 North Charles Street, Baltimore, Md. 21218.

Center for the Study and Education of the Gifted, Teachers College, Columbia University, New York, N.Y. 10027.

National Association for Gifted Children, 5100 North Edgewood Drive, St. Paul, Minn. 55112.

SUGGESTIONS FOR FURTHER READING

COX, JUNE, NEIL DANIEL, and BRUCE O. BOSTON. *Educating Able Learners.* Austin, University of Texas Press, 1985.

GALLAGHER, JAMES J. *Teaching the Gifted Child,* 3d ed. Newton, Mass., Allyn and Bacon, 1985.

HOWLEY, AIMEE, CRAIG HOWLEY, and EDWINA C. PENDARVIS. *Teaching Gifted Children.* Boston, Little, Brown, 1986.

STERNBERG, ROBERT J., and JANET E. DAVIDSON. *Conceptions of Giftedness.* New York, Cambridge University Press, 1986.

TANNENBAUM, ABRAHAM J. *Gifted Children.* New York, Macmillan, 1983.

Safety in Backpacking

Gerald O'Reilly

Once the unchallenged domain of dutiful Boy Scouts and grizzled mountaineers, backpacking is fast becoming a national pastime in the United States. Motor-home campers tired of crowded campgrounds, families no longer amused by amusement parks, city dwellers suffocated by the crush of daily life— all are now strapping on packs and striking out into the backcountry, building their bodies and stretching their souls in a world of rugged beauty just a few miles up the trail.

But some of the very elements that make backcountry life so appealing—physical isolation, self-sufficiency, communion with an often unpredictable Mother Nature—can also make backpacking a dangerous pursuit for the novice. As the Scouts learned years ago, the key to outdoor safety lies in being prepared. By reviewing a few general rules of backpacking safety and learning ways to avoid potential perils, even first-time trekkers will be well on their way to a lifetime of safe and rewarding journeys.

Equipment

Backpacking supply companies haven't let the sport's newfound popularity slip by unnoticed. Far from it. Catalogs thick as phone books and retail stores spanning city blocks now offer backpackers more kinds and styles of equipment than ever before—leaving the backpacking novice understandably bewildered. But choosing the proper equipment for the task at hand is perhaps the single most important step backpackers can take to minimize their chances of trouble on the trail. Fortunately, a number of excellent books provide comprehensive evaluations of some of the more popular equipment available and can help guide you through the critical selection process.

Match equipment to the task. If you're planning a trip through the foothills of the Sierra Nevada range during the heat of summer, there's no sense bringing an expensive down sleeping bag rated to five below zero; on the other hand, if you expect to be camping in cold weather, don't try to get by with the ragged cotton sack that saw you through summer camp 20 years ago. The same holds for

Gerald O'Reilly is a writer, editor, and frequent backpacker.

other equipment. Do you really need a four-season tent? If so, buy (or rent) one. But if you'll be camping in an area where there is no rain and there are few bugs, perhaps you don't need a tent at all. Will you be carrying a heavy load over rocky terrain? Then you'll probably want to opt for a pair of relatively heavy boots with thick rubber soles and steel-reinforced heels and toes. But for easy jaunts over well-maintained trails, a lighter pair will no doubt suffice.

With all equipment purchases or rentals, though, don't skimp on quality. It's obviously far better to spend a little more and err on the side of excess than to find yourself cold and exhausted in a collapsed tent 10 miles from the nearest road.

Learn how to use your equipment. There's nothing worse than standing in the dark in a downpour trying to figure out for the first time how to "just slide the tan pole through the horizontal sleeve and into the corresponding grommet. . . ." Practice setting up your tent in the living room a few days before your trip. Fire up your stove in the driveway and master the controls. If your boots need breaking in, wear them around the neighborhood for a week or two before setting out. Fully load your pack and try it on; if it's not comfortable, make necessary adjustments now. Don't try to carry too much—take only those articles that are really necessary for your trip.

Safety essentials. The box at left lists basic safety equipment you should not go backpacking without. Depending on your own particular needs and wants, you may well add to the list. But don't subtract from it, unless you bring an alternative piece of equipment that can perform the same function as the item you're leaving behind.

Map and compass. Learning how to read a topographic map and use a compass will contribute greatly to your enjoyment of backpacking— and in an emergency, these skills can save your life. A map allows you to gauge fairly accurately how much ground you can easily expect to cover in a single day. And if trouble strikes on the trail, a map and compass can help you find the quickest or easiest route to the roadhead, reveal a nearby water supply, or suggest an alternate campsite.

Proper use of map and compass is not difficult but does require some basic instruction and practice. *Be Expert With Map and Compass* by Bjorn Kjellstrom is widely considered the best book available on the subject.

First-aid kit. The box at left also lists the elements of a basic first-aid kit, although the size and contents of individual kits will vary depending on particular needs, size of party, length of trip, and degree of isolation.

Carrying a first-aid kit does you little good, however, if you are unfamiliar with its contents and unsure of how to use them. Regularly review the status of your kit, adding new items as necessary and replacing those that have been used up or have passed their expiration dates. Read through your first-aid book from time to time to familiarize yourself with basic first-aid procedures and the book's contents and layout, so that you can find needed information quickly in an emergency. Be sure to review basic first-aid procedures right before you set out. A number of medical guides geared specifically to the hazards of outdoor life can be found in most camping outlets.

ESSENTIAL GEAR

Waterproof ground cloth

Heat-reflecting "space blanket"

Lightweight tarp for emergency shelter (can double as ground cloth)

Reliable flashlight

Filled water bottle or canteen

Water purification tablets

30-foot length of lightweight nylon rope

Folding pocket knife with sharp blade

Fire-starter jelly or equivalent

Butane lighter

Strike-anywhere matches in waterproof container

Pliers or multi-function camping tool

Map and compass

Extra food and clothing

Distress whistle

First-aid kit

BASIC FIRST-AID KIT

Dozen Band-Aids

Several 3" × 3" sterile gauze pads

Roll of adhesive tape

Roll of gauze

Tube of triple antibiotic ointment

Aspirin or aspirin substitute

Moleskin for blisters

Small bar of soap for cleansing wounds

Small scissors

Tweezers

First-aid booklet

Nights are cold in the high country where the wind blows down from snow-covered peaks. Campers need to come prepared with a sturdy tent, warm sleeping bags, and plenty of layers of clothing.

Campfire starters. Although the use of campfires is now sharply restricted in many areas, the ability to light one in an emergency, whether for use as a heat source or as a signaling device, is essential. Since building a fire can be difficult and time-consuming even under the best of conditions, most safety-conscious backpackers now carry along a tube of fire-starter jelly or some other fire aid to ensure quick lights.

A few fire safety tips: Before building a fire, select an area away from anything that could burn, including tree roots and peat moss, and clear it down to bare ground or rock. If you decide to line the site with rocks, don't use any pulled from a stream; the more porous of these are full of water, and have been known to literally explode when heated. And when it comes time to put the fire out, douse it with water or smother it with dirt, leaving no ember unquenched.

Stoves. To compensate for the loss of the campfire, almost all backpackers now carry lightweight cooking stoves, fueled by either propane cartridges or liquid white gas. These stoves are actually much easier to set up and cook over than traditional fires. But like fires, the stoves, particularly the white gas variety, can be dangerous if handled improperly. To ensure their safe operation, read and follow all safety instructions, and take the same common-sense precautions you would around any open flame.

Planning for Safety

In addition to choosing the proper equipment and learning how to use it, a number of other steps can be taken during the planning stages of any backpacking trip that will significantly increase your margin of safety.

Work out before you set out. Try to get at least a few weeks of regular aerobic exercise under your belt before hitting the trail. Not only will this make the miles more enjoyable, but you'll be far less prone to fatigue and accidental injury.

Choose a manageable route. Using your topographic map, decide on a route that you can cover easily in the time available. Trying to cover too many miles each day defeats the whole purpose of a relaxing backpacking trip and increases the risk of injury.

Check out the weather. Never underestimate the weather; it represents by far the most common serious threat the backpacker faces. Before heading into the backcountry, make sure you know what the weather might be: is it likely to get cold at night? Are afternoon thundershowers typical? You might check with the weather service, park rangers, or other knowledgeable sources. Then, prepare for all reasonable possibilities.

Don't backpack alone. Many veteran backpackers insist that the only way to see and appreciate the subtler wonders of nature is to strike out

Developing skills in reading a map and using a compass can add to your enjoyment and keep you safely on the trail.

32

into the backcountry alone. Be that as it may, backpacking alone is many times more dangerous than backpacking in a group. The more people in a group, the easier it is to cope with a mishap.

Maximize your chances of rescue. At most U.S. state and national parks, backpackers are now required to apply for a backcountry permit before setting out, stating exactly where they plan to go, where they intend to camp, and when they expect to return. If the backpackers don't check in with the ranger station within a certain number of hours of their estimated exit time, a rescue party is sent out to look for them.

For most backpacking trips, however, you probably won't be required to register with authorities, so it's wise to take your own measures to ensure eventual rescue. The easiest method is simply to leave a copy of your itinerary with a family member or trusted friend, along with instructions to send help if you don't check in by a certain day and time.

Safety on the Trail

When at last you hit the trail, take care to observe the following common-sense guidelines:

Take it slowly. Backpacking is a form of enjoyment, not a test of endurance or a measure of machismo. Start off your trip at a comfortable, leisurely pace you can maintain over the long haul. Take rest stops whenever you need them; don't let yourself become exhausted. If you discover that you overestimated your speed and won't reach your target destination, don't worry; one of the great joys of backpacking is being able to stop and camp right where you're standing.

Keep your body fueled. Backpacking is strenuous work, and your body's reserves will need to be constantly replenished to ward off fatigue and dehydration. Stop frequently to eat and drink; a backpacking trip is no time to go on a diet.

Know when to turn back. If at any time during your trip conditions arise that make pushing on clearly dangerous—bad weather, a difficult stream crossing, injury, or the like—turn back. There's always next weekend.

Some of the potential hazards a backpacker should be prepared for are discussed below.

Hot Weather Hazards

When hiking in hot weather, follow a few common-sense rules. Drink plenty of water at frequent intervals to ward off dehydration (and remember that most people need to drink more liquids at high altitudes than they would at sea level). Minimize your exposure to the sun by walking in the shade wherever possible and by wearing light-colored, lightweight protective clothing, including a hat. Stop often to rest and cool off. And watch for warning signs of the following:

Heatstroke. The early signs of heatstroke, a usually fatal condition if not immediately recognized and treated, include high skin temperature, profuse sweating, irritability, fatigue, and sometimes headache,

Hikers sign in at the trailhead before setting out. In case they fail to return on time, park rangers will know to send out a search party.

33

dizziness, and nausea; eventually sweating stops completely, and the victim then soon collapses. At any stage, treatment is the same: get the victim out of the sun, strip off the person's clothes, and douse his or her body continuously with cold water until body temperature returns to normal. Get the victim to a doctor when the person is able to travel.

Heat exhaustion. Failure to replace lost fluids when exercising in warm weather can lead to a condition called heat exhaustion. Symptoms are similar to those for heatstroke except that the victim's skin will be pale, cool, and clammy with sweat. Treat victims by laying them in the shade with their feet slightly elevated and giving them slightly salted water to drink. Keep them cool, even after recovery.

Sunburn. Backpackers who try to work on their tans while on the trail usually end up regretting it. To avoid discomfort, use a sunscreen on exposed skin before heading into an open area where sunburn might be a problem.

Cold Weather Hazards

Even moderately cold weather, especially if wet or windy, can be hazardous.

Novice backpackers very often fail to realize that even moderately cool temperatures, if combined with wet or windy weather, can chill the unprotected body just as surely as bitter cold—and with equally serious consequences. Regardless of the time of year, if you plan to hike in a rainy, cool area, bring waterproof rain gear and plenty of wool clothing—several shirts, long trousers, a cap that covers your ears and neck, and mittens. Unlike cotton or down, wool retains its insulating properties even when wet (as do a number of fairly new synthetics, such as polypropylene and polyester pile). Dress in layers so you can strip down when hot to minimize sweating and put garments back on when it becomes chilly. And be sure to eat and drink frequently to reduce the risk of dehydration and fatigue, factors that sap the body of its ability to battle cold.

Hypothermia. Most people associate hypothermia, a condition in which the body's core temperature drops, with snowy winter nights and alpine expeditions. But the fact is, more cases of hypothermia occur between 30 and 50 degrees Fahrenheit than at temperatures well below freezing, simply because people don't realize the dangers of moderately cold and wet weather.

One of the most insidious aspects of hypothermia is that as the body's core temperature falls, the brain is one of the first areas affected—with the result that people in the early stages of hypothermia very often fail to recognize, or even deny, their symptoms and lack the simple reasoning skills needed to take quick action. Thus, it is critical to be aware of the warning signs of hypothermia and to keep a close watch for them in yourself and others whenever the weather turns cold. These signs include uncontrolled shivering, slurred or rapid-fire speech, confusion, lethargy, and overwhelming exhaustion.

If you observe any of these signs (even if the victim claims to be fine): Get the person into a tent or other sheltered area. Take off all wet clothing and place the victim in a sleeping bag with one or more other persons, also stripped to allow plenty of skin-to-skin contact (placing the

victim in a sleeping bag alone will do no good, since the person's body will have lost its ability to warm itself). Rub the victim's limbs vigorously and provide plenty of warm liquids to drink. Keep the person awake and talking until body temperature returns to normal.

Frostbite. Poor circulation and very cold temperatures can lead to a condition called frostbite, in which body tissue actually freezes. Extremities—hands, feet, nose, ears—are usually affected first and most severely. The first sign of frostbite, aside from intense cold, is very often pain in the affected area; sometimes, however, small patches of white, frost-nipped skin will appear on a victim's face or nose.

At an early stage, an affected body part should be warmed by placing it in contact with warm skin. But if the tissue has actually frozen, do not attempt treatment in the field; allowing a body part to remain frozen and numb until the victim can be treated in a hospital is far less dangerous than thawing in the field.

For some, backpacking alone may sound attractive, but it is not recommended. The presence of at least one other person significantly raises the chances of getting help in an emergency.

Lightning

If you're caught out in the open during a lightning storm, follow a few common-sense rules: Don't stand or sit directly under prominent trees or other prominent objects; stay at a distance equal to approximately twice the height of the object. If you are the most prominent object on the landscape, crouch down in a depression or ditch, making yourself as low as possible until the lightning moves away. Stay away from good conductors of electricity, such as metal tent poles and pack frames. And at no time take shelter from the storm under an overhanging crag or in the mouth of a shallow cave; lightning often jumps the gap within such openings, passing through whoever may be standing there.

Following the above guidelines will all but eliminate your chances of being struck by lightning. But in the rare event that someone in your group is struck, begin cardiopulmonary resuscitation immediately.

Polluted Drinking Water

The increased use—and misuse—of the backcountry has led to the widespread pollution of water sources. Today, the purity of all streams and lakes—even cold mountain springs—should be questioned before drinking. If there's the slightest chance that the water was polluted upstream, it should be treated.

Untreated, polluted backcountry water can contain a wide variety of viruses, bacteria, amoebas, and protozoa, many of which are capable of causing illness. The most common scourge of backpackers, however, is a protozoan parasite called *Giardia lamblia*, whose cysts are passed by human or animal excrement. These cysts can survive for months, not only in murky ponds, but in clear streams as well—and they can withstand freezing conditions, so that water should not be considered safe because it comes from a fresh snowfield. If a sufficient number of cysts are ingested, susceptible people (about half the population) may, after a short incubation period, contract giardiasis, an illness marked first by fever, chills, headache, vomiting, and fatigue and later by explosive diarrhea, cramps, and weight loss lasting a week or more. Usually the organism is expelled completely from the body in about a week, but giardiasis sometimes becomes a recurring condition that must be treated with powerful drugs.

Fortunately, *Giardia* cysts and other potentially harmful organisms can be killed by boiling questionable water for at least five minutes (at sea level—and an additional minute for every 1,000 feet of elevation above that) or by chemically treating the water, usually with iodine. Iodine tablets and crystals for this purpose may be found at camping retailers and through mail order catalogs; read the instructions carefully before using these products. Whether you boil your water or treat it chemically, it's a good idea to bring along a couple of canteens or water bottles.

A third treatment option is to strain the water through a special mechanical filter, by far the fastest and easiest method of water purification but also the most expensive. The better of these filters will strain out *Giardia* cysts, bacteria, and other oganisms, but none at present is able to strain out viruses. If you're in an area where contamination by the hepatitis virus is a problem (not in the United States or Canada at present), you should stick to the other methods.

Poison Ivy

Rare is the backpacker who hasn't stumbled across a patch of poison ivy, poison oak, or poison sumac on the trail, so it's a good idea to learn to identify these plants by sight. If you do touch one of them, immediately wash the affected area with soap and water if possible. Be sure to carry calamine lotion, cortisone cream, or a comparable medication if you're particularly sensitive.

Stomach ailments may be right around the corner for this hiker; even a crystal clear mountain stream can be polluted. Because there is no way of knowing, all water obtained in the wilderness should be purified before drinking.

Insects

Unless you restrict your backpacking to cold weather seasons, you'll no doubt contend with your share of insects. The most common of these—mosquitoes, black flies, and the like—are no more than a sometimes painful nuisance and can usually be kept at bay with an insect repellent containing the chemical N,N-Diethyl-meta-toluamide (DEET). Some other insects, however, may pose a health hazard, so it's worth knowing what to do if you get stung or bitten.

Bees and wasps. For most people, a bee or wasp sting is painful and causes local swelling but is not serious; for those allergic to the venom, however, such stings can prove fatal. If such a sting has caused you breathing difficulties or hivelike swelling in the past, you may be allergic and should purchase a sting kit, available by prescription, containing a preloaded syringe of adrenaline and a supply of antihistamine tablets. If you carry such a kit, be sure not only that you know how to use it, but that the other members of your party know of your allergy and also know how to use the kit.

Spiders. There are only three types of poisonous spiders in the United States whose bite is harmful to humans: tarantulas, black widows, and brown recluses. The bite of a tarantula is usually no more serious than a bee sting; in some cases, though, these bites can lead to serious complications, including bacterial endocarditis (inflammation of the lining of the heart and its valves).

Black widow or brown recluse bites, while rarely fatal, can cause a serious and painful reaction. Since there's no effective first aid for such bites, victims should be taken to a doctor for treatment if possible; if not, the victim should sit out the reaction in a cool place to slow the spread of venom.

Ticks. Ticks are usually found on tall grass or similar vegetation waiting for a warm meal to pass by. Once they latch onto a body, they crawl to soft, warm areas, burrow in with their heads, and begin sucking blood. Although most ticks are no more than a disgusting nuisance, a few species can transmit such serious illnesses as Lyme disease, a flu-like illness that can lead to arthritis or heart problems, and the potentially fatal Rocky Mountain spotted fever (a misnomer, since 95 percent of cases in the United States now occur in the East). If diagnosed early these diseases can be easily treated with antibiotics, but the best defense is to avoid picking up ticks or to remove them either before they attach themselves to the body or within the first few hours of contact, before they've had a chance to transmit disease.

If you will be traveling in an area where ticks are common (find out in advance whether that is the case), you can take precautions to minimize your chances of picking up ticks. Wear long pants tucked inside light-colored socks (which makes attached ticks easier to spot), and spray boots, exposed socks, and lower pants with an insect repellent containing DEET. For added protection, wear a long-sleeved shirt. Inspect your clothing and body regularly for ticks.

If a tick attaches to your body, the most effective way to remove it is with a pair of tweezers, being careful not to leave the head imbedded in the skin; this can still transmit disease. Complete removal is not

A good insect repellent is a necessity for backpackers.

usually a problem if the tick is found within a few hours of burrowing in, but if the head does break off and the skin becomes infected, see a doctor.

Snakes

From the Garden of Eden to the present day, snakes have been regarded by many people as sinister creatures. This is far from the truth. For the most part, snakes are rather timid animals that will go out of their way to get out of yours; they usually strike only when surprised and frightened. Moreover, of the many snakes found throughout the United States, only four are poisonous: the water moccasin (cottonmouth), found in wetlands of the South; copperheads, found widely throughout the East; various species of rattlesnakes, found throughout the country; and coral snakes, found only in the southeastern corner of the United States plus part of Arizona. The venom of the water moccasin and copperhead is rarely life-threatening, and even that of the rattlesnake will not kill most healthy adults. Coral snake venom, on the other hand, is highly lethal, but except for the large varieties found in Florida, these snakes rarely bite humans.

Preventing snakebites is far easier than treating them. Before heading into snake country, it's a good idea to familiarize yourself with the types of snakes you're likely to encounter there and to learn something about their particular habits. All snakes, however, are governed by a few basic biological rules that can help you determine when and where they're most likely to turn up.

Snakes are cold-blooded creatures, relying on the environment to maintain a stable internal temperature. They are often found sunning themselves on open trails during cool days or soaking up the trail's residual warmth at night; at warmer times they are more likely to be keeping cool in the shade of bushes, in rock crevices, or in similar protected places. At all times, watch where you put your hands and feet. Wear long pants and leather boots that cover your ankles, and try not to brush up against bushes on the side of the trail. Although snakes are technically deaf, they are highly sensitive to vibrations; in dense snake country, therefore, don't tread softly—but do carry a big stick if it will make you feel better.

If you're heading into an area where poisonous snakes may be a problem, you should carry a snakebite kit, whose purpose is to remove as much venom as possible and to slow its spread. Health experts warn, however, that more damage than good may be caused by a panicky first aider who doesn't know the proper use of the kit, so learn how to use it before an emergency exists.

Bears

More than one novice backpacker has struck out into bear country with visions of Gentle Ben on his mind and a roll of film in his camera, hoping for "just one shot." But Disney films aside, bears are extremely powerful and dangerous animals, and—as human activities encroach more and more heavily on their habitats—are becoming increasingly

Bears, like this menacing grizzly, are ferocious when provoked or hungry. Even cuddly looking bears should be avoided; they are wild animals that can severely maul or kill a human being.

Backpacking can be a fun family activity when safety precautions are heeded and the pace is kept comfortable for everyone.

unpredictable and increasingly likely to attack. To hike in bear country with any thought other than to avoid contact with these animals is foolish at best.

There are two main species of bears in the United States and Canada: black bears, found throughout the mountainous regions of the United States, in the Deep South, and across Canada and Alaska; and grizzly bears, also found throughout Canada and Alaska, but restricted primarily to the Yellowstone National Park and Glacier National Park regions in the contiguous United States. Of the two species, grizzlies are the larger and by far the more aggressive. Truly wild black bears are decidedly more timid and, except for instances where a mother is protecting her cubs, rarely attack humans. In many areas, however, particularly around state and national parks, years of interaction with tourists and their food supplies have made black bears—as well as grizzlies—far less fearful of humans; although they still rarely attack, black bears are now notorious campground raiders.

When traveling in bear country, there are a number of precautions a backpacker can take. Except for the semi-domesticated parkland variety, bears are generally shy animals who will, if possible, avoid all contact with humans. When hiking, therefore, talk or sing loudly, or attach a bell or similar noisemaking device to your pack—anything to warn a bear of your approach. Don't wear perfumes, hair sprays, or clothes with food spilled on them, and never bring a dog along. When you set up camp, be sure to pitch your tent at least 100 yards upwind from your cooking area—and never right beside a stream, since bears tend to prowl along streams at night. Clean all cooking utensils after you use them, and remove all traces of trash and food from your cooking area. Before retiring for the night, hang all food, trash, cosmetics, fishing tackle, and the like in bags at least 12 feet off the ground and well away from your tent, either from poles or cables specifically erected by park rangers for this purpose, from a rope strung between two trees, or from a tree limb reaching at least 10 feet out from the trunk.

If you do encounter a bear, however, the recommended course of action is far less straightforward. Many experts have long suggested hightailing it to the nearest tree, climbing it, and staying there until the bear loses interest. But other experts claim that running from a bear is one of the surest ways to encourage an attack. Some have suggested playing dead, still others that you kneel on the ground, press your head between your knees, clasp your hands behind your neck, and thus form a tight, well-protected ball.

The current advice among many park rangers and bear researchers in Alaska, however, is that if you encounter a bear, simply back away slowly and hope it doesn't follow. If it does, place your pack, jacket, or some other object that might distract the bear on the ground and continue to back away. If the bear still advances, draw yourself up into as imposing a figure as possible, shout menacingly, and wave your arms, in the hope that it will realize you're not its usual prey and retreat. If this still doesn't stop the bear, resort to the ball method discussed above.

Hang food and trash high above the ground to protect your campsite from raiding bears.

A Final Reminder

Any discussion of backpacking that focuses exclusively on spiders and snakes and other perils of the trail risks sending even outdoors enthusiasts quivering back to their motor homes. But it shouldn't. The only real danger in the woods is ignorance; conquer this, prepare for the risks, and you'll have nothing to fear. And a whole world to gain. ☐

SUGGESTIONS FOR FURTHER READING

FLETCHER COLIN. *The Complete Walker III.* New York, Knopf, 1986.

FORGEY, WILLIAM W., M.D. *Wilderness Medicine.* Pittsboro, Ind., Indiana Camp Supply Books, 1979.

KJELLSTROM, BJORN. *Be Expert With Map and Compass.* New York, Scribner's, 1976.

MANNING, HARVEY. *Backpacking: One Step at a Time,* 4th ed. New York, Vintage Books, 1986.

SCHUH, DWIGHT R. *Modern Outdoor Survival.* New York, Arco Publishing, 1983.

Raising an Adopted Child

Claire Berman

In a yellow room on the third floor of the gray-shingled building that houses the adoption agency, Doug and Kathy Sohmer are waiting. (The names of the Sohmer family members and their social worker have been changed.) Doug, 36, runs his fingers through his short, dark hair. Kathy, 32, keeps turning the gold wedding ring on the third finger of her left hand. The ring (and the marriage) are eight years old. Kathy turns to Doug. "How long has it been?" she asks. Doug glances at his watch. "Eight minutes," he replies. The last time Kathy asked how long they'd been waiting in this room, the answer had been five minutes. It has taken three years for the couple to reach this point, and now every second seems forever.

The doorknob is turned. Mrs. Horne, the couple's social worker, enters. In her arms is a three-week-old baby wrapped softly in a pink blanket. "Say hello to

A reunion of adopted youngsters and their families at the Chosen Children adoption agency.

43

Nontraditional Adoption

Nontraditional adoption arrangements are becoming more and more common. At left, a single mother and her adopted son; at right, an Oregon couple and their Korean daughter.

your new daughter," Mrs. Horne says as she places the baby in Kathy's outstretched arms. The couple stare down at the infant, marveling at the softness of her skin, at her dark eyes and long lashes. Doug reaches toward the blanket and gingerly touches the baby's small hand. "Oh, she's beautiful," the new parents say in unison. They cannot believe their good fortune, that this baby—whom they will name Alicia Ruth—has finally entered their lives. They are eager to spread news of the joyous event: *We have a daughter. A child has joined our family.*

When the Sohmers first considered adoption as a way to build a family, they did not realize that the process would be so thorough or that the wait would take so long. They began by glancing through the classified telephone directory, jotting down the numbers of several places listed under "Adoption Services," and then phoning some of the

Claire Berman is a writer whose books on children and families include We Take This Child: A Candid Look at Modern Adoption.

agencies listed. They quickly discovered that the number of people interested in adopting a healthy baby far exceeded the number of babies being placed. There were children waiting to be adopted, they were told. Many of these children were older, however, or had special needs of an emotional, educational, or physical nature. After some reflection, Doug and Kathy decided that they wanted their first parenting experience to involve a healthy baby. The first agency they approached said that its waiting list of potential parents was so long that it was no longer taking applications. At the second agency, they were invited to attend an informational meeting.

When they arrived, they found some half-dozen other couples assembled. The group was told about the children in need of adoptive parents, about the procedures involved in adopting, and about the possibility and process of adopting a child from another country. The caseworker who addressed the gathering did not provide cause for optimism for those who sought infants, but the agency *was* accepting applications, and so the Sohmers decided to pursue their dream.

The process they embarked on, called a home study, included medical examinations to verify that the couple was unable to have children biologically (a condition that does not apply when adopting a special-needs youngster). They had a series of meetings—jointly and individually—with a caseworker to talk about such things as their marriage, reasons for wanting a child, and feelings about adoption, as well as the expectations they had for the child they would adopt. They provided financial information (the caseworker was less interested in how much money the couple earned than in seeing that they were able to manage their income and meet their expenses) and references from people who could attest to their character. They completed the lengthy process successfully. And then they waited for two years.

There were times when they wondered if they had taken the right path. They questioned whether they should have pursued independent adoption and tried to locate a baby privately, perhaps using a lawyer as an intermediary. (This is often extremely expensive.) But their caseworker assured them that everything would work out well. And

In an open adoption, biological and adoptive parents may meet. Here, a young birth mother (right) prepares to say good-bye to her son, who will be raised by adoptive parents she herself chose.

here was Alicia Ruth to prove that they were right. There was no question that she was worth waiting for.

Kathy and Doug, like all parents, will be challenged by the everyday aspects of raising a child. As the years go by, Alicia Ruth, like all children, will experience both the pain and the pleasure that is involved in growing up. *Unlike* the majority of families, however, the Sohmers will have some special issues to consider along the way, matters that are unique to families that have been created through adoption.

There are no reliable statistics on how many such families there are in North America. Based on the dated and incomplete information that is available, it is estimated that 5 million to 7 million children are adoptees. To be an adoptee differs from being a child born into a family in a number of significant ways: the child does not share the medical or ancestral history of the family, the child may have different aptitudes and weaknesses, and the child may look different from other family members. But most important is the reality that the child has two sets of parents—one that gave him or her life, and another that has assumed legal and ethical responsibility for enhancing the quality of that life. Being an adoptive parent means that one has to acknowledge and accept these differences.

Accepting the Difference

"I love her so much, it's hard to believe she was not born to me," says one adoptive mother, expressing the closeness she feels toward her child. But the statement may also reflect the mother's wish that the adopted child *had* been born into the family and perhaps a desire to deny that there are any differences between her family and those based on a blood relationship.

Sociologist H. David Kirk, a pioneer in the study of parent-child relationships in adoption, has identified two contrasting responses of parents toward their adopted children: rejection-of-difference and acknowledgment-of-difference. In his insightful books *Shared Fate* and *Adoptive Kinship*, Kirk makes the point that rejection-of-difference inhibits the parent's capacity for empathy with the special problems that the adoptee experiences and diminishes communication between parent and child. Acknowledgment-of-difference, Kirk declares, allows for honesty, openness, and trust and is beneficial to family functioning.

Nature or nurture? Do children enter this world as human beings fully formed not only in body but in ways of behaving? Or do they come to us as clean slates upon which all of life's experiences have yet to be written? The question of the supremacy of nature or nurture has long been the subject of conjecture and study and is of particular interest in the case of adoption. How much influence on a child's life can an adoptive parent hope to have?

For much of the 20th century, almost all psychologists stressed the importance of environment in determining behavior. In the last 20 years, however, scientists have conducted many studies that have shown the importance of heredity. One study looked specifically at children who were placed for adoption, in order to determine how traits like intelligence, language ability, and temperament, including shyness,

Adoptive parents must acknowledge that their child differs from a child born into the family.

MARY JO AND HER BIRTHMOM, HELEN
FIVE (5) YEARS AFTER BEING REUNITED !!!

To help adopted children seek out their biological parents, a California woman who was successful in her own search for her birth mother co-founded a resource library in Garden Grove.

were developed. According to Robert Plomin, professor of human development at Pennsylvania State University, who conducted the experiment, shyness clearly proved to be an inherited trait. Such studies can be important in helping adoptive parents appreciate those attributes of the child—both bad and good—that the youngster has brought into the family.

However, "knowing that a child is born with certain attributes (such as shyness or an outgoing personality) and predispositions (to proficiency in sports or music, for example) should not lock the child in," cautions Dr. Plomin. "It's important for adoptive parents to see children not as a lump of clay to be molded, but perhaps as clay with certain markings in it. And it's also important to note that it's not that different for parents who have children biologically. These children, too, have certain characteristics that are unique to them and are not just clones of the parents."

The extended family. Until a few years ago, it was common practice in adoption to try to physically match a child as closely as possible with the adoptive parents—to place a red-headed child in a red-headed family, a tall child with tall parents, and so on. This was done so that, insofar as possible, the adoptive family would closely resemble the family that might have existed had the parents had their children naturally. In addition, it has been shown that the more closely children resemble the adopted family, the more readily are they accepted by members of the extended family. One problem with matching, however, is that it feeds into the fantasy that the adopted child *was* born into the family, and it works against fostering the acknowledgment of difference that is, in the long run, most healthful for adoptive parent-child relationships.

The more a child differs in looks from the adopted family—for example, when an interracial adoption takes place—the greater is the likelihood that there will be problems of acceptance on the part of the extended family. Often, these problems go away as the grandparents, aunts, and uncles get to know the child. If the problems persist, it is sometimes helpful to place some geographical distance between the adoptive family unit and those family members who do not welcome the child.

Telling the Child

How children learn of their adoption is often critical to its success. In fact, one of the major challenges adoptive parents face is how and when they will tell the child about the adoption. The prevailing practice over the past several years has been to tell children at an early age.

Too often, however, the story that is told is not open and honest; it is, instead, a fairy tale that has as its hero or heroine someone who is referred to as the "chosen child." The adoptee is told, "Other parents had to take whatever child was born to them, but we *chose* you." Children raised on this narrative tell of having fantasized their parents walking through a roomful of bassinets, spotting the child of their dreams, and proclaiming, "*This* is the one." Adoptive parents use this story to make up for any feelings the child might have of being second best. The moral of the chosen-child story is that adoption is not only as good as being born into a family, it is better.

One problem, though, is that being "chosen" places a burden on the child to measure up to what is perceived as the parents' special expectations. Also, it takes only a short while for children to figure out that in order for them to have been chosen, they first had to be given up. Of course, the reality is that the adoptive parents wanted a child and the adopted child needed a family. The true story of an adoption is miracle enough—it is the wonderful happenstance that, however and whenever it took place, fate brought these particular parents and this particular child together.

How and when to tell. "There are two very different approaches to telling," says Reuben Pannor, adoption consultant for the Vista Del Mar Child Care Service in Los Angeles and coauthor of *The Adoption Triangle.* "First, there is the secretive approach. The child is told the

It is easier today to find couples willing to adopt older children like these brothers.

49

bare facts in an almost furtive manner. It is made clear that the subject is never to be brought up again, that to do so would cause the parents discomfort. What this tells the child is that to be adopted is something shameful.

"At the opposite end," he continues, "you have the tell-them-everything-at-once approach, sometimes attempted when the child is as young as two or three. Here the parents seem more interested in unburdening themselves than they are in meeting the needs of the child."

More appropriate than either of these extremes, professionals agree, is gradually and continually conveying information as the child is ready to comprehend it. There is less agreement on when this process should start.

Herbert Weider, a psychoanalyst who played a major role in establishing an Adoption Study Center at New York City's Brookdale Hospital Medical Center, believes that "a child under three or four can't master the information. Telling too early creates confusion at a time when the developing conceptualization of the term 'mother' would apply to the image of a nurturing parent, and is then contradicted by introduction of another mother. At about four years of age, the child can accept less traumatically the concept of having grown in someone else's uterus." But, Dr. Weider cautions, children vary. "You have to . . . have some idea of the youngster's capability to handle distressing information."

As for the concept of the biological father, Dr. Vera Fahlberg, medical director of an Evergreen, Colo., psychiatric facility for children and adolescents, explains, "As children get older, their questions have to do with the part that daddies play in the birth process. Then one can get into the fact that there was a different father as well as a different mother."

Between the ages of five and six, after children have started school and entered an expanding world, they need to arrive at a better understanding about their birth parents. Dr. Fahlberg believes that "What do they look like?" is the most common question of adopted youngsters at this stage. If the adoptive parents have this information, she feels, they should share it. When children reach the age of nine or so, they move from concrete facts to more conceptual thinking. "What does it *mean* that I was adopted?" the child wants to understand. This is the time to explain some of the major issues involved.

Children's understanding of adoption. "Telling children about their adoption does not guarantee that they necessarily will understand the information provided," says psychologist David Brodzinsky of Rutgers University, who conducted a study that sheds light on the subject. He found that most preschoolers understand little about adoption, even though they have been told they are adopted and the children spontaneously use the word "adopted" when describing themselves.

By age six, most children differentiate between birth and adoption as ways of entering a family. Many also begin to be aware that a third party exists who acted as an intermediary in the adoption process. The children are likely to be interested in their parents' talk of "the agency where we got you," "the doctor we went to," and "when the judge said

One of the major challenges faced by adoptive parents is how and when to tell the child.

A couple at a Texas adoption agency looks at baby photos.

we were a family.'' Between ages 8 and 11, children's conception of adoption broadens considerably, Dr. Brodzinsky found. They begin to appreciate the uniqueness of their family status, especially such complexities as why people adopt and why children are placed for adoption. Much of the child's fantasy life becomes centered on whether the biological parents can return to reclaim the child. Children generally regain their certainty in the permanence of their place in the adoptive family toward the end of this period.

Open Adoption

A relatively recent option, open adoption has taken candor a giant leap further. In an open adoption the biological and adoptive parents may meet—sometimes before the child is born—and continue to communicate with and perhaps visit one another while the child is growing up. In other situations, the biological and adoptive parents do not meet but agree to exchange letters and photographs over the years, with the agency serving as an intermediary. (As in any adoption, the birth parents give up all legal rights to the child.)

Although slowly gaining acceptance among some parents and adoption agencies, open adoption remains controversial. Opponents

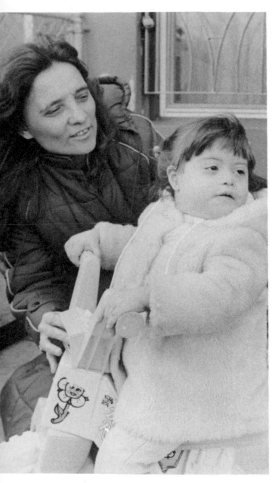

Until ten years ago, children with handicaps were considered unadoptable—a situation that has changed, as shown by this adopted girl with Down's syndrome.

argue that it threatens the privacy both of the mother who has relinquished her baby and of the adoptive parents, who may fear that she will want to take away the child. Opponents are also concerned that having two sets of parents will only confuse the youngster.

Supporters believe that keeping the door open is kinder to the birth parent and, over time, to adoptive parents as well. "The adoptive parents we have dealt with say that meeting the birth parent has allayed their fears of intrusion," says Kathleen Silber, author of a book on open adoption (*Dear Birthmother*) and state director of domestic adoption at Children's Home Society of California, a statewide private adoption agency. For the child, say those who favor the practice, an open adoption provides a sense of continuity. Proponents argue that when a youngster wants to know "Who do I look like?" or "Why couldn't my original parents keep me?" the new generation of adoptive parents will have adequate answers.

Continued communication between biological and adoptive parents also makes it possible for adoptees to obtain updated medical information, a need that is seldom considered at the time of placement but may become significant thereafter. In many adoptions, medical background is provided, but it is limited to what is known at the time that the birth parents relinquish the child and does not include the conditions and illnesses that are likely to develop as the birth parents grow older.

"People who take biological membership in their families for granted," says one adoptee, "may find it hard to imagine what it's like not to know that your grandfather died of cancer or that your grandmother lived to 101. They don't know how it feels, when you're asked to fill out a medical form for anything—school, a job, an insurance application—not to be able to fill in the blanks."

Special Situations

Older children. Children who are older at the time of adoption may have some of these questions answered. In addition, they do not need to be told that they are adopted—they know. Even so, they need help in understanding why they could not live with their original family or remain with previous caregivers, such as foster parents.

Less than two decades ago, a child of three or four was considered too old to be adopted. Today, many couples are eager to adopt healthy children up to around ten years of age. There are large numbers of preadolescents and teenagers, however, who are still waiting for a chance to become permanent members of a family through adoption. It remains difficult to locate individuals who will accept the special challenges often involved in adopting children over the age of ten. Such an adoption is in some ways similar to a marriage. Parents and child have to work at the relationship. Both have separate pasts that will take a long time to understand and to merge. Both may test one another's commitment. It can be hard work and take a long time to build satisfying relationships. Youngsters and parents who have come through the trial period successfully declare that the results are definitely worth the effort.

Children with handicaps. Adoption advocates often say that "no child is unadoptable, only unadopted," and over the past 15 or so years, they have been proven right. Up until the mid-1970's, a child born with a cleft lip and palate was considered too handicapped to be adopted. Children with mental retardation were routinely placed in institutions or with foster families. Since then, children with significant physical, mental, or emotional disabilities—even some known to be terminally ill—have been adopted by families committed to their love and nurture and to seeing that they develop to the utmost of their capabilities.

Children of other races. Transracial adoption is a very controversial issue in the United States. Those who are opposed to the practice of placing black or mixed-race children with white families hold a strong belief that it denies such children their racial identity and that greater efforts must be made to recruit families from within the minority community. Those who are in favor of placing children for adoption across racial lines assert that, while it is preferable for children to be placed in families of the same race, it is better for a child to be united with parents of a different race than to go from one foster home or institution to another.

There are special concerns, of course, for parents who adopt transracially. They need to learn about the child's background in order to instill in the youngster an appreciation of his or her own heritage. They would do well to live in an integrated community and to provide positive role models of the same race with whom the child can identify. Parents can also join support and friendship groups organized by agencies and other parents—for the benefit of both themselves and the child.

Children from other countries. Among the children being adopted by Americans is a sizable population from other countries. In 1986 close to 10,000 foreign-born children either were adopted abroad by U.S. citizens or came into the United States to be adopted. Of these, the largest groups came from Asia (predominantly South Korea) and Latin America.

Foreign-born adopted children have many extra adjustments to make—to a new climate, new foods, new language, new customs, and new ways of discipline. Just as the white family adopting a black child should help the child learn about and gain pride in his or her culture, so must the family adopting transnationally help the child become familiar with and proud of the country of origin. To assist in this process, in many communities families that have adopted children from other lands have organized special groups and programs to enable their children to meet others from similar backgrounds and to learn or continue the customs of their native peoples and countries.

Interest in the Biological Parents

Adopted children must be allowed to acknowledge the parents who gave them life. Many youngsters fear that even mentioning the biological parents would hurt their adoptive parents. Therefore, these children may be reluctant to raise the subject. Adoptive parents can

Children must be allowed to acknowledge their biological parents.

53

make it easier for the children if they themselves allude to the biological parents in a comfortable, natural way. "Mike, I don't know *where* you got your musical talent in this tin-ear family. You must have inherited it," an adoptive father might say. "I've always admired long lashes," an adoptive mother could tell her daughter. "Your birth mother must have beautiful eyes."

If children sense that their adoptive parents have not precluded discussion, their natural curiosity is bound to make them ask questions. Insofar as the adoptive parents are able, they should answer such queries openly and honestly.

The Search

Much attention has been focused in recent years on "the search," which is generally represented in the media as the adoptee's search for and eventual reunion with the birth parents, usually the birth mother. In fact, the search has different goals for different people. Some adoptees are interested solely in information: What is my heritage? What are the talents in my family of birth? Others seek to learn the reasons why their birth parents placed them for adoption. Some, especially those raised as only children, are interested in learning whether they have any sisters or brothers. Others want medical information. This is typically true of women who are about to give birth to their first child and wonder what they are passing on to the child. And many adoptees want to know, "Who do I look like?" Some would be happy with a onetime encounter with the birth parents in order to satisfy these feelings. Others embark on the search hoping for a meeting and ensuing relationship.

An adopted infant greets his new parents.

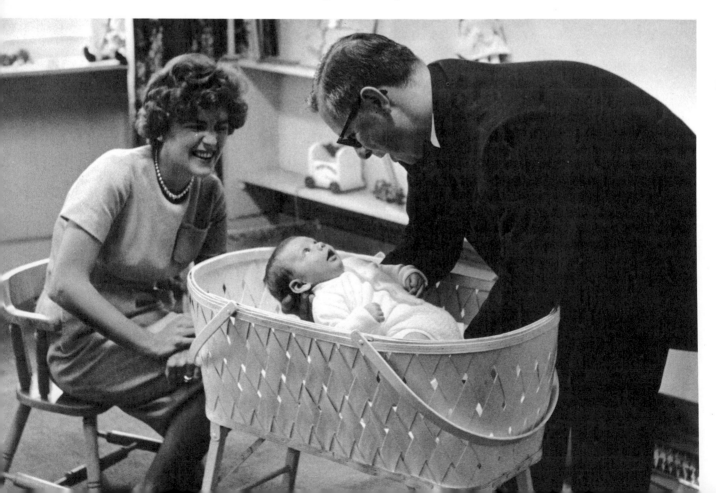

The seach for the biological family has become a highly controversial issue in contemporary adoption. In most states, records are sealed once an adoption has been legalized, and the information is unavailable. In a number of states, the laws have been changed so that once adoptees reach adulthood, they can receive nonidentifying information about their biological parents—such facts as the parents' ages at the time of birth; ethnic and religious background; general physical appearance; occupations, talents, and hobbies; health history (up to the time the child was placed for adoption); and circumstances surrounding the adoption. In other states, adoption registries have been established to facilitate the actual encounter between biological parents and their offspring on the condition that consent is obtained from the adoptee, the birth parents, and the adoptive parents.

"For some adoptive parents, the prospect of reunion brings on an emotional crisis," says Dr. Arthur Sorosky, professor of child psychiatry at the University of California at Los Angeles and coauthor of *The Adoption Triangle*. "The child they have raised to maturity suddenly declares a desire to contact the birth parents and may actively begin the search. All the old fears are brought back to the surface with much force. Does this mean we have failed as parents? Are we now to lose our children after all? But a look at reunions which have actually occurred puts these fears to rest. Their significance is entirely different from what many adoptive parents imagine," Sorosky notes.

"After I met my birth mother, I grew even closer to my adoptive mother," says one adoptee, whose search was made at the age of 32. "I suddenly started quoting her all over the place. And I had a lot of memories of myself as a small child with her and a lot of thoughts about what I was passing on to my daughter which came from her: songs, attitudes, interests, my way of speaking. . . ." She continues, "I also was helped to understand which attributes of myself came from none of my parents—which parts of myself were uniquely me." □

Adoption advocates say no child is unadoptable, only unadopted.

SUGGESTIONS FOR FURTHER READING

For adults:

GILMAN, LOIS. *The Adoption Resource Book*, rev. ed. New York, Harper & Row, 1987.

KIRK, H. DAVID. *Adoptive Kinship: A Modern Institution in Need of Reform*, rev. ed. Port Angeles, Wash., Ben-Simon, 1984.

KIRK, H. DAVID. *Shared Fate: A Theory and Method of Adoptive Relationships*, rev. ed. Port Angeles, Wash., Ben-Simon, 1984.

LIFTON, BETTY JEAN. *Lost and Found: The Adoption Experience.* New York, Dial, 1979.

MELINA, LOIS RUSKAI. *Raising Adopted Children: A Manual for Adoptive Parents.* New York, Harper & Row, 1986.

For children:

KREMENTZ, JILL. *How It Feels to Be Adopted.* New York, Knopf, 1982.

LIVINGSTON, CAROLE. *Why Was I Adopted?* Secaucus, N.J., Lyle Stuart, 1978.

POWLEDGE, FRED. *So You're Adopted.* New York, Scribner's, 1982.

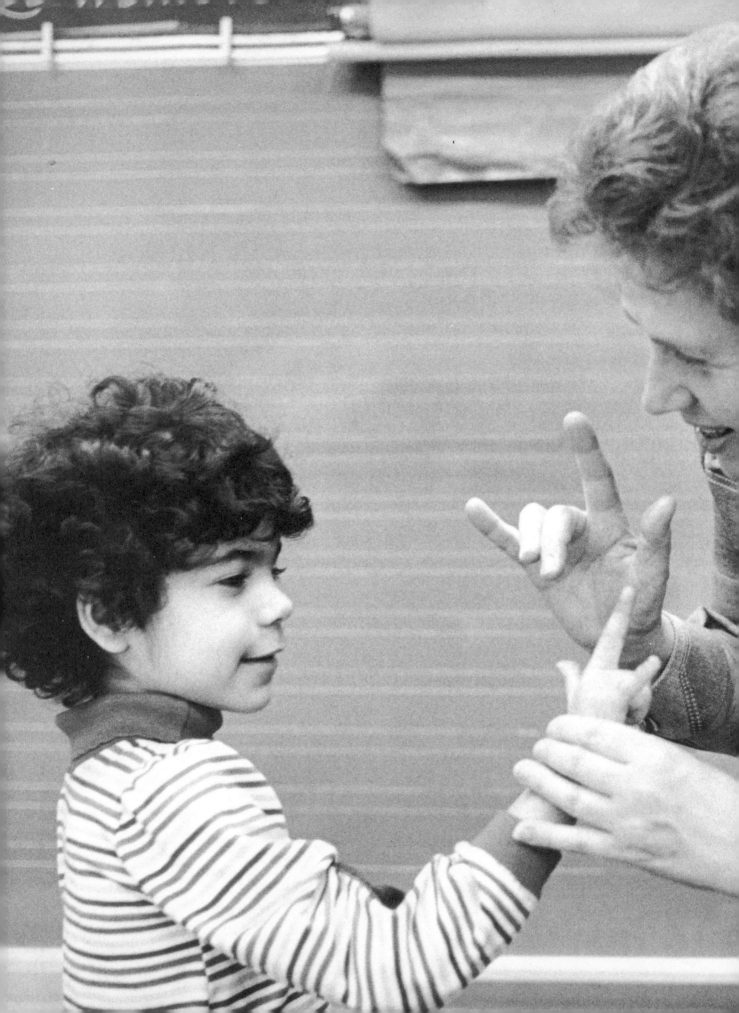

Educating the Deaf

Donald F. Moores, Ph.D.

Deafness has been called an invisible condition. Because deaf people have no problems moving about and are indistinguishable in appearance from others, they may not reveal their deafness until person to person communication is attempted. Also, early profound deafness—severe hearing loss from birth or a very early age, so that language development is affected—is fairly uncommon. Given the small number of individuals involved and the unique nature of deafness, it is not surprising that the difficulties often encountered by those who cannot hear are little understood by the general public. In fact, deaf people face many special problems in adapting to the hearing world. Fortunately, in recent years education for deaf individuals has provided new means for them to function successfully in that world.

Deafness should not be considered a handicap in itself, but rather an impairment or disability. It is caused by a physical *impairment* of the auditory mechanism, and *disability* is measured by tests of hearing. The *handicap* of deafness is more of a social and cultural concept. It refers to the extent to which an individual's functioning is limited by the disability of deafness. Two people might have the same level of disability, but one might be less handicapped than the other because of a greater development of skills for coping with the problem. Also, depending on the demands of the particular environment, a deaf individual may be handicapped in some situations and not handicapped in others.

The handicap of deafness is usually thought of in terms of limitations in communicating with hearing individuals. Deaf children have the same intellectual potential and range of physical abilities as hearing children. The only difference is in their access to a rich communication system from birth. Almost all deaf children have hearing parents who, because of the low incidence of deafness, have little understanding of its implications and have had little or no interaction with deaf children or adults. Only 3 to 4 percent of deaf children in the United States and Canada have deaf parents. Through early exposure to manual communication systems like American Sign Language and the different English-based sign systems, these children develop their linguistic and academic skills to a much higher degree than do deaf children with hearing parents. But they represent a small minority of the deaf population.

By the same token, when a deaf adult gets married—in most cases to another deaf adult—the probability is greater than 90 percent that any children will have normal hearing. The typical family pattern is for a deaf person to have hearing parents and siblings, a deaf spouse, and hearing children.

Since World War II there has been a virtual revolution in educational programs for the deaf.

Incidence of Deafness

There has been a great deal of confusion over the terms "deafness" and "hearing impairment," with resulting disagreement over the number of people that fall into each category. Quite simply, "hearing impairment" encompasses a complete range of hearing problems, from mild to profound hearing losses acquired at any time of life in one or both ears. Various studies have established the hearing impaired population in the United States at from 15 million to 20 million and in Canada at from 2 million to 3 million. The numbers have risen significantly in the last few generations because of an overall increase in population and growing life expectancy. The numbers of hearing impaired Americans will continue to grow as more and more people reach their 70's, 80's, and 90's and acquire the mild to moderate hearing loss associated with old age.

Deafness, or early profound deafness, accounts for a very small part of the hearing impaired population. It describes only those individuals with hearing losses that are present at birth or before the age of two, that occur in both ears, and that are so severe as to rule out the reception of spoken language even with the benefit of a hearing aid. There are approximately 250,000 such people in the United States. Thus, perhaps 1 American out of 15 has a hearing loss of some kind— usually mild—but only 1 out of 1,000 is in need of special educational services for the deaf.

The incidence of deafness varies from country to country and has

---

Donald F. Moores is director of the Center for Studies in Education and Human Development at Gallaudet University, a school exclusively for the deaf in Washington, D.C. He has published dozens of books and articles on the subject of deafness.

changed in the United Sates as a result of improvements in medical care, advances in hearing aids, and variations in marriage patterns (for example, the more isolated a community is, the greater the chance of concentration of recessive genes for deafness and other conditions). There is also the impact of epidemics. In the mid-1960's there was a worldwide rubella epidemic that affected untold numbers of expectant mothers, with deafness and other impairments occurring in the fetuses they were carrying. The number of deaf children born from 1963 to 1965 was double what might normally be expected. As they progressed from preschool to postsecondary levels, those children had a profound impact on educational programs.

At present there are approximately 45,000 children in educational programs for the deaf in the United States. The numbers have declined significantly since the early 1980's, as a result of the graduation of deaf children born during the rubella epidemic.

Deafness appears to be slightly more common among males, who constitute approximately 53 percent of the deaf school-age population. This percentage has remained remarkably stable for more than a century.

On a disturbing note, programs for the deaf enroll a higher percentage of minority children than might be expected. Almost one-third of the children in programs for the deaf are black, Hispanic, American Indian, or of Asian/Pacific Island background. This is a larger proportion than in the general school-age population. Because there is no reason to believe that deafness is more common in one racial or ethnic group than in another, it is likely that the differences are largely the result of environmental factors. A greater proportion of minority group members live in poverty and may not have access to adequate prenatal and postnatal medical care. Conditions that might be treated medically or through simple surgical procedures can, if neglected, lead to serious hearing loss. Also, deaf children born into poor families may not have their deafness identified early on; as a

Students come from all parts of the United States to attend a summer reading clinic at Gallaudet University, the world's only liberal arts college exclusively for the deaf.

result, they might not be fitted for a hearing aid that might significantly boost hearing.

A Revolution in Education

There has been a virtual revolution in educational programs for the deaf which began shortly after World War II, received impetus from the rubella epidemic, and accelerated in the United States under the influence of Public Law 94-142, the Education of All Handicapped Children Act of 1975. Traditionally, deaf children had been educated either in residential schools for the deaf or in special schools for the deaf in large cities, which the children commuted to daily. The increase in the American birthrate after World War II produced a larger number of deaf children, placing a strain on the resources of existing programs for the deaf. Rather than build new separate facilities, many state and local educational agencies chose to place some deaf students within standard public schools. Sometimes the deaf students were clustered in a separate part of the building, and sometimes classes for the deaf were scattered throughout the school. This trend was reinforced by the effects of the rubella epidemic. At a time when the baby boom had finished and empty classrooms were appearing in schools for the first time in decades, there was an increase in the young deaf population. Since the rubella epidemic was viewed as a onetime phenomenon and public schools were underutilized, state legislators were reluctant to commit funds for the construction of special schools. Instead, increasing numbers of deaf children were accommodated within standard public school settings, or to some extent "mainstreamed" in classes with hearing children.

A final major thrust toward the mainstreaming movement was

Communicating

A family whose members are all deaf (left) conducts a lively and freewheeling group conversation. At right, hearing parents and a deaf brother and sister tend to keep their exchanges separate.

provided by mandates contained within PL 94-142. The most important of these is the statement that each handicapped child is entitled to a free appropriate public education. The law lists procedures that must be followed to protect the rights of handicapped children and their parents. Among these are nondiscriminatory testing and an annual individualized education plan suited to the child's unique needs at that point of development.

The result of these dramatic changes has been a range of program placement options. Deaf children can still attend residential schools for the deaf or separate day schools for the deaf. But they also have available to them:

• one or more self-contained classes within a public school, in which they receive all academic instruction in a class with deaf students;

• one or more resource rooms within a public school, where they receive special instruction from a teacher of the deaf and are integrated with hearing students for one or more academic classes, frequently with the support of sign interpreters; and

• what are called itinerant programs, in which they are integrated with hearing students and receive support on the basis of need from an "itinerant" teacher of the deaf serving children in several schools.

Approximately 30 percent of deaf children in the United States now attend residential schools for the deaf, and 5 percent attend separate day schools for the deaf. Most deaf children today are educated in resource rooms or in self-contained classes for the deaf in public schools. The number who are mainstreamed completely into hearing classes remains relatively small.

After evaluating educational placement of deaf students, several researchers (including myself) have concluded that it is not beneficial to argue over which is better, mainstreaming or segregation. The

situation is not black or white, and the question can be answered only in relation to a particular child and the range of services available locally. The results to date indicate that educators in general have been quite conscientious in making placement decisions on the basis of the child's needs, contributing to an overall improvement in school achievement among deaf students.

Different Ways to Communicate

At the same time as the movement toward education in public schools developed, the education of the deaf experienced another revolution: the change to the use of manual communication, employing gesture instead of voice, in the classroom. A generation ago, almost all day and residential school programs used only oral instruction for children, at least up to age 12. Children read their teachers' lips and then spoke in response. Signs and finger spelling were not allowed. (Signs and finger spelling are different forms of manual communication. For example, it is possible either to use a single sign to signify *cat* or to use the manual alphabet and finger spell *C-A-T*.) Some residential schools employed what was known as the combined system for students of junior and senior high school age. Students who were judged to be successful in oral-only classes continued to be taught orally; those who fell behind were assigned to "manual" classes, which sometimes were taught through sign alone and sometimes with the simultaneous use of speech and sign.

The complete reliance on oral-only education for young deaf children and the restrictions on the use of manual communication came under attack from a number of sources. One of the earliest was linguist William Stokoe's pioneering analysis of American Sign Language (ASL)

Students at New York City's Lexington School for the Deaf rehearse for the annual dance recital.

GIVING MEANING TO SOUND

In recent years many products and services have been developed to make deaf people's lives easier and safer. Below are some examples of these items and how they work.

Closed Captioning. Closed captions are essentially subtitles for TV programs, appearing at the bottom of the screen. Most major network television programs are now closed captioned, but the captions can be seen only by viewers who have a special decoding device attached to their TV set.

Over 160 hours a week of cable programming and over 600 videocassettes (as well as thousands of TV commercials sponsored by major advertisers) also are closed captioned.

TDD. This device, to be attached to an ordinary telephone, has a keyboard for sending and a printer for receiving messages, enabling a deaf person to carry on phone "conversations" in printed form. (Both parties must have a TDD for the system to work.)

A new addition to the TDD is the TDD Announcer, a recorded message from the caller's machine that tells a hearing receiver (should the caller not speak well) to connect the phone to his or her TDD.

Doorbells. A special device installed at the door flashes a light when the doorbell is pressed. This device can also be attached to a lamp, causing it to flash on and off.

Alarm Clocks. Specially designed alarm clocks can be connected to lamps to cause them to flash at the set time. Also available are lamps that can take bulbs of up to 300 watts, to ensure that the person is awakened.

Baby Cry Boxes. A special device placed near a baby's crib will pick up the sound of the child's crying and flash a light to alert the deaf parents. This device can also be attached to lamps throughout the home.

Security Alarms. A device attached to the windows in a deaf person's home will do several things should a window be forced open: it will set off a loud horn to frighten intruders and alert passersby, flash a lamp attached to it to awaken the sleeping deaf person, and automatically dial and give messages to several emergency numbers. The security system is portable and can be taken along on vacations and business trips.

in the late 1950's and 1960's, which clearly demonstrated that a sign language could have all of the range, power, and subtlety of a spoken language. Stokoe's work challenged the long-held prejudices of many educators who believed that ASL was concrete and did not have the properties of a real language. His studies reduced the resistance of many educators to the use of manual communication in the classroom.

At the same time Stokoe was conducting his analysis of ASL, several independent researchers across the United States were reporting that deaf children of deaf parents were superior—academically, socially, and in their use of English—to deaf children of hearing parents. Because deaf parents almost without exception signed to their deaf children, the reports stunned educators of the deaf. The practice of restricting the use of signs at least until adolescence had been based on the unproven belief that manual communication detracted from the development of speech, skill in using English, academic achievement, and social adjustment. However, the scientific evidence from outside the field of education of the deaf clearly showed that children were actually benefiting in many ways from early manual communication; it seemed to have no effect—either positive or negative—on speech development.

By 1970 educators of the deaf were engaged in a painful reevaluation of their policy against the use of manual communication. Evidence in favor of its use was just too strong and came from too many different sources. At about this time the "total communication" movement began to gain strength. The philosophy behind the movement was that

Children are taught the different manual signs used in finger spelling.

all types of communication are appropriate and should be used, depending upon the individual needs of a child. Speech, lipreading, hearing, ASL, reading, writing, gesture, and English-based sign systems are all legitimate means of communication and may be encouraged.

Sign Systems

In adapting manual communication to the classroom, the types of signing developed since the early 1970's have followed an English-language model. It may surprise many people to learn that ASL—as used by deaf adults—is employed relatively infrequently in classrooms for the deaf. Although it has been heavily influenced by English, ASL is a separate language, with its own unique syntax (word order) and morphology (word forms). Since most teachers of the deaf, 85 percent of whom are hearing, are simply not fluent in ASL, many felt that it would be easier for them to learn a sign system based on English. Also, educational programs had a substantial commitment to oral communication and preferred to instruct students through simultaneous oral-manual communication (meaning that teachers would be expected to sign and speak at the same time; children also signed and spoke, though their speech is sometimes not intelligible). This could not be done with ASL and English because the word order is not always the same.

Several English-based sign systems have been developed for classroom use. The most widely used are Signing Exact English, Seeing Essential English, and Signed English. Each of these systems has its unique features, but each follows English word order and was designed for use in coordination with spoken English. The systems share a basic vocabulary drawn from ASL. A person using one of the systems can understand someone using another.

One way in which the English-based systems differ, to some extent, from each other—and differ from ASL—is in their "invented" signs: those created to show aspects of English grammar such as tense and number.

For example, all languages have mechanisms for expressing features such as present and past tense (in English, *walk, walked*), number (*girl, girls*), and continuous action (*work, working*). ASL has such mechanisms, but it does not express them through signs that correspond to English's *-ed, -s,* or *-ing.* ASL also may incorporate into one sign a concept that requires two English words, so that the English *sit on* or *stand on* might require only one ASL sign. The English-based

The deaf can communicate manually through finger spelling or signs. Here, illustrations from a book for young children show how some common words can be expressed in two different ways.

systems have added "sign markers" such as -s, -ed, -ing, -en, -ly, and -ment to follow English forms. In a case where ASL might use one sign for the English *climb up* or *walk around*, the invented systems use two.

Evidence from experimental studies, which began appearing around 1975, indicated that young deaf children taught through English-based signs and speech were doing better in English and academic subjects than children educated in oral-only classrooms, with no differences in speech intelligibility. The results led to a rapid change in the acceptance of manual communication in classes for deaf children. By 1978, between two-thirds and three-quarters of classes for deaf children used both manual and oral communication. Large school programs tend to have oral-only and oral-manual options, depending on the individual needs of the child. By high school, signs and speech are used in conjunction with 80 percent or more of deaf students. The content and academic demands of subjects such as algebra, literature, and science are such that most deaf students are using oral-manual communication, which is more efficient. In fact, the majority of deaf high school students mainstreamed for academic classes receive support from sign interpreters.

Realizing Their Potential

As might be expected, in educating deaf children, special attention is given to the development of communication skills. Teachers of the deaf receive training in areas such as anatomy and physiology of the speech and hearing mechanisms, methods of developing speech, manual communication, and the use and monitoring of hearing aids. Within the limited school day, deaf children usually spend less time than hearing children on subjects such as reading, math, and science. Educators of the deaf face a very difficult dilemma in deciding what the appropriate mix should be between regular academic subjects and instruction in communication skills. Both clearly are important in helping deaf children realize their potential.

In the past, teaching communication was considered the primary task of educators of the deaf, with academic achievement of secondary importance. Now that most deaf children are being educated in the same school buildings, if not the same classes, as hearing children, the priorities are starting to change. Mainstreamed deaf students must meet the same academic standards as hearing students, and educators of the deaf today are highly influenced by the push for excellence in the public schools. The education of the deaf corresponds much more closely to the general education of hearing students now than it did when most deaf children were educated in separate schools.

Since the first systematic studies were conducted in the 1920's, using standardized tests developed for hearing children, the academic achievement of deaf children has been reported to be far behind that of hearing students. Over a long period of time there have been reports that the average deaf adolescent (from the eighth or ninth grade on) reads at around the fourth-grade level and has mathematics abilities at the sixth-grade or seventh-grade level—a serious educational lag.

Fortunately, there is reason to believe both that the educational

Deaf actress Marlee Matlin won an Oscar for her performance in the 1986 film Children of a Lesser God; *here, she signs the words "I love you."*

achievement of deaf students has been improving and that the tests used to measure achievement may have underestimated the abilities of deaf students. In 1974 the Stanford Achievement Test, which is used for nationwide achievement testing, was restructured to establish deaf norms for its test batteries. This was a major breakthrough because the scores of a deaf child on the test then could be compared to norms for both hearing children and deaf children. In 1983 new norms for deaf children were set. Although many new questions were added, substantial parts of the 1983 test were the same as in the 1974 version. An analysis of how deaf children in 1974 and deaf children in 1983 scored on the test items that were the same on the two batteries found that the scores were significantly higher in 1983 than in 1974. There thus appears to have been substantial improvement in academic achievement in deaf children over that time. The two biggest contributions probably were the increased flexibility in placing children in different types of classes (from self-contained to integrated) and in communication options (from oral-only to oral-manual).

Moreover, many educators now believe that deaf students may always have been achieving at higher rates than test results showed. Dissatisfaction has been expressed for some time over the standardized tests of reading as applied to the deaf. Such tests commonly present one sentence or a short paragraph and then ask the student to respond to a set of multiple choice questions. Many educators of the deaf have felt that such tests may expose grammatical difficulties that many deaf children have with English but may not be true measures of how a deaf reader would comprehend a narrative over several pages, a chapter, or a book, where the reader is able to use context and prior knowledge. There have been some efforts to assess the reading ability of deaf students by having them read narratives and then, with videotaping, check their understanding by means of story retellings, questions, and prompts. Results to date have been quite promising. Deaf adolescents who score at a fifth-grade level on standardized tests demonstrate clearly that they can read tenth-grade material with good comprehension.

The trend appears to be toward higher educational achievement by deaf children, and there is reason to anticipate the future with optimism. ☐

The educational achievement of deaf students has been improving markedly.

SUGGESTIONS FOR FURTHER READING

GANNON, JACK. *Deaf Heritage: A Narrative History of Deaf America.* Silver Spring, Md., National Association of the Deaf, 1981.

HIGGINS, PAUL C. *Outsiders in a Hearing World: A Sociology of Deafness.* Beverly Hills, Calif., Sage, 1980.

MEADOW, KATHRYN P. *Deafness and Child Development.* Berkeley, University of California Press, 1980.

MOORES, DONALD F. *Educating the Deaf: Psychology, Principles and Practices.* Boston, Houghton Mifflin, 1987.

SCHILDROTH, ARTHUR, and MICHAEL KARCHMER. *Deaf Children in America.* San Diego, College Hill Press, 1987.

Medical Complications of
Alcoholism

—————————*T. M. Worner, M.D.* —————————

In the United States, approximately 7 percent of the adult population, or well over 10 million people, are alcoholics. In Canada, about half this percentage, or about 600,000 people, are alcoholics. The disease of alcoholism takes a heavy toll on the individuals affected, their families, and their friends. Its long-term physical complications include liver disease, various types of cancer, and other potentially fatal conditions. It takes a staggering economic toll as well. The annual economic cost, in terms of lost work productivity, law enforcement costs, and treatment and other healthcare costs, totals more than $100 billion in the United States and over Can$5 billion in Canada.

The disease of alcoholism is one that knows no prejudices. There is no "typical" alcoholic: alcoholism breaches all ethnic, economic, sex, age, and social barriers. The popular image of the alcoholic as a sleazy down-and-out drunk on skid row is misleading. In fact, skid row alcoholics make up only a very small percentage of the alcoholic population.

Statistics do show that alcoholism is more common among men than women and that women who are full-time homemakers are more likely to be heavy drinkers than married women who work. Many teenagers have a drinking problem; nearly 5 percent of American high school seniors drink every day.

What Constitutes Alcoholism?

According to the *Diagnostic and Statistical Manual of Mental Disorders*, a standard reference work, an alcoholic is someone who drinks pathologically—for example, who consumes more alcohol over longer periods than originally intended or who continues to drink despite

68

The typical alcoholic American

young   old   male   female

black   white   rich   poor

employed   unemployed   executive   laborer

student   doctor   immigrant   native born

There's no such thing as typical.
We have all kinds. Ten million alcoholic Americans.
It's our number one drug problem.

NATIONAL
INSTITUTE
ON ALCOHOL
ABUSE AND
ALCOHOLISM

70

physical disorders either caused or made worse by drinking. An alcoholic also has difficulties in social functioning (misses work, loses jobs, fights with family and friends) and develops *tolerance* and *withdrawal*. Tolerance is defined as the need for increased amounts of alcohol to achieve the desired psychological effect and withdrawal as the development of symptoms such as the "shakes" after stopping or reducing drinking.

Early warning signs of alcoholism include blackouts (the inability to remember events that occurred during periods of heavy drinking), surreptitious drinking, feeling guilty about drinking, and inability to control one's drinking behavior. Ultimately, dependence on alcohol, as well as other medical and/or psychiatric complications, develops.

New Attempts at Diagnosis

Unlike people with most other medical problems, those suffering from alcoholism often deny that they have a problem. For this reason, attempts have been made to find "objective markers" for the disease. Such markers, their users hope, would be roughly analogous to using blood sugar levels for diagnosing and treating diabetic individuals.

Alcoholism breaches all ethnic, economic, sex, age, and social barriers.

Objective criteria for the diagnosis of alcoholism have been developed by the U.S. National Council on Alcoholism and include a blood alcohol level at any time of 300 milligrams per deciliter. This level is three times the level legally defined as intoxication in most states. An alcohol level of 150 milligrams per deciliter, in the absence of signs of intoxication (slurred speech, difficulty in walking, incoordination), is also considered a criterion, since the lack of signs of intoxication at this level indicates that tolerance has developed.

Because alcohol levels in the blood decrease over several hours following alcohol consumption, attempts have been made to identify other abnormalities in the blood that would indicate chronic heavy drinking. Unfortunately, most of the abnormalities proposed to date may also be present in people with conditions other than alcoholism, such as liver disease, or may be absent in some people who are actually alcoholics. A marker recently identified by Swedish researchers, however—elevated levels of carbohydrate-deficient transferrin, a protein synthesized in the liver—appears to be effective in diagnosing actively drinking alcoholics.

In addition to biological markers, simple screening questionnaires have been developed to diagnose alcoholism. One of these, the Brief Michigan Alcoholism Screening Test (MAST), consists of ten questions whose yes or no answers are assigned point values. Anyone who scores more than five points is considered an alcoholic. Questions include "Have you ever gotten into trouble at work because of drinking?" and "Have you ever been arrested for drunken driving or driving after drinking?"

T. M. Worner is assistant professor of medicine at Mount Sinai School of Medicine and director of alcoholism treatment services at Long Island College Hospital, both in New York City.

A Genetic Factor

Although alcoholism may well develop in individuals as the result of numerous environmental, sociocultural, psychological, and physiological factors, a considerable body of recent research has investigated a genetic factor in the disease. An inherited predisposition to alcoholism was noted by both Aristotle and Plutarch. Throughout the 19th century both medical and religious works referred to the transmission of alcoholism from one generation to the next.

Recent studies of adopted children conducted in Denmark, Sweden, and the United States support the idea of a genetic factor in alcoholism. All of these studies involved children who were adopted by nonrelatives. Alcoholism was found to be more likely to develop in children whose *biological* parents were alcoholic and was *not* statistically linked to alcoholism or other psychiatric disease in the adoptive parents. Sons of alcoholic men were three times more likely than sons of nonalcoholic men to become alcoholics themselves, and one study also found a threefold excess of alcohol abuse among daughters of alcoholic women. The incidence among sons of alcoholic women, however, was found to be not significantly higher than among sons of nonalcoholic mothers. Since alcoholism is much more common in males, researchers have been able to evaluate much larger groups of males than of females.

Support for genetic transmission is also provided by studies of twins. Scientists have observed that both twins develop alcoholism nearly twice as often among identical twins (whose genes are all the same) as among fraternal twins (about half of whose genes are the same).

Liver Disease

Liver disease is a common complication of alcoholism and accounts for more than three-fourths of the deaths attributed to alcoholism in the United States and Canada. Cirrhosis, in which liver cells are destroyed and replaced by scar tissue, causes the majority of these deaths. The total number of deaths annually from cirrhosis of all causes peaked in 1973. Since then it has declined steadily and now is at its lowest level since 1959. Possible explanations for this decrease include earlier diagnosis, better treatment of complications, and improvements in prevention of viral hepatitis.

The earliest stage of alcoholic liver injury is steatosis, or the accumulation of fatty deposits in the liver. Such deposits have been observed after as little as one week of heavy alcohol consumption. Although most alcoholics have no symptoms at this stage of liver disease, hepatomegaly (enlargement of the liver) may be found by physical examination in some individuals. If a liver biopsy is then done, fat accumulation can be seen in the liver cells. Cells with fatty accumulation will usually be replaced with healthy cells if the person stops drinking.

The next and more severe stage of liver injury is alcoholic hepatitis. The alcoholic may experience a loss of appetite, have a painful, enlarged liver, and have jaundice (yellowish skin); blood tests will

Cirrhosis of the liver is the leading cause of deaths attributed to alcoholism.

72

indicate that the liver is functioning abnormally. However, a diagnosis of alcoholic hepatitis should be made only by examining tissue from a liver biopsy under a microscope. The death rate for alcoholic hepatitis may approach 40 percent. At present there is little evidence that drug therapy improves short-term survival rates. Recently, however, the steroid drug oxandrolone (marketed under the brand name Anavar) has been shown to improve long-term survival rates, which are also improved by abstinence from alcohol.

The majority of patients with hepatitis who continue to drink progress to the most severe stage of alcoholic liver injury, cirrhosis. It is estimated that 50 percent of men who consume the equivalent of one pint of whiskey daily for 30 years will develop cirrhosis. In addition to the damage from alcohol, other causes such as nutritional deficiencies and genetic or immunologic factors may play a role in the development of this stage of liver injury. Alcoholic women, despite consuming lesser quantities of alcohol than men for shorter periods of time, appear to be at particular risk of developing cirrhosis. Symptoms of cirrhosis include enlarged breasts, spider angiomas (blood vessels on the skin that take on the appearance of spiders), and accumulation of fluid in the abdomen. These signs occur because the liver, with much of its normal tissue replaced by scar tissue, is unable to perform its usual functions. Again, a biopsy showing this scar tissue in the liver is required to make the diagnosis. There is no medication available to dissolve the scar tissue. Abstinence from alcohol improves an individual's chances of survival.

With early detection by liver biopsy, progression of cirrhosis often may be halted—through abstinence from alcohol and the adoption of a proper diet—before severe complications occur. However, in more

The old belief in an inherited predisposition to alcoholism has been confirmed by various studies. The Berkeley, Calif., surgeon shown above and his son (left) and daughter (second from right) are all recovered alcoholics; his other daughter and adopted son are not alcoholics.

An instructor at the Betty Ford Center in Rancho Mirage, Calif., leads patients in therapeutic exercises in a heated pool. Named for and co-founded by the former First Lady who overcame her addiction to both alcohol and prescription drugs, the center is perhaps the best-known U.S. facility for treating these and other drug dependencies.

severe cases two major complications may develop: encephalopathy (mental confusion accompanied by a flapping tremor of the hands) and internal bleeding. Encephalopathy often improves with the restriction of dietary protein, although medication may be required. Bleeding may occur from ulcers or gastritis (inflammation of the membrane of the stomach) in actively drinking alcoholics or from esophageal varices (enlarged veins in the esophagus), which bleed into the stomach. The one-year mortality rate once bleeding from these esophageal veins has begun has been reported to approach 70 percent. Survival rates have been improved by new treatments such as endoscopic sclerotherapy, which involves repeatedly injecting a solution into the veins to cause them to clot and gradually disappear.

Increased Cancer Risk

Evidence suggests an association between heavy drinking and cancers of the mouth, larynx, and esophagus, and smoking appears to further increase the risk of these cancers. Heavy smokers (more than 20 cigarettes a day) who are also heavy drinkers (more than eight drinks a day) have a risk of developing cancer of the esophagus 44 times that of nonsmoking nondrinkers. (A commonly used definition of a drink is a beverage containing the amount of alcohol found in 1¼ ounces of 80 to 90 proof liquor, a 5-ounce glass of wine, or a 12-ounce glass of beer.)

Alcoholics, especially those with underlying cirrhosis of the liver, also have an increased incidence of liver cancer. Infection with the hepatitis B virus may also predispose alcoholics to the development of this cancer. More recently, alcoholism has been reported to increase the risk of breast cancer—even among nonalcoholic women who consumed as little as three drinks a week. (One recent study, however, found no association between alcohol consumption and an increased risk of breast cancer.)

Blood and Heart Problems

Anemia (decreased number of red blood cells) is common in alcoholics and has been reported in up to 70 percent of hospitalized alcoholics. There are several possible reasons for this anemia. First of all, alcohol in some individuals damages the cells in the bone marrow that manufacture blood. Second, alcoholics often eat poorly when drinking and therefore may become deficient in folic acid, a B vitamin necessary for the production of red blood cells. Besides stopping drinking, these people may need to take folic acid in a pill form until their blood counts return to normal. Third, bleeding from ulcers, gastritis, and esophageal veins is common in actively drinking alcoholics. When more blood is lost than the body is able to manufacture, anemia occurs. If blood is lost rapidly, transfusions may be necessary; if it is lost more slowly, iron supplements may be all that is required. In addition, the source of bleeding must be identified and treated.

Aside from its effect on red blood cells, alcohol may also decrease the number and impair the functioning of the white blood cells, which help the body defend itself against infections. This is one of the reasons that actively drinking alcoholics are more prone to infections, such as pneumonia.

Platelets, the third blood component that may be affected by alcohol, are essential for the proper clotting of blood. Alcohol is known to damage the cells in the bone marrow that make platelets. Fortunately, after about one week's abstinence, the platelet count usually returns to normal. However, during the time when the count is low, the alcoholic who is bleeding internally or has been injured in an accident is at an increased risk of developing complications.

Hypertension, or high blood pressure, has been known since 1915 to be associated with alcohol consumption. The consumption of three or more drinks daily may account for 11 percent of cases of hypertension in males (and a much smaller percentage in females). Hypertension is a known risk factor for strokes. Indeed, the risk of stroke is increased in alcoholics. Thus, total abstinence from alcohol should be the first treatment for control of blood pressure in both heavy drinkers and alcoholics.

Smaller amounts of alcohol (less than two drinks a day) have been reported to protect against heart attacks, but more than five drinks daily may increase the risk. Although is has been suggested that the protective effect of low doses of alcohol may be in part related to elevated blood levels of high-density lipoproteins, which apparently help remove cholesterol from the blood, the part of the lipoprotein structure that performs this function is unchanged by alcohol.

Abnormalities in the heartbeat (arrhythmias) may also occur following heavy alcohol consumption. In the original 1978 report on these abnormalities, a very large percentage of the cases had occurred between December 24 and January 1; hence, the name "holiday heart" has been applied to such arrhythmias. Although they may cause palpitations, dizziness, or fainting, many will disappear with abstinence alone. A more severe cardiac problem is cardiomyopathy, a disorder that may involve thickening of the heart's muscle tissue and a lowered

At Crossroad Hall in Erie, Pa., people picked up by the police for public drunkenness are given shelter, food, therapy, and other services—along with frequent reminders that they have to take responsibility for themselves.

75

WHERE ALCOHOLISM DOES ITS DAMAGE

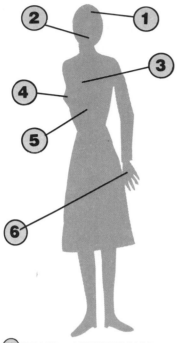

(1) BRAIN and CEREBELLUM
Depression; difficulty in walking

(2) MOUTH, LARYNX,
and ESOPHAGUS
Increased risk of cancer

(3) HEART and BLOOD
Increased risk of heart attacks;
irregular heartbeat; lowered blood
output; hypertension; anemia;
damage to white blood cells;
lowered platelet count

(4) BREASTS (women)
Increased risk of cancer

(5) LIVER
Fatty deposits; hepatitis; cirrhosis;
increased risk of cancer—liver
disease accounts for most deaths
attributed to alcoholism

(6) HANDS and FEET
Numbness or pain from
impaired functioning of nerves

blood output. In the United States, this is a disease primarily of black males. Symptoms include shortness of breath, coughing, palpitations, and loss of appetite. Although the course of the disease may be reversed with abstinence if it is detected early, the ten-year mortality rate for those in late stages of the disease is reported to approach 70 percent.

Neurological and Psychological Problems

Peripheral neuropathy (impairment in the functioning of the nerves in the limbs) has been reported in up to 10 percent of hospitalized alcoholics. Although when mild the condition may have no symptoms (it is detected during physical examinations only by abnormal reflex responses or by the loss of sensation to pinpricks), in more severe cases sensations of numbness and/or pain may be present. Symptoms are usually more prominent in the legs but may also occur in the hands. Although alcohol has been shown to be directly toxic to nerves, most evidence suggests that peripheral neuropathy occurs when alcoholism is accompanied by a deficiency of B vitamins. Symptoms may take months to years to eliminate, even though the patient stops drinking and takes vitamin supplements.

Another common neurological complication of alcoholism is degeneration of the cerebellum, a cauliflower-shaped organ at the back of the brain. In alcoholics, the top of the front portion of the cerebellum is damaged. Initially, the ability to walk placing one foot directly in front of the other is impaired. In the most severe cases, those affected are unable to stand. Improvements in walking occur after a person stops drinking.

Depression occurs in up to 50 percent of alcoholics when they are drinking. Although depression may result from the adverse consequences of drinking (for example, job loss, ill health, or family problems), it may also be the direct result of alcohol on brain cells. This alcohol-induced depression usually disappears within a few days to a couple of weeks following complete abstinence from alcohol. Treatment with antidepressant medication is not required to alleviate the symptoms.

Despite the fact that the majority of depressed alcoholics improve with abstinence, the danger of depression in an actively drinking alcoholic should not be underestimated. More than one-third of all suicides in the United States have been linked to alcohol. The elderly alcoholic is at highest risk.

Fetal Alcohol Syndrome

References proscribing the use of alcohol during pregnancy date back to the Old Testament. Yet, it was not until 1899 that Dr. William Sullivan, working at the Liverpool prison in England, scientifically described the deforming effects of alcohol on unborn children. The modern era of research into what is now called fetal alcohol syndrome (FAS) began in the late 1960's when researchers described typical malformations in several children of alcoholic women. FAS is estimated to occur in from 1 to 3 of every 1,000 live births in American and European cities; blacks and certain American Indian tribes are apparently at greater risk.

Maternal alcohol consumption has been linked to a broad spectrum of infant abnormalities, ranging from the slow growth of the fetus to the full-blown syndrome, which has been defined by the following criteria: retarded growth, before or after birth, in height, weight, and/or head circumference; abnormalities in the shape of the body, especially the face; and abnormalities of the central nervous system, especially mental retardation. The likelihood of miscarriage in the second trimester of pregnancy has also been noted to increase with increasing alcohol consumption.

Although FAS is clearly linked to maternal alcohol consumption, other factors may influence the development of the syndrome, including poor nutrition, genetics, and the mother's health. Despite the early identification of FAS in children, the long-term outlook remains grim. Mental retardation does not appear to improve significantly, even though a child is educated in a stimulating environment.

In New York City, restaurants are required to post a sign warning pregnant women of the danger that drinking poses to the fetus.

Drug Interaction

The interaction of alcohol with both legal and illicit drugs has several medical consequences for alcoholics, which are affected by whether they are drinking or abstinent and also by whether they have liver disease. Taken in large quantities over a period of hours or days, alcohol may interfere with the body's ability to break down and eliminate some drugs, thereby prolonging or enhancing their effects, as the combination of alcohol and barbiturates illustrates. The lethal dose of barbiturates is almost 50 percent lower in the presence of alcohol than when the drug is used alone.

In the case of chronic alcohol consumption, however, alcohol activates the enzymes in the liver that break down some drugs. Thus, to obtain the same therapeutic effect, a higher dose of medication may be needed by the recently abstinent alcoholic, whose liver may be metabolizing the drug too quickly, than by the nondrinker. Examples of drugs that are affected by chronic alcohol consumption include medications used to treat seizures and diabetes.

Because of alterations in the breakdown of drugs, alcoholics are also prone to adverse reactions to nonprescription drugs, even when these drugs are used in the recommended doses. One important example of this is acetaminophen (the pain reliever in such products as Tylenol). This drug is commonly used instead of aspirin by alcoholics, since it does not cause bleeding and is not irritating to the stomach. However, it is now known to cause liver damage, sometimes severe, in alcoholics.

Treatment Strategies

The consensus among professionals involved in alcoholism treatment is that total abstinence is to be encouraged. Attempts at controlled drinking, except for the rare patient, usually have dismal outcomes. The first step in treatment is detoxification—that is, the gradual withdrawal of alcohol from the patient. Detoxification must be carried out under the supervision of trained personnel to prevent withdrawal symptoms, which can range from mild (nausea, anxiety, tremors, insomnia) to severe (seizures, hallucinations, or delirium tremens, a state characterized by confusion, agitation, and severe shaking).

In recent years, detoxification has been carried out more frequently in an outpatient setting. For severe cases, however, the admission of the patient to a hospital is mandatory. Mild tranquilizers such as diazepam (Valium) or chlordiazepoxide (Librium) are used to treat the symptoms, which usually disappear in three to five days. Thiamine is often administered by injection to prevent the development of Wernicke's syndrome (which involves difficulty in walking and moving the eyes and problems in thinking).

After detoxification has been completed, the challenge of lifelong abstinence faces the alcoholic. To provide assistance along this journey, aversive therapy and self-help groups have been developed.

Aversive therapy for alcoholism was first proposed in 1937 when it was observed that workers exposed to tetramethylthiuram disulfide developed hypersensitivity to alcohol. However, it was not until 1948, when two Danish physicians who were studying the related compound tetramethylthiuram disulfide became ill after drinking an alcoholic beverage at a cocktail party, that rapid progress was made in developing this drug for treating the alcoholic. Now known as Antabuse, it is considered "aversive" treatment because it causes symptoms such as severe headaches or nausea if alcoholic beverages are consumed while the drug is present in the body. Since it remains in the body for several days, a daily dose of it "buys time" when the urge to drink becomes overwhelming. A recent study, however, has shown that the patient's willingness to cooperate in this treatment may be as important as taking the medication.

Alcoholics Anonymous (AA) is a voluntary worldwide fellowship of men and women who meet together for the purpose of attaining and

At a support group for children of alcoholics, youngsters receive counseling; such therapy may help prevent their becoming alcoholics themselves.

maintaining sobriety. The group was founded in 1935 by William Griffith Wilson, a New York stockbroker, and Robert Holbrook Smith (Dr. Bob), an Ohio surgeon, in an effort to help other alcoholics as well as to remain sober themselves. Membership is currently estimated at more than 1 million, with groups in 114 countries. The group has no affiliation with other organizations and neither endorses nor opposes other causes. Fully self-supported, it neither seeks nor accepts contributions from nonmembers.

The only requirement for membership in AA is a desire to stop drinking. Sobriety is maintained through group sharing at AA meetings, as recommended in the Twelve Steps, which call for alcoholics to admit that they have become powerless over alcohol and to turn for help to a greater "Power"; to admit past errors and try to make amends; and to share their recovery experiences with others in need of help. At meetings, feelings of fear, guilt, and worthlessness are relieved by constant reassurance that one suffers from a disease over which one can gain control. By sharing their personal histories, members help build each other's self-respect. The meetings also provide a nonalcoholic environment for members to meet new friends and acquaintances. Meetings can be either open (anyone may attend) or closed (for alcoholics only). Meeting information can be obtained by calling the Alcoholics Anonymous listing in any telephone directory.

Al-Anon is a support group for the families and friends of alcoholics. Although it was originally founded by families of alcoholics who were sober in AA, today Al-Anon's membership includes families and friends of actively drinking alcoholics. The goals for the Al-Anon member are to grow spiritually through living by the Twelve Steps, to give encouragement and understanding to the alcoholic, and to give comfort and enlightenment to the families of alcoholics. Another support group, Alateen, provides teenage relatives of alcoholics a place to share their experiences with their peers. □

SOURCES OF FURTHER INFORMATION

Al-Anon and Alateen: AFGINC, P.O. Box 862, Midtown Station, New York, N.Y. 10018.
Alcoholics Anonymous General Services Office, 468 Park Avenue South, New York, N.Y. 10016.
National Council on Alcoholism, 12 West 21st Street, 7th Floor, New York, N.Y. 10010.
National Institute on Alcohol Abuse and Alcoholism (NIAAA), 1776 East Jefferson Street, Suite 400 South, Rockville, MD 20852.

SUGGESTIONS FOR FURTHER READING

JELLINEK, E. M. *The Disease Concept of Alcoholism.* New Haven, Conn., The New College and University Press, 1960.
One Day at a Time in Al-Anon. New York, Cornwall Press, 1972.
THOMSON, ROBERT. *Bill W.* New York, Harper & Row, 1975.
Twelve Steps and Twelve Traditions. New York, Alcoholics Anonymous Worldwide Services, 1953.

Old-time sports stars like the mighty Babe Ruth could be known for both athletic feats and displays of gluttony. Here, the Babe celebrates his 39th birthday with a cake topped by a baseball diamond in multicolored frosting.

Nutritionists on Call

"Diet and nutrition are one of the real keys to maximizing performance," says Bill Walton of the Boston Celtics, a magnificently conditioned athlete who nevertheless has been plagued by injuries throughout his career. "It's one of the things an athlete has control over himself. An athlete owes it to himself to do research on it."

And if athletes don't research the subject themselves, their teams are likely to do it for them. Many teams, both professional and collegiate, have a nutritionist on call, and most bring in an expert to discuss dietary concepts at some point. In general, teams also require their trainers to be knowledgeable about diet and nutrition.

It was not always so. Until fairly recently, athletes in America tended to eat what they wanted, believing that training and strategy were far more important than the right combination of carbohydrates and proteins. Indeed, many coaches were as distrustful of nutritionists as they were of women, agents, and independent thinking.

Consider the "training table," a staple of American athletics for the last 50 years. Until recently, no one listened to the claims of nutritionists that eating heavy foods like steak and eggs before a game might be harmful. "Eating at the training table was something you just did without thinking about it," says New York Giants quarterback Phil Simms, the Most Valuable Player in the 1987 Super Bowl. "*Now* you think about it."

Athletes started thinking about diet sometime in the early 1970's, affected, like everyone else, by the fitness revolution brought on by the running boom. "It kind of happened all of a sudden," said Bill Walton. "I never heard much about nutrition when I was in high school, but when I got to UCLA [in 1970] there were courses on nutrition."

The evidence that athletes are paying more and more attention to diet is everywhere. It used to be axiomatic that World Series champions from the previous year would float into spring training, bloated and overweight from an off-season spent on the banquet circuit. Management wasn't happy about it, of course, but complained very little, particularly since the team manager, gut protruding, was generally the worst offender. But at spring training in 1987, the New York Mets (World Series champs in 1986) came in looking lean and tough. Pitcher Doug Sisk had lost 25 pounds. First baseman Keith Hernandez was trimmer. Another pitcher, Ron Darling, had opened a restaurant in New York City and had still lost weight. It is no longer fashionable to eat your way through the rubber chicken circuit. "When I'm invited to a banquet, I eat before I go," says the Giants' Simms, "and I haven't as yet missed any memorable meals."

Dietary Gurus

Each time a well-known athlete delivers a paean to the benefits of diet and nutrition, a hundred others fall in step. Tennis has become particularly important to the diet revolution in this regard. In the

Jack McCallum is a senior writer for Sports Illustrated.

early 1980's, Martina Navratilova was a depressed, chubby, 167-pounder when the call for help went out to Robert Haas, a Florida-based sports nutritionist. After following Haas's regimen of high-carbohydrate, low-fat meals, as propounded in his book *Eat to Win*, Navratilova, who is 5'7½" tall, is now an almost svelte 145 pounds, with 8.8 percent body fat (the average nonathletic woman's body is 20 to 25 percent fat).

Ivan Lendl was the next tennis star to work with Haas, who changed him from a junk-food junkie to a lean and mean tennis machine. Haas recommended that Lendl eat skim milk and sugarless cereal for breakfast, and clear soup, fresh fruit, and pasta for lunch and dinner. The rest is history—Lendl all but gave Haas complete credit for his breakthrough 1985 victory in the U.S. Open.

New Orleans-based nutritionist and trainer Mackie Shilstone commanded the attention of the boxing world in 1985 when he transformed Michael Spinks from a light heavyweight to a heavyweight, adding 25 pounds without, according to Shilstone, adding any body fat.

A tennis great of the '80's, Martina Navratilova, has credited the careful diet prescribed for her by sports nutritionist Robert Haas (below) with much of her success in recent years.

A new diet and training regimen put pounds but not fat on Michael Spinks, enabling him to move up a class and win the International Boxing Federation's heavyweight crown.

He did it with fewer miles of roadwork than are traditional in boxing training regimens, to cut down on Spinks's calorie expenditure, and with a 4,500-calorie-a-day diet. Spinks consumed mammoth meals; a typical breakfast consisted of three eggs, shredded wheat, whole wheat toast, fruit, and tea, and lunch might be broiled fish, a baked potato, green vegetables, more wheat toast, a salad tossed with lemon juice and vinegar, fruit, and tea. Spinks got 65 percent of his total calories from carbohydrates (starch and sugar), 20 percent from protein, and 15 percent from fat. This is not far from the dietary guidelines set out by nutritionists for all Americans, athletes and sedentary individuals alike (55 to 60 percent carbohydrates, 25 to 30 percent fat, and 15 percent protein). Spinks went on to defeat Larry Holmes for the International Boxing Federation's heavyweight crown.

Shilstone's next project was 7'6¾", 189-pound Manute Bol of the NBA's Washington Bullets. Bol spent all of the summer of 1986 with Shilstone, bulking up on 5,500 calories per day served at 11 different meals and snacks. Bol left at 230 pounds, better prepared, presumably, for the guerrilla warfare that takes place near the basket in the NBA.

Not everyone is enamored of such "miracle" physical transformations through diet, however. Spinks, it was said, looked slow and merely caught a slower boxer on the way down. Some observers believe that Bol's added weight cost him whatever limited quickness he had to begin with. And Eamonn Coghlan, probably the world's best indoor miler, does not hold Haas in such high regard. "I went on the *Eat to Win* diet," said Coghlan, "and lost." Once Coghlan went off the diet, he started winning races again.

Indeed, many nutritionists are skeptical of aspects of Haas's diet. No one challenges his central concepts of eating foods high in complex carbohydrates (starches rather than sugars) and low in fat. But Haas also recommends specific diets for specific sports, diets experts say have no basis in fact. Moreover, he recommends a variety of supplements to improve stamina and performance. Others say this is nonsense: no one, including athletes, needs to take vitamin or other supplements if the diet is balanced. Plus, there is no scientific evidence to support the claims for such "energy enhancers" as honey, bee pollen, wheat germ oil, and yeast powder. (Navratilova has since moved on to another nutritionist, who she says has discovered that particular foods affect her body in certain ways. She currently avoids certain vegetables and eats little sugar and red meat, concentrating on complex carbohydrates.)

There is no doubt that once they got interested in nutrition and diet, athletes became more vulnerable to fads and trends than the average person because they search constantly for the little edge that will give them optimum performance. "They are frequently willing to try any dietary regimen or nutritional supplement that promises to provide the 'magic bullet,'" says Peter Van Handel, director of the Sports Physiology Laboratory at the U.S. Olympic Training Center.

Singing the Praises of Carbohydrates

If there is one real trend that has transcended all others, it is this: Athletes are now singing the praises of complex carbohydrates and doubting the long-held assumptions about the value of protein-rich (and high-fat) red meat.

Body physiology is a complicated subject, but any athlete with an interest in nutrition now knows that the body breaks down complex foods, like starches, more slowly than it breaks down simple sugars supplied by so-called energy foods like candy bars and soft drinks. The body converts both types of carbohydrates into glucose, which is carried by the blood to the liver and muscles. Excess glucose that is not needed immediately for energy is converted into glycogen, which the liver and muscles store. When simple sugars are eaten, glucose is quickly released to the body cells for immediate energy needs; the remainder floods the liver, in effect overwhelming it. But when complex carbohydrates are eaten, there is a slower release of glucose so that the liver can better synthesize glycogen.

For light to moderate exercise, such as walking, having stores of glycogen is not particularly important, because the body will use stored fat as its primary fuel. But as exercise increases in intensity, the body switches to glycogen. So, the greater the glycogen store in the body, a store best stocked by complex carbohydrate consumption, the better the athlete's energy level during long-term, intense exercise.

A key role of protein in the diet is to build and maintain muscle and other body tissues. Certainly, therefore, some protein is needed by an athlete for strength. But nutritionists now know that except in the case of athletes (weight lifters, for example) whose needs are extraordinary, a balanced diet provides enough protein for muscle growth. Protein is the least important nutrient as an energy source.

In the endurance sports, such as long-distance running, carbohydrate intake has become almost a religion. Witness the ritualistic pasta

For Peak Performance

To maintain overall fitness and attain peak performance, professional and weekend athletes alike would do well to follow these guidelines.

- Eat a balanced diet composed of 55 to 60 percent carbohydrates (mostly starches rather than sugars), 25 to 30 percent fat, and 15 percent protein. Vitamin and mineral supplements should not be necessary, with the possible exception of an iron supplement for women.

- While competitors in some sports (like weight lifting) may need slightly more protein to help muscle growth, the average diet contains enough protein to meet most athletes' needs.

- Take in more calories during periods of rigorous training or competition; eat less when not actively competing or working out.

- Drink plenty of fluids before, during, and after competition (even if not thirsty). Cool water is the recommended drink.

- The precompetition meal should be light (about 500 calories) and composed mostly of carbohydrates. To make sure your stomach is empty during competition, eat about three hours before the event.

- Salt tablets are not necessary to replace salt lost through sweat. Your regular diet should give you all the salt you need.

- There is no evidence that "energy enhancers" like honey, bee pollen, or wheat germ oil are of any value.

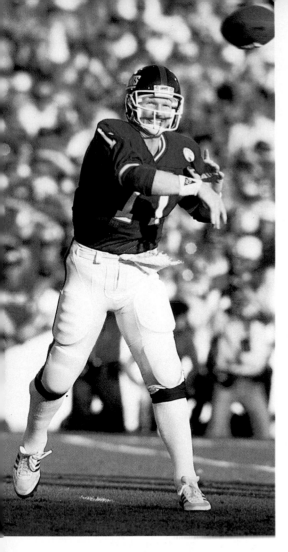

PHIL SIMMS

CONNIE CARPENTER

consumption before marathons. "Carbohydrate loading" is widespread, though some sports nutritionists question its benefits. The practice is generally credited to a Swedish exercise physiologist, Erik Hultman, who during the late 1960's was searching for a way for cross-country skiers to build up their glycogen reserves. (Only a limited amount of glycogen can be stored; Hultman's aim was to find a way to increase that amount.) He drained his skiers' muscles of glycogen several days before competition through strenuous training and a diet low in carbohydrates, then put the athletes on a "carbo binge" a couple of days before the meet. The results were considered dramatic at the time, though many now believe that the first part—carbohydrate starvation—can be downplayed.

Some Real Diets

There is still much fiction and fad surrounding athletes and their diets, but there is much knowledge, too. Consider the following testaments by five athletes from very different sports. Their diets may not always be perfect—they may not always follow what nutritionists preach—but their comments illustrate the extent to which, for serious competitors, thinking about diet and nutrition has become a way of life.

PHIL SIMMS: New York Giants quarterback.

The Giants' pregame training table on the road looks pretty much the same as it did ten years ago—steak, eggs, cereal, bread, jello, and so on. The only difference is that the players are likely to ignore it. "The coaches and other team personnel pretty much eat it all," says Simms.

Simms says he has become much more nutrition conscious in the last three or four years, "simply because it's the right thing to do. Athletes will do anything to help their performance, take care of themselves, and this is one of those things."

A steak or burger will cross Simms's palate from time to time, "just because I think I should," but in general he confines his main meal to chicken or pasta. "I thought meat and eggs was the way you were supposed to do it," says Simms, "and now that I know it's not, I feel better." He stays away from desserts on all but the rarest of occasions and makes his pregame meal a simple one—dry toast, tea, and maybe some fruit juice. He even goes so far as to practice a limited form of carbo loading, eating a lot of pasta and bread in the couple of days before a game.

"I'm not obsessed with diet," says Simms, "and there have been times when I've wanted something that might not be good for me and I've eaten it. But basically, I've found that I feel better watching my diet pretty carefully."

CONNIE CARPENTER: cyclist; gold medalist in the 1984 Summer Olympics in the 79-kilometer women's individual road race.

A little while before she was to nip fellow American rider Rebecca Twigg at the wire in the 1984 Olympics, Connie Carpenter ate a bagel ("good for me") with cream cheese ("has a little bit of fat but not too bad for me"). "That's what I like to eat," says Carpenter, "so I ate it. I look at diet the same way I look at equipment. You have to use what's best for you. You can't compromise the functional for a fad diet. I never believed you are what you eat. I believe you should eat what is best for you."

What is best for Carpenter, however, would be good for almost anyone. Like most endurance athletes, she eats a lot of pasta, bread, and rice to get the carbohydrates, and she stays away from red meat completely. "Cyclists in general don't have a lot of protein in their diet," says Carpenter, who runs training camps in Copper Mountain, Colo. "But it [not eating red meat] is more of a general health consideration than a competitive thing for me. I feel lighter and leaner when I don't eat red meat." Not surprisingly, she also stays away from fried foods and doughnuts, "foods that aren't easily digested. Fruits, salads, vegetables, light foods: that's pretty much my diet."

Would she recommend that for any athlete who wants to win an Olympic gold medal? "Well, Eric Heiden, who was a gold medal speed skater and a top cyclist, ate almost anything," she says. "There's no other explanation than some of us just have cast-iron guts."

BRUCE BAUMGARTNER: 1984 Olympic wrestling champion and 1986 world champion in the superheavyweight division.

Surely, Bruce Baumgartner is a guy who gobbles hot dogs and hamburgers and puts away a case of beer at a single sitting, right?

BRUCE BAUMGARTNER

87

BILL WALTON

After all, the U.S. wrestler weighs 275 pounds and is considered the scourge of Soviet heavyweights.

"Well, I come from a red-meat family," says Baumgartner. "Beef was definitely the most liked, most served meal. It took a long time for me to discover that that wasn't the way to go, but I've come around. I've cut red meat almost all the way down. Rice, potatoes, carbohydrates—now they serve as my energy source." Baumgartner had a head start in the nutritional game: his wife, Linda, is a trainer. "She let me know about certain things, and I learned a lot myself," says Baumgartner.

His diet goes in cycles. When he's not in training, Baumgartner may lapse a little, eating a small dessert with dinner. But he still stays away from alcoholic beverages and soft drinks completely. "I feel alcohol hurts conditioning in general, and you certainly don't need it to enjoy life," says Baumgartner. "And the carbonation [in soft drinks] is no good at all."

When Baumgartner moves into a training cycle, a couple of months before a major competition, his diet changes slightly. He tries to stay away completely from sugars and feels he needs a little more protein, "but not too much, not like in the old days." He does believe in getting energy from food on the day of competition. "About five or six hours before I wrestle, I might have pasta, pancakes, or waffles, something like that. And always wheat bread, instead of white."

Baumgartner is also a strong advocate of drinking a good deal of water. "If you sweat off a pound," he says, "you should replace a pound with water." Coaches used to consider water a detriment to athletic performance. But most nutritionists now agree with Baumgartner and recommend lots of water.

BILL WALTON: center, Boston Celtics.

The Boston Celtics had just beaten the Los Angeles Lakers, and Bill Walton was celebrating with a dozen or so friends at a restaurant near Boston Garden. "Give me the biggest steak you've got," said Walton with a big smile, "and keep the beer coming." A couple of people in Walton's entourage were aghast. "I thought you were a vegetarian," they said.

Indeed, Walton had confounded the NBA establishment years ago when he eschewed meat and, moreover, criticized anyone who did not share his vegetarian views. "But for practical purposes I gave it up," Walton says today. "Too many road trips, too many strange places. Plus, I found out that you can enjoy some red meat and not have it harm you."

Walton eats a balanced diet with an emphasis on fresh, natural fruits and vegetables. And he stays away from candy and other kinds of junk food completely. Walton, however, eats great quantities of food, as many as six full meals a day. "Most of the guys eat like that because we can burn it off," he says. "Also, I'm not averse to having a beer or two. Or six. If you stay away from junk and fried foods, there is no reason an athlete cannot enjoy a lot of different kinds of food and still be successful."

DAVE MAGADAN: infielder, New York Mets.

At the end of the 1986 baseball season, Dave Magadan, a young infielder and clutch hitter who figured prominently in the Mets' plans for the future, packed only 180 pounds on a 6'3" frame. The Mets felt he needed more power, so Magadan went to work on his diet. "The Mets had always had a nutritionist talk to us in spring training, and I felt I could design my own off-season program," says Magadan. "Basically, my philosophy was to eat three full meals, healthy portions, and to continue my workouts."

For breakfast, Magadan either had pancakes or had French toast (with a little syrup) and eggs. "I never emphasized the eggs, though," he said. "They're not good for you in large quantities." He's right. Another myth has died. For lunch, Magadan usually had a ham sandwich and macaroni and cheese. If he couldn't get a home-cooked meal, he stopped at Wendy's and ordered two hamburgers and a baked potato "with a lot of trimmings." For supper, he had a variety of main dishes—lots of lasagna and spaghetti, fried chicken, and steak. Unlike many athletes, "I'm still a meat eater," he says. (His diet is also somewhat high in fat.)

The result? Magadan managed to get his weight up to 210 pounds and has been able to maintain it with basically the same diet during the season.

But nobody's perfect. "I'm still guilty of the old practice of eating hot dogs or some other kind of junk food a couple of hours before the game," says Magadan. "And after the game sometimes presents a problem. They give us a big spread in the clubhouse—meat loaf, lunch meats, lasagna—but I don't always like to eat that. First of all, it's not as good as a meal you can get at a restaurant, and I just like getting away from the field and eating.

"I do my best on the road, put it that way. And I think most of my teammates do. We all know about diet and good nutrition, even if we don't always follow it."

And that realization in itself is a long way from the days of Babe Ruth. ☐

DAVE MAGADAN

SUGGESTIONS FOR FURTHER READING

CLARK, NANCY. *The Athlete's Kitchen: A Nutrition Guide and Cookbook.* New York, Van Nostrand Reinhold, 1981.

HENDERSON, DOUG. "Nutrition and the Athlete." *FDA Consumer,* May 1987, pp. 18-21.

KATCH, FRANK, I., and WILLIAM D. McArdle. *Nutrition, Weight Control, and Exercise.* Philadelphia, Lea & Febiger, 1983.

SMITH, NATHAN J. *Food for Sport.* Palo Alto, Calif., Bull Publishing, 1976.

WILLIAMS, MELVIN H. *Nutrition for Fitness and Sport.* Dubuque, Iowa, William C. Brown, 1983.

WILLIAMS, MELVIN H. *The Nutrition for Fitness Answer Book: A Companion for Your Active Lifestyle.* Dubuque, Iowa, William C. Brown, 1985.

Biking for Fun and Fitness

Jennifer Bernard

Question: What vehicle has two wheels, provides excellent aerobic exercise, and has presented a so far unsolvable riddle to physicists and mechanical engineers? The answer is the bicycle, and the riddle is why it stays up when it's ridden. Theories abound, but there is as yet no unanimous agreement. While scientists continue to investigate the issue, the rest of us can just be glad that bikes do stay up. For biking can be a convenient way to get from one place to another or a great way to relax and enjoy the scenery on a country road. And if done regularly for a sufficient length of time, biking can condition the heart and skeletal muscles and help you keep down your weight.

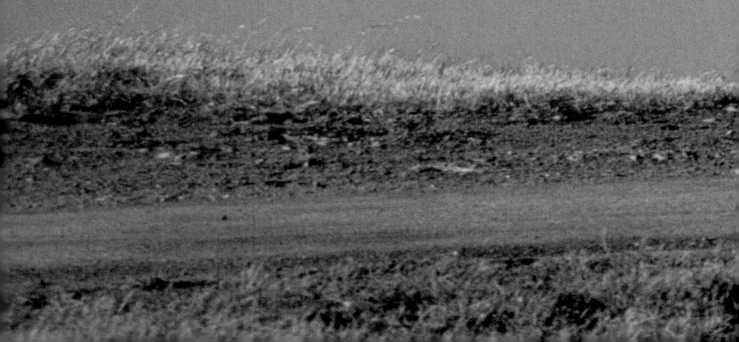

the next week, increase to 15 minutes a day, still riding only three days. The week after that, aim to increase to 20 minutes, and so on. Do not take on too much; increase your time only when you can do so comfortably. In addition, always be sure to rest for at least a day between rides.

While 30 minutes is the minimum length of time needed for aerobic benefit, to keep improving your fitness, you can continue to increase the time you spend exercising. When you have worked up to 35 minutes at your target heart rate, you can increase the number of weekly workouts to four, still taking care to rest every other day. Continue the periodic five-minute increases until you reach the point where you can ride for an hour every other day at your target heart rate. Regular hour-long workouts will keep you at peak aerobic fitness.

You may, however, want to branch out and increase your strength and endurance. This can be done through sprints and hill work. A sprint is an all-out effort at top speed for about a quarter of a mile. Begin by doing ten sprints in a day, resting between each until your heart rate is down to 120 (above your resting heart rate but below your target range). Hill work involves riding up a quarter-mile hill ten times. A basic conditioning program might consist of three days of steady riding for about an hour, one day each of hill work and sprints, and two days of total rest. You can gradually increase the number of sprints and hill climbs as you feel able. Sprints and hill work will increase your overall endurance, speed, and strength; meanwhile, the hour or more of steady riding provides excellent cardiovascular conditioning.

Always warm up before a workout and cool down afterward. To warm up and cool down, do stretching exercises and ride for a while in a lower gear or at a slower rate. Stretching makes the muscles more flexible, relaxed, and less likely to become strained. "Static" stretching is the best method to employ; you must hold the stretching position, without bouncing, for 30 to 60 seconds, about five times. Do not stretch until it hurts; you should feel no pain.

Tools of the Biking Trade

Anyone buying a bicycle will be presented with an utterly bewildering variety of frame materials, saddle shapes, accessories, and handy gadgets that will do anything from measure heart rate to automatically remove nails from tires. Should you get a bike with Sun Tour "Road VX" rear derailleurs? Or what about the Superlight Campagnolo Super Record crankset? And how much double butting does the run-of-the-mill rider need? As in any sport, the better you get, the fancier the equipment you will want. For a beginner, the best thing to do is go to a reputable bicycle shop—with financial limits firmly in mind—and follow the advice of the salespeople. It is possible to buy a perfectly fine bike for a manageable price.

There are several different kinds of bicycles to choose from, but the best for exercise purposes are 3-speed and 10-speed (or 15-speed) bikes. (The higher speed models are also called derailleur bikes; a derailleur is a gear-shifting mechanism.) The 3-speed bikes are sturdy, rather slow, and better for short trips. The only problem with 10-speed bikes is that

Use of the proper equipment—helmet, shoes, gloves, and even toe clips—in addition to a thorough understanding of your bike and its maintenance, makes for a safe and enjoyable ride.

they can be difficult to ride on rough or unpaved roads. However, they are fast and excellent for long trips.

Bicycle frames are made from a variety of materials; the selection changes frequently. Chrome-molybdenum, manganese, and vanadium alloy are among the steel alloys currently in use. The bicycle shop specialists should know which is the best material to buy.

There are only two kinds of frame construction, however: straight-gauge and double butted. Straight-gauge frames are not reinforced at the joints, while double-butted frames have all the joints welded with a double thickness to the frame. Double-butted frames are of higher quality, but a beginner does not need a bike that is completely double butted. Some frames also have "lugs" (fitted metal sleeves) to join the tubes. Buy a frame that is lugged and that has double-butted tubing on the main tubes (for instance, the tube that connects the seat to the pedals), but anything more than that is probably too fancy for the average bike rider.

Of the two kinds of brakes, coaster (foot-operated) and caliper (hand-operated), only the latter can be used on 10 speed bikes. Good wheel spokes, preferably made of stainless steel, are an excellent investment, since broken spokes can be a real headache. Of the two kinds of tires, clincher (which are wired onto the wheel rim) and tubular (which are sewn up and glued on), the clincher tires are more practical for the average rider, though less popular with the bicycle fanatic. Another choice you must make is whether to use dropped or raised handlebars. Dropped handlebars are much better for the lower back because when you are in the bent-over position that they require, less weight is placed on the spine, and there is less chance of the vertebrae being pinched together. However, choose whichever is most comfortable. Once again, the bicycle shop may help customers cope with these many options.

An uphill climb such as the one pictured above presents an excellent test of the biker's strength and endurance.

95

Probably more important than what kind of bike you buy is what size you buy. Riding a bike that is the wrong size can cause all kinds of problems, from backaches to saddle sores. To get the right frame size, straddle the bike while barefoot. The distance between your crotch and the top tube should be between a half-inch and an inch. To get a rough estimate, another method is to measure your inseam (from crotch to floor—again, while barefoot) and subtract 10 inches. Bicycle frames are generally from 19 to 27 inches; a six-footer would probably need a bicycle frame of around 24 or 25 inches.

Saddle height is as important as frame size. When you are sitting in the saddle, your heel should just rest on the pedal when it is at its lowest point, with the leg fully extended and the pelvis level. If your leg feels cramped when you are riding, or if the heel drops lower than the pedal, the saddle should probably be raised. If you rock from side to side when pedaling, the saddle is too high, and saddle sores could be the sad result.

The saddle should be essentially horizontal. If the nose is too low, more weight is placed on the hands, which will make them tired and numb. On the other hand, back pain can result from a saddle being angled with the nose too high. If you feel any of these symptoms, simply adjust the saddle angle. Make all adjustments in very small increments since radical readjustments that cause body weight to shift can result in knee pain.

What about accessories? One piece of equipment that should not be considered a mere accessory is a helmet. Always wear a helmet, especially in traffic. While a helmet may seem cumbersome, there are crash helmets available that sit lightly on the head, cause no discomfort, and may save your life.

The recreational and fitness benefits of biking can be enjoyed the world over by young and old alike.

Many serious cyclists swear by toe clips that hold the feet to the pedals and allow the back leg muscles to do more work. Half clips can also serve the same function while making it easier to extract your foot for a sudden stop. Proper biking shoes are a must for any extended ride; they should have cleats that fit snugly onto the pedals. Good cycling shoes spread the pressure over the whole foot, sparing the fragile metatarsal bones (between the toes and ankle).

Fingerless biking gloves, which usually have padded palms, can prevent the hand numbness that occurs during long rides. Biking gloves should be worn for any ride longer than half an hour.

When riding at night, wear a reflector. The bike should also have a reflector and lights; in fact, most states require them. In addition, bright clothing, perhaps fluorescent if your taste will allow it, will increase your visibility, both at night and in traffic. A reaview mirror that can be attached to the handlebar or clipped onto the helmet is another essential piece of safety equipment.

Some optional but recommended accessories if you are biking for fitness include a speedometer to tell you how fast you are going, an odometer to tell you how far you have traveled, and a stopwatch to measure your pulse. A bicycle pump to help repair flat tires and a horn or bell to warn pedestrians or other cyclists are also good ideas. A final word of accessory advice: buy a good lock.

Some Tips on Technique

Avoidance of accidents and injuries hinges on proper biking technique. Mastering the fine points of bike riding will not only give you greater control, but it will also help you to get more aerobic benefit from the exercise.

A very basic principle that surprisingly few people think about is to ride in a straight line. Wandering all over the road is inefficient and may be dangerous, while riding in a straight line makes it easier to maintain a steady heart rate. Riding straight demands concentration and discipline. Sit still in the saddle. Do not move your body around or flap your elbows. Let your legs do the work, and concentrate on controlling the bike.

The first technique you master should be pedaling. "Ankling," as some call it, is the most efficient way to pedal. Place the ball of the foot (not the arch) on the pedal, with your foot flat. During the downward stroke the foot should remain perfectly flat. At the bottom of the stroke, the heel should be slightly lower than the rest of the foot, so that the heel can be pulled up during the upward stroke. At the top of the stroke the foot should once again be flat. In this way the leg muscles are used rather than the toes, and power is applied throughout the stroke. Practice this until it is automatic. The pedal spin should be perfectly round and smooth, not jerky. Racing cyclists wear toe clips, cleats, and straps in order to ensure that they are ankling through the whole stroke.

"Cadence" is the term used for the rate at which a rider pedals. Each person has his or her own cadence, or most comfortable pace. The important thing is to pedal as regularly as possible and concentrate on maintaining a smooth, consistent pace. Cadence is measured in

Roughing It on a Mountain Bike

Not all cyclists like to do their riding on paved roads and paths. For those who prefer biking up hillsides, through woodlands, or across rocky beaches, there's a new breed of bicycle on the market called the mountain bike or all-terrain bicycle. These vehicles have sturdy frames, large, knobby tires, wide, upright handlebars, and up to 18 gears— all of which makes them well suited to rough terrain. The bikes cost anywhere from $400 to over $2,000. So many Americans have taken to mountain biking in recent years that hikers and horseback riders have complained, as have environmental groups that charge the bikes contribute to erosion. After a number of accidents, mountain bikes have been banned from certain wilderness trails in California, Colorado, and other areas. Not that this limits their growing appeal. Because they can negotiate bumps and potholes with jeep-like ease, mountain bikes are now enjoying popularity on the streets of city, suburb, and town.

Hand Signals
for Cyclists

Use hand signals when turning or stopping, to alert others on the road as to your movements. Practice signaling so that you can control your bike with one hand, and always make your signals as clear as possible.

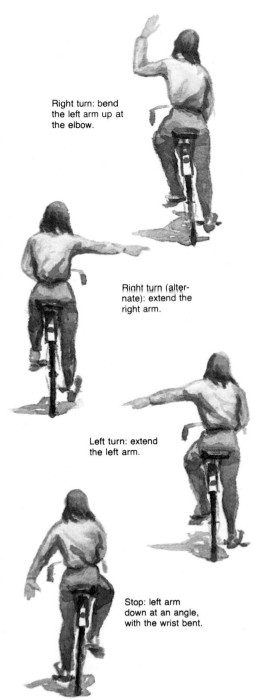

Right turn: bend the left arm up at the elbow.

Right turn (alternate): extend the right arm.

Left turn: extend the left arm.

Stop: left arm down at an angle, with the wrist bent.

rotations per minute, or rpm. To compute your cadence, ride at your accustomed pace, count the number of pedal rotations in 30 seconds, and multiply by two. Beginners should pedal at about 70 to 80 rpm, later moving up to the 80 to 90 rpm range.

Gear shifting should help to maintain this cadence. If it becomes hard to keep the same cadence, shift down; if you begin to feel little or no resistance when you pedal, shift up. Bicycle gears, unlike automobile gears, do not allow greater speed. They should be used only to adjust to the terrain, the weather, or simply to how you are feeling. If you are riding uphill or on a rocky stretch, you should shift down. You might also need to shift down if it is muggy, and if you are tired, shift down to the point where you feel that you are riding comfortably. Three-speed bicycles can be shifted while the bike is at a standstill or while it is moving, but if it is moving, do not pedal while you shift. The gears on 10-speed bikes can be shifted only while the bike is in motion and while you are pedaling. Simply let up slightly on the pedals when you shift.

Riding downhill can be frightening, since the bicycle can reach speeds as high as 55 miles per hour. Sometimes front wheel "wobble" or "shimmy" occurs: the front wheel wobbles and the handlebars begin to shake, making it very hard to control the bicycle. The way to prevent this is to grip the handlebars below the brake levers and hold your forearms firmly against the back part of the handlebars, just where they begin to curve downward.

Downhill riding can also make the brakes heat up, which causes the tire rim to overheat and the air in the tire to expand. This can result in a blowout—not pleasant to experience while hurtling down a hill. To avoid this, alternate braking with the front and rear brakes and control your speed so that you do not have to brake suddenly.

While rounding corners or making turns, freewheel (that is, do not pedal) and keep the inside leg bent and the outside leg straight. Slow down a bit before taking the turn, but do not brake in mid-turn. Many more accidents result from using the brakes in that situation than from not using them.

Feel free to ride your bicycle in the cold, rain, and snow, as long as you are properly bundled up, but do not ride if there is ice on the road. Most accidents not caused by collisions with automobiles are due to icy road conditions.

Avoiding Accidents

Clearly, making sure that your bike is in good repair is the first step to biking safety. Beyond that, the most obvious danger for bike riders is the possibility of colliding with one of those unaerobic metal monsters of the road, cars. The only way to protect against an error on the part of the driver is to be as careful as possible not to give any car a chance to be dangerous. It is important to remember that it may be difficult for drivers to see the bike. Drivers mainly keep an eye out for vehicles their size or larger, and a bicycle can easily be missed. Do not assume that the driver of the car coming right at you knows you are there; be ready to take quick evasive action. Following a few sensible guidelines will reduce the risk of collisions:

• Always ride with the traffic rather than against it. The main purpose of this is to reduce the impact should a collision occur. It is also better not to have to dodge oncoming traffic. Ride in as straight a line as possible so as not to unsettle or confuse neighboring motorists.

• Follow all traffic regulations. From the legal standpoint, bicycles are considered motor vehicles, and as such they are subject to the same rules as cars. Do not run red lights or stop signs, even if it looks safe.

• Be very careful at intersections. Most collisions between bikes and cars happen at intersections. Even if the stop sign or traffic light is in your favor, cars have been known to ignore these little details and barge on through. Be aware that this may happen, and be prepared to swerve out of the way.

• Remember that at intersections, cars to your right have the right of way.

• Signal very clearly when you make a turn, taking care to make yourself and your hand signals as visible as possible. (See the box on page 98 for hand signals cyclists should use.)

• In the city, keep your hands near the brake levers, if not on them, at all times, and keep your toe straps loose in case you do come to a sudden stop.

• Do not ride on highways or freeways. On long trips in the country, use the roads that run parallel to the main routes, which, in any case, are more pleasant.

• Do not wear a Walkman or listen to any kind of radio while riding a bicycle. In traffic you need all the clues you can get to what is going on.

• Other things to watch out for are doors of parked cars being opened ahead of you; driveways, from which cars can emerge with little or no warning; and pedestrians, who always have the right-of-way.

The other big threat to biking safety is the deep hatred that dogs seem to harbor for anyone on a bike. Dogs will almost invariably run barking after moving bicycles and will sometimes even try to bite the front wheel. This canine characteristic poses a real problem for cyclists out for a spin in the country. There is no real solution. Some people carry a can of repellent or a small whip. However, these measures seem extreme, if not cruel, and are by no means recommended. The best advice is simply to ride as fast as you can and outrun the dog.

If you do get bitten, get treatment quickly. It is also important to try to find out who owns the dog or at least be able to accurately describe it so that it can be identified. The law is on the side of the cyclist, since dog owners are required to keep dogs that will bite off the streets. Dogs will usually head home after they bite someone, so try to follow it home, if at all possible.

Biking in Good Health

Some injuries, of course, have nothing to do with cars or dogs but are instead a matter for discussion between you and your bicycle. You may need to make some adjustments in saddle height or angle. Pain in the knees can result from sudden increases in the distance or speed at which you are riding.

Strengthening your muscles is a good way to prevent certain injuries.

Although city riding presents a challenge even to the most experienced cyclists, accidents can easily be avoided if the proper precautions are taken.

99

For summer bikers, an off-season weight training program can be useful in this respect. Weight training can also complement a bike riding exercise program. It can, for instance, help develop the upper body, which does not derive as much benefit from cycling as the legs. If you choose this route, do so under supervision—and start slowly.

As a general rule, do not ride in pain. If you suffer an injury, take a brief vacation from biking. If the pain persists or is severe, see a doctor.

For minor muscle pain, many physicians recommend ice applications. Hold the ice against the affected area—but only for about 20 minutes three times a day, to be sure that you do not add to your problems by giving yourself a case of frostbite. Also, aspirin and ibuprofen have an anti-inflammatory effect that reduces muscle pain.

Saddle sores are an occupational hazard of cycling. These painful open sores or boils are brought on by friction between the rider and the saddle. Improper saddle position is usually the cause of the problem, so the best defense is to make sure that your saddle is correctly positioned. If you do suffer a saddle sore, do not ride until it is healed. Many ointments are available that both provide relief and help the boil to heal. If it gets worse, go to a doctor.

Biking clubs, a common feature of towns across the United States and Canada, can enhance the rider's enjoyment of this popular sport by organizing bicycle tours and other group activities.

Another frequent problem, especially for neophyte bikers, is overtraining. Overtraining is an easy trap to fall into: you may not know, as you start out, how much you are capable of doing. Even if you want to ride 20 miles in half an hour—and even if, by some miracle, you succeed in doing so—the price will be the exhaustion you feel later on. The symptoms of overtraining are a high resting heart rate, awakening frequently during the night, and irritability. If your legs feel heavy when you ride, and if, in general, you feel tired rather than strong on the bike, you are probably overtraining. The solution: take a few days off. When you start training again, do less and only very gradually increase milage or speed. Overtraining not only makes you tired and more prone to injuries, but it can also destroy the enjoyment that biking should provide.

Where to Bike

Biking is a sport for all ages and for all places. Where and when you bike should depend on how much free time you have, where you live, and how ambitious you are. Commuters may want to try riding to work. Small-town dwellers should have no trouble finding country roads to bike on. Many cities now have trails with distances marked off that are set up for cyclists. City parks are also good biking locales.

The United States Cycling Federation, which oversees amateur racing in the United States, has a district representative for every region in the country. The federation's address is 1750 E. Boulder, Colorado Springs, Colo. 80909; phone number: (303) 578-4581. The federation will be happy to tell you who to contact in your area. The representatives have information on trails, on local biking clubs, and, of course, on races. In Canada, contact the Canadian Cycling Association, 333 River Road, Vanier, Ontario, K1L 8I19; phone number: (613) 748-5629.

The best way to find out about biking clubs is to inquire at the local bicycle shop. Local youth hostels or YMCA's may also organize biking tours. If possible, it is a good idea to join a biking club. Clubs serve several purposes: they organize long trips, they create a biking community with which to exchange information on the newest frame alloys and helmet models, they provide you with companions to bike with, and they encourage you to get all the benefits and enjoyment you can out of the sport of biking. □

SUGGESTIONS FOR FURTHER READING

Bicycling Magazine's Fitness Through Cycling. Emmaus, Pa., Rodale Press, 1985.

BURKETT, LEE N., and PAUL W. DARST. *Cycling.* Glenview, Ill., Scott, Foresman, 1987.

SANDERS, WILLIAM. *The Bicycle Racing Book.* Chicago, Domus Books, 1979.

SLOANE, EUGENE A. *The All New Complete Book of Bicycling.* New York, Fireside, 1983.

WOODFORDE, JOHN. *The Story of the Bicycle.* New York, Universe Books, 1971.

FACTS ABOUT FAT

Eleanor R. Williams, Ph.D.

ILLUSTRATION BY LEE RENNER

The word "fat" strikes terror into the hearts of many, whose image of the perfect body is the sylphlike figure in a magazine ad or the taut, trim physique of a dancer. Overweight adults are constantly dieting, trying in vain to achieve these elusive shapes, while fat children endure ridicule and isolation from their peers. At the same time, dietary fat occupies center stage in the news media, and educational campaigns about its role in heart disease and breast and colon cancer are sponsored by government agencies and health organizations. Yet the North American diet is particularly high in fat. In 1985 fat accounted for 43 percent of total calories, a jump of 11 percent since early in the century.

There are many questions about dietary fat. Are all fats unhealthy, or do some serve useful purposes? How much fat can safely be eaten? How does it contribute to heart disease? What is the relationship between fat and cholesterol? This article provides some perspective on the complex subject of fat in the diet and in the body.

Fats, including oils, play many roles in the diet. To begin with, the first thing you would miss if there were no fats or oils would be certain flavors. Particular fats lend characteristic flavors highly prized in the world's cuisines: olive oil is favored in Greek, Italian, and Spanish dishes; Mexican refried beans require lard; and butter cookies just aren't the same when made without butter. Fats readily take up other flavors as well; for example, onions and garlic are sautéed in fat before they are mixed

103

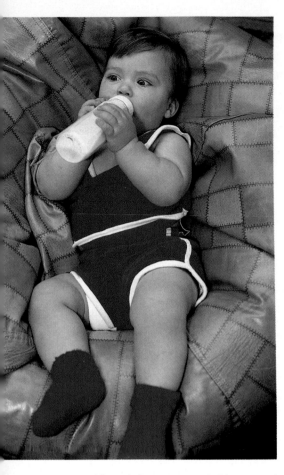

Unlike adults, young children need the fat and cholesterol in whole milk.

with other ingredients to allow their flavors to permeate an entire dish. Fats also impart textural characteristics to food. The smooth, rich "mouth feel" of ice cream or hollandaise sauce, and the crispness of potato chips and french fries, come from fat.

In addition to savory differences, a fat-free diet wouldn't "stick to the ribs" very well. Fat stays in the stomach longer than carbohydrates or protein, causing one to feel satisfied longer. In addition, since fat contains more than twice as many calories per unit of weight as carbohydrates or protein, a person on a fat-free diet would have to eat a larger volume of food to get enough calories to maintain normal weight.

People can't live on fat-free diets for long because the body needs to obtain certain essential fatty acids from fatty foods. These basic chemical units are required for normal body functions, yet the body is unable to manufacture them. Furthermore, fat-free foods fail to furnish vitamins A, D, E, and K, which are present in the fatty portions of food. Dietary fat is also needed for absorption of these vitamins, as well as for absorption of cholesterol, a fat-like substance. From a practical viewpoint, however, it would be impossible to put together a diet free of fat using traditional foods; a completely fat-free diet would have to be synthetic.

The Good and Bad of Body Fat

Just as dietary fat is important for many reasons, body fat also serves several purposes. It accumulates around certain organs like the kidneys, holding them in place and protecting them against jostling and jarring. Fat also collects beneath the skin (subcutaneous fat), providing insulation against the cold. Body heat is generated deep within the body, and because fat is a relatively poor heat conductor, subcutaneous fat effectively helps to maintain adequate body temperature.

Stores of body fat provide a ready energy source in times of famine or when an illness prevents or lessens food consumption. This is because large amounts of energy are packed into a relatively small space: only a half-pound of pure fat furnishes 2,000 calories, compared with more than a pound of pure carbohydrate. Thus, the body would need to carry much more weight around to supply emergency energy if carbohydrates were the main nutrients stored.

The ability to store body fat played an essential role in human survival during prehistoric and historical periods of food scarcity. But today, with food readily available to most North Americans, this natural ability has led to a high incidence of obesity. Being overweight can be dangerous, since it increases one's chances of developing diabetes, high blood pressure, gallstones, a common type of arthritis, some forms of cancer, sleep apnea (abnormal breathing during sleep), and coronary heart disease (clogging of the arteries carrying blood to the heart muscle).

Only recently have scientists understood that obesity is particularly related to dietary fat. It has long been known that taking in more total

Eleanor R. Williams is an associate professor in the Department of Food, Nutrition, and Institution Administration at the University of Maryland.

calories than the body needs leads to excessive weight gain. But it was not realized until recently that a high-fat diet is more fattening than a high-carbohydrate diet. Once inside the body, 100 excess calories from dietary fat are efficiently converted into 97 calories of body fat, with a mere 3 calories used up to make the conversion. Yet 100 excess calories from carbohydrates are converted into only 77 calories of body fat, with 23 calories used up in the process.

The Cholesterol Connection

Fat and cholesterol are interrelated in the diet, in the body—and in their effects on health. They both belong to a class of compounds called lipids, although cholesterol is entirely different from fat in chemical structure.

Cholesterol plays many important roles in the body. It is an essential component of all membranes in body cells. It is required for normal development of the brain and other nervous system tissues, and the liver uses it to form bile acids, which are necessary for fat digestion. Cholesterol is also the parent substance from which the body makes many hormones, such as those secreted by the adrenal glands, ovaries, and testes, as well as a substance found in the skin called 7-dehydrocholesterol, which is converted into vitamin D when the sun's rays strike it.

However, the human body (at least after the first months of life) can manufacture all the cholesterol it needs—without our consuming any cholesterol in food. Totally avoiding dietary cholesterol would be quite difficult, though, since it is present in many animal foods: milk, cheese, eggs, other dairy products, red meat, poultry, organ meats, and fish (especially shellfish). Foods highest in cholesterol are liver and egg yolks; meat and poultry are also high. (See the table on page 111 for the cholesterol and fat content of various foods.)

Unfortunately, both dietary cholesterol and dietary fat are related to coronary heart disease, through their influence on the amount of cholesterol in the blood. The major types of fat are saturated and polyunsaturated (the names refer to the chemical composition of the fats). According to current theory, a diet high in total fat, saturated fat, and cholesterol, and low in polyunsaturated fat, leads to atherosclerosis, a type of hardening of the arteries in which cholesterol and other fatty substances in the blood are deposited inside artery walls as raised, rough material called plaque. Plaque can narrow the opening through which blood travels and can even totally block blood flow—resulting in a heart attack if the blood supply to the heart is affected or a stroke if flow to the brain is interrupted. Sometimes a blood clot is responsible for finally plugging the narrowed section of an affected artery.

Studies have clearly established that high blood cholesterol levels, high blood pressure, and cigarette smoking are major risk factors for coronary heart disease—that is, they increase one's chances of developing the disease. Thus, not smoking, keeping blood pressure within normal limits, and maintaining low blood cholesterol levels can all help to prevent coronary heart disease.

Fast food french fries may taste good— but they contain unhealthy amounts of fat.

Atherosclerosis and coronary heart disease are directly related not only to high total blood cholesterol levels but, more specifically, to high levels of a major carrier of cholesterol in the blood called LDL's. (LDL stands for low-density lipoprotein.) High blood levels of LDL's are believed to injure the tissues lining the artery wall; the lipoproteins are then able to penetrate the lining, accumulating within the wall. This triggers the release of a variety of substances, eventually resulting in the development of atherosclerotic plaque.

LDL's are formed in the blood from other lipoproteins, synthesized by the liver, called very-low-density lipoproteins (VLDL's). Normally, LDL's are removed from the blood by so-called receptors located chiefly on liver cells. The proper number of efficiently functioning LDL receptors is necessary for maintaining low LDL levels and, consequently, low total cholesterol levels in the blood.

If LDL's are "bad" lipoproteins, there are also "good" ones. High blood levels of another cholesterol carrier, HDL's (high-density lipoproteins), are associated with a lower risk of coronary heart disease. Presumably, HDL's aid in the removal of excess cholesterol from the blood and are instrumental in transporting it to the liver for eventual elimination through the bile. In this way, HDL's help to protect against heart disease.

Different Kinds of Fat

How do the various types of fat influence blood cholesterol levels and LDL levels? Dietary fats can be categorized as saturated, monounsaturated, and polyunsaturated; these designations are important since the different types have different effects on blood cholesterol.

Saturated fat, which is not needed in the diet, is found in all animal fats and in shortening and margarine made from hydrogenated vegetable oil (hydrogenation converts oils and softer fats into more solid forms). Palm oil, coconut oil, and cocoa butter (the fat in chocolate) are also high in saturated fat.

Saturated fat is the worst type of fat: more than any other dietary factor, saturated fat raises blood cholesterol levels and increases LDL levels. For every 1 percent of the total calorie intake contributed by saturated fat, cholesterol in the blood increases by 2.7 milligrams per 100 milliliters of blood. For an average person taking in 2,000 calories a day, one teaspoon of butter will have this effect. A person taking in 15 percent of total calories in the form of saturated fat (15 percent is the average intake for Americans) is apt to have a blood cholesterol level that is 40 milligrams higher than if the person consumed no saturated fat.

Apparently, saturated fat raises LDL and total blood cholesterol levels because it has a negative effect on the LDL receptors, resulting in the failure to remove LDL's from the blood. Whether the fat does this by reducing the number of receptors or by decreasing their efficiency is not known at present. Saturated fat also tends to make blood clot more easily. Thus, it can contribute to coronary heart disease in two ways: by promoting atherosclerosis and encouraging blood clotting.

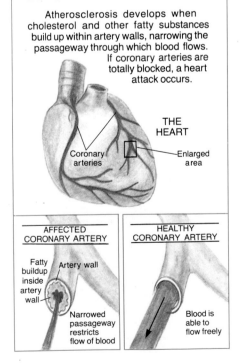

DANGEROUS FATTY DEPOSITS

Atherosclerosis develops when cholesterol and other fatty substances build up within artery walls, narrowing the passageway through which blood flows. If coronary arteries are totally blocked, a heart attack occurs.

THE HEART

Coronary arteries

Enlarged area

AFFECTED CORONARY ARTERY

Fatty buildup inside artery wall

Artery wall

Narrowed passageway restricts flow of blood

HEALTHY CORONARY ARTERY

Blood is able to flow freely

Choose cooking oils high in polyunsaturated or monounsaturated fat, like olive, corn, or safflower oil.

Monounsaturated fat is also not required in the diet. By far the most common source of it in food is oleic acid, a major component of olive oil and rapeseed oil (commonly used in Canada). Oleic acid is also found in nuts, meat, poultry, milk, cheese, and other fats and oils used in cooking.

Eating monounsaturated fats can have a healthful effect. When, in experiments, oleic acid is substituted for saturated fat in the diet, total blood cholesterol and LDL levels fall, but HDL levels do not. These drops are apparently the result, not of any positive effect of monounsaturates, but simply of the lower intake of saturated fat. People living in Mediterranean countries, such as Italy, Greece, and Spain, show significantly lower average blood cholesterol levels and lower rates of coronary heart disease than people in the United States; they consume large amounts of oleic acid but relatively small amounts of saturated fat.

Polyunsaturated fat, unlike other types of fat, is needed in the diet so that the body can obtain fatty acids that are vital constituents of cell membranes. These fatty acids are also building blocks for prostaglandins, compounds having a variety of effects in the body. (Specific prostaglandins cause blood vessels to either narrow or widen, promote or prevent blood clotting, and counteract inflammation in body tissues.) The two important classes of polyunsaturated fatty acids are called omega-6 and omega-3. They have a major beneficial effect on blood cholesterol levels.

Omega-6 and Omega-3

The most common omega-6 fatty acid in food is linoleic acid, found in large quantities in soft margarines; in corn, safflower, cottonseed, sunflower, and soybean oil; and in oils made from wheat germ. Linoleic acid cannot be produced by the body and is required in the diet at levels of 2 to 3 percent of total calories. (About 1½ teaspoons of corn oil provide 2 percent of calories in a 2,000-calorie daily diet.)

But there is good reason to take in more than 2 to 3 percent of one's calories in the form of polyunsaturated fats, for replacing dietary saturated fat with linoleic acid has been found to lower blood cholesterol levels dramatically. Studies also indicate that linoleic acid reduces blood pressure, the tendency for blood clots, and the death rate from coronary heart disease. However, authorities do not recommend intakes of linoleic acid higher than 10 percent of total calories because no population group anywhere in the world is known to have habitually consumed a diet with such a large amount. Very high intakes of linoleic acid lower HDL as well as LDL levels and may result in the development of gallstones in people with high blood levels of fats. There is also concern among doctors, based on animal studies, that very high intakes may be detrimental to the immune system and may increase the risk of cancer. However, including linoleic acid in the diet at levels under 10 percent of total calories does not affect HDL levels or have other detrimental effects and does have important beneficial results.

The omega-3 family includes linolenic acid (found in leafy vegetables and in soybean, walnut, and rapeseed oil). It also includes two substances found in fatty fish—eicosapentaenoic acid (EPA) and

Salads, fruits, and vegetables are on the menu for a healthful diet. These foods are low in fat and high in vitamins and minerals.

DIETARY SUGGESTIONS

Eat less of the following foods:
- whole milk and high-fat cheeses
- meats, especially those high in fat
- fried foods
- added fat (butter, bacon fat, lard, shortening)
- high-fat baked products (cakes, pies, cookies)
- ice cream
- foods containing palm and coconut oil
- egg yolks (only three each week)

Eat more of the following foods:
- low-fat milk and cheeses
- poultry with skin removed
- low-fat dried bean dishes
- fish, especially fatty fish such as salmon and mackerel
- dark green and deep yellow vegetables
- fruits
- low-fat whole grain breads and cereals, including pasta
- margarines made primarily from such oils as corn, soybean, sunflower, cottonseed, or safflower
- olive oil and oils such as corn, safflower, cottonseed, sesame, and soy bean

docosahexaenoic acid (DHA)—recently found to be particularly beneficial in reducing the risk of coronary heart disease. The richest dietary sources of EPA and DHA are fish such as salmon, eel, and mackerel and fish liver oils.

The chief effect of EPA and DHA on blood lipids is to reduce the levels in the blood of triglycerides (fats) and of their major lipoprotein carrier, VLDL's. They do this by decreasing the production of VLDL's by the liver. The acids also raise HDL levels, while lowering LDL levels to the same extent as other unsaturated fatty acids. In addition, these fatty acids from fish oils may play a role in preventing heart attacks because they increase production of certain prostaglandins that diminish the tendency of blood to clot. They also lower blood pressure.

Although omega-3 fatty acids do many good things in the body, their overall effects are poorly understood, and experts recommend that people get them by eating a reasonable amount of fish. They advise against taking any of the omega-3 or EPA supplements now widely available in capsule form. The consequences of taking such supplements over a long period of time cannot currently be predicted.

Effects of Dietary Cholesterol

The role of dietary cholesterol in raising blood cholesterol levels is increasingly seen as significant by health specialists. The effect of

Although salmon is a fatty fish, it contains substances shown to be beneficial in reducing the risk of heart disease.

dietary cholesterol varies with each individual. Some people show substantial increases in blood cholesterol levels when they consume high amounts of cholesterol; others do not. Experts estimate that at least a third of the U.S. population responds to dietary cholesterol with elevated total blood cholesterol levels, as reflected by elevated LDL levels. The explanation for differing responses to dietary cholesterol probably lies in our differing abilities to break down cholesterol in the liver or in a failure to shut down the body's production of cholesterol after large amounts of cholesterol have been consumed.

Normally, only about half of a person's dietary cholesterol is absorbed; this cholesterol quickly enters the liver, even if the amount in that organ is already quite high. Once inside the liver, dietary cholesterol normally prevents that organ from producing more cholesterol.

The liver may do one of three things with its accumulation of cholesterol. It may convert it into bile acids, which are subsequently excreted in bile; it may excrete small amounts of cholesterol in bile; or it may incorporate cholesterol into VLDL's. Then, VLDL's proceed into the bloodstream, where they may result in the formation of LDL's. Moreover, if the liver's biochemical mechanism for converting cholesterol into bile acids is inefficient, or if the mechanism to shut off production of cholesterol fails, large amounts of cholesterol accumulate in the liver. This lowers the number of liver LDL receptors, so that less LDL is removed from the blood. These are the ways in which dietary cholesterol causes elevated LDL levels in the blood.

Many experts are concerned that dietary cholesterol also causes the formation of unusual lipoproteins that appear in the blood only after meals. They would not therefore be detected on blood tests, since blood samples are usually taken when the patient has not eaten for at least several hours. These unusual lipoproteins may play some sort of important, previously unrecognized role in the development of atherosclerosis.

Dietary Tips

To escape the dangers of a diet high in saturated fat, people would do well to increase their consumption of carbohydrates. Low-fat diets are by definition high-carbohydrate diets, since calories must come from fat, carbohydrates, or protein, and in many cases protein is too expensive to be a major calorie source. Many population groups around the world consuming low-fat, high-carbohydrate diets have low incidences of coronary heart disease. Experimental studies show that substituting carbohydrates for saturated fat in the diet causes a fall in blood LDL levels similar to those seen when either monounsaturated or polyunsaturated fat is substituted for saturated fat. The exact reason why this occurs is not known for sure; it could be the result either of decreased formation of LDL's or of accelerated removal of LDL's from the blood.

Experts estimate that if the blood cholesterol level of the U.S. population were reduced from the present range of between 175 and 300 milligrams per 100 milliliters of blood to a range of between 130

THE FAT IN FOOD

Food	Serving Size	Total Fat (grams)	Saturated Fat (grams)	Cholesterol (milligrams)
DAIRY PRODUCTS				
Whole milk (3.3% fat)	8 oz.	8.1	5.1	33
Low-fat milk (2% fat)	8 oz.	4.7	2.9	18
Low-fat milk (1% fat)	8 oz.	2.4	1.5	10
Skim milk	8 oz.	0.6	0.4	5
Cottage cheese, creamed	½ cup	5.2	3.3	17
Cottage cheese, dry	½ cup	0.3	0.2	5
Cheddar cheese	1 oz.	9.4	6.0	30
Sour cream	1 Tbsp.	2.5	1.6	5
Yogurt, plain, low-fat	8 oz.	3.5	2.3	14
Cream, table or light	1 Tbsp.	2.9	1.8	10
Coffee creamer, made with coconut or palm oil, dry powder	1 tsp.	0.7	0.6	0
MEAT, POULTRY, AND EGGS				
Chicken, light meat, skin removed	4 oz.	5.2	1.4	96
Turkey, light meat, skin removed	4 oz.	3.6	1.2	78
Beef rump, choice grade, lean only	4 oz.	10.6	5.0	104
Ground beef patty, lean	4 oz.	12.8	6.2	106
Pork loin, lean only	4 oz.	16.0	5.8	100
Liver (beef), cooked with added fat	4 oz.	12.0	3.4	496
Egg yolk	1	5.6	1.7	274
Egg white	1	trace	0.0	0
FISH AND SHELLFISH				
Halibut, broiled	4 oz.	1.6	0.2	47
Cod, broiled	4 oz.	1.0	0.2	63
Tuna, light, oil-packed, drained	4 oz.	9.2	2.4	33
Crabmeat, cooked	4 oz.	1.8	0.2	114
Oysters, cooked	4 oz.	3.0	0.8	124
Shrimp, steamed	4 oz.	1.8	0.2	221
FATS AND OILS				
Butter	1 Tbsp.	11.5	7.2	31
Margarine, stick	1 Tbsp.	11.4	2.1	0
Corn oil	1 Tbsp.	13.6	1.7	0
Peanut oil	1 Tbsp.	13.5	2.3	0
SALAD DRESSING				
Mayonnaise	1 Tbsp.	11.0	1.6	8
French	1 Tbsp.	6.4	1.5	0
Italian	1 Tbsp.	7.1	1.0	0
Thousand Island	1 Tbsp.	5.6	0.9	4
SNACK FOODS AND DESSERTS				
Ice cream, vanilla	½ cup	7.2	4.4	30
Frozen yogurt	½ cup	1.5	1.0	6
Sherbet, orange	½ cup	1.9	1.2	7
Chocolate chip cookies	2	4.4	1.3	8
Brownie, frosted	1	6.6	2.2	12
Cupcake, chocolate-frosted	1	4.5	1.8	17
Potato chips	10	8.0	2.0	0
French fries, salted, large	10	10.3	2.6	0
Peanuts, dry-roasted, salted	¼ cup	17.6	3.1	0
Peanut butter	2 Tbsp.	15.3	2.8	0

Source: *Food 3*, published by the American Dietetic Association, based on material originally developed by the U.S. Department of Agriculture, 1982.

and 190, the rate of coronary heart disease would be reduced by 30 to 50 percent. No longer is there any doubt among scientists that high blood cholesterol levels are dangerous and that lowering them is important. Making changes in the diet is the best way for most people to lower blood cholesterol. (For individuals with very high cholesterol levels, prescription drugs are available that reduce blood cholesterol. They are not to be taken, however, in place of a diet low in cholesterol and saturated fat. Rather, they should be taken at the same time a person follows a proper diet.)

Specific guidelines on testing for and more aggressively treating high blood cholesterol levels were issued in October 1987 by the U.S. government and more than 20 health organizations. All Americans were urged to have their cholesterol levels checked (done through a blood test) once they reach age 20. Those whose levels were below 200 milligrams per 100 milliliters of blood were considered at the desirable point; they need only have their levels rechecked every five years, the government panelists said. People with cholesterol levels from 200 to 239 milligrams were considered borderline high. Those in this group who had no further risk factors for coronary heart disease should follow a low-fat, low-cholesterol diet and have their levels checked every year. It was recommended that those individuals deemed borderline high who did have risk factors—as well as all people with cholesterol levels of 240 milligrams or higher—have their LDL levels checked too. The panelists urged people in these categories to follow a low-fat, low-cholesterol diet (under a doctor's supervision) for three months, followed if necessary by a stricter diet for another three months. If cholesterol levels are still too high at this point, patients should take prescription drugs—possibly for life—to lower their levels to an acceptable range.

Various organizations, including the National Cancer Institute, the National Academy of Sciences, and the National Heart, Lung, and Blood Institute, have issued recommendations on how to reduce fat and cholesterol in the diet. Following these suggestions may help lower blood cholesterol levels (and thus decrease the chances of coronary heart disease) and also decrease the chances of colon and breast cancer. The recommendations are:

● Maintain normal body weight.

● Hold down fat intake to no more than 30 percent of total calories.

● Of that 30 percent, saturated fat should make up no more than a third, polyunsaturated fat no more than a third, and monounsaturated fat the balance.

● Consume no more than 250 to 300 milligrams of cholesterol a day.

Maintaining normal weight is important because excessive body fat frequently results in overproduction of VLDL's by the liver, leading to increased conversion of VLDL's to LDL's; at the same time, HDL levels are reduced. Losing excess weight is often essential to achieving normal blood lipid levels; therefore, this guideline is basic to all of the others.

How do you know if your diet gives you 30 percent or more of total calories as fat? In the United States the average daily calorie intake for females is 1,800 for ages 12-17, 1,600 for ages 18-54, and 1,500 for ages

FAKE FATS

Consumers may soon be able to eat ice cream, french fries, or cookies without undue guilt or worry about fat and cholesterol. Two new low-calorie, cholesterol-free fat substitutes are ready to enter the market—perhaps as early as 1989.

One of the products, Simplesse, is made from natural protein sources like egg whites and milk. The protein particles are heated, chopped, and blended until they are the same shape (round) and size as fat particles—creating the smooth, rich "mouth taste" of fat. Simplesse cannot be used in baking or frying but could find a place in such prepared foods as ice cream, salad dressing, mayonnaise, and yogurt. The Nutrasweet Company, the maker of Simplesse, contends that since the fat substitute is made from natural ingredients, it requires no approval by the U.S. Food and Drug Administration—something the FDA announced it would determine on its own.

Meanwhile, Procter & Gamble has asked the FDA to approve its fat substitute, Olestra. Olestra is a synthetic product—technically classified as a sucrose polyester—made from sugar and vegetable oil. Its molecules are too large to be digested and thus pass through the body unchanged. Olestra can be used in cooking oil and shortening (and therefore in the preparation of foods like potato chips and french fries). Both Simplesse and Olestra will probably not be used entirely on their own but in combination with other substances; Procter & Gamble, for instance, is working on a product that is one-third Olestra with the remainder composed of a Crisco-like shortening.

Of course, while fat substitutes can make occasional treats less likely to ruin one's cholesterol count, they will not make junk foods any more nutritious. These foods will, at best, be largely empty calories, and eating a balanced, healthful diet will be as important as ever.

55 and over. Thirty percent of calories as fat would amount to 540, 480, and 450 calories, respectively, or 60, 53, and 50 grams of fat. (There are nine calories in every gram of fat.) Males daily consume on average 2,600 calories for ages 12-17, 2,400 calories for ages 18-54, and 2,000 calories for ages 55 and over. Thirty percent of calories as fat would be 780, 720, and 600 calories, respectively, or 87, 80, and 67 grams of fat.

A man who maintains his normal body weight by consuming 2,000 calories each day will get 30 percent of his calories as fat if he eats 67 grams of fat. It is all too easy to exceed this amount. A typical fast-food triple cheeseburger supplies 68 grams of fat, all of the man's fat allowance for an entire day, and most of the fat is saturated. Obviously, the man needs to choose foods lower in fat to stay within his allowance. In addition, an effort should be made to decrease sources of saturated fat. The table on page 111 lists the amount of total fat and saturated fat in various foods.

Reducing cholesterol intake to recommended levels can be achieved by consuming no more than an average of three egg yolks a week, using low-fat milk and cheese products, and eating only limited amounts of those meats and shellfish that are high in cholesterol. It should become easier for people to keep track of their cholesterol intake if recently proposed regulations by the U.S. Food and Drug Administration go into effect. The rules would require food manufacturers to list cholesterol content on food labels.

To achieve a healthful diet, it is not enough to simply reduce fat and cholesterol to recommended levels. What is needed is a varied diet containing a great many different kinds of foods. Compared with the way most Americans have been eating, the recommended diet would increase the consumption of low-fat foods and decrease that of high-fat foods, as indicated in the list on page 109. This diet has long been advocated by the American Heart Association, which will provide details upon request. The diet can do no harm and is one a person can live on happily the rest of his or her life, for it includes a wide variety of foods that invite adventurous dining. ☐

SUGGESTIONS FOR FURTHER READING

BRODY, JANE, *Jane Brody's Good Food Book: Living the High-Carbohydrate Way.* New York, Norton, 1985.

CONNOR, SONJA L., and WILLIAM E. CONNOR. *The New American Diet: The Lifetime Family Eating Plan for Good Health.* New York, Simon & Schuster, 1986.

GOOR, RONALD, and NANCY GOOR. *Eater's Choice: A Food Lover's Guide to Lower Cholesterol.* Boston, Houghton Mifflin, 1987.

JACOBSON, MICHAEL F. *The Complete Eater's Digest and Nutrition Scoreboard.* Garden City, N.Y., Doubleday/Anchor Press, 1985.

LECOS, CHRIS W. "Cutting Cholesterol? Look to the Label." *FDA Consumer*, February 1987, pp. 9-13.

LECOS, CHRIS W. "Planning a Diet for a Healthy Heart." *FDA Consumer*, March 1987, pp. 29-36.

Lung Cancer

Prevention and Treatment

Don V. Jackson, Jr., M.D.

Cancer is the second leading cause of death in the United States, and lung cancer is the most common cancer. It also causes the most deaths due to cancer. It is a highly lethal disease, killing 85 to 90 percent of its victims within a five-year period after diagnosis despite surgery or other treatments such as radiation or chemotherapy. The majority of patients die within one year of their diagnosis. The poor overall survival rates indicate the systemic nature of the disease in most patients at the time of diagnosis.

Lung cancer originates in the bronchial tubes. It commonly spreads (metastasizes) very early in the illness to other parts of the body, such as lymph nodes, the liver, bone, other parts of the lung, and sometimes the brain or other sites. Because of this early spreading of cancerous cells, which occurs through the bloodstream and lymphatic vessels, a cure is often impossible.

The lung is also a common site to which other cancers metastasize. When cancer of the breast or colon is advanced, lung involvement is common. (Cancers which originate in other organs and metastasize to the lung are not considered to be lung cancer.)

In 1987 approximately 136,000 Americans died as a result of lung cancer. Tobacco smokers overwhelmingly constitute the biggest population at risk, with the risk highly correlated to the degree of exposure to tobacco smoke. Important risk factors include the age when smoking starts, the total number of cigarettes used, the duration of smoking, the depth of inhalation, and tar levels in the tobacco. An American Cancer Society study of 200,000 people over seven years demonstrated the relationships between the degree of smoking and the development of lung cancer. In nonsmokers there were 3.4 deaths due to lung cancer per 100,000 population. For people smoking less than half a pack of cigarettes a day, there were 51.4 deaths due to lung cancer per 100,000 population. This ratio increased to 143.9 deaths for smokers of one to two packs per day. Smokers of cigars and pipes also had a marked increase in death rate compared to nonsmokers. With respect to levels of tar, there does not appear to be any safe cigarette. The use of any type of tobacco has been associated with a marked increase in the lung-cancer death rate.

A smoking machine is used at the U.S. National Institutes of Health to analyze the ingredients of tobacco smoke.

About 80 to 85 percent or more of lung cancer victims smoke or have smoked tobacco. When passive, or secondhand, smoking—inhalation of smoke caused by someone else's smoking—is taken into consideration, even more cases of lung cancer are linked to tobacco. It has been estimated that 500 to 5,000 nonsmoking Americans die each year as a result of passively inhaling tobacco smoke.

In a review of research findings, published in 1986 by the U.S. National Academy of Sciences, it was stated that approximately 20 percent of the lung-cancer deaths occurring annually in nonsmokers are attributable to passive smoking. A 1986 U.S. surgeon general's report on the health consequences of passive smoking reached three major conclusions. Passive smoking is a cause of disease, including lung cancer, in healthy nonsmokers. Compared with children of nonsmoking parents, children whose parents smoke have an increased frequency of respiratory symptoms and infections, and they also have slightly smaller rates of increase in lung function as the lungs mature. Simple separation of smokers and nonsmokers within the same airspace may reduce, but does not eliminate, environmental tobacco smoke.

On a broader scale, tobacco smoking is considered to be the largest single preventable cause of illness and premature death in the United States, accounting for approximately 350,000 deaths annually. It has been estimated that between two and four of every ten smokers will die because of their habit as a consequence of diseases such as cancer, including cancers other than lung cancer; heart disease; or lung diseases other than cancer. Furthermore, perhaps as many as 10 million Americans currently suffer from debilitating chronic disease caused by smoking.

The peak incidence of lung cancer is in the sixth decade of life. However, 1 in 50 lung cancers occurs in the age group under 40. Smoking appears to be the cause of lung cancer in this age group, since heavy smoking has generally been noted among the victims. Unfortunately, this young group of patients does not survive lung cancer any better than older patients do.

Don V. Jackson, Jr., a specialist in lung cancer and antitumor agents, is associate professor of medicine at the Bowman Gray School of Medicine of Wake Forest University in Winston-Salem, N.C.

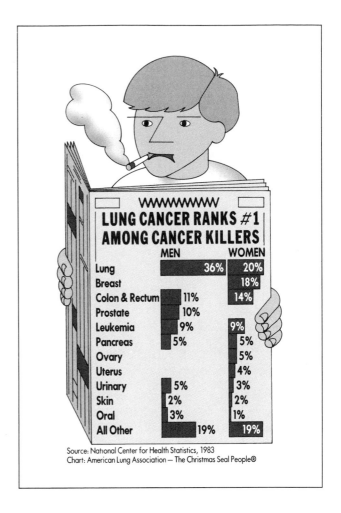

Source: National Center for Health Statistics, 1983
Chart: American Lung Association — The Christmas Seal People®

A Growing Problem

Since the 1930's, the incidence of lung cancer in the United States has increased dramatically in both men and women. This has paralleled the increase in tobacco usage by both sexes since World War I. The death rate among males has increased 200 percent since 1954. Cancer of the lung was responsible for approximately one out of five cases of cancer in males during 1987, according to the American Cancer Society. The estimated total new cases among men was 99,000. Lung cancer in men was responsible for 92,000 deaths in 1987, or 36 percent of deaths due to cancer, and was the leading cause of cancer death.

An alarming increase in the lung cancer death rate among women has recently been observed. This may relate in part to the fact that there was a period of 25 to 30 years when widespread use of cigarettes among women lagged behind that of men.

116

Between 1954 and 1984, the mortality rate of lung cancer in women rose nearly 400 percent, according to the American Cancer Society. Cancer of the lung was responsible for 11 percent of cases of cancer in women during 1987, the Society reported; the estimated total new cases among women was 51,000. In 1986 deaths due to lung cancer exceeded those due to breast cancer, the most common cause of cancer death among women until that time. Lung cancer was responsible for one out of five cancer deaths in women during 1987, accounting for 44,000 deaths. Lung cancer appears to be as lethal in women as it is in men.

Results of a recent Canadian survey have shown a difference in the sexes with respect to the age at which lung cancer is diagnosed. Females were, on average, younger at the time of diagnosis than males. Whereas the diagnosis was made at an average of 67.6 years for males, it was made at an average of 63.5 years for females. During this study another interesting feature was observed. Women smokers who developed lung cancer did so after smoking fewer cigarettes per day and for fewer years than men who developed lung cancer.

Racial differences have been noted for lung cancer. Compared to whites, blacks have a substantially higher mortality rate from cancer, according to a recent report from a U.S. government task force on black and minority health. Black men experienced a 58 percent higher incidence of lung cancer than white men. The 1985 National Health Interview Survey showed that 41 percent of black men smoked cigarettes, compared with 32 percent of white men. That survey also showed that more black women smoked than white women.

In March 1987 a joint committee, with representatives from both the private sector and the U.S. government, met concerning the health hazards of tobacco use. The Interagency Committee on Smoking and Health was established by Congress and chaired by Surgeon General C. Everett Koop. Experts voiced concern over the advertising of cigarettes to the black and Hispanic populations. Cigarette advertisements in publications aimed at minority groups, tobacco company sponsorship of cultural and entertainment events that drew large minority audiences, and the use of billboards to advertise cigarettes in minority neighborhoods are all common. In his closing remarks, the surgeon general stated: "We must place cigarette smoking in the total context of minority health, but in doing so

we must give it its proper place in the hierarchy of risks. It ranks very high indeed. Two of the six leading causes of excess death observed among blacks and other minorities are cancer and cardiovascular disease, both of which are smoking-related, and a third is infant mortality, to which cigarette smoking contributes."

Lung cancer is also a major health problem outside the United States, as shown in the table on page 119. At the Sixth International Symposium on Prevention and Detection of Cancer, Dr. Jan Stjernsward, the chief of the World Health Organization Cancer Unit in Geneva, Switzerland, stated that "globally during the 1980's, we estimate that lung cancer will surpass gastric cancer as the most common tumor, as a direct result of smoking."

The researchers during this conference focused on ways to prevent smoking-related cancers. It was

A health-conscious New York pharmaceutical company enforces a smoke-free environment by compelling its workers who smoke to step outside if they want a drag on a cigarette.

noted that more than 60 countries had enacted legislation to control smoking. As an example of the possible effectiveness of such legislation, the tobacco act of 1975 in Norway was cited. It includes a total ban on advertising and requires health warnings on packages. After its passage, there was a marked decline in smoking by young people. In 1974 in Norway, 40 percent of boys between 16 and 20 and 41 percent of girls were smoking daily. However, only 21 percent of boys and 26 percent of girls in that age range were smoking daily in a 1983 survey.

The Causes of Lung Cancer

There are many cancer-causing chemicals, or carcinogens, in the tar of tobacco smoke. Some of these are benzopyrene, dibenzanthracene, 5-methylchrysene, benzofluoranthenes, N-nitrosonornicotine, nickel, cadmium, and polonium-210, which are found in solid particles in tobacco smoke. There are also carcinogens in the gases, including hydrazine, vinyl chloride, urethane, formaldehyde, nitrogen oxides, and notrosodiethylamine.

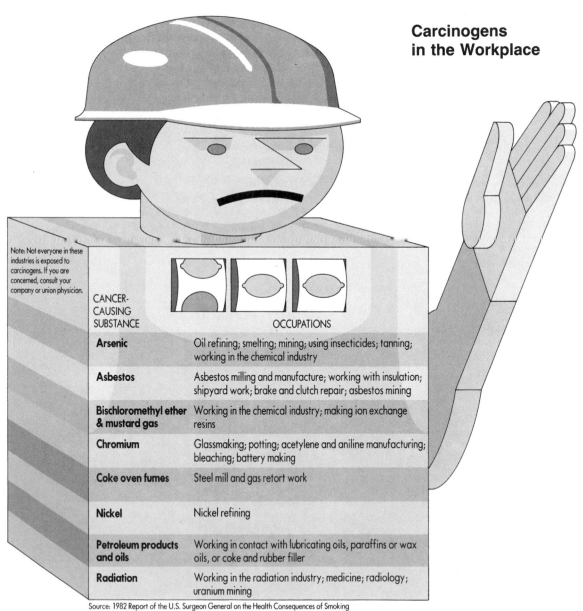

Carcinogens in the Workplace

Note: Not everyone in these industries is exposed to carcinogens. If you are concerned, consult your company or union physician.

CANCER-CAUSING SUBSTANCE	OCCUPATIONS
Arsenic	Oil refining; smelting; mining; using insecticides; tanning; working in the chemical industry
Asbestos	Asbestos milling and manufacture; working with insulation; shipyard work; brake and clutch repair; asbestos mining
Bischloromethyl ether & mustard gas	Working in the chemical industry; making ion exchange resins
Chromium	Glassmaking; potting; acetylene and aniline manufacturing; bleaching; battery making
Coke oven fumes	Steel mill and gas retort work
Nickel	Nickel refining
Petroleum products and oils	Working in contact with lubricating oils, paraffins or wax oils, or coke and rubber filler
Radiation	Working in the radiation industry; medicine; radiology; uranium mining

Source: 1982 Report of the U.S. Surgeon General on the Health Consequences of Smoking
Chart: American Lung Association — The Christmas Seal People®

AN INTERNATIONAL PROBLEM

Area	Lung Cancer Cases per 100,000 Population
Scotland	101.0
England and Wales	88.5
Netherlands	75.0
Belgium	73.1
Czechoslovakia	71.9
Finland	68.6
Northern Ireland	64.0
United States	63.4
Austria	58.8
Luxembourg	57.9

Source: Mann, S. G. "Epidemiology of Lung Cancer." In Scarantino, C. W., ed., *Lung Cancer*. West Berlin, Springer-Verlag, 1985.

Other carcinogens besides tobacco smoke have been less commonly implicated as potential causes of lung cancer. Some of these carcinogens are asbestos, radon, nickel, chromium, arsenic, chloroethers, vinyl chloride, coal tar products, and uranium dusts. These chemicals pose a particular hazard for those involved with them in the workplace. Also, radon gas seeping into homes from underground rock formations is increasingly being recognized as a significant problem in some parts of the United States; according to a 1988 National Academy of Sciences report, such radon exposure may account for 13,000 lung cancer deaths annually.

There may be a complex interaction between other carcinogens and cigarette smoking. A well-studied interaction is that of asbestos with cigarette smoking. Among asbestos insulation workers who have been employed 20 years or more, nonsmokers are five times more likely to develop lung cancer than nonsmokers who have not been exposed to asbestos in their occupation. Without a history of exposure to asbestos, the risk for development of lung cancer by a regular smoker is about ten times that of a nonsmoker. However, an asbestos insulation worker who smokes is 50 times more likely to develop lung cancer than a nonsmoker who does not work with asbestos. The combination of asbestos and cigarette smoking produces more than an additive risk for development of lung cancer. In fact, it is multiplicative, supporting the concept that an interaction of chemicals causes cancer.

Another example in the workplace has been found among uranium miners who smoke. The risk of death due to lung cancer in such individuals is 442 times greater than that of nonsmokers who are not uranium miners. By comparison, the risk for nonsmoking uranium miners is only five times greater than normal. Moreover, there appears to be an acceleration of the development of lung cancer: uranium miners who smoke are diagnosed as having lung cancer at an earlier age, on average, than their nonsmoking counterparts.

Does air pollution cause lung cancer? Probably not. More uban dwellers do develop lung cancer than those living in rural areas. But when tobacco use is taken into account, there is no difference in the incidence of lung cancer between the two groups. Also, studies of Seventh-Day Adventists provide additional evidence for the low likelihood that air pollution is an important risk factor. This religious group strongly adheres to a no-smoking policy. Members have a very low rate of lung cancer even when living in an urban setting.

Is there a genetic predisposition to lung cancer? The disease does not seem to run in families. According to some investigators, there may be an increased risk in close relatives of lung cancer patients compared to other adults in the general population. However, these same investigators acknowledge that the situation is complex. Variables such as a common environment and similar personal habits may play important roles.

The weight of the evidence points to tobacco use as the most important variable in the development of lung cancer.

Symptoms and Diagnosis

Coughing is the most common early symptom of lung-cancer victims, but it is often present in patients who have smoked for a long time and do not have lung cancer. A change in the amount or intensity of coughing might signal cancer. Shortness of breath might occur, but it, too, is often present after smoking for many years. Greater breathlessness than usual might be noticed. Occasionally, blood will be present in the phlegm. Chest pain, hoarseness, recurring bronchitis or persistent pneumonia despite antibiotics, loss of appetite, weight loss, and loss of strength are other possible symptoms.

Commonly, a tumor seen on chest X rays is the

first definite sign of lung cancer. Sometimes old X rays are available and a comparison shows a definite change, which suggests that a cancer is growing. However, accurate diagnosis requires microscopic analysis by a pathologist of a piece of tissue (a biopsy). The tissue is often obtained with a bronchoscope, an instrument that is a very flexible fiber-optic tube with a small cutting tool attached. The bronchoscope is passed down the airway into the bronchial tube of the lung. An inspection of the lung is made through it, and samples for biopsy are taken with the cutting tool.

Occasionally, more aggressive techniques to obtain tissue for biopsy will be necessary, such as opening the chest or inserting a scope into the middle of the chest. Less aggressive surgical procedures, such as removal of superficial lymph nodes in the lower neck area or passage of a needle through the chest wall and lung into the lung mass, can provide adequate material for diagnosis.

Examination of washings of the bronchial tubes may also reveal malignant cells. Sometimes looking carefully for malignant cells in the patient's early morning phlegm will be necessary to establish the diagnosis. This is called sputum cytology.

With the use of a microscope, the pathologist examines the suspect tissue after it has been chemically treated and stained. In addition to establishing the presence of cancer, the pathologist will determine the particular type of lung cancer. There are four major types: squamous or epidermoid (30 to 40 percent of cases), adeno-carcinoma (20 to 25 percent), small or oat cell (15 to 20 percent), and large or giant cell (15 to 20 percent).

Staging and Treatment

Following a tissue diagnosis, the physician caring for the patient will determine the extent of disease by a variety of blood tests and X rays and scans of various organs. This process is called staging. It is important because different treatments are more successful at different stages of the disease. Relatively new techniques used to scan for disease, such as computerized tomography (CT) and magnetic resonance imaging (MRI), can greatly assist in staging and improve its accuracy. Recently, use of monoclonal antibodies (genetically engineered substances that can seek out tumors) has

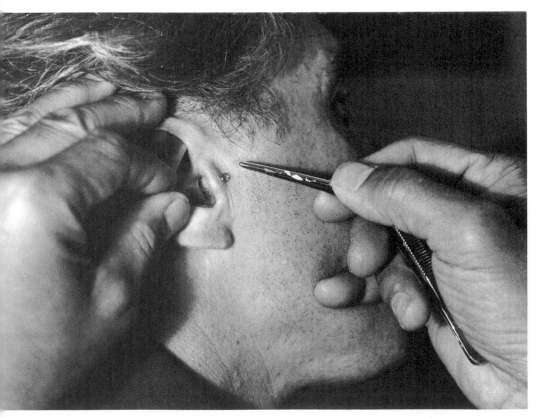

Smokers who want to kick the habit may try anything from cold turkey to behavioral counseling or nicotine gum. At left, a patient undergoes acupuncture to ease the desire to smoke. Hypnosis, right, helps a smoker focus her thoughts on quitting rather than reaching for a cigarette.

been explored as a staging procedure in small-cell lung cancers.

For most types of lung cancer, it is important to establish the potential for surgical removal of the cancer, since surgery provides the greatest chance for cure. Unfortunately, the disease will have often spread out of the lung by the time the diagnosis is made, making surgery an impossible treatment choice. For instance, if involvement of the liver is established, surgical removal of the lung tumor and surrounding normal tissue would have no potential for cure. In such a situation, other treatment options, such as radiation and chemotherapy, might be considered.

In most cases of small-cell lung cancer, surgery is not considered. Surgery has produced generally poor survival results for small-cell lung cancer with or without evidence of spreading from the lung. However, there has been a resurgence of interest in the use of surgery for very carefully staged patients who have limited-disease small-cell lung cancer. Chemotherapy is considered to be standard treatment for this type of cancer, sometimes coupled with radiation treatment of the chest. Chemo therapy has been very effective in controlling this

type of lung cancer temporarily and prolonging survival, producing an apparent cure in some cases. When surgery is attempted in cases of small-cell lung cancer, chemotherapy and radiation are often used as well. On the other hand, chemotherapy is not generally helpful in patients with non-small-cell types of lung cancer, although some may benefit temporarily from it.

Even when non-small-cell lung cancer shows no evidence of spread from the lung, surgery may be impossible to carry out. This may be because of other risky medical problems such as heart or lung disease. Often the ability of the patient's lungs to provide oxygen for body tissues is impaired because of chronic bronchitis or emphysema, diseases associated with prolonged cigarette smoking. Frequently, breathing tests and a measurement of the concentration of oxygen in the blood are done prior to surgery in order to determine the severity of existing lung damage. In some cases, removal of one lung or even a portion of a lung could not be tolerated in terms of resulting breathlessness. In such a situation, high-dose radiation is generally used, providing temporary control of the lung cancer in most patients, and cure in a small percentage of cases.

In some cases, doctors find during surgery that the diseased tissue in the chest cannot totally be removed. This may be a consequence of finding more extensive disease than was previously detected by X rays and scanning or being unable to remove some diseased tissue because of involvement of vital structures such as major blood vessels.

Other potential treatments include laser therapy, therapy in which light is used to activate chemicals added to the bloodstream (photodynamic therapy), or treatment with genetically engineered equivalents of substances (such as interleukins) naturally produced in minute quantities by the body's immune system. All of these approaches, however, must currently be considered as either experimental or very limited in their capacity to make a major impact in cases of lung cancer.

Can Lung Cancer Be Cured?

Some lung cancer patients can be cured, but most are not. The five-year survival rate is less than 15 percent when all stages and all types of the disease are considered. For the non-small-cell types, which constitute some 80 percent of lung cancer cases, the

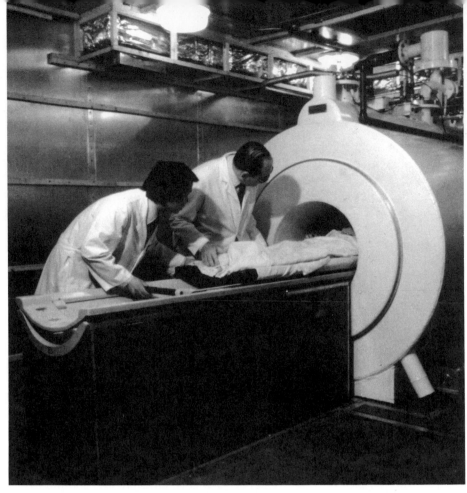

A relatively new scanning technique, magnetic resonance imaging, helps doctors determine the stage of lung cancer and therefore the best treatment approach.

best chance for cure is surgery. However, even in the best of circumstances, when there is no preoperative evidence of spread from the lung and the operation reveals clear margins with no cancer cells around the tumor that is removed, the five-year survival rate is only 20 to 30 percent. For patients with small-cell lung cancer, perhaps 5 to 10 percent may be cured using chemotherapy with or without radiation treatments or surgery.

In both small-cell and non-small cell types of cancer, the extent of disease at the time of diagnosis is the most important determinant of subsequent survival. The more extensive the disease, the less chance there is for cure. As an example, the finding of lymph node involvement greatly decreases the likelihood of a cure, despite the common practice of postoperative radiation treatment in such cases.

Sometimes lung cancer causes death when the lungs can no longer provide oxygen to body tissues as the cancer progresses. More commonly, a generalized illness characterized by multiple organ involvement and progressive weakness results in death.

Often the main role of the physicians and other medical personnel is helping the patient (as well as family and friends) through this process, attending to problems as they arise and offering supportive care. The patient and family members must realize the many limitations and stresses, both physical and emotional, caused by this disease. Problems should be dealt with as openly as possible by all concerned. There is a great variety of supportive treatments and aids, but none surpasses the warmth and caring extended by others. The universal success of hospice programs for the terminally ill across the United States attests to that; in such programs, the patient often remains at home or goes to a more "home-like" institution rather than a hospital, and the emphasis is on making the individual as comfortable as possible rather than on aggressive medical treatment.

What Can Be Done?

It seems logical that high-risk individuals—particularly tobacco smokers—would benefit from an annual or a semiannual chest X ray and checkup. Unfortunately, this practice has not been helpful. The disease has generally spread from the lung by the time lung cancer is seen on a chest X ray. In the Philadelphia Pulmonary Neoplasm Research Project (1951-1965), where semiannual chest X rays were used, the five-year survival rate was still only 8 percent overall and 16 percent for those undergoing surgery. The Cooperative Early Lung Cancer Group, organized by the U.S. National Cancer Institute in 1971, has thus far shown no major improvement in survival rates, even where patients had phlegm specimens checked for cancer cells in addition to undergoing frequent chest X rays.

Because of the poor results thus far of treatment and early detection efforts, the focus must be on prevention. Given the economics associated with growing and selling tobacco, progress in this area has been slow. Nevertheless, public awareness of the health hazards associated with smoking is growing, and 37 million Americans are now ex-smokers. From 1976 to 1985, according to the U.S. National Center for Health Statistics, adult male smokers dropped from 42 percent of the population to 32 percent, while women smokers decreased from 32 percent to 28 percent. By late 1987, the Centers for Disease Control reported, only 26.5 percent of Americans were smokers. However, more than 50 million Americans still do smoke, and some of them are unaware of the potential health hazards. According to a Federal Trade Commission staff report, more than two in five Americans do not know that smoking causes most lung cancer, and one in five does not know it can cause cancer at all.

Because most adult smokers began smoking as teenagers, public education efforts directed toward prevention of lung cancer should be focused to a large extent on youths. According to the American Cancer Society, a 1984 survey of high school seniors showed that 20.5 percent of girls smoked and 16.0 percent of boys smoked. This represents some improvement compared to a survey done in 1976 in which 28 percent of both boys and girls smoked.

Existing smokers should be told that numerous programs are available to help them stop smoking. Usually, it is quite difficult to stop, but the health rewards can be many. Quitting smoking reduces one's cancer risk substantially. Ex-smokers experience decreasing lung cancer death rates that approach those of nonsmokers after 10 to 15 years of not smoking.

Passive smoking and the associated potential health risks, including lung cancer, have received a great deal of recent attention. Over 40 U.S. states and more than 400 municipalities restrict smoking in public places. More than 20 states have enacted laws that limit smoking in the workplace. Smoking restrictions were put into effect in 1987 in many United States government buildings. In 1986 the U.S. Army adopted a new policy banning smoking in Army facilities, except in established smoking areas. A 1986 nationwide survey of 662 private employers showed that 36 percent had policies on employee smoking. Another 21 percent had policies under consideration. Eighty-five percent of the existing rules had been introduced in the previous five years and 60 percent within the past two years. Hotels, motels, and car rental agencies continue to set aside more rooms and vehicles for nonsmokers. Realizing that tobacco smoking in tightly confined spaces, such as airplanes, is dangerous to nonsmoking passengers and personnel, in 1987 the U.S. Congress passed a measure, effective in April 1988, prohibiting smoking on commercial flights of two hours or less.

With increasing awareness of the potential health hazards associated with both active and passive smoking, it is quite likely that tobacco consumption will continue to decline, followed by declines in the rates of lung cancer incidence and mortality, at least in countries stressing public health. However, it is not likely that lung cancer statistics will improve in the immediate future because of the long period of 20 to 30 years between the onset of smoking regularly and the development of lung cancer in those who become afflicted. Were it not for this largely preventable disease, the strides made in the war declared on cancer would appear much more striking than they do today. □

SUGGESTIONS FOR FURTHER READING

The Health Consequences of Involuntary Smoking. A Report of the Surgeon General. Washington, D.C., U.S. Department of Health and Human Services, 1986.

LASZLO, JOHN. *Understanding Cancer.* New York, Harper & Row, 1987.

SOURCES OF FURTHER INFORMATION

American Cancer Society, 19 West 56th Street, New York, N.Y. 10019.

American Lung Association, 1740 Broadway, New York, N.Y. 10019-4374.

U.S. Office on Smoking and Health, 12420 Park Lawn Drive, Room 110, Rockville, Md. 28057.

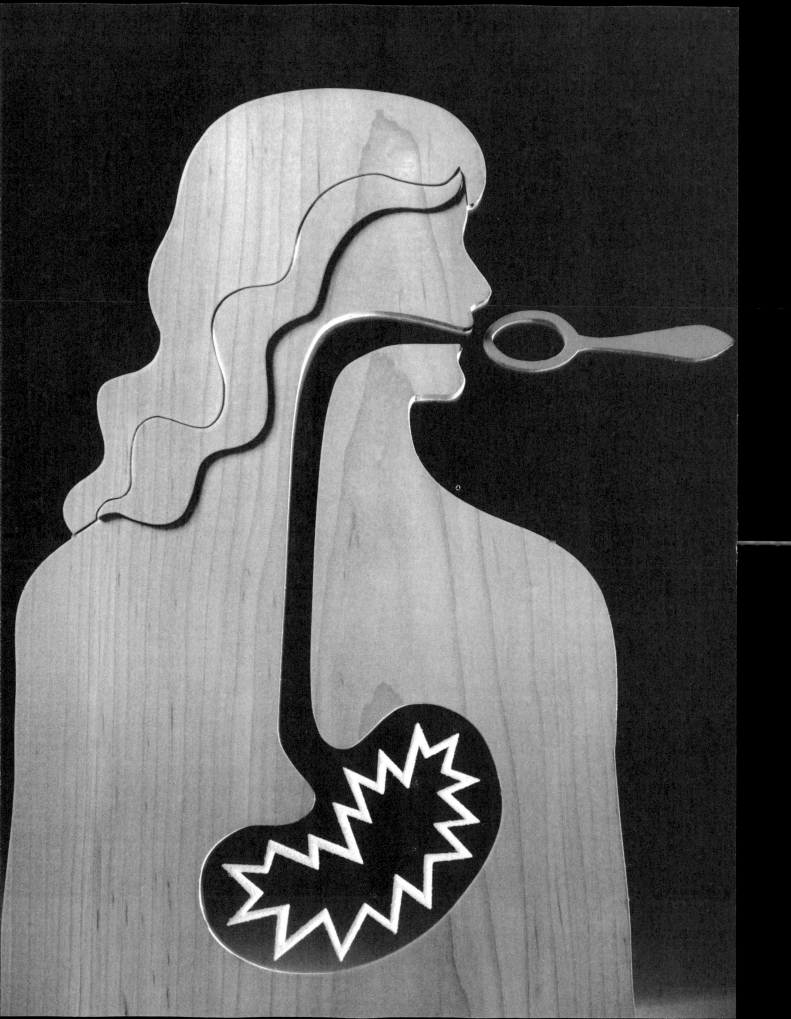

Protection From Food Poisoning

— Terrence Adolph —

ILLUSTRATION BY LEE RENNER

In the spring of 1985 over 16,000 people in the midwestern United States were infected with one of the many strains of *Salmonella* bacteria that can cause food poisoning. The outbreak, the largest and most publicized in recent years, was traced to improperly pasteurized milk from a dairy in Melrose Park, Ill. Six people died either directly from the infection or from other conditions aggravated by it.

Also in the spring of 1985 more than 80 people (some estimates ranged as high as 100) died from food poisoning caused by the bacterium *Listeria monocytogenes*, which can infect milk and cheeses and causes blood poisoning, fever, chills, and meningitis (inflammation of the membranes surrounding the brain and spinal cord). Most of the cases occurred in Southern California and were traced to fresh cheeses produced in a suburb of Los Angeles.

In October 1983, 28 people in Illinois were hospitalized with the neurologic signs of botulism, a sometimes deadly form of food poisoning. One person died, and 12 needed breathing support to survive. Health officials traced the outbreak to sautéed onions served in a local restaurant.

In 1982, two large outbreaks of gastroenteritis, caused by an organism known as the Norwalk virus, occurred in Minnesota. In one outbreak over 3,000 people became ill after eating frosted baked goods; in the other, over 2,000 people became ill from eating cole slaw. Gastroenteritis is the medical term for the inflammation of the stomach and intestinal lining that is involved in most forms of food poisoning and that usually results in diarrhea.

125

Food poisoning is a widespread and potentially serious health problem in North America, and the number of cases reported in the media represents only a tiny portion of the number of people affected each year. In 1986, one U.S. Food and Drug Administration (FDA) food safety expert went so far as to say that virtually everyone in the United States has at least one episode of food-borne diarrhea each year. For some of those people, the health consequences can amount to considerably more than a few days of discomfort.

Our food can be contaminated by many things, including chemicals, natural poisons, and numerous types of microorganisms. Some of these contaminants may actually pose little danger. According to the FDA official, although in recent years the public has become greatly concerned about the possible dangers from chemicals (such as preservatives, coloring agents, and pesticides) in commercial foods, the likelihood of experiencing illness or health damage from them is very slim. Likewise, while serious illness can be caused by the natural poisons contained in certain foods, such as some varieties of mushrooms, such cases are rare. The greater danger for greater numbers of people stems from infections by the bacterial, viral, or parasitic microorganisms that attack food improperly processed, handled, stored, or prepared. Many of the resultant cases of food poisoning could be prevented if the public were more aware of some simple steps that can be taken to keep foods from becoming infected with these microorganisms.

How Many Cases?

A study published in November 1985 by two food safety scientists at the FDA estimated that between 21 million and 81 million cases of food-borne diarrheal disease occur in the United States each year, diarrhea being the symptom common to almost all forms of food poisoning. Yet in 1982, the most recent year for which statistics are available, only 19,380 cases of food poisoning were reported to the Centers for Disease Control (CDC) in Atlanta, which collects and analyzes data from state and local health agencies, the FDA, the U.S. Department of Agriculture (USDA), the U.S. armed forces, and private physicians. Among those cases were 2,056

Terrence Adolph is a staff editor.

caused by *Salmonella* bacteria. However, some scientists estimate that *Salmonella* probably causes between 1 million and 2 million cases of food poisoning a year.

The extent of the underreporting of food poisoning cases can be explained in a number of ways. The FDA scientists estimated that at most 1 out of 25 people, and perhaps only 1 out of 100, actually seeks medical attention for diarrhea. The common symptoms of food poisoning—nausea, vomiting, fever, diarrhea—often resolve themselves fairly quickly, so that those afflicted may dismiss them as a passing stomach "flu" or as the result of nervous tension, which can cause similar symptoms.

Also, cases of food poisoning may go unreported because local laboratories cannot identify the pathogen responsible for the infection. In over half the cases that actually got reported to the CDC in 1982 the pathogen was not identified. Many laboratories do not have the sophisticated equipment needed to identify some pathogens, especially many of the newly discovered ones. Some microorganisms may not be identified because the proper tests are not run. And, too, by the time food poisoning is suspected, the contaminated food may no longer be available for laboratory analysis.

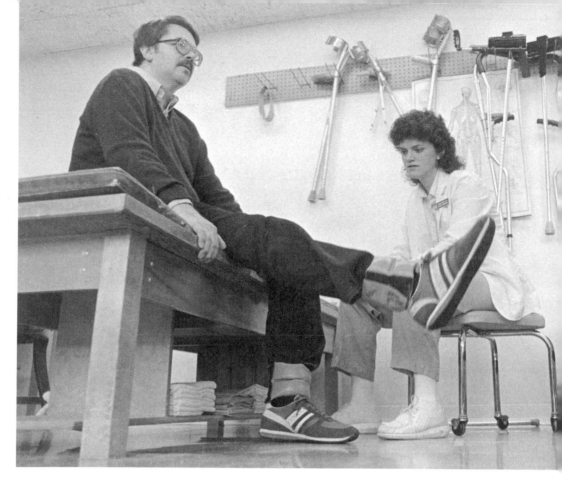

Tainted cheese (left) caused numerous deaths in California in 1985; at right, an Illinois man receives therapy for paralysis from a 1983 botulism outbreak.

Some Cause for Concern

Most cases of food poisoning go away by themselves in a few days and leave their victims with no discernible aftereffects. However, scientists have known for some time that recurrent bouts of diarrhea can impair the functioning of the intestines, affecting the body's ability to absorb essential nutrients, and can weaken the immune system. Food poisoning is therefore especially dangerous for those who already have relatively weak immune systems—the elderly, young children, and the chronically ill or malnourished.

Moreover, some scientists suggest that there is evidence that recurrent bouts of diarrhea may contribute to long-term health damage even in people with strong immune systems. This would mean that individuals who suffer frequent diarrheal attacks from other causes should make a special effort to avoid food poisoning. Diarrheal disease may be a factor in the development of chronic conditions such as allergies, cardiovascular disease, and autoimmune disorders (in which cells of the immune system attack and destroy other cells of the body) like rheumatoid arthritis.

With all our medical technology, food poisoning remains one area over which science seems to have gained little control. One of the reasons that the number of cases each year remains so high is the increasing concentration of the food industry. In the past, outbreaks of food-borne diseases would likely affect only local markets served by small dairies and food production plants. Now, as larger companies buy up the smaller ones, they control larger shares of the consumer market. Consequently, should something go wrong in their production process, they have the ability to affect greater numbers of people over wider areas. This was demonstrated in the case of the Melrose Park dairy, which served 2 million to 3 million people. Some public health scientists estimated that that one incident may actually have affected as many as 200,000 people, many of whom, again, never reported their illness.

Recognizing the seriousness of food poisoning in the United States, the CDC has three objectives in monitoring the problem: to identify and treat those people suffering from food-borne pathogens; to identify contaminated foods as soon as possible and remove them from the commercial market; and to improve food preparation practices in restaurants and in the home.

What You Can't See

Because so few cases of food poisoning are identified as such, it is difficult to estimate which microorganisms most commonly cause illness. However, various food safety experts, including those at the FDA, have identified a number of microorganisms that have "the greatest potential" to produce food poisoning. These organisms are so common in the environment that government inspection agencies cannot ensure that food is free of contamination by them.

Salmonella. These bacteria, which are commonly found in raw meat, poultry, seafood, milk, and eggs, account for more reported cases of food poisoning than any other type of organism. The key to eliminating the risk of *Salmonella* infection is to cook foods thoroughly. The USDA recommends that poultry be cooked until it reaches an internal temperature of between 180° and 185°F (check with a meat thermometer) or until the juices run clear. Other meats should be cooked until they reach an internal temperature of at least 160°F. (The USDA recommends that no meats be eaten raw or rare.) Partial cooking may leave enough bacteria in the food to cause illness. Also, within only a few hours, any bacteria that are not killed can multiply in food left at room temperature, almost guaranteeing a bout of illness.

Symptoms of poisoning—diarrhea, abdominal cramps, vomiting, and fever—usually appear within 48 hours and last from two to seven days. Many people are hospitalized each year with *Salmonella* poisoning, and as many as 500 people in the United States die from it each year.

Staphylococcus aureus. This bacterium gets into food through improper handling and releases a toxin that causes poisoning. Since the bacterium is commonly found on people's hair and skin and in their nasal passages, food handlers can transfer it to food, where it multiplies at room temperature in such items as meat, poultry, egg dishes, potato salad, cream-filled pastries, and gravy. Symptoms include vomiting, diarrhea, abdominal cramps, and prostration and usually appear from one to seven hours after eating contaminated food and last one or two days.

Clostridium perfringens. This bacterium produces a toxin that causes diarrhea, gas pains, and, less frequently, nausea and vomiting. Symptoms set in between 8 and 14 hours after

eating contaminated food and usually last a day or two. Cooking is not enough to protect you from this bacterium; the bacteria's spores commonly survive in food that has been thoroughly cooked. If the food is left standing at room temperature, the spores can germinate, developing into new bacteria that then produce the toxin.

Clostridium botulinum. This relative of the more common *C. perfringens* causes botulism, the most severe illness associated with food. Before better methods of detecting botulism poisoning and antitoxin to treat it were developed, between one-half and two-thirds of all cases were fatal. Now the mortality rate is about 10 to 15 percent. This bacterium produces a deadly nerve toxin, the deadliest poison known. As little as a pint of it could kill everyone living today. The symptoms of poisoning, however, are distinctive enough to alert anyone suffering from them to go immediately to a doctor or hospital emergency room. The toxin causes the usual nausea and vomiting, which can appear anywhere from a few hours to eight days after infection, but it also causes blurred or double vision, difficulty in swallowing, and paralysis.

Botulism usually results from eating improperly canned commercial or home-canned foods, especially meat, fish, poultry, and low-acid vegetables (such as corn, beans, carrots, spinach, and asparagus). However, scientists are finding new and previously unrecognized food sources of this infection. In the example of the outbreak in Illinois from sautéed onions, health experts suspect that the onions could have been contaminated with botulism spores, which are common in the soil, before they reached the restaurant. The spores may not have been destroyed when the onions were first fried. After frying, the onions were apparently placed in a pan, covered with a layer of margarine, and not reheated before serving. The covering of magarine on the grill could have provided the warm, moist, oxygen-free environment the bacteria need to thrive.

Where to Go Looking for Trouble

Although improperly prepared food of many kinds can cause food poisoning, certain types of foods consistently account for many reported cases. Foods most likely to cause trouble are undercooked meats and poultry, raw milk, and shellfish.

Meat and poultry. Recently, researchers at the Centers for Disease Control have found evidence that certain strains of *Salmonella* bacteria have developed a resistance to some of the antibiotics commonly given to livestock in the United States and Canada to prevent disease and promote growth. Since the drugs kill off competing bacteria in the animals, the *Salmonella* that are resistant to the drugs can thrive. Unfortunately, many of these antibiotics are the same ones used to treat bacterial infections in people. Therefore, if people become infected with antibiotic-resistant *Salmonella*, the resultant food poisoning will be increasingly difficult to treat.

In May 1985 the Los Angeles County Health Department noticed a marked increase in the number of reports of antibiotic-resistant *Salmonella* food poisoning cases and traced them to raw or undercooked hamburger from dairy cattle slaughtered when they could no longer produce milk. Health Department workers found that 95 percent of the animals had been given penicillin, and 86 percent had been given another common antibiotic, tetracycline. Among the patients afflicted with food poisoning, several had taken penicillin or tetracycline in the month prior to the onset of their illness. Scientists suspect that the antibiotics gave the *Salmonella* bacteria a selective advantage in both the cattle and their human hosts.

The problem of antibiotic-resistant *Salmonella* poisoning is not a minor concern. A 1986 report from the congressional Office of Technology Assessment estimated that feeds containing antibiotics are given to approximately 90 percent of the pigs, 60 percent of the cattle, 90 percent of the calves raised for veal, and almost all the poultry in the United States. That means that potentially all those animals could become infected with *Salmonella* strains that are not killed by those antibiotics.

A recent report from the Natural Resources Defense Council, a nongovernmental organization, predicted that the routine use of just two antibiotics—penicillin and tetracycline—could account for more than 270,000 cases of *Salmonella* poisoning each year, including between 100 and 300 deaths. The CDC said that light cooking, especially preparing hamburger rare, does not kill all the *Salmonella* bacteria.

In 1977 the FDA tried to impose a ban on the use of antibiotics in livestock feed, but Congress, under pressure from pharmaceutical companies and farmers, blocked the action. In 1987 a bill was

It is important to wash thoroughly utensils used on raw meat or poultry, which may harbor Salmonella *bacteria.*

introduced in the Senate that once again proposed limiting the use of such antibiotics.

Another common form of food poisoning acquired from eating undercooked meat, particularly pork, is trichinosis, caused by the *Trichinella spiralis* roundworm. Once ingested, the parasites move from the intestines to the blood and muscles and cause fever, swelling (especially around the eyes), diarrhea, and muscle pains. Symptoms usually appear 3 to 30 days after infection and disappear after about three months. Various drugs can be used to attack the parasites directly and to treat complications caused by them.

Raw milk. Reports of food poisoning outbreaks from pasteurized milk usually mean that mistakes in the production process caused contamination rather than that pasteurized milk is unsafe to drink.

In the Melrose Park dairy case, for example, a malfunctioning valve on a connecting pipe allowed unpasteurized milk to mix with pasteurized milk. Milk can also become contaminated after it is pasteurized and leaves the dairy.

However, raw, or unpasteurized, milk is a common source of *Salmonella* poisoning and can transmit (and cause poisoning from) the *Campylobacter jejuni* and *Listeria monocytogenes* bacteria. Before the development of pasteurization (which involves heating a liquid to destroy the pathogens in it), raw milk was the leading cause of death among infants. Now the American Academy of Pediatrics recommends that no child be given raw milk or raw milk products. In 1987 the FDA issued regulations prohibiting the interstate sale of raw milk in the United States. This would not ban local sales of raw milk but could limit sales significantly. Some people claim that raw milk is healthier than pasteurized milk, but, according to FDA officials, there is no evidence to support such claims. The minor differences in nutritional content between the two kinds of milk in no way justify the risks associated with drinking raw milk.

Raw milk has also been linked recently to a previously unrecognized illness characterized by chronic diarrhea that in some cases continued for over one year. Over 100 people in at least seven states were affected with the syndrome in 1983 and 1984. No pathogen was identified as the causative agent in any of the cases, yet raw milk consumption was found to be a common link among all the afflicted persons.

Shellfish. Clams and oysters feed off debris on the ocean floor and so can be contaminated by sewage and pollutants in runoff. They have been known to transmit cholera, typhoid fever, the Norwalk virus, various bacteria, and hepatitis A. These shellfish are usually collected from beds in waters certified by state agencies as safe, but fishing boats sometimes stray into polluted waters. Also, shellfish can be contaminated through improper handling or refrigeration after they have been collected.

In 1982, New York State, a leading harvester of clams and oysters, experienced a sharp increase in the number of cases of food poisoning associated with the shellfish. Though those numbers have since declined, the New York State Health Department still recommends that people not eat raw or undercooked shellfish. Most restaurants cook these bivalves only until the shells open, which can take as little as one minute. Food safety experts recommend, however, that they be cooked for at least four to six minutes to kill possible pathogens.

Treating Food Poisoning

Mild cases of food poisoning require little more from the patient than a few days' rest in bed and drinking plenty of fluids, since diarrhea can cause dehydration. If symptoms are more severe, of course, or if they last more than a few days, the patient should see a doctor. Antibiotics and other drugs can help eliminate many pathogens from the body, once the specific pathogen has been identified (usually through the laboratory analysis of stool samples).

Doctors doubt the wisdom of using over-the-counter antidiarrhea medications. Some claim they do nothing, while others suggest that, since diarrhea is the body's attempt to flush out irritating microorganisms, antidiarrhea medications prevent this natural process by keeping the pathogens in the body and possibly extend the course of the illness.

As for whether patients should eat solid food, the general advice is, if they can tolerate it, it probably will not hurt. Bland foods like white rice, clear broth, gelatin, dry toast, and salty crackers are least likely to cause distress. Other foods that may be considered are bananas, which contain potassium, one of the body's fluid regulating substances that may be depleted by diarrhea, and applesauce, which contains pectin, a natural antidiarrhetic.

An Ounce of Prevention

Avoiding food poisoning is a tricky business, especially since so many of us eat so many meals away from home and have little control over how that food is prepared. When eating out, especially at delicatessens and salad bars, try to avoid foods allowed to sit out in the open or any dishes not kept hot or cold enough. This is particularly true of those foods most likely to attract microorganisms, such as egg dishes, potato salad, cream dressings, cold cuts, and meat, poultry, or fish dishes. Contrary to common opinion, commercial mayonnaise is not a likely source of food poisoning because it is too acidic. Also, since undercooked meat and chicken are more likely to cause infection, it may be wiser not to order meat rare in restaurants and to send back meat and chicken that have any pink left inside.

Storing food. At home keep in mind that moisture, warmth, and oxygen encourage food spoilage. Except for such things as bananas, acidic fruits like oranges and apples, potatoes, and squash, most fresh foods should be stored in the refrigerator. Make sure that the temperature inside your refrigerator stays at or below 40°F, even if you have to buy a special thermometer to gauge it. Use fresh foods in three to five days after purchasing them, and use the most perishable foods—poultry, meat, fish, leftovers, and milk and egg dishes—within a day or two (unless you freeze them). Even canned goods, usually the most durable, can spoil if kept in too warm a place. Do not store them under the kitchen sink or in cupboards next to the oven. Ideally they should be stored in a cool, dry place

- Keep your refrigerator at or below 40°F.

- Do not let foods stand for any length of time at room temperature.

- Do not defrost foods at room temperature; thaw them in the refrigerator.

- Divide up large portions of cooked food into smaller units before refrigerating so that the interior portions do not remain warm too long.

PREVENTION AT HOME

- Wash your hands before handling foods and after handling meat and poultry.

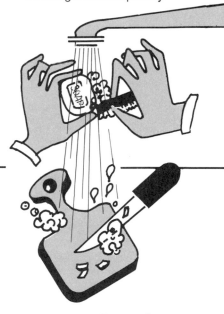

- Reheat all leftovers thoroughly; do not just warm them.

- Cook all foods thoroughly, especially meat and poultry. The internal temperature should reach 160°F for beef (for medium well-done) and 180° to 185° for poultry, which should have no pink remaining.

- Wash utensils, such as knives and cutting boards, after each use, particularly if they come in contact with meat and poultry.

Foods left unrefrigerated for long periods of time are often sources of food poisoning. On summer picnics, dry or acidic foods are safest, and hot foods should be kept hot and cold foods cold until they are served.

Safe Summer Eating

Food poisoning reports increase during July and August, when foods are often left unrefrigerated for hours, particularly on picnics. Below are some suggestions for making outdoor summer activities less risky.

- On picnics, take along dry or acidic foods, which are less likely to spoil in warm weather. These include breads, cookies, crackers, raw fruits and vegetables, hard cheeses, and peanut butter.

- Leave at home in the refrigerator those foods most likely to spoil—potato salad, cream-filled pies, chicken, ham, egg salad, and tuna—unless you can be certain that they can be kept cold enough in coolers or thermos bottles.

- Since facilities needed to clean utensils are often unavailable at picnics, stick to foods that require a minimum of handling.

- Cook meat and poultry until there is no sign of pink. Quick barbecuing can leave foods crisp on the outside and underdone on the inside.

- Don't leave foods standing on the table at picnics. Keep hot foods hot until they are served, and return cold foods to the cooler when they are not being used.

outside of the kitchen. If canned foods show signs of spoilage, such as bulging lids, odd odors, mold, or foam, do not use them.

Many people assume that foods are safe almost indefinitely in freezers. But the length of time foods should be stored there depends on the type of freezing unit used. Generally, foods should not be stored in the freezer compartments of refrigerators for more than a few weeks, because a low enough temperature is difficult to maintain consistently with so small a unit exposed to higher temperatures each time the refrigerator door is opened. In two-door refrigerators, foods can be stored in the freezer side for several months; in separate freezer units, they will keep up to a year.

Preparing food. Most food poisoning results from the improper handling of food during its preparation and serving. As general rules, keep hot foods hot, cold foods cold, and thoroughly clean all utensils that come in contact with foods.

Meat and poultry should be cooked long enough so that the internal temperature at the thickest part of the roast reaches at least 160°F and the bird, at

132

least 180° to 185°F. Again, buy a meat thermometer to be sure. (If you have any questions about storing, handling, or preparing meat and poultry at home, call the U.S. Department of Agriculture's toll-free hotline from 10 A.M. to 4 P.M. Eastern Standard Time. The number is 800-535-4555.)

Once the food has been cooked, keep in mind that the temperature range in which microorganisms thrive in foods is roughly between the extremes of room temperature—about 60° to 125°F. According to the USDA, foods left for more than two hours at those temperatures may be unsafe to eat. Even fully cooked foods can become infected from microorganisms in the air, on countertops, even on people's hands. The foods most likely to spoil at such temperatures are the same ones likely to spoil soonest when refrigerated: meat, poultry, fish, leftovers, and foods containing milk or eggs.

Foods should not be left on counters at room temperatures to cool after cooking; they should be refrigerated. If large portions are involved, they should be split up into smaller storage units so that the interior portions do not remain warm too long. The same is true for stuffing in birds; it should be removed before the bird is refrigerated so that it does not stay warm too long. (It should also be made and put into the bird's cavity just before roasting, not kept overnight in the bird in the refrigerator.) Foods should not be left at room temperature to thaw; again, thaw them in the refrigerator. Reheat all leftovers thoroughly before serving; do not just warm them. One of the times of year when food poisoning reports increase is the holiday season in November and December. This may well be because at those times leftovers are often left out at room temperatures and not properly heated before being eaten. (The other time of year when food poisoning reports increase is in July and August, perhaps because foods are left unre-frigerated for long periods of time, especially on picnics. The list on page 132 offers suggestions for safe summer eating.)

A serious example of the danger of eating foods not reheated before being served occurred in 1982 in California. A young man prepared a commercial pot pie for his mother's dinner. His father came home with take-out hamburgers, and the pot pie was set aside on an unrefrigerated shelf. More than two days later the mother ate the pot pie without reheating it and developed botulism poisoning.

Besides keeping foods at appropriate

temperatures, you should keep the utensils that come in contact with foods scrupulously clean, especially utensils used on meat and poultry, which are increasingly likely to be infected with *Salmonella* bacteria. Wash your hands before handling food and after handling raw meat or poultry. Never place cooked food on an unwashed platter that held raw meat—and possibly bacteria. Wooden cutting boards should be washed thoroughly after contact with meat and poultry. Every few days they can be cleaned with a bleach and water solution to kill bacteria possibly trapped in cracks and pores. Nonporous plastic boards may be less likely to become infected.

As an example of what can happen when such precautions are not observed, if a person used a knife to cut up raw chicken on a cutting board and then chopped up vegetables for a salad with the same knife and cutting board without washing them in hot soapy water, *Salmonella* bacteria left from the chicken could easily be transferred by the knife and cutting board to the salad ingredients; there, because the salad ingredients would not be cooked, the bacteria could proliferate. If after the chicken was cooked it was again transferred to the unwashed cutting board, it could become reinfected with the bacteria.

With all the caution you can muster, there probably is no likelihood of eliminating all sources of food poisoning. But if governmental agencies thoroughly monitor food production procedures and food service establishments, and you exercise care in storing and preparing foods at home, the number of cases of food poisoning each year can be significantly decreased. □

SUGGESTIONS FOR FURTHER READING

DACK, G. M. *Food Poisoning.* Chicago, University of Chicago Press, 1982.

FOULGER, RICHARD, and EDWARD ROUTLEDGE. *The Food Poisoning Handbook.* Bromley, England, Brookfield Publishing Company, 1981.

Home Canning of Fruits and Vegetables, G-8. Available for $1.50 from the Superintendent of Documents, U.S. Government Printing Office, Washington, D.C. 20402-9325.

LECOS, CHRIS. "The Public Health Threat of Food-borne Diarrheal Disease." *FDA Consumer*, November 1985, pp. 19-22.

The Problem of Teenage Pregnancy

Lorraine V. Klerman, Dr.P.H.

Teenage pregnancy is not a new problem nor one of increasing magnitude, like **AIDS**; nor is it usually a problem with a potentially fatal outcome. Yet it has captured the attention of the American public and held it for a decade. Why are Americans so concerned about it?

There are several reasons. First, an early pregnancy is more likely to result in health problems for mother and child. Second, a girl's prospects for an adequate education (at least completing high school) are reduced by motherhood before age 19. Third, a large proportion of the young women who give birth as teenagers end up on welfare. But perhaps the single most important reason for the public's concern is that teenage pregnancy most commonly takes place outside of marriage. Although Americans have become accustomed to movie, television, and rock stars having children out of wedlock, the thought of an unmarried teenage girl not only having intercourse but becoming pregnant and then delivering and raising a child is morally unacceptable to many people.

Teenage pregnancy is undoubtedly a serious problem in the United States, and studies suggest that it is more widespread there than in many other industrialized nations. In order to define the problem's dimensions, however, we must first identify the central issue. For example, although this matter is usually discussed in terms of pregnancy, many people are really concerned about what they consider precocious sexual activity. Most health professionals are concerned about births, not

135

Sexual activity among American teenagers has been increasing in recent decades.

pregnancies, about the potential medical complications for mother and child during or after delivery. Many pregnancies end in miscarriage or abortion, with few if any lasting health consequences for the mother. Also, are we really concerned about the pregnancies of married women who are 18 or 19 and have finished high school? No one considers such pregnancies immoral, they cause few health problems, and the child will not usually need welfare support. Thus, it seems that not all teenage pregnancies are problems requiring public attention.

Sexual activity among American teenagers has been on the rise at least since the 1970's. While in 1971 it was estimated that 32 percent of females aged 15 to 19 had experienced premarital sexual intercourse, by 1982 the figure was 44 percent. Among teenage boys, the percentage is much higher. There are major statistical differences by race in the age at which adolescents begin sexual activity. Blacks start earlier, and consequently almost 85 percent of black women have become sexually active by age 20, as compared with slightly over 70 percent of white women.

In contrast to the trend in sexual activity, the number of teenage pregnancies has actually been declining in the 1980's. A total pregnancy count is difficult to obtain, since it would include not only those teenagers who gave birth to a live infant, but also those who had miscarriages or stillbirths and those who had abortions. The count of live births is fairly accurate; of abortions, less so; and of stillbirths and miscarriages, questionable at best. Nevertheless, it is estimated that in 1978 there were over 1.14 million teenage pregnancies in the United States. By 1984, the number was only slightly over 1 million—a decline of 10 percent. Despite this decline, though, in 1981 approximately two out of every ten 18-year-old girls had become pregnant at least once, as had four out of ten 20-year-olds. The rate among blacks was four out of every ten 18-year-olds and six out of ten 20-year-olds.

Births to teenagers have declined during the 1980's even more than teenage pregnancies. In 1978 there were over 554,000 such births. By 1985 the number was under 470,000, a decline of 15 percent. If only those mothers under 18 are considered, the number of births dropped from more than 213,000 in 1978 to 178,000 in 1985.

Perhaps the most important reason for the lower number of pregnancies and births in the 1980's has been a decline in the number of teenagers, as the last of the baby boom generation reached their 20's. An increase in premarital sexual activity, coupled with the large number of women available to become pregnant, had caused a temporary increase in teenage pregnancies and births during the 1970's. Contraceptive use has played a lesser but important role in the recent decline in pregnancies, and the availability of abortion is another major factor in the decline in births. By the mid-1980's approximately 40 percent of pregnancies among women 15 to 19 were being terminated by an abortion. Among those under 15, the rate was over 50 percent.

Lorraine V. Klerman is professor of public health at the Yale University School of Medicine.

When marital status is considered, the overall statistical picture changes. The birthrate among unmarried teenagers and the proportion of teenage mothers who are unmarried have increased in recent years. In 1978, 873 of every 1,000 live births to women under age 15 were to unmarried women, and 441 of every 1,000 live births to those aged 15 to 19 were to unmarried women. In 1985 the corresponding figures were 918 and 580.

Since 1970, over two-thirds of the first children born to mothers aged 15 to 19 have been conceived outside of marriage. For blacks, this figure is more than 90 percent. Marriages of couples after conception of a child are more frequent among whites than among blacks, and among older rather than younger teenagers. Overall, however, legitimization of premarital pregnancy is not as common as it was in the past, presumably because of a lessening of the stigma attached to illegitimate birth and the availability of financial support from the federal Aid to Families with Dependent Children (AFDC) program.

Adoption, once the answer to unwanted pregnancy, is now rarely used by teenagers. It is estimated that fewer than 10 percent of the babies of unmarried mothers aged 15 to 19 are surrendered for adoption, marking a considerable decline over earlier decades. Abortion appears to have replaced adoption as the method of solving the problem of unwanted pregnancy.

San Francisco teacher Robert Valverde congratulates a new "father" on his five-pound "baby"—a bag of flour. To pass Valverde's course in family life and learn about the responsibilities of being a parent, students have to care for their sack 24 hours a day for three weeks.

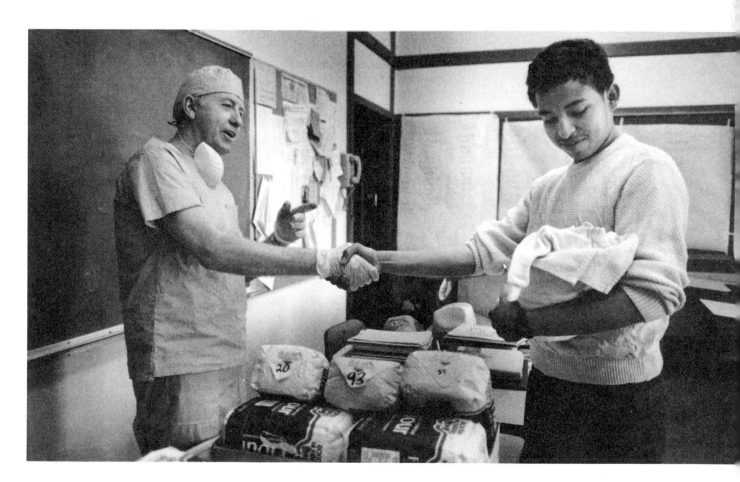

Pregnant teenagers at the Edna Gladney Home in Fort Worth, Texas, are enrolled early in a program of prenatal care that includes nutritional supplements, health education, and social support.

What Are the Reasons?

Many reasons have been offered for what the public perceives as an "epidemic" of teenage pregnancy. Actually, the figures just reviewed suggest that there has been no such epidemic. Only the *rate* of *births* to *unmarried* teenagers has increased. Explanations for this increase and for the substantial, although declining, number of teenage pregnancies often depend on the point of view of the person providing them.

For example, those alarmed about pornography and its effect on morals believe that the increase in unwed teenage mothers is due to a rise in the amount of sexually explicit material to which adolescents are exposed. This would include the sexually suggestive appeals in many advertisements, the sexual themes in many television soap operas, the explicit sex scenes in movies, and the clear sexual message in the lyrics of much rock music. Although this theory seems reasonable, the fact that teenage pregnancy rates are lower in Sweden and other European countries where teenagers are exposed to even greater amounts of sexually explicit material suggests that other factors are involved.

Critics of the U.S. welfare system suggest that teenage girls have babies in order to "get on welfare," thus enabling them to live independently of their families. Yet studies have shown that the rate of teenage pregnancy is highest in the states in which it is most difficult to become eligible for welfare and in which benefits are the lowest.

People who perceive a breakdown of family values believe that sex education in schools and the availability of contraceptives and abortion without parental consent encourage teenage sexual activity and therefore pregnancy. However, research has shown that those who attend sex education classes are *not* more likely to become pregnant before marriage. Also, most teenage girls seek family planning advice and contraceptive devices after they have been sexually active for many months, and sometimes only when they are afraid they are pregnant.

Teenagers themselves do not always provide clear answers as to why they become pregnant. When asked why they have not been using contraceptives, the vast majority answer that intercourse was unplanned, that they did not think or know about contraceptives, or that they didn't want to use contraceptives. More rarely, they say that they thought pregnancy was impossible, wanted the pregnancy, or didn't care whether they became pregnant.

There is increasing speculation about the role of rape and incest in teenage pregnancy. Some doctors and researchers believe that a substantial number of teenage girls, especially young ones, are forced to have sexual relations with members of their household, other older men, or even dates. Since contraceptives are rarely used in such intercourse, pregnancy may occur.

Currently, sociologists and social welfare experts are examining the reasons for teenage pregnancy from the perspective of socioeconomic environment. Teenage women from middle-income and upper-income families begin sexual activity later, are more likely to use effective methods of birth control, and are more likely to resort to abortion if they become pregnant. It is the teenage female who lives in poverty or close to it who is most likely to begin sexual activity early, to use contraceptives ineffectively, sporadically, or not at all, and to carry a child to term if she becomes pregnant.

The differences between these two groups lie not only in income, but also in expectations. Young women who have educational or occupational aspirations and a firm belief that they can achieve them are less likely to bear children regardless of income. But those having few such goals in life that they realistically believe they can reach may find having a baby a positive substitute. If they feel unloved or unwanted, a baby to love, and to be loved by, may be very appealing. One teenager, asked about her reason for having a baby, said "someone to always be there." Similarly, teenage men with few career aspirations or expectations may find fathering a child a way to bolster their self-esteem or their standing among their peers.

The problem of teenage pregnancy is further compounded in the black community by a shortage of suitable marriage partners. Adolescent black males have a high rate of death from homicide, significant numbers are imprisoned, and even larger numbers have dropped out of school and are not working in legitimate occupations. Marriage to such males does not appear to have any advantage over being on welfare. Nor do the prospects for a dependable husband improve markedly for black women in their early and middle 20's, so there is little incentive to postpone childbearing until then.

American society thus appears faced with a continuing teenage pregnancy problem for many reasons. Being an unwed teenage mother has become an easier role with the reduction in the stigma associated with out-of-wedlock childbearing, the presence of role models for sex

Adoption, once the answer to unwanted pregnancy, is now rarely used by teenagers.

and childrearing outside marriage, and the availability of financial support through welfare, which lessens the economic problems of raising a family at a young age without a husband. Moreover, among some segments of society the scarcity of suitable partners for marriage and the lack of powerful aspirations toward education or career make these alternatives appear less feasible. Finally, the belief that the teenager will be loved and respected by peers, boyfriend, and the baby if she is a mother increases the lure of early motherhood.

What Are the Consequences?

While several negative consequences are associated in the public mind with teenage pregnancy, it is difficult to distinguish between those problems caused by early pregnancy per se and those caused, regardless of age, by poverty, lack of education, and single parenthood. The first negative effects often mentioned are health-related. Pregnant teenagers are known to have more health problems during their pregnancies, to give birth to more preterm and low-birthweight babies, and to have more of their infants die in the first year of life than do older women. Recent studies have shown, however, that at least among those aged 15 to 19, these problems are the result not primarily of age at time of pregnancy but rather of inadequate prenatal care, poor nutrition, or unhealthy behavior such as smoking or drug use. These, in turn, are related to the mother's poverty, possible denial of pregnancy, and lack of education. When enrolled early in a program of prenatal care that includes nutritional supplements, health education, and social support, most teenage mothers have as healthy pregnancies and babies as do older mothers.

Pregnant teenagers often drop out of school. Some mothers return to classes after their child is born, and others receive a high school equivalency diploma when their children are older. But many remain without the education required for all but the most menial employment. Although when compared with women of similar economic status, those who give birth as teenagers complete less education than those who wait to have children, it should not be assumed that all women who delay having children will necessarily graduate from high school. Many teenagers drop out of school before they become pregnant, and others would have done so even if they did not bear a child.

Welfare dependency is often another direct result of teenage pregnancy. The oft-quoted figure is that about half of the money spent on AFDC goes to households in which one or more women had their first child as a teenager. There can be little doubt that when a poor teenager has a child some household will need welfare benefits, whether it be the one in which she is residing or an independent one which she chooses to form. Many young women, however, will seek employment once their children are old enough to be in day care or attend school. Few teenage mothers want to remain on welfare, but their efforts to find a job may be hampered by lack of adequate day care facilities or their insufficient education. Moreover, "getting off" welfare also means losing medicaid coverage. Since many of the jobs for which teenage

Teenage childbearing has significant economic repercussions for society.

mothers are eligible do not carry health insurance benefits, taking such a job leaves the mother vulnerable to high medical bills.

Young mothers have tended to have a second child early (often within two years of the first) and to have a fairly large number of children. In recent years, however, the trend to high fertility has slowed. Many young women who have difficulty using contraceptives effectively are turning to abortion or sterilization to avoid having more than two or three children.

Unwed women who have their first child before they reach their 20's are also more likely to have later marital problems. Although most of them do eventually marry, their marriages tend to be less stable than those of their peers who delayed childbearing.

However, the consequences of teenage motherhood are not limited to the mother herself. Low birthweight, a condition that is more common among the infants of teenage mothers, has many negative effects. Such babies are either preterm, growth-retarded, or both. They are more likely to have cerebral palsy, seizure disorders, and other neurodevelopmental problems, as well as lung conditions that make them especially susceptible to respiratory infections.

Children of young mothers are likely to score lower on standardized intellectual achievement tests than the offspring of older mothers and tend not to do as well in school. The precise reasons are unknown, but the intellectual problems may be related to the mother's own educational deficiencies, to the absence of a father, or to growing up in a poor neighborhood with inadequate schools. Behavior problems and child abuse are also somewhat more common among the children of young mothers.

Finally, teenage childbearing has significant economic repercussions for society. Recent estimates have been made of the annual cost to the AFDC, food stamp, and medicaid programs that is attributable to families established as a result of teenage childbearing. That cost is close to $17 billion, or approximately 53 percent of the total public expenditure for these programs. The estimate of the 20-year public costs resulting from all first births to teenagers in 1985 is over $5 billion. However, the potential savings if all births were delayed until the mothers were 20 or older would be only $2 billion, or 40 percent, because some women would require public support even if they delayed having their first child.

For girls who feel unloved or unwanted, the idea of a baby to love and be loved by has a strong appeal.

What Can Be Done?

In a recent report, the U.S. National Research Council's Panel on Adolescent Pregnancy and Childbearing made numerous recommendations for policies and programs that it believed would accomplish the following goals:

• reduce the rate and number of unintended pregnancies among adolescents, especially those of school age;

• provide alternatives to adolescent childbearing and parenting;

• promote good health and social, economic, and educational opportunities for adolescent parents and their children.

The first strategy suggested by the panel for reducing teenage

Job-training programs help teenagers stay in school and set career goals.

pregnancy is enhancing the options of teenage girls and boys. This would be accomplished through programs to improve school performance and provide role models for careers, as well as employment programs and life-planning courses.

A second strategy is to try to convince teenagers not to become sexually active so early. Educational programs about sex and family life are certainly one approach, but these should be bolstered, the panel said, by training in decision-making, the provision of positive role models for family life, and a change in the way sexuality is treated in the media.

The final pregnancy reduction strategy recommended by the NRC panel is encouraging effective contraceptive use. Sex education programs should include information on the use of contraceptives and how they can be obtained. Birth control services should be easily available, with neither cost nor distance being a barrier. The panel saw school-based clinics and condom distribution programs as particularly likely to be effective.

Recognizing that prevention will occasionally fail, the panel urged that abortion and adoption be available as alternatives to teenage childbearing and parenting. In order for these alternatives to be used with the minimum of emotional trauma, pregnancy testing as well as counseling should be readily available.

For those who choose to become parents, the panel recommended a wide variety of programs to ensure that mother and child develop to their fullest potential. In the health area, prenatal, labor, and delivery services, nutritional counseling and supplementation, and pediatric care are essential. Economic support should be available through AFDC, medicaid, food stamps, and other programs. Moreover, fathers should be encouraged to support their children, or required to by the courts if necessary. Since the children of teenage parents appear to have more problems than others, special efforts should be made to promote their social, emotional, and intellectual development. Providing education to parents about the tasks and problems of parenthood is one useful step. Child care programs, Head Start, and other specialized services can also help. Finally, teenage parents will need special educational and employment programs if they are to assume meaningful roles in American society.

Teenage Pregnancy: Cause or Symptom?

Many see teenage pregnancy as the cause of numerous social ills, including high infant mortality and school dropout rates and high welfare costs. Alternatively, these ills can be viewed as symptoms of poverty and alienation—and teenage pregnancy itself can be perceived as just another such symptom. Those who hold this view would argue that society must certainly treat the symptom; it must provide the services that are needed to prevent teenage pregnancy and to assist young parents. But it must also treat the underlying problems by encouraging young men and women to stay in school, become employed, and plan their children so that both parents and offspring will enjoy their lives to the fullest.

SUGGESTIONS FOR FURTHER READING

ALAN GUTTMACHER INSTITUTE. *Teenage Pregnancy: The Problem That Hasn't Gone Away.* New York, The Institute, 1981.

FURSTENBERG, FRANK F., JR., J. BROOKS-GUNN, and S. PHILIP MORGAN. *Adolescent Mothers in Later Life.* Cambridge, Cambridge University Press, 1987.

JONES, ELISE F., et al. *Teenage Pregnancy in Industrialized Countries.* New Haven, Conn., Yale University Press, 1986.

NATIONAL RESEARCH COUNCIL. *Risking the Future: Adolescent Sexuality, Pregnancy, and Childbearing.* Washington, D.C., National Academy Press, 1987.

Booklets on various aspects of teenage pregnancy are available from the Adolescent Pregnancy Prevention Clearinghouse of the Children's Defense Fund, 122 C Street, N.W., Suite 400, Washington, D.C. 20001.

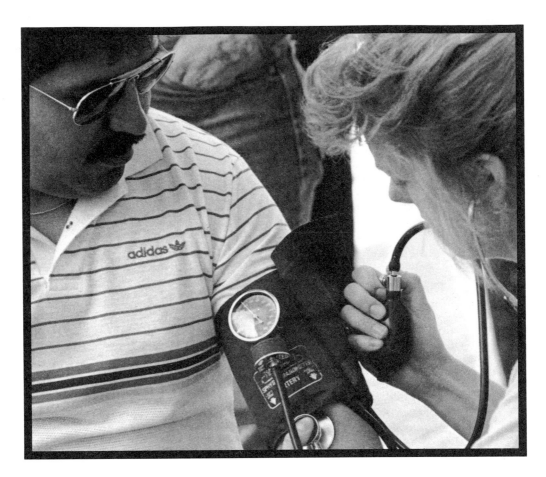

HYPERTENSION
The Silent Killer

John H. Laragh, M.D.

As many as 20 percent of adult Americans suffer from some form of hypertension, or continuing high blood pressure. The most common forerunner of stroke, heart attack, and kidney failure, hypertension is American society's leading risk factor for sickness and death.

All of us have bursts of high blood pressure from time to time, as we exercise or deal with situations that challenge us or require unusual effort. But when high blood pressure is sustained over time, it is considered established hypertension and should be treated. Unfortunately, hypertension can remain asymptomatic for some time, going quietly about its unpleasant business until the damage it has done is very great. It is sometimes referred to, therefore, as "the silent killer."

Understanding Blood Pressure

The heart constantly pumps blood throughout the body under pressure and within a closed network of expandable veins and arteries. The arterial system can be likened to a hose that is made of soft, balloonlike rubber. Essentially, two factors determine the pressure within the hose: the amount of water coursing through it and the inward squeeze of the stretched rubber. Pressure can be increased in two ways: by sending more water through the hose and by increasing the squeeze of the rubber. Conversely, pressure can be lowered by decreasing the amount of water in the hose or lessening the squeeze of the rubber.

In the human body, as long as the heart is pumping normally, blood pressure can be increased either by increasing the volume of blood in the blood vessels or by narrowing the channels through which the blood travels, through a process called vasoconstriction. The walls of the small arteries, or arterioles, are lined with muscles that, on signal, can contract, narrowing the arterial channel. Pressure can be lowered by decreasing blood volume or by relaxing the muscles of the arterial walls, thus enlarging the inner channel.

Sometimes the signal that triggers vasoconstriction is conveyed through what is known as the autonomic nervous system in response to a short-term demand for unusual effort—whether running a race or coping with a crisis on the job. The best known chemical messengers, or neurotransmitters, for activating this intermittent kind of elevated blood pressure are epinephrine and norepinephrine (also known as adrenaline and noradrenaline, respectively). For reasons not as yet entirely clear, some people react to even the most ordinary stresses of daily life by continually sending such signals. As a result, they keep themselves in a prolonged and inappropriate state of high blood pressure.

Most people with high blood pressure, however, have some defect in the structure or functioning of the marvelous regulatory system that normally keeps blood pressure at the steady level needed for healthy blood flow and everyday functioning. Something goes wrong either with the way this system perceives and attempts to regulate the level of sodium in the blood—an important factor in certain cases of high blood pressure—or with the way it tries to keep the arteries in the proper state of constriction or relaxation.

A Complex Regulating System

The chief managing agents of the body's blood-pressure regulating system are the kidneys, which clean the blood of wastes and adjust its volume. For these dual tasks the kidneys receive an enormous flow of blood, and they are highly sensitive to the state of that flow. Responding to certain chemical signals in the blood, specialized cells in the kidneys work either to retain sodium in the bloodstream or to excrete it from the body through the urine. The kidneys provide the main route for the elimination of dietary salt. Sodium (a major component of table salt) has the special ability to attract and retain water in the body; increasing the blood's sodium content, therefore, leads to a rise in its fluid volume. This fact is the basis for the action of drugs called diuretics, which are still probably the most frequently used type of antihypertensive drug. Diuretics force the kidneys to eliminate salt, and with the salt goes water. As a result, volume drops, and so, generally, does blood pressure.

By releasing their own chemical messenger, renin, the kidneys can also stimulate a powerful vaso-constrictive effect in the arterioles, and this sharply increases blood pressure. When renin is secreted into the bloodstream, it triggers a chain of chemical reactions by other components of the renin system.

Renin is released or withheld by the kidneys as they react to changes in blood pressure or blood flow. Just what triggers the kidneys' actions is not yet completely understood. Some scientists think that special cells lining the renal arteries (those leading to the kidneys) secrete renin into tiny pockets, the openings to which are kept closed by the blood pressure in the surrounding blood vessels. When blood pressure falls, these pockets may open and release renin into the bloodstream. Renin may also be secreted by the kidneys when they detect a decrease in the amount of sodium being retained by the body; conversely, renin secretion is turned off by a rising store of body sodium.

Whatever its cause, the release of renin is followed by a wonderfully effective series of events. Renin reacts with a substance in the blood called the renin substrate, a protein that is manufactured and

John H. Laragh is director of the Cardiovascular Center and chief of the Cardiology Division at The New York Hospital-Cornell Medical Center. He has written more than 650 articles and has edited 8 books on hypertension and related topics in cardiovascular medicine.

released by the liver. This chemical interaction releases another substance called angiotensin I. By itself, angiotensin I has no effect on blood pressure. However, it very quickly encounters, in the lungs, a special converting enzyme that changes it to angiotensin II, which is the most powerful vasoconstrictive hormone yet discovered. The heart immediately delivers angiotensin II to the network of arterioles, where it causes the walls of the arteries to contract, raising blood pressure.

At the same time, angiotensin II gets busy on another front. Its chemical signal to the cortex, or outer layer, of the adrenal glands—which lie on top of the kidneys—triggers the secretion of the hormone aldosterone from these glands. The final messenger of the renin system, aldosterone slowly but steadily causes the kidneys to retain sodium in the body rather than clear it out in the urine. The retained sodium increases the sensitivity of the muscles of the arterial wall to angiotensin's action, enhancing vasoconstriction. By attracting water, sodium increases the volume of fluid in the bloodstream and elsewhere in the body. These combined actions, of vasoconstriction and increased volume, raise pressure and improve blood flow—and nutrition—to the vital organs. The raised, or restored, blood pressure then stops the release of renin by the kidneys, turning off the entire operation at its origin.

The Heart's Hormone

An exciting discovery in the early 1980's stimulated a new area of research that holds great promise for better understanding of the cardiovascular and renal systems and for better treatment of hypertension and related disorders. The discovery was a hormone secreted by the heart. This atrial hormone works with the renin system in regulating sodium balance and blood pressure.

Atrial hormone causes a great increase in sodium excretion, while at the same time it lowers pressure by acting directly on the blood vessels. A lack of this hormone may be important in causing certain forms of hypertension. Researchers are working hard to improve the understanding of precisely how atrial hormone works with the renin system in regulating blood pressure and to develop possible new treatments for hypertension that are based on analogues (that is, synthetic equivalents) of this substance.

When the System Goes Wrong

Nature designed the blood pressure control system to keep pressure at a healthy, normal level. But sometimes things go wrong, causing blood pressure to be maintained at an abnormally high level. The resultant hypertension must be taken seriously. Although many people with very high blood pressure live long and untroubled lives, others may succumb with little or no warning to cardiovascular illness or death.

Like fever, hypertension is a symptom of disorder; it is not, in itself, a specific disease. A continuing state of high blood pressure can be brought about by a number of conditions and events. There are two major categories of hypertension—secondary and essential. In secondary hypertension, elevated blood pressure is a by-product of some other abnormal condition. In the far more common essential hypertension, no specific cause for the higher blood

Some Patterns of Hypertension

systolic hypertension: systolic blood pressure is elevated and the heart's work is excessive only when the person is challenged; this type of hypertension is often seen in the elderly and results from decreased elasticity of the larger arteries.

labile hypertension: blood pressure is elevated on some occasions and normal on others; people with labile hypertension tend to have average blood pressure readings that are higher than readings for the general population, but it is not known whether such people are likely to develop sustained hypertension.

borderline hypertension: blood pressure readings are only slightly elevated or at the high end of the normal range; people with borderline pressure sometimes develop true hypertension, so they should be checked regularly by their physicians.

hypertensive vascular disease: persistent and severe hypertension that produces enlargement of the heart, failure of the heart's left ventricle, and damage to the arterioles of the kidneys, eyes, and brain; the walls of the small arteries and arterioles become thickened, narrowing the channels through which the blood flows, and hardening of the larger arteries may also occur.

malignant hypertension: a severely accelerating condition in which the retina, optic nerve, and kidneys are damaged and the walls of the arterioles become inflamed and may actually die; this syndrome can occur by itself, but it is most often a complication of untreated essential or secondary hypertension.

pressure can be identified. Whether secondary or essential, hypertension can manifest itself in various ways, which are described in the box on page 146 entitled ''Some Patterns of Hypertension.''

In many cases, permanent control of blood pressure can be achieved only with long-term or lifelong medication; however, hypertension can sometimes be cured. For this reason, one or more screening tests for possible causes should be performed on every person whom a physician suspects may have high blood pressure.

Diagnosing High Blood Pressure

In 1896 a prototype of the modern blood pressure-measuring instrument, the sphygmomanometer, was developed. The technique for measuring pressures was perfected in 1905, with a description of five characteristic sounds that can be heard through a stethoscope as arterial pressure is artificially reduced.

The classic sphygmomanometer includes a cuff that is wrapped around the upper arm; a pump that inflates the cuff, tightening it so as to stop the arterial blood flow temporarily; and a pressure gauge—a glass column filled with mercury. One can take a blood pressure reading by listening, with the stethoscope, to the sounds that occur over the artery as the cuff is slowly deflated and the blood begins to flow again. Of the five sounds, the first and last are usually used to assess blood pressure. This is done by reading the height of the mercury column at the occurrence of each sound. The first reading, known as *systolic blood pressure*, is based on the abrupt, sharp sound as pressure is reduced to just below the highest pressure, exerted as the heart forces blood into the arteries. The second reading, the *diastolic blood pressure*, is based on the total disappearance of the

sound of the heartbeat, indicating that the heart is resting. Normal blood pressure is considered to be about 120 systolic and 80 diastolic, or 120/80. Although it is generally accepted today that blood pressures over 160/95 are high, what is normal varies with age, the condition of the arterial system, and a patient's medical history.

About 85 percent of all hypertensive patients have what is called primary or benign essential hypertension, whose hallmark is a raised diastolic pressure. This blood pressure pattern is the result of a generalized vasoconstriction of the arterioles. The diagnosis of essential hypertension, however, should be made only when all other known causes for the elevation in diastolic blood pressure have been excluded.

Hypertension is a major risk factor for stroke, heart attack, and kidney failure.

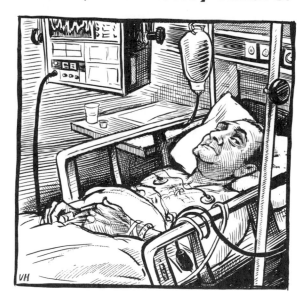

The most basic of several tests designed specifically to screen for different forms of hypertension is the renin-sodium profile test. This test can identify patients whose hypertension is curable, and it can categorize other patients according to the amount of circulating renin in their blood, information that can be very helpful in devising effective plans for those whose hypertension, though not curable, is treatable.

Secondary Hypertension

When the renin-sodium profile reveals very high or very low levels of renin, the possibility of secondary hypertension—in which elevated blood pressure is secondary to some other condition—should be considered. Many of these conditions are curable, and additional tests can be done to clarify or confirm a diagnosis.

A tumor in the adrenal cortex sometimes produces excessive amounts of aldosterone or similar hormones that cause the body to retain salt. In this disease, called primary aldosteronism, the blood pressure is high and the levels of renin and potassium in the blood are low. In the condition called pheochromocytoma, a tumor in the medulla, or central portion, of the adrenal gland causes the continual or episodic release of epinephrine or norepinephrine, constricting the arteries and speeding up the heart. Both types of tumors can usually be removed, resulting in a permanent cure.

In the condition known as renovascular hypertension, a diminished or blocked blood supply to one or both kidneys may rob these organs of the pressure they need either to turn off renin release or to eliminate sodium. It is crucial to identify this fairly common condition, which can frequently be cured by means of a new, nonsurgical technique called balloon angioplasty. In this procedure, a balloon is threaded through a catheter and into a narrowed artery where the balloon is inflated to widen the arterial channel.

These are the most common curable forms of secondary hypertension. Causes of other types of secondary hypertension include kidney injuries, tumors, or inflammation; various disorders of the adrenal glands; injuries to the spine or nervous system; and drug and alcohol abuse. Screening tests for various forms of hypertension are described in the box on page 149.

Essential Hypertension

The hypertension of some 85 percent of high blood pressure patients cannot be attributed to a specific cause. In the past, the only way the conditions of these millions of patients with essential hypertension could be distinguished was by blood pressure level. Thus, patients were classified as benign (if the level was barely above normal), not too serious, fairly serious, and malignant or extremely serious (if the level was very high). Treatment was a trial-and-error affair in which various combinations of a salt-free diet, diuretics, and drugs of one kind or another were used in an attempt to lower blood pressure. This type of treatment often resulted in unwanted side effects, including impairment of physical, mental, and sexual functioning.

It has now been demonstrated that patients with essential hypertension are by no means all alike. In fact, their hypertension can arise from very different biochemical disorders. Two quite distinct forms of essential hypertension have been identified. One type is characterized by high levels of renin in the blood, lowered blood flow, and a "dry" vasoconstriction in which blood supply is greatly reduced. The other type is characterized by low renin levels, higher blood flow, and a "wet" vasoconstriction associated with a higher body sodium content. "Dry" hypertension leads much more often to complications such as stroke, heart attack, kidney damage, retinal disease, and symptoms such as vomiting, headache, and convulsions.

Armed with this new knowledge about types of essential hypertension and aided by tests such as the renin-sodium profile, physicians can now often provide patients with far more specific treatments, directed precisely to their underlying biochemical defect. The modern array of anti-hypertensive drugs that act on particular structures and processes within the cardiovascular and related systems gives the physician many new options.

Risk Factors for Hypertension

Studies involving large population groups have helped researchers determine both normal blood pressure ranges and various risk factors for hypertension, including age, race, and sex. Both systolic and diastolic pressures tend to rise with age in all but a few isolated populations. Hypertension is somewhat more prevalent in women and, for reasons as yet unexplained, is much more common in blacks. Genetic factors have

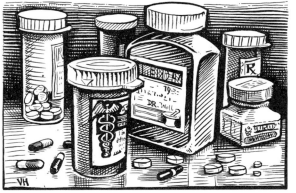

Many types of medication are available to treat high blood pressure.

long been suspected of playing a role in essential hypertension. However, environmental factors may also play a role.

For a long time it was thought that a high intake of dietary salt caused high blood pressure. This hypothesis was based chiefly on the observation that hypertension and related disorders are far more common in societies with high salt intake than in those with lower sodium consumption. But efforts to correlate individual variations in salt intake and blood pressure have been unsuccessful.

It seems probable that dietary sodium is a causal factor only when intake is extreme or, perhaps, in certain people who are for some reason particularly sensitive to sodium. And low salt intake may not always be good. The Yanamamo Indians of South America eat practically no salt and show very little hypertension, but their physiological characteristics suggest chronic dehydration.

It has been shown, principally in studies of migrating populations, that stress produces increases in blood pressure. Advocates of the environmental stress theory suggest that elevated blood pressure reflects a prolonged inability to adapt to stressful surroundings. But, animal studies have not demonstrated the development of chronic hypertension in response to stressful stimuli.

Whether essential hypertension has a single origin in an individual or is the result of many factors, whether it is largely genetic or develops in response to environmental and psychosocial factors, remains to be revealed. But the failure so far to expose essential hyptertension's specific cause or causes has not prevented the accumulation of new knowledge about the physiological characteristics of the

Screening for Hypertension

The *renin-sodium profile test* is a simple test in which samples of the patient's blood and urine are analyzed for renin and sodium levels, respectively. The levels of renin circulating in the blood, measured against the rate of sodium excretion (which reflects dietary sodium intake), form the basis for categorizing patients as high-renin, medium-renin, or low-renin types. This information alerts physicians to the possibility of curable forms of hypertension and also may predict what type of drug therapy will be most effective in treating patients with essential hypertension.

The *captopril test* can be employed to confirm the presence of renovascular hypertension. The converting enzyme inhibitor captopril is given orally to the patient, and the reaction to this drug is measured through blood pressure readings and analysis of blood samples. Patients with renovascular hypertension show a sudden rise in renin level in response to captopril.

Further tests that permit the doctor to visualize the renal arterial network (*digital subtraction angiography* or *arteriography*) and that evaluate renin levels in the renal veins themselves (*renal vein renin studies*) can confirm a dangerous narrowing of a renal artery or other pathologic change and can localize the problem in one or the other kidney.

Blood and urine tests that assess the levels of other substances (for example, aldosterone, cortisol, epinephrine, and norepinephrine), as well as other assessment techniques, can reveal the presence of primary aldosteronism or an adrenal tumor.

disorder, and it has not prevented the development of useful therapies.

Why Treat High Blood Pressure?

Statistics have long shown that having relatively higher blood pressure might shorten one's life. It has been hypothesized that the risk of early death from hypertension varies greatly among individuals and that, in fact, this risk may be incurred by only a small, as yet unidentified fraction of hypertensive patients with special vulnerability. It may be that the majority of people with hypertension are not at greater risk of premature death than anyone else. However, until the high-risk subgroup can be identified, treatment must be offered to all hypertensive patients to save those at special risk.

What can happen to people with elevated blood pressure if they are given no treatment? Excessive blood pressure, if it persists over a long period of time, can produce harmful effects in a variety of ways. Some of the same mechanisms responsible for the high blood pressure may cause arteries to harden—to become stiffer and less resilient—and thus reduce the flow of blood. Tissues deprived of blood—and these include the blood vessels themselves—may weaken and be unable to function properly. The smaller arteries eventually become susceptible to rupture, a common cause of stroke.

The kidneys are particularly vulnerable to such subtle and cumulative damage. And because these organs play such a crucial role in regulating blood pressure, a vicious cycle may be set up in which the damage intensifies the hypertension and the hypertension worsens the damage. The heart itself, working harder to support higher-than-normal pressure, may ultimately weaken and fail.

MAJOR CLASSES OF ANTIHYPERTENSIVE DRUGS

Class	Representative Drugs	Advantages	Possible Side Effects
USEFUL PRIMARILY WITH MEDIUM- TO HIGH-RENIN HYPERTENSION			
Converting enzyme inhibitors	captopril, enalapril	Maintain blood flow and rate at which blood is filtered; lower resistance of small arteries to blood flow	Proteinuria (excess protein in the urine), low blood pressure, reduced number of white blood cells
Beta blockers	propranolol, nadolol, atenolol, pindolol	Reduce cardiac output and the heart's work	Cardiac failure if the heart's action is too depressed, nausea, vomiting, diarrhea, light-headedness; may exacerbate angina
USEFUL PRIMARILY WITH LOW-RENIN HYPERTENSION			
Calcium antagonists	nifedipine, diltiazem, verapamil	Dilate blood vessels; maintain blood flow; lower resistance of small arteries to blood flow	Low blood pressure, peripheral swelling from fluid accumulation, dizziness, flushing, headache; may exacerbate angina
Diuretics	thiazides, such as hydrochlorothiazide; "loop" diuretics, such as furosemide	Eliminate excess body salt and water	Reduced blood flow; excess loss of potassium, sodium, and calcium; low blood pressure
	aldosterone antagonists, such as spironolactone	Maintain body potassium, blood flow	Overload of potassium, nausea, vomiting, menstrual irregularities
Alpha blockers	prazosin, terazosin	Maintain cardiac output, blood flow, and rate at which blood is filtered	Low blood pressure, excess loss of sodium, dizziness, headache, lack of energy, palpitation, nausea

Many individuals who blithely proceed through the years with very high blood pressure somehow escape these kinds of complications, but why and how, no one knows. Thus, to protect those at risk, doctors are often forced to lower blood pressure to more normal levels and to keep it there in the group as a whole. Studies have shown that hypertensive patients whose blood pressure has been held under control generally live longer than those who are not controlled.

Managing Hypertension

As noted earlier, some forms of secondary hypertension can be treated very effectively. And even for the great majority of patients whose hypertension cannot so easily be cured, there are many more treatment options today than ever before. A few individuals can control their hypertension by means of nondrug regimens that include such things as lowered salt intake and weight control through diet and regular exercise. For many people, however, some form of medication is necessary. The current array of antihypertensive drugs offers the physician the possibility of achieving the primary goals of all drug therapy: to give the smallest number of drugs, in the lowest possible dosages, and with the least possible frequency.

Currently, the five drug types shown in the table on page 150 are the most widely used. Because each type acts on different physiologic mechanisms, the physician can target therapy much more efficiently than before.

Converting enzyme inhibitors are bringing about important changes in the way hypertension is understood and treated. These drugs block the conversion of angiotensin I to angiotensin II, thus preventing the final effects of the renin system in constricting blood vessels. The effectiveness of these drugs demonstrates the involvement of the renin system in a large fraction of hypertensive patients.

Converting enzyme inhibitors are very powerful and alone can often replace three or four other drugs. By themselves, they lower pressure and yet improve blood flow to the heart, brain, and kidneys. Moreover, because of their specifically targeted action, they are free of the unwanted side effects of some older drugs.

Beta blockers work by occupying what are called beta receptor sites in the heart and kidneys and thus blocking communication between these receptors and the nervous system. In this way they depress heart rate and reduce cardiac output, reducing the heart's work. Because beta blockers also inhibit the secretion of renin, they are particularly effective in lowering the blood pressure of hypertensive patients with medium or high levels of renin in their blood; they are not effective in patients whose renin levels are low.

Calcium antagonists are particularly effective in treating hypertension in patients with low renin levels. The observation that these drugs also may produce significant blood pressure reductions in patients with high renin levels underlines the likelihood that some sort of defect in calcium metabolism is involved in all excessive vaso-constriction. At present a great deal of research is being focused on the question of how interactions among calcium, magnesium, and sodium metabolism and the renin system affect the hypertensive process.

Diuretics speed up the body's elimination of sodium and, with sodium, water. Some diuretics act directly on the special sodium-retaining cells in the kidneys; others interrupt the chemical signals that turn these cells on or off. Although probably the most frequently used type of hypertensive drug, diuretics are appropriate only if the patient's hypertension can be shown to be due to excessive retention of salt and water. It is a popular misconception that everyone with high blood pressure should take a diuretic: this is emphatically *not* true. Diuretics may even be harmful in patients with hypertension caused by high renin levels that produce "dry" vasoconstriction; they may tend to reduce blood volume even more and to intensify the vasoconstriction and hypertension.

Alpha blockers, like beta blockers, act to counter the kind of vasoconstriction that is mediated by the sympathetic nervous system. Although these agents are most effective in the low-renin forms of hypertension, they are not usually powerful enough to be used by themselves in the long-term control of high blood pressure. These drugs do have a special use in cases of pheochromocytoma, where they are very effective in managing the hypertension until corrective surgery can be performed.

What's in the Future?

Researchers continue to explore the precise role of atrial hormone in the regulation of blood pressure, as well as the therapeutic possibilities of analogues of this newly discovered substance. A number of investigators are working with several new drug types that cause vasodilation by increasing the cell membrane's permeability to potassium. This is important because potassium plays a critical role in vasoconstriction, influencing the contraction of the muscles that line the arterial walls. Researchers are also studying some renin-inhibiting substances that, unlike the converting enzyme inhibitors, act at an earlier point in the renin system's cycle. As a result, these drugs may not trigger the reactive renin secretion that converting enzymes sometimes set off, sabotaging their own usefulness. □

AIDS
UPDATE

The relentless spread of AIDS—in spite of modern medical techniques—has aroused many of the deep-seated fears that accompany world epidemics. This article examines the current state of knowledge about AIDS and summarizes attempts to date to control the disease. The article that follows provides some perspective on the history of epidemic illnesses.

Steven D. Helgerson, M.D., M.P.H.
James F. Jekel, M.D., M.P.H.

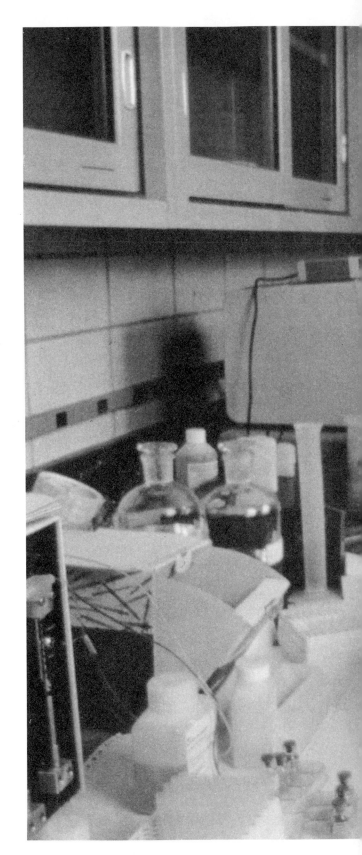

The AIDS epidemic is neither the first nor the largest worldwide epidemic to challenge the ingenuity of scientists, the dedication and ethical values of physicians, the tolerance and reason of the general public, and the fortitude of those with the disease. Nor has the virus that causes acquired immune deficiency syndrome been responsible for as much death and disability as bubonic plague or smallpox or even the contemporary scourge of tobacco smoking, with its array of related diseases. Since 1981, when AIDS was first identified, more has been learned about the disease, its cause, the ways it is transmitted, and the measures necessary for its control than was ever before learned about a similarly pestilential disease in such a short time. But it is not this rapid accumulation of knowledge that most distinguishes AIDS from other epidemics. Rather, it is its extraordinary notoriety, made possible by late-20th-century communications technology. AIDS is the most publicized disease in history.

As a result, there are two simultaneous epidemics:

the disease itself and the unwarranted fear of the disease in people at very little risk. Both epidemics have continued to spread, and there seemed to be a new hurdle for every one investigators surmounted.

The Nature of the Disease

Polls have shown that more than nine out of ten people in the United States recognize the term AIDS. Many also know by now that AIDS destroys the body's immune system, leaving its victims prey to a variety of otherwise rare infections and cancers, which often kill within a matter of months. These include pneumonia caused by the organism *Pneumocystis carinii*, a skin cancer called Kaposi's sarcoma, and cancer and infections of the brain. AIDS patients also show various symptoms of a weakened immune system, such as weight loss, night sweats, fatigue, and swollen lymph nodes.

AIDS is caused by a virus known as human immunodeficiency virus type one, or HIV-I (the virus is also known as HTLV-III and LAV). Viruses similar to HIV-I have been identified, one of which (called HIV-II) has caused an AIDS-like disease in Africa, another of which (called HTLV-I) causes a rare form of leukemia. So far, however, only HIV-I is known to cause AIDS in North America.

Not everyone infected with HIV-I has developed AIDS, although an estimated 20 to 30 percent of virus carriers develop AIDS within five years of initial infection. By March 1988, more than 57,000 AIDS cases had been reported in the United States, more than 1,600 in Canada, and at least 60,000 in other countries around the world. (The last figure probably is far too low because of less adequate diagnostic facilities and intentional underreporting in some countries.) More than half of those diagnosed as having the disease have died. In New York City, AIDS is the leading cause of death for men 25-44 years of age and for women 25-34.

Since U.S. and Canadian blood supplies began to be screened for HIV-I in 1985, greatly reducing the risk of transmission of the virus through trans-fusions of blood or blood products, the primary routes of transmission have been by direct exchange

Steven D. Helgerson is senior epidemiologist at the Indian Health Service in Tucson, Ariz. James F. Jekel is professor of epidemiology and public health at the Yale University School of Medicine.

of body fluids in sexual contact, through the sharing of hypodermic needles and syringes, or from mother to child during pregnancy or delivery (and possibly through breast feeding). Many studies have shown that the virus is not spread by casual contact at home or in the workplace, or by food, air, or water.

Who Is at Risk?

In 1987 experts estimated that 1.5 million Americans were infected with HIV-I. In the United States, about 95 percent of AIDS victims and people estimated to be infected with the virus are members of risk groups that were identified by scientists within a year or two after AIDS was first recognized. These risk groups include homosexual and bisexual men; intravenous drug users; people who received blood transfusions or blood-clotting factors for hemophilia prior to 1985; and heterosexual partners of persons in the preceding groups. A disproportionate number of U.S. AIDS cases, including most of the heterosexual cases, have occurred among blacks and Hispanics. The rate among these groups is at least twice that for whites and probably reflects greater intravenous drug use among urban minorities. Concerns about AIDS breaking out of the recognized risk groups and into the general population were expressed often in 1987, but there was no clear evidence that such a spread had occurred.

Even though, according to many experts, most people in the United States are at very low risk of being exposed to HIV-I, some simple precautions taken during sexual activity can reduce the possibility of transference of the virus. So-called safe sex—using a condom or avoiding the exchange of body fluids—with any partner whose HIV-I status cannot be known for certain is advised by most medical experts.

There is some evidence against the probability of a major increase in the heterosexual spread of HIV-I in the United States. Since October 1985 all civilians applying to the U.S. military and all active-duty military personnel have been tested for the virus. The rates of positive blood tests have remained constant at about 1.5 positives for every 1,000 applicants tested and 1.6 positives for every 1,000 active-duty personnel.

As many as 10 million people in more than 100 countries outside the United States and Canada are probably infected with HIV-I. The burden of AIDS cases is particularly heavy in central Africa. Unlike the United States, where more than 90 percent of those afflicted with AIDS are male, cases in some developing countries are equally divided between males and females, and heterosexual contact is probably the dominant means of transmission in those countries.

Why is the spread of AIDS among heterosexuals apparently so common in developing countries, yet so rare in the United States? The answer to this question is not known for sure, but much of the difference in transmission patterns can probably be explained by certain factors. Unlike most Americans, but like many members of the major U.S. risk groups, many heterosexuals in developing countries have had repeated infections with bacteria, parasites, and viruses; a constantly stimulated immune system may increase the likelihood that a person infected with HIV-I will develop AIDS. Urban men and women in developing countries may have more sexual partners than Americans outside the established risk groups and may be more likely to be exposed to unsterile needles used by traditional healers and in poorly equipped hospitals and clinics. These factors lead to more infected heterosexuals and increase the risk of infection for their sexual partners.

Before the cause of AIDS was known, it was necessary to establish a descriptive definition of the illness in order to allow physicians to report cases. The definition emphasized the occurrence of infections and cancers that were very rare except in people with severely damaged immune systems. Once HIV-I was discovered and blood tests were developed to identify antibodies to it, AIDS could be more clearly defined by combining the results of blood tests with the presence of key signs and symptoms as well as of rare infections and cancers. In September 1987 the U.S. Centers for Disease Control (CDC) in Atlanta expanded the definition of AIDS to include adults with dementia (intellectual deterioration) or severe weight loss when these conditions are accompanied by a blood test showing infection with HIV-I. With this wider definition the number of cases of AIDS reported in the United States since 1981 will increase an estimated 20 percent once the CDC finishes compiling new statistics. The added cases will almost certainly have the same risk group characteristics as previously reported cases.

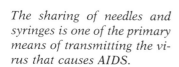

The sharing of needles and syringes is one of the primary means of transmitting the virus that causes AIDS.

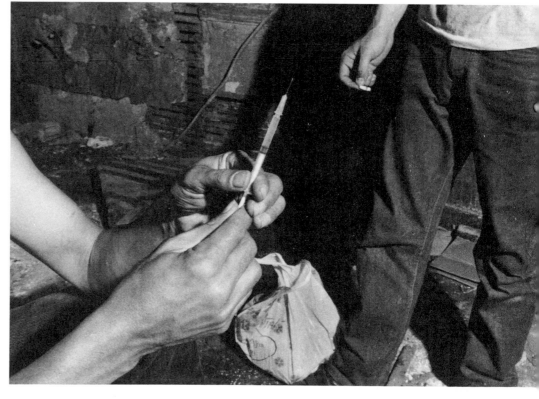

Three Florida brothers (shown at left with their father), who contracted the virus responsible for AIDS through contaminated blood products taken for their hemophilia, were rejected by their community; they were eventually forced to move when their house was destroyed in a suspicious fire. At right, a poster emphasizes that children afflicted with AIDS need affection—and that the disease cannot be spread by nonsexual physical contact.

Fighting the Virus

Further strides in understanding the biology of HIV-I have been made. Scientists now know that the virus that causes AIDS consists of an outer envelope made up of two substances, called glycoproteins, and that inside the envelope are eight genes that regulate the virus's structure and its ability to replicate. Knowing the chemical structure and functions of the virus's parts is very promising; scientists can use this knowledge to identify or design drugs to treat people infected with HIV-I. Unfortunately, once treatments are developed, they are not likely to eradicate the virus, but only to suppress it. Since infection probably persists for a lifetime, lifelong drug treatment will probably be needed.

The search for drug therapies for AIDS has focused on two areas: (1) identifying drugs that have a direct effect against the virus, and (2) using agents that generally enhance the functioning of the infected immune system.

In March 1987 the U.S. Food and Drug Administration approved the first treatment shown to fight HIV-I in patients with active AIDS: zidovudine (brand name, Retrovir), formerly known as azidothymidine, or AZT. The drug blocks the virus's ability to reproduce itself. While it is not a cure, zidovudine increases the length and quality of life of some AIDS patients. It also crosses the so-called blood-brain barrier; that is, it moves from the bloodstream into the brain and thus could possibly stop the virus from damaging the brain. The drug does have drawbacks. Some patients suffer such severe side effects that they must stop taking it. Also, the drug must be taken every four hours and may cost about $8,000 a year per person (after a 20 percent cut by the manufacturer in the drug's wholesale price in December 1987).

Many other drugs are being investigated, but none have been proved yet to be effective. As is the case with zidovudine, the potential for long-term use of these investigational drugs may be limited by severe side effects that unavoidably accompany their use. The toxic effect of one promising drug, dideoxycytidine (DDC), were found to be reduced when it was alternated with zidovudine.

Infection with HIV-I becomes an active case of AIDS when the immune system is so damaged it can no longer fight off exposure to otherwise harmless

I HAVE AIDS
PLease hug me
I can't make you sick

J.keeter

AIDS HOT LINE FOR KIDS
CENTER FOR ATTITUDINAL HEALING
19 MAIN ST, TIBURON, CA 94920, (415) 435-5022

organisms, which in AIDS patients cause life-threatening illness. Sometimes treating these so-called opportunistic infections is as difficult as trying to treat the underlying HIV-I infection. The most common of these infections is *Pneumocystis carinii* pneumonia. Many AIDS patients cannot tolerate the standard treatments for this pneumonia; however, a report published in October 1987 presented preliminary evidence that an innovative treatment may provide an effective alternative. Researchers used an anticancer drug, trimetrexate, to fight the pneumonia, in combination with another drug, leucovorin, to diminish the undesirable side effects of the first drug. In February 1988 the Food and Drug Administration announced that trimetrexate and leucovorin would be distributed free to patients who could not be treated with the standard pneumonia drugs.

Developing a Vaccine

The quest to develop a preventive vaccine has brought scientists head-to-head with a major AIDS problem. Standard vaccines work by stimulating the body's immune system to produce antibodies that identify and destroy invading organisms. However, HIV-I tends to change the structure of the antigens on its surface proteins. These antigens are the substances that trigger immune response and enable antibodies to recognize the virus as foreign to the body. When the antigens change, antibodies formed to fight the original antigen structure will not recognize the virus or attack it. Also, within the body HIV-I seems able to spread directly from cell to cell without being exposed to antibodies in the blood. The virus can lie dormant within cells for years before replicating and causing disease. If the virus can hide within cells and can change its antigen structure so that antibodies do not recognize and destroy it, a standard vaccine may be useless. Investigators now realize too clearly that developing a vaccine to protect against AIDS will be even more difficult than many had thought.

One of the most troubling aspects of developing a vaccine is the potential danger from making one using live but weakened HIV-I that would stimulate the body's immune system to make antibodies against the virus. (Typically, vaccines are made from viruses or bacteria grown and killed in the laboratory or from weakened, live microorganisms.) Although a vaccine made from the live virus might be the most effective type, it is possible that the altered HIV-I could mutate back to the original virus and actually cause AIDS, or mutate to another type of virus and produce a different disease. It is thus likely that candidate vaccines would use killed whole viruses or parts of certain viral proteins.

In spite of all these difficulties, potential advances were announced. The first clinical trials in humans in the United States of a potential AIDS vaccine were approved by the Food and Drug Administration in August 1987 and began the following month. The vaccine, called VaxSyn HIV-I, is manufactured by MicroGeneSys, Inc., of West Haven, Conn. (The first months of tests were to determine the vaccine's safety and whether it stimulated the production of antibodies, not its effectiveness in preventing AIDS.) A second potential vaccine, developed by the Bristol-Myers Company, received FDA approval in November for initial testing. In both products genes coding for different proteins from the virus's outer cover are inserted into another virus using genetic engineering technology—an ingenious effort to avoid the potential dangers associated with a live whole-virus vaccine.

Also in 1987 a French scientist, Dr. Daniel Zagury, and his fellow researchers in Zaire announced that late in 1986 they had begun the first tests of experimental AIDS vaccines in humans. Dr. Zagury even injected himself, a time-honored and sometimes very dangerous experimental practice, with a candidate vaccine. The ultimate test for all the candidate vaccines is whether or not they actually succeed in preventing or perhaps helping control HIV-I infections. Most experts feel the answer to this question will not be known for at least five to ten years.

Dr. Daniel Zagury, a French scientist, acted as his own guinea pig when he injected himself (as well as human volunteers in Zaire) with an experimental AIDS vaccine late in 1986.

Alternative Treatments

Many critics of governmental efforts to fight AIDS have proposed changing the usual rules of drug testing and approval if for no other reason than to offer hope to AIDS patients who otherwise have very little to hope for. One proposal has been to make available without clinical trials investigational new drugs to treat certain kinds of disease, including AIDS. A related proposal would allow pharmaceutical companies for the first time to charge for investigational drugs. Still other proposals call for even more funding to stimulate development of anti-AIDS drugs than is currently available from federal and state governments. The FDA did adopt new regulations in 1987 under which investigational new drugs that showed promise in preliminary tests could be given free or sold at cost to patients with life-threatening illnesses. Trimetrexate, in February 1988, became the first drug made available under the new regulations.

Many AIDS patients turn elsewhere for potential treatments. Persons infected with HIV-I, with and without AIDS, travel to other countries to obtain treatments not easily available in the United States, such as the antiviral drug ribavirin. (Late in 1987 the FDA authorized clinical trials of this drug to determine whether it would delay the onset of AIDS in HIV-infected people.) Other patients stay home and use probably harmless, but also probably ineffective, remedies. These therapies can be costly and may lead patients to delay seeking needed medical attention. But very dangerous alternative treatments also exist. Injections of untested substances can be contaminated by poisons or infectious agents, and the last thing an AIDS patient needs is another infection. Yet, the desire to do something about an apparently hopeless situation must be compelling.

Testing Controversies

Almost every AIDS screening issue swirled in controversy in 1987. Few question the wisdom of testing blood or other body tissues before they are donated to other people, to learn whether they contain antibodies to HIV-I; the presence of antibodies means that the virus itself is also present. Since 1985 all blood donated in the United States and Canada has been screened for this purpose. However, studies in 1987 showed that some people

Protesters gather outside the White House in June 1987 to call for increased government action on AIDS research, treatment, and education.

might be infected for 14 months or more before they develop antibodies. If this is the case, is new testing needed for donated blood?

In 1987 physicians began offering the HIV-I antibody tests to persons who had received blood transfusions from 1978 to 1985, before national blood screening began. It was hoped that people testing negative would be relieved of understandable anxiety, while those testing positive could be offered counseling and take appropriate precautions to avoid infecting others.

Such limited testing is uncontroversial, but some people are arguing for widespread mandatory testing programs. They have proposed various groups for testing, including all people being admitted to hospitals and all applicants for marriage licenses. (Testing of the latter group has already begun, with Illinois and Louisiana becoming the first states to require testing of marriage applicants.) At issue here are questions of confidentiality and privacy; also, the proposed benefits must be weighed against the cost of testing large groups.

It should be noted that the tests themselves are

"Safe" social clubs have opened, like this one in New York City. To become members, people must pass blood-screening tests for antibodies to the virus that causes AIDS.

not wholly reliable and sometimes yield false positive results. Even when the follow-up tests are negative, people may suffer fear and mental anguish and could face discrimination from those around them. In the early months of HIV-I infection, false negatives can also occur. Such a finding could give people who are infected a false sense of security. Also, the test results are out-of-date as soon as they are done. A person not infected on the day of the test may become infected later that day or at any time in the future.

Even if testing were completely accurate, mandatory screening could easily promote discrimination in such areas as housing, jobs, and insurance if the results were not kept confidential.

Since no specific treatment is currently available for people infected with HIV-I but without symptoms, the only benefit of screening and identifying asymptomatic individuals is to protect others. (Several drugs, including zidovudine, are being investigated for their possible effectiveness in preventing virus carriers from developing AIDS, but so far none has been shown to be useful.) Virus carriers could be made aware of their infection and be more cautious in their sexual activities. However, unlike people who volunteered to take the test, those who were forced to take it might well be unwilling to change their behavior.

And finally, widespread mandatory screening would be enormously costly. With limited funds available for research and public education, many experts think it unwise to devote to mandatory testing money that might better be used elsewhere, especially since the rate of infection among many groups proposed for testing is likely to be very low.

A study done by investigators from Harvard showed that at the present time a one-year, universal premarital testing program in the United

States would find that fewer than 0.1 percent of those tested were actually infected with HIV-I. Such a program would cost more than $100 million. Of even more concern is the likelihood that, because of false negative results, 100 infected persons would be told they were not infected and, because of false positive results, another 350 or more would be told they were infected when they were not.

Some mandatory testing programs have been instituted in recent years. The Pentagon now screens all prospective military recruits for HIV-I and rejects applicants who test positive. However, it has some special justifications for doing so. Many medical experts suspect that in people infected with HIV-I, intense stimulation of their immune systems can activate the virus, causing these people to develop AIDS or AIDS-related complex (a milder form of the disease). All new inductees undergo extensive immunization procedures and face many new environments where they are exposed to new organisms. Their immune systems are therefore constantly stimulated. If recruits were infected with HIV-I, that stimulation could cause them to develop the actual disease. A reason for testing both potential recruits and active-duty personnel is that blood may be needed on the battlefield for transfusions.

In the United States, all potential blood donors and applicants for certain federal jobs are also required to be tested. Attorney General Edwin Meese announced in June 1987 that all prisoners entering or scheduled to leave federal facilities would be tested for infection with HIV-I. After about 3 percent of the first 16,000 prisoners screened showed evidence of HIV-I infection, the Federal Bureau of Prisons began to segregate prisoners who tested positive and who also displayed "predatory or promiscuous behavior." The Immigration and Naturalization Service added AIDS to the list of conditions that all persons applying for temporary or permanent residence in the United States must be tested for; those testing positive could be denied legal status.

Entrepreneurs are ever present, and the AIDS screening controversies offer fertile fields for those with a little marketing expertise. At least one U.S. company began marketing at-home test kits for people wishing to screen their own blood. The confidentiality of the results needs to be weighed carefully against the possibility of inaccurate test results.

In some cities people looking for "AIDS-negative" partners were being encouraged to join "safe" social clubs. The implied safety was based on the presumably accurate results of the always out-of-date AIDS blood tests prospective members were required to undergo.

The Financial Costs

What will be the cost of the AIDS epidemic? The economic impact is potentially staggering, although the rending of the social fabric of many nations may be even more costly in the long run. The U.S. Public Health Service has projected that by 1991 the total number of AIDS cases reported in the United States alone may reach 323,000, and the total number of deaths, about 200,000. Without advances in treatment more than 20 percent of the estimated 10 million HIV-infected people in the world will develop AIDS by 1992.

Also, the occurrence and severity of other diseases are showing troubling patterns. The tuberculosis rate in the United States increased significantly in 1986 for the first time since reporting began in 1953. At least some of the increase was due to the occurrence of the disease in HIV-infected people, cases that probably would not have developed in the absence of HIV-I infection. And an advanced form of syphilis that attacks the nervous system and is usually very responsive to antibiotic treatment did not respond to antibiotics and caused severe complications in HIV-infected men.

Health economists estimate that by 1991 the AIDS epidemic will cost the United States $66.4 billion in lost personal income from illness and premature death. At the same time, the cost of providing necessary healthcare to AIDS patients will be enormous. Researchers estimate that personal medical costs for AIDS patients in the United States may be $8.5 billion in 1991. Government officials have projected that medical costs charged to medicaid alone will reach nearly $1 billion in 1988. (Medicaid is the joint federal and state government healthcare financing program for the poor.)

A recent study of more than 5,000 U.S. AIDS patients found that in a single year (1985) these patients accounted for more than 8,800 hospital admissions averaging 19 hospital days per admission. The average cost per hospital day for these patients was $635, but since insurance coverage was incomplete, the hospitals actually received only $482 of revenue per hospital day. The authors of this study cautioned that the costs of treating the growing number of AIDS patients could profoundly affect the U.S. hospital system, especially public hospitals for which restrictive medicaid programs are a major source of financing.

One of the industries feeling whiplashed by the AIDS epidemic is the insurance industry. Many companies would like to screen the blood of insurance applicants for evidence of HIV-I infection, in order either to refuse policies to infected people or to charge such individuals higher rates for life or health insurance coverage. Several states have passed laws or established guidelines to prevent companies from doing this. However, a study by the congressional Office of Technology Assessment revealed that most insurance companies do screen applicants for the HIV-I, asking questions about AIDS, requesting medical information, and sometimes requiring applicants to be tested for the virus. The National Association of Insurance Commissioners has issued guidelines prohibiting companies from questioning applicants about their sexual preference or orientation.

The issues here will not be easy to resolve. What is a proper balance between an applicant's right to privacy and a company's right to know about factors that could significantly affect insurance costs? To what extent can insurance companies pass on the huge cost of AIDS to the entire pool of insured people? Will there come a time when government-funded programs will need to finance all AIDS-related care?

Physicians and AIDS

As extraordinary as are the financial projections, even greater problems may be developing. Just as some members of the general public have reacted to AIDS with irrational fear, so too have some healthcare workers. Although HIV-I, like other blood-borne infections, can be transmitted to healthcare workers, it is generally agreed that precautions such as the use of gloves or, in some situations, masks or goggles will protect these workers from the potential hazard of HIV-I infection. However, in 1987 some surgeons and other healthcare workers publicly announced that they would not treat AIDS patients. Both the U.S. surgeon general and the executive vice president of the American Medical Association have denounced

physicians who refused to care for AIDS patients. In fact, the AMA in November 1987 issued a strongly worded statement emphasizing that doctors, in times of medical emergency, have an ethical obligation to treat afflicted patients without regard for their own health.

Doctors with AIDS, as well as doctors fearing AIDS, were in the news. At issue was the possibility of a healthcare worker's transmitting HIV-I to a patient, although such transmission has not been documented. A Texas pediatrician saw his patient load dwindle dramatically after a public announcement in September 1987 that he had tested positive for HIV-I. He soon closed his practice.

It is exceedingly unlikely that a physician would transmit HIV-I to a patient while providing healthcare, so long as standard precautions are followed and invasive procedures, like surgery, not performed. Whether physicians infected with the virus should tell their patients about the infection is controversial; given the experience of the Texas

pediatrician, there will be little incentive for them to do so.

The Epidemic of Fear

The effect of AIDS on the public continued to be one of the most extraordinary consequences of the dual epidemic. Public health leaders struggled to increase the public's knowledge in the hope that facts would allay fears. But misconceptions were hard to fight.

A 1987 Gallup Poll found that more than 78 percent of Americans felt "AIDS sufferers should be treated with compassion." But the same poll also found that 60 percent felt "people with AIDS should be made to carry a card to this effect" and one-third thought employers should be able to dismiss employees based solely on a diagnosis of AIDS. Other polls found that nearly half of adolescents and adults continued to mistakenly believe that donating blood puts one at risk of acquiring AIDS.

Several public school students and some teachers with HIV-I infection were overwhelmed by hostile reactions fueled by unnecessary fear. HIV-I cannot be spread by casual contact, but fear can. Three Florida brothers and their family were subjected to hysterical rejection in one community before being welcomed with understanding acceptance in another. The boys, aged eight, nine, and ten, were hemophiliacs who contracted the AIDS virus from contaminated blood products. They were showing no symptoms of AIDS but had tested positive for HIV-I antibodies. When the blood test results became known in their small community, they were expelled from school, only to return under a federal court order and with a police guard. Despite assurances from health experts that the boys posed no risk to their classmates, they were reportedly shunned by playmates, their barber, and their minister, and their home was destroyed in a suspicious fire.

In Orange County, Calif., a teacher was reportedly

Public education efforts to combat the spread of AIDS include classroom instruction on the disease (at left, a California junior high school) and warnings on precautions to take during sexual contacts (at right, a sign in a London subway).

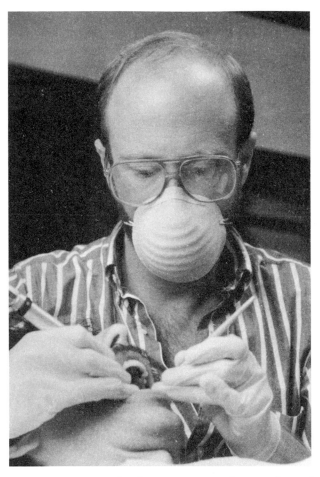

It is now common for dentists to wear face masks and rubber gloves to protect themselves from possible infection with the virus that causes AIDS.

reassigned from the classroom to writing grant proposals because he had AIDS. He successfully challenged the reassignment in court.

The list of probably unnecessary reactions to AIDS grew steadily longer in 1987. The request of an AIDS patient to marry in New York City's St. Patrick's Cathedral was first refused, but eventually granted. An increase in assaults on homosexual men was reported in several cities. A 14-year-old Florida boy was quarantined in a hospital psychiatric ward because he had HIV-I antibodies and was sexually active. A Westchester County, N.Y., judge moved the hearing of a drug defendant from the courtroom into the street because the defendant was suspected of having AIDS. During a Fresno, Calif., court hearing for a prostitute diagnosed as having an AIDS-related

condition, bailiffs wore rubber gloves and the defendant was forced to wear a mask.

A number of more constructive public responses began to emerge as well. Several star-studded gala AIDS benefits were held across the United States. Sensitive and educational performances about AIDS victims appeared in theaters and on television. TV stations accepted commercials about condoms. Individuals and organizations opened their hearts— and in some cases, homes—to help support AIDS babies and adults.

AIDS was an issue in a number of court cases. Two U.S. Army personnel faced court-martial because they allegedly had sexual encounters after learning they were infected with HIV-I. One of the men was dishonorably discharged and sentenced to five months in the stockade. The court-martial of the other was delayed by a series of appeals to determine whether HIV-I test results could be used as evidence. In the civilian legal system, a Los Angeles psychiatric patient who police said tested positive for HIV-I was booked for investigation of attempted murder after he allegedly raped a woman in a hospital mental ward. An HIV-infected Minnesota prison inmate who bit two guards was convicted of assault with a deadly and dangerous weapon—his mouth and teeth.

Raising Public Awareness

Throughout 1987 considerable resources were focused on controversial public education efforts directed toward combating AIDS. The Centers for Disease Control held the first national conference on AIDS and minorities to highlight the need for expanded drug treatment and AIDS education programs. To decrease drug abuse and as a result cut down on the chances of infection, more openings in drug treatment programs are needed. Information about the danger of sharing needles must be disseminated, and some public health leaders have advocated distributing clean needles as well. While it is unlikely that the sexual partners of intravenous drug users will abstain from sex, as urged by some national leaders, the wide use of condoms would almost certainly decrease the frequency of transmission of HIV-I infection. Many critics have pointed out that support from Washington and from local governments for these preventive measures has been woefully inadequate.

Public health and other leaders face a distinct

challenge in formulating AIDS education programs. Certainly, messages for high-risk groups need to be explicit and sometimes grim in order to portray the danger that exists and the control measures that need to be taken. Educators are not concerned about stimulating too much anxiety in these groups. But what is the best approach in messages for the general public? If the risk is overstated, will more fear and denial be the result? If the low risk for AIDS is stressed, will the result be a false sense of security?

October 1987 was designated AIDS Awareness Month by the U.S. government. Private organizations, such as the American Medical Association, joined local, state, and federal agencies in disseminating as much accurate AIDS information as possible to the public. Despite moves by some prominent national leaders like Senator Jesse Helms (R, N.C.) to dismantle federal educational efforts by cutting government funding—because of objections to explicit discussions of homosexuality, premarital sex, and drug use—important messages were spread. U.S. Surgeon

CAUTIOUS ADVICE

In 1987, U.S. Surgeon General C. Everett Koop issued guidelines, summarized below, to help physicians in both allaying their patients' fears about AIDS and cautioning patients against behavior that could put them at risk of acquiring HIV-I. Physicians were urged to tell their patients the following:

- HIV-I cannot be transmitted through casual, non-sexual contact.
- Ideally, refrain from having sex with an individual when you cannot be certain the person has not been infected.
- If in doubt about the status of a sexual partner, at least use a condom.
- Do not practice anal intercourse; the mucous membrane in the rectum bleeds easily and provides a ready means for the entry of HIV-I.
- Never use an unsterilized or previously used needle.
- A pregnant woman infected with HIV-I can transmit the virus to her unborn children.
- If in doubt about whether you are infected, seek a blood test for HIV-I from a physician or health-care facility. Physicians are required to keep test results confidential.

General C. Everett Koop urged all physicians to tell their patients, among other things, that AIDS cannot be transmitted by casual, nonsexual contact; that pregnant women infected with HIV-I can pass the virus on to their unborn children; and that people should abstain from sex if they cannot be certain their partners are uninfected. If people have doubts about their partners, they should at the least use condoms.

There was evidence in 1987 that educational efforts had increased public awareness about AIDS and the precautions necessary to avoid it; unfortunately, evidence suggested, too, that a gap between knowledge and practice persisted. Studies found that homosexual males had become more knowledgeable about the disease, had decreased the number of sexual partners, and were generally contracting fewer sexually transmitted diseases. However, a New Jersey study of female partners of intravenous drug users found that although the women were fully aware of the risk of exposure to HIV-I from infected sexual partners, they continued to practice unsafe sex just the same. The fear of being abandoned or beaten by a partner asked to wear a condom was apparently stronger than the fear of AIDS.

Has AIDS come of age, politically? By 1987 the disease had become an issue at all levels of government. Members of President Ronald Reagan's cabinet disagreed publicly on how to control the AIDS epidemic. The president himself for the first time stated the need for a national AIDS policy. He called for compassion and by midsummer appointed a controversial 13-member AIDS commission.

The main tasks of the commission were to advise the president on the best ways to protect the public against AIDS and to make recommendations on the best ways to find a cure for the disease and to improve the care of AIDS patients. By October 1987 the commission's chair, another member, and its executive director had left. The president later filled the vacancies, and in December the commission produced an interim report. It stated that four areas should be immediately investigated: the lack of low-cost home or hospice care for AIDS patients, the scarcity of AIDS drugs, the insufficient number of treatment programs for intravenous drug users, and the lack of data on the actual extent of the AIDS epidemic. The commission's final report was scheduled for June 1988. □

A History of Epidemics

Guenter B. Risse, M.D., Ph.D.

The spread of acquired immune deficiency
syndrome, or AIDS, throughout the world raises
questions about the appearance, behavior, and
impact of infectious diseases. History shows that
previously unknown diseases or diseases new to a
particular population have frequently ravaged large
areas of the globe. In many cases, patterns can be
seen in how humankind produced conditions that
led to the disease or contributed to suffering after
the disease began to strike specific elements in
society.

   To study past and present disease patterns,
scientists look at the dynamic relationship that
exists between people and the environment—an
ecology of disease—that leads to the appearance and
departure of specific health problems. The first task
of historians of epidemics is to find explanations for
why the ecology of disease has changed over time,
giving us successive epidemics of plague, syphilis,
smallpox, yellow fever, cholera, influenza, polio, and
now AIDS. What biological and social factors can

*A mass burial of bubonic plague victims in 14th-century
Belgium.*

be detected that may have been responsible for such diseases?

Historians also need to look at how epidemics have been handled by various populations. How did past societies cope with the problem of mass disease?

Especially important for our understanding of the social dimensions of AIDS are questions regarding past judgments of individuals who became victims of epidemics. Who sets standards of health and sickness, and what relevance do they have for members of a community? Why are the victims of disease stigmatized? Society has often been ambiguous about the meaning of illness, and perceptions of moral responsibility for becoming sick have shifted with each epidemic. Perhaps lessons from history will help us deal better with our latest plague.

Significant epidemics began to afflict humankind only after the onset of the agricultural revolution around 8000 B.C. and the establishment of civilized life around 4000 B.C. Relying on a limited number of crops, agriculturalists became vulnerable to malnutrition and even famine, which decreased their resistance to sickness. The geographic immobility resulting from this new way of life contributed to an expansion of the population and greater population density. More and closer contacts between persons facilitated the transfer of air-borne germs. Domesticated animals, now living in close proximity to humans, began to transmit their own parasites and disease-producing microorganisms to human masters.

The Plague of Athens

A new and more lethal phase in the history of disease began around 500 B.C. Previously isolated populations of Europe, Asia, and Africa, each with their separate infections, increasingly came into contact with each other as a consequence of expanded trade and warfare. One result was the epidemic described by the Greek historian Thucydides in his book *The Peloponnesian War*. In the summer of 430 B.C., a year after the outbreak of

---

Guenter B. Risse is professor and chairman of the Department of the History and Philosophy of Health Sciences at the University of California, San Francisco.

war between Sparta and Athens, the Spartan forces were on the offensive, invading the region around Athens. As a result, large numbers of refugees from the countryside crowded into Athens, and severe overcrowding ensued.

Suddenly, fever broke out among inhabitants of the Athenian port of Piraeus. This early epidemic was attributed to poisoning of wells by the invaders. As the Athenian metropolis came under siege, the disease quickly spread to the entire city. Its fever-ridden and thirsty victims began to shed their clothes and plunge themselves into rain tanks. More than a third of the thousands of sick died about a week after the onset of the "plague"; many had gangrene of the genitals, fingers, and toes. Neither prayers nor medicines were of any use.

Reactions to the epidemic were intense. According to Thucydides, there was a general breakdown of law and order. Many of the sick were abandoned. With many of the homeless strangers from the countryside seriously ill, streets and temples were full of the dead and dying. Corpses were summarily thrown onto burning funerary pyres—a serious violation of traditional burial rites and thus a reflection of the social collapse and chaos prevailing in the city. "Great licentiousness" occurred among hopeless people, who cast away their inhibitions for final gratifications before the arrival of pestilence and death. Such fatalism was fueled by a religious sense of collective punishment inexorably claiming its victims. "Neither the fear of gods nor the laws of men awed any man," commented Thucydides.

The epidemic felled the great statesman Pericles and severely weakened the political and economic power of Athens. Suffering and degradation scarred the Athenians' sense of honor, self-confidence, and civic responsibility. Although the war with Sparta lasted for another 20 years, this plague decisively contributed to the collapse of the "golden age" of Greek civilization.

It is not known to this day exactly what disease caused the Plague of Athens. Candidates have included smallpox, typhus, influenza combined with toxic shock syndrome, and Rift Valley fever.

The Black Death

From about 1200 to 1650, the people of Europe made changes that profoundly affected the ecology of disease. Expanding populations caused severe crowding in walled medieval towns. Living quarters lacked sanitary facilities: waste and garbage were simply thrown into streets, and city wells were often contaminated. Houses with half-timbered walls and earthen floors fell prey to rats, which found ideal nesting and feeding places among household grain storages.

While such conditions created multiple opportunities for sickness, the bubonic plague clearly dominated the European panorama of disease after its reappearance in 1347 as a pandemic known today as the Black Death. (A pandemic is an epidemic with a wide geographical range.) Since plague is primarily a disease of rodents that only occasionally is transmitted to humans, reasons for its arrival must be found in the movement of infected black rats across the elaborate East-West trading system established during the 12th century.

Most victims of the disease acquired the infection through bites from fleas that are usually associated with rats. Person-to-person transmission was also possible; droplets exhaled by individuals suffering from a form of plague that produced pneumonia could be inhaled by others. High fever, total exhaustion, and the appearance of "bubos"—swollen lymph nodes in the groin—were common. Dark blotches produced by multiple hemorrhages under the skin made the sick appear "black."

From Messina, Venice, and Genoa, where infected travelers and cargoes had come ashore from the Black Sea, plague traveled northward, reaching Scandinavia and northern Russia three years later. It is estimated that in those three years nearly 25 million people perished, about a fourth of the entire European population. Hardest hit were the poor, who lived in the most crowded sectors of cities in substandard housing with no sanitation.

Reaction to the massive die-off was swift. The affluent simply left town as the epidemic approached, relocating in the adjacent countryside. Their absence often contributed to administrative and economic chaos. Interpreting the disaster as collective punishment by God, many sought atonement for their sins by attending special religious services and participating in penitential processions. Frequently the objects of Christian prejudice, Jews were blamed for causing the disease by poisoning city wells. Foreigners and travelers were also suspect. Panic and terror severely strained family relationships, often leading to the abandonment of victims. Immorality and crime

"Plague doctors" in 18th-century France wore fanciful protective clothing in an effort to prevent disease; the beak was filled with aromatic herbs.

flourished. Looting houses of the dead and stripping corpses of valuables were widespread practices. The large number of victims and the perceived danger of contagion created problems in the disposal of the dead, who were often dumped into huge pits outside city walls.

Not all was despair, however. As early as 1348, Venice appointed new officials as "overseers of public health." These officials coordinated efforts to prevent the appearance and spread of epidemic disease. Ships, goods, and individuals suspected of carrying plague were conveyed to an island in the lagoon and detained there in isolation for 40 days—*quarantenaria*, or quarantine. In other places, following the expulsion of foreigners, city gates were closed to travelers and commerce. Within the walls, dusk-to-dawn curfews were imposed to stem the waves of disorderly conduct, including crime. Those suspected of harboring the disease were marched off to makeshift out-of-town pesthouses or locked up in their homes. The dead were quickly removed from the streets for fear of further contamination. Their houses were closed and many of their possessions burned. Towns and villages hired physicians and surgeons to care for the sick;

such "plague doctors" made house calls to diagnose the disease and provide treatment in pesthouses. The goal was to ease the atmosphere of fear and apathy created by the epidemic.

Plague continued to reappear in epidemic form well into the 18th century, although there was a gradual retreat of the disease from Western Europe. The reasons for such a disappearance are far from clear. Better housing, food storage, and changes in rat species probably played minor roles. More important were environmental changes such as deforestation and draining of swamps, which placed agricultural lands between the wild reservoirs of plague and those rodents living close to humans. Strict quarantine of goods may also have played a role.

Syphilis

As successive plague epidemics took their toll, Europe in the early 16th century was confronted with a seemingly new disease: syphilis. Its acute character, fast spread, and high mortality imply that syphilis had been introduced into the Old World from another continent, presumably America. Indeed, there is evidence suggesting that returning crew members from Columbus's 1492 expedition were infected and that the disease spread quickly in several Mediterranean ports.

At this time, European society had inadvertently created optimal conditions for syphilis to thrive.

Rulers waging war against each other depended on hired soldiers, mostly foreigners, whose principal compensation was derived from plunder and rape. Exchanges of soldiers and deserters between opposing armies were common. These undisciplined mercenaries were followed by large contingents of female companions and prostitutes. Ex-warriors, in turn, scattered throughout the countryside, mostly as beggars or robbers who spent much of their time in taverns and bordellos.

Syphilis first gained notoriety as the "French disease" during the expedition of Charles VIII of France to Italy in 1495. Naples at that time was the capital of a state that had been ruled for many years by Spain. As the French army entered Naples and laid siege to the royal palace, the Spaniards defending the fortress released a number of noncombatants, including prostitutes infected with syphilis, who freely participated in festivities celebrating the occupation of the city. Deserting Spanish soldiers, presumably also sick with syphilis, contributed to the outbreak, which acquired epidemic proportions in the spring of 1495. As the forces of Charles VIII withdrew to the north, syphilis spread rapidly through the Italian peninsula before crossing the Alps and infecting northern Europe. By 1500 most countries in Europe were affected, including Scotland and Scandinavia. At the same time, syphilis spread to Africa and the East, surfacing in India in 1498 and China in 1505.

The venereal character of syphilis was only

Seventeenth-century victims of syphilis—like this Spaniard afflicted in Naples—were placed in fumigation chambers to expel the poison presumed to infect them.

gradually recognized, and the disease acquired its present name from a poem, *Syphilis or the French Disease*, written by the Italian physician Girolamo Fracastoro in 1530. In the poem, Syphilis was the name of the first person to suffer the disease.

In the first 50 to 80 years of the epidemic, syphilis produced not only obvious genital sores but also high fever and exhaustion, with frequent skin eruptions and painful inflammation of the bones. All social classes were affected, and mortality was quite high before 1520. Both the Tudor dynasty in England and the Valois in France may have died out as a result of syphilitic infections.

Syphilis was feared like bubonic plague and at first considered as another collective punishment imposed by God on a sinful humanity. When the connection with sexual intercourse became widely known, however, individual sufferers were singled out as the offenders, and their moral transgression was punished by drastic medical treatments, including mercury ointment, profuse sweating, and a starvation diet, all designed to expel the presumed venereal poison.

After 1540 the explosive nature of syphilis abated somewhat and the disease ceased to be so acute in its primary stage, but the stigma surrounding its acquisition increased. The disfiguring nature of some symptoms and high mortality rate sustained the horror. Public baths were closed, common drinking cups were avoided, and even kissing fell out of favor. Hospitality was denied to those with suspicious skin lesions. Sexual relationships became fraught with danger, fear, and mistrust. Women, especially prostitutes, were seen as convenient scapegoats. Already stigmatized by society as evil seductresses, they were now additionally blamed for conveying a fatal disease. There are indications that even the contemporary witch burnings owed much to the appearance of syphilis.

The presence of syphilis in epidemic proportions throughout Europe undoubtedly contributed to a more rigorous enforcement of sexual morality. Premarital chastity, marital fidelity, and clerical celibacy were newly stressed. This change probably strengthened previous ideals of asceticism and played an important role in the rise of Protestantism, especially Puritanism.

Syphilis remains present in society but can now be cured in most cases by penicillin, which came into use during World War II.

Smallpox, a killer of millions, was effectively controlled in developed countries during the 1800's. Here, children are vaccinated on a street in Jersey City, N.J.

Smallpox

Smallpox was probably an ancient disease, common in India, but the first undisputed indication of its presence is a description by an Arab physician of the 10th century. This is not surprising since the disease can be transmitted only between humans and needs a fairly large population to establish itself. There are suggestions that this highly contagious disease was present centuries earlier, moving rapidly with the expansion of the Arabs from the Middle East to Northern Africa and

THE FIRST MOUNTAIN TO BE REMOVED

Yellow fever long threatened the construction of a canal across Panama. A contemporary cartoon shows Uncle Sam and Theodore Roosevelt planning the campaign to eliminate the disease.

entering Europe through Spain. From the surviving descriptions, smallpox was apparently rather benign—perhaps the clinical variety now called *variola minor*—with low mortality and infrequent facial scarring.

In 1518 smallpox was identified for the first time in the New World, during an epidemic among Indians on the island of Hispaniola. Surprisingly, it apparently killed a third of the island's inhabitants, although some deaths were probably from starvation and other illnesses. A virulent strain of smallpox virus presumably caused this more severe form of the disease—*variola major*. Whether that strain came from Europe or Africa remains unknown. In any case, shortly after the Hispaniola outbreak, most other Caribbean islands were affected, virtually wiping out the highly susceptible native Arawaks. From the West Indies, smallpox traveled to the Yucatán peninsula and joined the forces of the Spanish conquistador Hernán Cortés in 1520. With the Spanish in retreat at the most critical moment in their campaign, the disease broke out among the Aztecs defending the capital of their empire, Tenochtitlán. The severe epidemic caused havoc among the natives, killing a great number of them. This episode allowed Cortés to regroup his troops and undertake a successful siege of the city, thus sealing the fate of the Aztec empire.

Not unexpectedly smallpox rapidly spread south from Mexico, first reaching Guatemala, then the isthmus of Panama, and in 1525 the northern border of the Inca Empire. Its ruler, Huayna Capac, was stricken early and died from the disease together with his designated heir. Without a proper successor, the empire became embroiled in a bloody civil war, which allowed a small contingent of Spanish troops under the command of Francisco Pizarro to conquer it. Thus, two powerful native empires in the Americas yielded to the onslaught of smallpox. Lack of immunity, fear, and social disorganization all contributed to their fall.

By contrast, severe smallpox epidemics occurred in Europe only after 1550. In 1570, Venice reported 10,000 cases and a high mortality rate; similar outbreaks began to occur in Spain and Holland. In the next century, such major epidemics continued to proliferate, suggesting a replacement of the previously benign smallpox virus with a more virulent one. In the American colonies, such outbreaks of the disease decimated the Indians—first in New England, then Delaware and Virginia—making way for white settlers. By 1700 smallpox had become the leading epidemic disease in most European countries, killing an estimated 60 million people in the next hundred years.

In 1796, Edward Jenner demonstrated that inoculation with the cowpox virus would prevent smallpox. During the 1800's, Jenner's approach, called vaccination, effectively controlled smallpox in developed countries. In the 20th century an extensive World Health Organization program eradicated smallpox throughout the world. The last naturally acquired case was in 1977.

Yellow Fever

A primarily tropical illness acquired epidemic proportions in the New World: yellow fever. Probably introduced from Africa to the Caribbean during the slave trade, the disease first struck the island of Barbados in 1647, soon spreading to nearby Guadeloupe and St. Kitts before moving on to Cuba and the Yucatán peninsula.

Here again a series of human developments created favorable conditions for yellow fever to occur. The most important was the colonization of the West Indies by European countries during the 17th century and the establishment of a plantation system for the production of sugar. To be successful, this enterprise demanded the continuous import of slave labor from Africa, a process that unwittingly brought into the New World the yellow fever virus as well as its carrier, the *Aedes aegypti* mosquito. After arrival, these mosquitoes multiplied in great numbers because of plentiful supplies of their basic diet: sugar. On most islands, thousands of open clay pots employed in the draining and drying of sugar are available throughout the year. Subsequent movements of soldiers, merchants, slaves, and goods helped spread the virus and its carrier. Predictably, yellow fever victims were white settlers and American Indians; most of the blacks recently brought from Africa were immune.

Not surprisingly, major epidemics of yellow fever can be closely linked to the establishment of trade with the Caribbean, including epidemics that assailed the East Coast ports of Boston (1691), New York (1668), Philadelphia (1690), and Charleston (1690). After independence, American traders reestablished their profitable contacts with the West Indies, causing a new wave of yellow fever epidemics, which began with Philadelphia's severe outbreak of 1793. In time, most towns and cities on the southeastern coast and Gulf shore were regularly affected since the mosquitoes could easily survive the winters and did not need to be periodically reintroduced. During the 19th century, New Orleans suffered almost yearly onslaughts; 20,000

people died of yellow fever in the 1850's, including 11,000 within a five-month period of 1853.

In Philadelphia the epidemic of 1793 killed nearly 15 percent of the population, about 7,000 persons, between August and November of that year. Panic and fear gripped the inhabitants, encouraging 20,000 simply to flee the city. Ignorant of the true cause, physicians and laypersons vigorously debated the causes of the fever, one group arguing for a contagion from person to person brought in from the outside, the other blaming local conditions— corruption of the air by decaying materials. The former, called contagionists—composed mostly of Federalists—blamed the British and French West Indies for importing the disease and supported quarantine and trade restrictions to end it. Those in favor of a domestic origin, or anticontagionists— generally Republican merchants—feared restrictions on their lucrative foreign trade. The anticontagionists argued for a massive city cleanup. In the Philadelphia outbreak a compromise was reached, and measures representing both viewpoints were adopted.

In 1853 yellow fever caught the New Orleans authorities unprepared. In spite of a mounting toll from the disease, city officials denied the existence of an epidemic and adjourned without establishing a temporary board of health for the summer. Many residents then fled the city. By August the crisis could no longer be ignored, and officials ordered a comprehensive cleaning program. Since the highest incidence of yellow fever occurred among recently arrived European immigrants, mostly Irish and Dutch, they were not only blamed for introducing the disease, but their susceptibility was explained as the consequence of immorality and lack of hygiene.

In 1900 scientists established the true cause of yellow fever. Campaigns to eliminate breeding places for *Aedes aegypti* mosquitoes virtually eliminated yellow fever from urban areas, although the virus persisted in tropical rain forests, using other species of mosquito and monkeys as hosts. By 1942 a safe and effective vaccine was available, removing the risk for vaccinated individuals of contracting yellow fever in the rain forests.

Cholera

During the 19th century, Europe and America faced a new disease: cholera. There is still much speculation about its origin. One hypothesis argues that a relatively harmless water-borne germ, easily destroyed by stomach acid, mutated in India early in the century. The mutated form suddenly acquired the capacity to produce a powerful toxin that affects the bowels and leads to an enormous loss of body fluids. The spread of cholera throughout the world occurred because of improved means of transportation and the existence of favorable ecological circumstances in metropolitan centers. Indeed, rapid urbanization linked to the Industrial Revolution created ideal conditions for the spread of cholera. Transmission through fecal matter was easy when water supplies were contaminated with sewage and hygienic standards among the poor were dismal.

Reports from West Bengal suggest that the first cholera pandemic originated there in 1817, spreading throughout the region with help from traders, soldiers, and pilgrims. Within a few years the disease extended to Persia, East Africa, China, Japan, and the Philippines. A new and much more extensive pandemic also began in India during 1826, moving into Russia (1830), Germany and England (1831), and France (1832). In 1832 cholera crossed the Atlantic, affecting Canada, the United States, and, by 1833, Mexico. In 1840 a third pandemic broke out in India, again spreading to Europe, the Far East, and eventually North and South America. These epidemics were followed by another wave in 1863-1875 and a final one in 1883-1894. Since then, smaller and localized outbreaks of cholera have occurred throughout the world, although Europe and the United States have remained relatively cholera-free in the past decades. All five pandemics killed millions of people, especially the poor.

Reaction to the cholera epidemics is illustrated by the first impact of the disease in New York City, then a metropolis with a population of 200,000. Anticipating the appearance of sickness in 1832, thousands fled the city in stagecoaches, steamboats, carts, and even wheelbarrows. As the first cases were reported, the local Board of Health reluctantly assumed a number of governmental responsibilities, including the establishment of a blanket quarantine against all European and Asian travelers; the removal of garbage, manure, and dead animals from the streets; and the spreading of lime for disinfection. Compulsory evacuation of the poor from cholera-ridden slums to makeshift shanties was accomplished with the aid of police. Individual houses harboring the sick were isolated. Clothes and bedding of the dead were burned and houses fumigated with burning tar. Such measures still reflected the widespread belief in atmospheric pollution as the cause of the epidemic, a triumph of those medical authorities defending an anticontagionist point of view. By the time the epidemic was over, the death toll had reached about 3,500; an estimated 20,000 people, or 10 percent of the city's population, had contracted cholera.

According to American religious leaders, the three prominent "abominations" that could lead to cholera were Sabbath-breaking, intemperance, and debauchery. Only those who willfully weakened their constitutions through unwholesome life-styles were thought to be susceptible to cholera. Anyone dying of the disease was morally suspect, especially the starving Irish immigrants who in large numbers had fled the potato famine and now suffered from cholera in greater numbers than wealthier people.

In many countries, notably France, the poor believed that cholera was part of a deliberate mass poisoning ordered by the authorities. Violent clashes with police and riots ensued as the poor expressed resentment about the manifest social inequality of the disease and protested stigmatizing public health measures. In the end, such protests did much to promote governmental responsibility for health and social reform.

As early as 1854, John Snow, a physician in London, showed that cholera was carried by contaminated water, but his work was not widely recognized. Eventually, urban sewage disposal systems helped to rid much of the world of cholera.

Epidemics have occurred in our own century, notably the influenza pandemic of 1918-1919 and the polio epidemic of the 1940's and 1950's. How can history help us to understand what is happening with our current epidemic, AIDS? We now have a number of well-developed instances of mass diseases that have time and again afflicted humankind, decimating populations and challenging the fabric of society. One important step would be to review the ecology of those diseases and attempt to construct an accurate epidemiological model for AIDS, which could help in controlling the disease.

We must also look at the social dimensions of AIDS in terms of past epidemics, perhaps gaining insights into the judgments society made and makes about the victims of disease. There are lessons to be learned from studying the past that may help us deal better with our latest plague. □

SPOTLIGHT
ON HEALTH

INSOMNIA

Anthony Kales, M.D.

Throughout history, people have complained of insomnia. The elusiveness of sleep is noted in the Bible in Job's lament, ". . . nights of misery have been assigned me . . . the night drags on and I toss till dawn." A character in a 17th-century play commented, "Sleep is as nice as woman: The more I court it, the more it flies me."

The word "insomnia" is derived from the Latin *insomnis*, or sleepless. Actually, it refers to a relative deficiency in the amount or quality of sleep—a problem that is encountered by most people at some time during their lives.

A Common Problem

Millions of Americans have difficulty falling asleep or staying asleep. Physicians report that insomnia is a problem for nearly 20 percent of their adult patients; psychiatrists report that 34 percent of their patients complain of insomnia. Large-scale surveys of the general population indicate that about a third of those questioned complain of difficulty sleeping. Insomnia is a more frequent problem for women and elderly people. One study found that close to 40 percent of people over 50 years of age currently had a problem with insomnia.

There are two types of insomnia. The first, short-term insomnia, is usually a response to temporary stresses that may be work related, stem from financial problems, or result from major life changes such as marriage, birth of a child, or death of a loved one. Transient sleep difficulty may also be due to jet lag or some other situation that results in an irregular schedule of activity and rest, such as shift work.

Medical conditions—particularly those associated with high levels of pain, discomfort, anxiety, or depression—often result in difficulty sleeping. Prescription medications, such as those used to treat hypertension, often result in disturbed sleep as a side effect. Even drugs prescribed for insomnia can produce sleep difficulty. When the underlying condition is taken care of or the medication changed, the insomnia should disappear.

The second type of insomnia is chronic. The most frequent problem here is difficulty falling asleep. This may occur on its own or in combination with other problems, such as interrupted sleep (difficulty staying asleep) or early final awakening in the morning. Interrupted sleep and early awakening can also occur independently.

In most people with chronic insomnia, sleep difficulty starts before the age of 40. Generally, those whose primary complaint is difficulty falling asleep begin having this problem earlier in life than those whose problem is interrupted sleep or early awakening.

Characteristics of Insomniacs

As a group, chronic insomniacs show many similarities in behavior and physiology. At bedtime they are tense and anxious and dwell on unresolved issues of the day, personal problems, and concerns regarding work, health, death—and getting enough sleep.

Compared to good sleepers, insomniacs feel considerably worse when they awaken in the morning. Significantly more of them feel sleepy, groggy, physically and mentally tired, depressed, worried, tense, anxious, and irritable. They often lack self-confidence and fear losing control of their emotions.

Psychological Factors

Psychological problems are the most common factor in chronic insomnia. Studies and psychiatric assessments of patients with long-standing insomnia reveal high levels of emotional distress and distinct personality patterns, which are characterized by chronic anxiety, rumination, neurotic depression, emotional inhibition, and an inability to express anger outwardly.

Typically, the individual with chronic insomnia has difficulty expressing and controlling aggressive feelings and may see going to sleep as a loss of control against which insomnia becomes a defense. On occasion, the chronic insomniac's bedtime fears may result from suppressed memories of traumatic childhood experiences associated with sleep.

Problems with interpersonal relationships are closely linked to both the development and persistence of chronic insomnia. For example, insomniacs may avoid sexual relations because of a fear of aggressive impulses or as an attempt to control the spouse through the insomnia (for instance, by claiming that they are "too tired to have sex").

Because chronic insomniacs

generally handle stress and conflicts by internalizing their emotions, they tend to be in a constant state of emotional arousal or excitement. This emotional arousal causes various physiological responses, such as an increased heart rate and muscle tension. In this state of hyperarousal, the person has difficulty falling asleep, whether upon first going to bed or when trying to return to sleep after awakening during the night. Soon, fear of sleeplessness develops, intensifying emotional arousal and creating a vicious circle that perpetuates insomnia.

Impaired work performance, such as repeated absence or lateness because of poor sleep, may provoke resentment from coworkers, lowering the insomniac's self-esteem and increasing anxiety and emotional distress. Family members may make the insomniac's condition worse. They sometimes have their own needs met in some way through the patient's role as an "insomniac." By providing undue sympathy and support, they may reinforce the persistence of insomnia.

Long-standing and severe sleep disturbance is often perceived by insomniacs as the chief source of their distress and as a distinct disorder rather than only a symptom. When this occurs, the patient becomes preoccupied with the condition of insomnia, minimizing or denying the underlying psychiatric or medical conditions.

Treatment

For the treatment of chronic insomnia, a complete history that assesses sleep, medication use, and medical and emotional factors is critical. Treating short-term or situational insomnia requires identification of the stressful conditions that interfere with restful sleep. Physical conditions frequently associated with disturbed sleep should be ruled out, including disorders of the heart, kidneys, glands, and gastrointestinal, respiratory, and nervous systems.

Chronic insomnia is most successfully treated with a multidimensional approach combining general measures for improving sleep habits, psychotherapy, and, where appropriate, the use of sleep-inducing drugs (called hypnotics) or antidepressant medication.

General measures include having the patient gradually increase daily activity and exercise; these activities, though, should be completed long before bedtime to minimize any arousing effect. Sleep will be facilitated by a favorable environment—that is, a comfortable, dark, quiet room. Times to go to bed and to awaken should be regularized, yet flexible. Naps during the day should be discouraged. Caffeine-containing beverages and cigarettes should not be taken close to bedtime. The doctor may also suggest methods of managing stress and have the patient stop using medications that may be disturbing sleep.

A type of therapy called insight-oriented psychotherapy is highly effective in helping the patient to recognize and resolve the conflicts that underlie insomnia. Such therapy provides insomniacs with a means for interrupting the vicious circle of insomnia (emotional conflicts, physiological arousal, emotional arousal, and sleeplessness).

Most people whose primary complaint is chronic insomnia have some type of depression. In some of these people, the depression is severe; a class of drugs called tricyclic antidepressants, some of which have sedative side effects, are often beneficial in these cases.

For most insomniacs, when temporary symptomatic relief of sleeplessness is needed as a secondary part of the overall treatment plan, drugs that are related to the tranquilizer Valium may be prescribed for a few weeks. These drugs are usually effective and safe.

Over-the-counter sedatives are not recommended. They are ineffective and, when taken in large dosages, may result in troublesome side effects. ☐

Breakfast Cereals

Mary T. Goodwin

Ready-to-eat breakfast cereals, as we know them, came into existence late in the 19th century, often developed by doctors and promoted as health foods. The now ubiquitous corn flakes were the brain child of a Michigan physician, John H. Kellogg, who began serving them around 1902 to patients in his Battle Creek sanatorium. Soon the cereal was marketed to the general public, and the breakfast cereal business began to flourish. It is still flourishing today—to the tune of $4 billion a year in the United States alone.

For some people, ready-to-eat breakfast cereal is just a quick, convenient meal, an easy way to start the day. But cereal can be—and should be—a good source of various elements of a healthful diet, including vitamins, minerals, carbohydrates, and particularly fiber. Some cereals, though, are high in sugar, salt, or fat. It is important therefore to pay attention to the ingredients list and nutritional information printed on the package.

The Gifts of Grains

A grain kernel is made up of three parts: the germ, or embryo, which is the part that sprouts; the endosperm, which makes up the starchy bulk of the grain; and the bran, or husk, which is the tough outer coating protecting the grain. Cereals made of whole grains contain all of these parts and tend to be the most healthful.

But some cereals are made from refined rather than whole grain. When grains are milled and refined, the endosperm, containing starch and some protein, is retained, but all or most of the germ and bran are removed. This is a nutritional mistake since the germ and the bran contain many important nutrients: minerals (notably iron, magnesium, phosphorus, and potassium), vitamin E, and B vitamins (niacin, thiamine, riboflavin, folic acid, pantothenic acid, and vitamin B_6), as well as a little protein.

By removing the germ and the bran, the manufacturer is able to make a finer flour with a longer shelf life, but also provides a significantly less nutritious product.

Manufacturers generally enrich cereals made from refined flour by adding back a small number of nutrients—thiamine, riboflavin, niacin, and iron—in the same amounts that occur in whole grain.

In Praise of Fiber

The bran lost in the refining process also contains large amounts of fiber, the indigestible part of a plant's cell walls. The type of fiber that predominates in most whole-grain and bran cereals adds bulk, which helps to move food waste out of the body quickly. It therefore helps prevent or alleviate such problems as constipation, hemorrhoids, and intestinal disorders like diverticulosis.

Although the research is not yet conclusive, there is good evidence that a high-fiber diet will also reduce the risk of colon cancer. Most populations that eat fiber-rich diets have lower rates of colon cancer, which is second only to lung cancer as the leading cancer killer in North America.

The National Cancer Institute recommends that Americans eat 20 to 30 grams of fiber each day. Eating a high-fiber cereal is a quick and easy way to help reach this amount, with some products providing 10 or more grams of fiber per serving. It should be noted, though, that eating too much fiber can be a problem. A diet too high in fiber can reduce the absorption of essential minerals and cause intestinal discomforts like gas and diarrhea. The National Cancer Institute recommends that people eat no more than 35 grams of fiber a day.

Healthful as a whole-grain or bran cereal can be, it is not likely to take care of all fiber needs. There are important types of fiber supplied by beans, fruits, and vegetables that are not abundant in most grains.

Putting Starch in the Diet

Health authorities agree that carbohydrates (sugar, starch, and fiber) should supply 55 to 60 percent of total daily calories. Most of this should be complex carbohydrates, the kind found in starch. Complex carbohydrates supply many essential nutrients in addition to calories. Simple carbohydrates, found in sugar, provide virtually no nutrients besides the calories.

Cereals can be excellent sources of complex carbohydrates, but it may take some investigation to determine which products are best. The nutritional information on some packages specifies the quantities of complex and simple carbohydrates. Often, though, the package gives only the total carbohydrate content per serving. In that case, you need to look at how high up on the ingredients list sugar and other sweeteners are. (Ingredients must be listed in descending order by weight—that is, most plentiful first.)

Fortified Cereals

Many cereals are now fortified with nutrients such as vitamins A and B_{12} not present in the original grain. This is, in most cases, wasteful and costly for the consumer. It is best to meet nutritional requirements through a balanced, varied diet rather than through one or a few highly fortified foods. Theoretically, people who eat a sensible diet should not need the extra vitamins or minerals in fortified cereal—and should not have to pay the premium prices these products often carry. (Another unfortunate aspect of fortification is that some people mistakenly assume that a cereal fortified with 100 percent or more of the Recommended Daily Dietary Allowances for *particular* nutrients is actually meeting their daily need for *all* nutrients.)

Sweeteners

While the growing number of adult cereals made from whole grains are a step in the right direction for cereal manufacturers, products targeted at the children's market are often not very health-

ful. Sugar and other sweeteners (for example, dextrose or honey) may account for 50 percent or more of these cereals by weight. Foods high in sugar curb appetite and displace more nutritious foods from the diet. Highly sweetened cereals foster poor eating habits, and frequent snacking on such cereals promotes tooth decay and obesity.

Weaning children away from sugary cereals can be no easy task. Not only do such cereals appeal to the sweet tooth, but they are heavily advertised, especially on children's TV programs.

Cereal is big business in the United States. In general, for every dollar in sales, cereal makers

Read the Box

The ingredients list and nutritional information on the cereal box can steer you toward the most healthful product.

- **The shorter the ingredients list, the less processed and better for you the cereal is likely to be.**

- **Grain (wheat, corn, or oats, for example) should be the first ingredient; sugar should not be near the top of the list, and there should not be many different sweeteners in the product.**

- **Choose a whole-grain or bran cereal, not one made from refined flour.**

- **Look for high fiber content, but don't use cereal to fill your entire daily requirement.**

- **The vitamins and minerals added to a cereal should not be a key factor in your choice; you should not rely on cereal to supply all of your daily needs.**

- **Note sodium content if salt is a concern for you.**

- **Check for artificial sweeteners like aspartame (NutraSweet) if you are concerned about them. Also, note whether added fruits are real or imitation.**

- **Don't choose a cereal by protein content. All cereals provide relatively little protein.**

spend a dime on advertising, a significant part of it directed specifically at children. With prizes, promotions, giveaways, and tie-ins with cartoon and other characters, the manufacturers enhance the appeal of their least nutritious products.

If you're concerned about sugar, make sure it's not one of the first ingredients listed on the package—and that there aren't a number of different sweeteners on the ingredients list.

Some cereals are now being artificially sweetened with aspartame. The efficacy and safety of this product are still being questioned, although U.S. government studies have concluded that aspartame poses no serious problems for people unless they have a particular sensitivity to it.

Dried and other fruits are also being added to give a sweet touch. Natural fruits like raisins and dates can add to nutritional value. Some "fruits," though, are imitation. Read the package carefully.

Other Ingredients

Be on the lookout for various other ingredients in breakfast cereals. While some products contain no sodium (salt) or very little, others have up to 370 milligrams per 1-ounce serving. Check the package ingredients list and nutritional information if sodium intake is a concern for you.

Cereals in general are low in fat, except for some granola cereals. Coconut oil, a saturated fat, is often added by the manufacturer to keep the granola moist. Granola can also be relatively high in calories—many of them coming from fat and sweeteners. (In general, "puffed" cereals have the fewest calories.) To keep down the fat content of any bowl of cereal, use low-fat or skim milk.

Regarding hot cereal, in general, the longer the preparation time, the better the product nutritionally. Instant hot cereals are likely to contain a great deal of sugar and salt. □

What Is AUTISM?

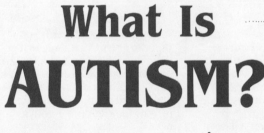

Eric Schopler, Ph.D.

Autism is a developmental disorder characterized by impaired social interaction and communication. Although the condition cannot be cured, significant improvement can result from appropriate education and treatment.

Aspects of Autism

Autistic children show three primary characteristics: an inability to form social relationships, a failure to communicate appropriately with others, and persistently repetitive and restricted play activities. These characteristics are not always apparent in infancy but usually become evident by age 3½. Unless successfully treated, the disorder persists into adult life.

Other types of behavior frequently seen in autistic children include peculiar and repetitive body movement. There also may be unusual responses to sensory stimulation, such as a fascination with lights and shiny materials and an unawareness of pain. Many children with autism have extreme and anxious reactions to change in expected routines or interruptions in their play. They may also have seizures and sleep disturbances.

The majority of autistic children show some degree of mental retardation. A recent study of some 400 youngsters in the North Carolina TEACCH program (for the Treatment and Education of Autistic and Related Communication-Handicapped Children) showed 33 percent with an IQ below 40, 38 percent with an IQ between 40 and 70, and only 29 percent in the borderline-to-above normal range. (Normal IQ is considered to be 100.) The retardation may go unrecognized because autistic children may have unusual "splinter" skills, such as early reading and math abilities and an exceptional memory for music or television commercials.

Incidence

Autism is generally considered to occur in 15 children in 10,000. The condition is four times more frequent in males than in females. It occurs equally among people of all races and economic and educational backgrounds. Although these three factors do not influence frequency, they may affect the speed and type of treatment the children receive.

The problems seen in autism are not new. Old diaries found in France and India describe similar children, called "wild" or "feral" and said to have been suckled by wolves in the wilderness. However, the diagnostic classification of autism is relatively new, with the designation first used in the 1940's. Although the healthcare professionals at that time lacked sufficient knowledge and the tools needed to appropriately diagnose and treat children with autism, today the condition is one of the best studied and understood of psychiatric disorders. In the past considered primarily an emotional problem, it is now recognized as a developmental disability with biological causes. Healthcare professionals can now refer an autistic child to the proper centers for further evaluation and educational treatment.

Behavior in Autism

The primary problem in autism is a lack of awareness in social interaction. A young child may not seek comfort during periods of distress and may fail to imitate or may avoid looking at others. The child may consistently prefer to play alone and may form no friendships with other youngsters. Older children may show little interest in pleasing others and may be unaware of emotional reactions to their behavior. They may also fail to understand or develop common manners, such as waiting in line and not interrupting others.

Communication. Autistic children tend not to use simple gestures or to communicate wants or emotions. Their facial expressions may remain flat or show exaggerated and inappropriate fluctuations. When scared or punished, such children may laugh. They do not look to adults when they need assurance. However, an autistic child may take an adult's hand and try to use it as a tool, to open a door or to work a toy. Appropriate pointing, eye movements, and postures are often lacking. Instead of nodding or shaking the head to indicate a preference, these children may grab or throw away items.

When the child uses speech, abnormal pitch, rate, rhythm, and intonation are often used, resulting in a flat tone. Speech may be much too rapid and articulation slurred. Even when there is adequate speech, meaning is often obscured by the child's repeating phrases such as those from memorized TV commercials. Pronouns and verb tenses are often confused, and conventional word sequences are mixed up. The child is unable to engage in normal conversation.

Repetitive activity and interests. An autistic child may perform repetitive body movements, such as rocking back and forth. The need for repetition is seen as the child lines up toys the same way, follows the same order in daily routines, and becomes upset by any interruptions or changes in expected routines. Parents report that their child screams out if they take a different route on the way to grandmother's house or if a chair is moved from its customary place.

Some children form strong attachments to objects like a piece of string or a hairbrush. This need for sameness is evident also in very rigid and limited food preferences, with unusual aversions to changes in color, texture, or smell of food. Extreme examples include children who will eat only white food or who insist on french fries only from McDonald's. Similar resistance to change is evident in the dislike of certain clothing, especially new clothes.

At a higher level of functioning, an autistic child may amass facts about a particular subject or mem-

> **Autism was once viewed as an emotional illness, but it is now recognized as a disability with biological causes.**

orize timetables or baseball scores. These children may ask questions over and over about time, birth dates, the make of automobiles, and TV channel numbers. Their questioning reflects another aspect of repetition rather than a request for new information. (Nonautistic children may also show some of these traits, but autistic children persist in them longer and may exhibit them more strongly.)

Sensory peculiarities. The first cause for parental concern frequently is a suspicion of deafness, since young children suffering from autism do not respond to others' voices and may ignore loud noises in the room. Hearing tests commonly show hearing to be within normal limits, and closer observation shows that children are selective in their hearing. The child may be alert to the sound of a candy bar being unwrapped or may notice sounds of footsteps or a door closing in another room. Some children form excessively fearful reactions to the sounds of a vacuum cleaner, a washing machine, or a flushing toilet. They often have difficulty integrating two sensory stimuli, thus acting deaf when they are visually occupied or being unable to maintain visual attention while they are listening.

Unusual visual responses can also often be observed. The child may inspect objects at unusual angles, become overly excited by shiny surfaces, or flick light switches. Peculiar sensory reactions are often seen, such as the lack of response to pain or a tickle and a strong aversion to being touched or held. Some children scratch surfaces, lick or smell objects, or bite and even chew apart inedible objects like clothing, sticks, and even furniture.

What Are the Causes?

In the past some researchers assumed that autism had a single cause, most likely rooted in parental mismanagement. However, more recent research has shown that parents of autistic children are not significantly different from parents of "normal" children, except that they have to cope with the stresses of a handicapped child. Autism is not caused by the parents, but they can be instrumental in reducing its effects.

Current research indicates that a number of biological mechanisms may be implicated in autism. These include one of several possible genetic factors, such as the so-called Fragile X phenomenon, a structural weakness in the X sex chromosome that causes mental retardation. Other factors that may help contribute to autism are prenatal infections such as rubella. High levels of uric acid and difficulty in metabolizing crystalline compounds called purines, which are derived from uric acid, may also be involved, as well as structural abnormalities such as tuberous sclerosis, in which there are growths in the brain.

With Other Handicaps

It is not uncommon for autism to exist in combination with other handicaps. As already mentioned, it is found with all levels of retardation. Occasionally, it is seen in the blind and deaf and in children with cerebral palsy and with epilepsy or other seizure disorders.

Autism has been confused in the past with childhood schizophrenia. More recent studies have shown that early-onset autism (from infancy) rarely develops into schizophrenia in later years, with the accompanying hallucinations and delusions. On the other hand, children afflicted during adolescence with late-onset symptoms tend to develop schizophrenia instead of autism.

Prospects for Improvement

The prognosis for any individual child depends on a number of factors, including the severity of mental retardation, the availability of appropriate educational services, and the understanding and involvement of the family and community. Recognition of and appropriate programs to deal with the underlying handicaps, combined with environmental adjustments and support, can result in the child's optimal adaptation to normal life, including varying degrees of productive employment in adulthood.

Follow-up studies of the North Carolina TEACCH program showed that the rate of institutionalization for autism could be reduced, with appropriate community support, to less than 8 percent—compared with a possible high of 78 percent indicated by studies published in 1960. It is widely believed that early diagnosis and intervention are key factors. The early development of language or an alternate communication system and the development of normal social behavior increase the child's potential for adapting to the family, school, and community.

Treatment

A number of different therapies have been studied or used to help autistic children achieve optimal adaptation to community living.

Drugs. A wide variety of medications have been used in treating autism. These include the so-called neuroleptic group (antipsychotic drugs and tranquilizers) and fenfluramine, a medication that lowers levels of serotonin—a substance that transmits impulses between nerve cells. Megavitamin therapy (massive doses of vitamins) and special diets have also been tried.

Reports have been published showing some improvement for a few children given drug therapy. For example, medication may oc-

> While autism cannot be cured, patients can show considerable improvement if provisions are made for appropriate education and treatment.

casionally be helpful for a limited time in controlling seizures, sleep disturbances, and extreme behavior. However, there is much individual variation in response to the same drug, and the various drugs used may have undesirable or unexpected side effects. For these reasons, drug therapy must be considered on a case-by-case basis, preferably be employed for a limited time period, and evaluated according to whether the benefits outweigh the adverse effects and risks. Drug therapy cannot produce a "cure" for autism, nor should it be used as a substitute for special education and related programs.

Other therapies. A number of other therapies are available, including behavior modification, speech therapy, sensory integration, aversive therapy, music and dance therapy, and residential treatment. The names of programs using one or more of these approaches can be obtained from the Autism Society of America, 1234 Massachusetts Avenue, N.W., Suite 1017, Washington, D.C. 20005 (202-783-0125). Many of these programs have been publicized in the media, which often give the impression that the treatments are proven and established. In fact, they are actually in the experimental phase, and publicized accounts of treatment success may reflect only exceptional progress in single cases but no more.

Education. There is general agreement that appropriate education, including the involvement of parents, is currently the treatment of choice for autistic children. This usually involves placing the children in small, structured classrooms and devising individualized educational programs. Teachers must understand principles of behavior management and have special training for teaching communication and social skills. Educational goals and curricula are based on the child's anticipated vocational and residential needs in later life. The first and most comprehensive state program for autistic children is TEACCH at the Department of Psychiatry, University of North Carolina School of Medicine, Chapel Hill, N.C. 27514 (919-966-2175). For information about other services, contact the Autism Society of America.

Community and family resources. The autistic person needs access to recreational programs in the community and can benefit from contact with normal peers if the necessary supervision is provided. Family relations are also important. Autistic children need to develop close ties to their siblings as well as their parents. Extended family, church groups, and friends can also be important assets in helping autistic children to develop social skills, communication, and adjustment to community life. □

Dealing With
HEARTBURN

Daniel Pelot, M.D.

Each day some 24 million Americans suffer from heartburn, an uncomfortable burning sensation that originates in the middle of the chest behind the breastbone and radiates up the throat toward the mouth. At least one out of three people experiences this discomfort at some time, but occasional episodes of heartburn need not be worrisome. Frequent occurrences, however, may produce complications and thus are a cause for concern.

What Causes Heartburn?

The esophagus, the passageway for food and liquid to the stomach, is a ten-inch tube connecting the mouth to the stomach, with a valve (or sphincter) at each end. The valve at the upper end prevents food from backing up into the throat and possibly being taken into the lungs. The lower valve, or lower esophageal sphincter (LES), relaxes when food is swallowed to allow it to pass into the stomach. The LES then closes to prevent food from backing up. However, sometimes the LES is very weak or relaxes inappropriately so that it does not close off the lower esophagus. In these cases, stomach contents do flow back into the esophagus, a condition called gastroesophageal reflux.

The contents of the stomach are acidic, and when they flow backward, they directly irritate the esophageal lining or cause abnormal contractions in the wall of the esophagus. This is what produces the discomfort of heartburn. The pain usually occurs within an hour after eating and is made worse by bending over or lying down.

A Weak LES

What causes the LES to become weakened or to relax and open inappropriately? A variety of foods, hormones, and drugs may be involved. Fatty foods, chocolate, alcohol, peppermint, and coffee are known to have such an effect. Cigarette smoking can cause the problem. Sedatives like Valium, as well as a class of drugs called anticholinergic agents, also have this adverse effect on the LES.

Up to half of all pregnant women experience heartburn during the third trimester. This is due primarily to the relaxing effect on the LES of certain hormones present during pregnancy.

Some people who have had repeated attacks of heartburn develop a chronic inflammation of the lining of the esophagus from the continual exposure to stomach acid. These people then experience heartburn symptoms when they drink citrus juices or eat tomato products or spicy foods—all of which have a direct irritating effect on the inflamed lining of the esophagus.

Diagnostic Tests

A number of diagnostic tests can be done on people frequently suffering symptoms of heartburn. These tests can determine whether gastroesophageal reflux actually occurs, whether the LES is functioning normally or is weak, whether the esophageal lining has been damaged, and how sensitive the lining is to acids. Not all of these tests need to be performed before the patient can be treated. Instead, diagnosis and treatment can be approached together on a step-by-step, trial-and-error basis.

A barium X ray of the upper gastrointestinal tract is usually the first examination performed. X rays are taken after the patient has swallowed a solution containing barium, to outline the stomach and esophagus more clearly. The X rays can rule out or reveal other conditions—such as a stomach ulcer—that may be responsible for the patient's symptoms. They can also show evidence of chronic reflux, like esophageal ulcers or narrowing of the esophagus.

If none of these abnormalities are present, the patient may be given a trial treatment. Foods or other substances known to produce gastroesophageal reflux are restricted, and antacids are given to neutralize the stomach acid. Drugs may also be prescribed to decrease the amount of acid produced in the stomach.

If this approach fails to relieve the patient's heartburn, additional tests become necessary. (Further testing is also necessary in cases where the initial X rays showed some abnormality or where the patient complains of difficulty in swallowing.) The next test is generally endoscopy. In this procedure the physician inserts an endoscope—a flexible, optical tube—down the patient's throat and into the esophagus and upper gastrointestinal tract, in order to actually see the lining of the esophagus, stomach, and duodenum (the first part of the small intestine). Endoscopy not only enables the doctor to detect inflammation, ulcers, tumors, and other lesions, but allows for the removal of small pieces of tissue for microscopic examination.

A test known as the Bernstein test may also be done. Here, a tube is run into the patient's esophagus, and a dilute solution of hydrochloric acid and then a salt water solution are alternately allowed to drip through. The test is positive—indicating reflux is the problem—if the patient's symptoms are exactly reproduced during the acid phase of the test and then disappear during the salt water phase.

Esophageal manometry is a test in which the patient swallows a small tube connected to a special recording device. This test determines the amount of pressure generated by the LES and the presence of abnormal contractions in the wall of the esophagus.

If the patient's symptoms persist after treatment based on the results of the above tests, the 24-hour pH monitoring test may be necessary. In this procedure—the most objective means of demonstrating esophageal reflux—the patient swallows a tiny device that measures acid and monitors the number and duration of reflux occurrences throughout a 24-hour period.

In many cases, making simple changes in the diet will be sufficient to prevent the uncomfortable sensation of heartburn.

Something that should be kept in mind when testing for heartburn is the possibility of heart disease. In some instances heartburn may result in severe chest pains that radiate to the neck or jaw or down one or both arms, simulating angina pectoris—the chest pain associated with coronary artery disease. If drinking milk or taking an antacid relieves the pain within 10 or 15 seconds, then the likelihood is that esophageal reflux caused the discomfort. However, specific testing for heart disease should be done when there is any uncertainty about the origin of the chest pain.

Treatment

The initial treatment of heartburn resulting from uncomplicated gastroesophageal reflux includes removing from the diet fats, alcohol, coffee, and all other foods known to cause heartburn. Patients should stop smoking (if they do smoke) and, if possible, stop taking drugs that weaken the LES.

Since obesity is strongly associated with gastroesophageal reflux, those who are overweight should lose weight. Patients should be warned against overeating and having the evening meal within three hours of going to sleep. Taking an over-the-counter liquid or tablet antacid (such as Mylanta, Maalox, or Gaviscon) after meals and at bedtime is usually beneficial, as is elevating the head of the bed by 4 to 6 inches.

In many cases, dietary changes alone will be sufficient to prevent heartburn. An occasional episode may be relieved by drinking a liquid, especially milk, or taking an antacid.

Drug Therapy

If heartburn persists in spite of dietary changes, then drugs can be added to the regimen. Medications can be prescribed that will decrease acid production in the stomach, such as cimetidine (brand name, Tagamet), ranitidine (Zantac), and famotidine (Pepcid). Other drugs strengthen the LES; these include bethanechol (Urecholine) and metoclopramide (Reglan). Another effective drug is sucralfate (Carafate). This medication promotes healing of the esophageal lining and increases its resistance to the corrosive effects of stomach acids.

Following this treatment approach, 95 to 97 percent of patients with heartburn will improve.

Surgical Repair

For the small number of patients whose symptoms resist all forms of dietary and drug treatment, surgery may be needed. The procedures used are designed to correct the underlying cause—a poorly functioning LES. The main objective is to strengthen the LES so that it closes properly. This can be accomplished by surrounding the lower end of the esophagus with a portion of the upper part of the stomach. Anti-reflux surgery has produced good results in the vast majority of patients. □

HOW TO SELECT A DOCTOR

Susan Carleton

Few decisions have more far-reaching implications for overall health and well-being than the decision to become the patient of a particular doctor. The primary care physician determines, in a very real sense, what kind of care one will receive in the event of a serious illness, as well as how thorough one's routine medical treatment will be. The doctor should be familiar with a patient's medical history and life circumstances and knowledgeable about the kinds of health problems the patient is likely to encounter. Most of all, the physician should be someone with whom both physical and emotional problems can be frankly talked over, not an awe-inspiring figure one would hesitate to bother with questions that may seem silly.

Having a trusted personal doctor means that when you do get sick, you know where to go, whether the malady is a simple case of the flu or a more complicated condition requiring specialized treatment. Yet many people look for a doctor only after illness strikes, when worry and time constraints make it difficult or impractical for them to choose wisely. The time to find a doctor is while you're still healthy.

How do you go about finding a doctor? It's tempting, of course, to take the simplest route and see any physician who happens to have an office nearby and an appointment available. But, while convenience is a factor to consider, it should not be the sole criterion. Other factors, including the doctor's credentials, accessibility when questions or problems arise, and personal rapport with you, should have at least equal weight. It may also be important to you whether the doctor practices alone or is part of a group; in the latter case, you may not always be cared for by the same physician.

Listing Candidates

First, get the names of several physicians in your community. The names of internists and family practitioners, who make up the bulk of primary care physicians, are available from both hospitals and state or county medical societies. The department of internal medicine or family practice at the nearest medical school also is a good source of information; many physicians in academic positions also maintain private practices, and their medical school affiliations mean that they are well respected by colleagues and abreast of the latest advances in medical

science. Company personnel offices and insurance carriers sometimes provide lists of physicians. Finally, consumer groups in some cities have compiled directories of physicians, listing not only their names and telephone numbers but also such information as their fees, billing practices, and office hours. To find out whether there is such a directory in your area, contact the Public Citizen Health Research Group, 2000 P Street, N.W., Washington, D.C. 20036.

It is important to find out a physician's credentials and certification, as well as which hospitals the doctor is affiliated with.

One can also get doctors' names from friends and relatives, from the yellow pages, or from ads announcing new practices, but these sources seldom give much information about the doctor's credentials or standing in the medical community. Friends' recommendations, though, help you get a sense of the doctor's personality and the way the practice is run, so don't discount them entirely. If you know any physicians socially, they might make helpful recommendations; also, if you're moving and looking for a new doctor, your current doctor may be able to provide you with the names of a few physicians in your future community.

Checking Credentials

When you have a list of names, check each doctor's credentials. Two reference books that give detailed information about individual physicians' training and qualifications are the *American Medical Directory*, published by the American Medical Association, and the

Directory of Medical Specialists, published for the American Board of Medical Specialists. Both are available in most public libraries. These books list physicians by location and specialty and give such data as the physician's medical school and year of graduation, residencies completed, type of practice and office address, and subspecialties. Generally, the best medical schools and residency programs are affiliated with major universities.

An M.D. (doctor of medicine) degree means that the doctor has completed four years of education at an accredited medical school. In most U.S. states, an M.D. must complete at least one year of postgraduate training in order to be licensed and usually must train for two or more additional years to specialize. Canadian M.D.'s undergo similar training.

A small minority of U.S. doctors have an O.D. (doctor of osteopathy) degree rather than an M.D. O.D.'s have graduated from an accredited college of osteopathy and practice osteopathic medicine, which differs in philosophy from the medicine practiced by M.D.'s, placing greater emphasis on the body's natural defenses against disease. O.D.'s maintain their own hospitals in the United States; they are not licensed in Canada and do not have admitting privileges in Canadian hospitals.

Family practitioners and internists approach patient care from slightly different angles. Family-practice training programs are more eclectic than internal-medicine programs, usually covering gynecology, pediatrics, minor surgery, orthopedics, and preventive medicine, as well as disorders affecting the cardiovascular, gastrointestinal, and endocrine systems. Internal-medicine programs focus mainly on these systemic problems. Whether one prefers a family practitioner or an internist, then, depends on individual healthcare needs.

The *American Medical Directory* and the *Directory of Medical Specialists* also indicate whether doc-

tors are board-certified, which means they have passed the examination given by the specialty board, such as the American Board of Internal Medicine, in a particular field. (Examinations are also given for subspecialties, such as cardiovascular medicine and gastroenterology.) Board certification is an added assurance of competence, although some older doctors may not have gone through the certification process, and some younger ones may not yet have taken the examination. For doctors who are not certified, ask their offices if they are board-eligible, meaning that they have completed the appropriate training program that would allow them to take the certifying exam.

It is important to find out which hospitals have given admitting privileges to the doctors you are considering. The hospitals should, at a minimum, be accredited by the Joint Commission on Accreditation of Health Care Organizations, a nonprofit organization in Chicago that promulgates standards and conducts surveys to determine whether hospitals meet them. To learn whether the hospital is accredited, make inquiries at its administrative office. It's a plus if the hospital has a medical school affiliation and a teaching

---

One factor to consider is how accessible the doctor is if you have a question or problem to discuss.

---

program that trains doctors in various specialties. Such hospitals generally have the most highly regarded specialists on their staffs.

On the other hand, some community hospitals also provide excellent care without many of the hassles associated with larger institutions. If possible, however, avoid any hospital with fewer than

100 beds, since studies have shown that institutions of this size have disproportionately high death rates when compared to larger hospitals treating similar cases.

The First Visit

Once you narrow your list of doctors to two or three candidates, call each office to find out if the doctor is accepting new patients, and if so, what the usual wait is to get an appointment. Occasionally, a practice is "closed"—so full that new patients are referred elsewhere. By the same token, you may be asked to wait several weeks for an appointment with the doctor, another sign that the practice is busy.

A patient should be able to have frank discussions with the doctor on both physical and emotional problems.

Find out if you can schedule a nonmedical visit to meet the doctor. Some physicians—pediatricians and obstetricians in particular—set aside a few hours each week for such visits and may not bill for their time. Others will fit you into their regular office schedules and, most likely, will charge their usual consultation fees.

Here are some questions to ask on the first visit:

- Do you have any weekend or evening office hours? (As competition among doctors increases, many physicians are tailoring their schedules to their patients' convenience.)
- How do you schedule appointments? How much time do you allot for an initial visit and for follow-ups?
- If there is a question, can you be reached by telephone? Do you have special hours for telephone questions during the week?

- Who covers your practice on your days off?
- Do you have laboratory and X-ray facilities in your office?
- Do you provide written materials on prevention, medications, and specific ailments? Is patient education your responsibility or your nurse's?
- What is your billing policy? Will you take payment directly from an insurance company? Can special arrangements be made to pay over time in the event of extraordinary expenses?
- What is your fee schedule for routine office visits and common office procedures?
- Do you take medicare assignment—that is, accept medicare fees as full payment for your services?

Two-way Communication

A physician can communicate with a patient only as well as the patient communicates with the doctor. When visiting a doctor for the first time for a medical reason, the patient must be truthful and accurate in giving his or her medical history and should ask for information and clarification during the examination when either is needed. Some people are hesitant to discuss their sexual practices or drug and alcohol use with doctors, even though these habits can provide important insights into the sources of many ailments. Job or marital stress, family problems, and other emotional upsets should also be reported to the doctor, since these difficulties may affect physical health.

When reporting a specific symptom or illness to the doctor, try to give concrete information. For instance, describe the location, nature, duration, and intensity of pain as precisely as possible. Also keep track of any accompanying symptoms so you can tell the doctor about them; if you have trouble remembering them, write them down.

Many people, out of fear of annoying their doctors, claim they have followed orders to change their diets, cut out smoking, or

---

Many people look for a doctor only after illness strikes, but the right time to find a physician is while you're still healthy.

---

take medication when, in fact, they haven't. Such misinformation can harm your relationship with a doctor and, especially in the case of medication, pose a serious threat to health. If a prescribed drug disagrees with you, the best course is to inform the doctor of the side effects immediately. Often, an alternative treatment is available.

Second Opinions

In certain circumstances, it is good practice to consult more than one doctor for the same condition. In general, a second opinion should be sought if your doctor recommends almost any type of surgery (some insurance companies encourage or require another opinion in this case) or if a rare or serious disorder has been diagnosed. A second opinion can also be helpful if, after several visits, no cause can be found for your symptoms, or if you are told the symptoms have an emotional or psychological basis.

Most physicians will readily give a patient the name of a specialist if asked about a second opinion. After seeing you, the specialist will forward a report to you and your doctor. When surgery is recommended, it may be advisable to seek an opinion from a surgeon who is not on the staff of the hospital where the operation will be performed.

If you prefer not to ask your doctor for a referral for a second opinion, you can call the appropriate surgical or medical subspecialty department at the nearest teaching hospital for a list of physicians to consult. □

TONSILS

Raymond B. Karasic, M.D.

To keep or not to keep—
That is the question.
Anon.

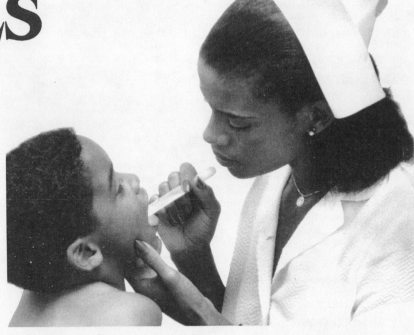

You might think that after centuries of experience, doctors could agree by now on whether the tonsils should be left in or taken out. But in fact, the controversy still rages. Some authorities claim that tonsils are an important part of a person's immune system and thus should be left alone, whereas others believe that removing the tonsils will lead to fewer sore throats and perhaps other benefits. Who is right? As you might expect, there is some truth in each argument. In order to understand the issues and draw reasonable conclusions, it is worthwhile to review some basic facts about the tonsils and summarize what we know about the benefits of tonsil surgery.

Location and Function

The palatine tonsils—tonsils for short—are two roundish masses of tissue that protrude from shallow sockets (called the tonsillar fossae) on either side of the throat. They have an irregular surface, covered with craters and deep grooves, or crypts. Each tonsil is composed of lymphoid tissue, which contains infection-fighting cells known as B and T lymphocytes.

Situated near the tonsils are two other collections of lymphoid tissue: the adenoids, which are located above the palate, deep within the nasal cavity, and the lingual tonsils, at the base of the tongue. Together, these three strategically located clusters form a protective barrier to ward off unwelcome bacteria and viruses that enter the throat or nose. Because of the important role that tonsils play, there has been growing agreement in recent years that they should not be removed unless there is a good reason to do so. The question is: what constitutes a good reason? Although there is no simple answer, we can shed some light on the issue by considering what can go wrong with tonsils. Two of the commonest problems are enlargement and infection.

Enlarged Tonsils

Big tonsils are not necessarily bad tonsils. All collections of lymphoid tissue—including tonsils, adenoids, and lymph nodes—tend to increase in size during childhood, then shrink again around adolescence. Not only do children's tonsils get larger with age, but they also grow in response to infections, especially within the throat. Fortunately, most children with enlarged tonsils come through the school years without any difficulty at all. Therefore, unless they are causing trouble, there is no more reason for taking out big tonsils than for removing, say, a big nose.

Occasionally, the tonsils become so huge that they block the throat, making it hard to swallow and breathe. Most experts agree that in such cases the tonsils should be taken out. If the blockage is severe enough, it can eventually lead to heart failure, caused by lack of oxygen in the blood.

Although the two tonsils are usually about the same size, occasionally only one becomes markedly enlarged, raising the possibility of a tumor, either benign or malignant. In such cases, it is generally necessary to remove and examine the affected tonsil.

Tonsillitis

As gatekeepers of the throat, the tonsils usually are successful in fending off microscopic invaders, but not always. Sometimes they are overwhelmed and become infected. This condition, called tonsillitis, is generally caused by either bacteria or viruses; distinguishing between the two is useful because antibiotics are effective only against bacteria.

The commonest and most important bacterial cause of tonsillitis is the group A *Streptococcus*. In addition to causing the common "strep throat," this organism can produce a number of early and late complications. Early complications occur when the *Streptococcus* spreads from the throat and tonsils to the ears, sinuses, lymph nodes, skin, lungs, bones, bloodstream, or other sites. The late consequences of strep infections—glomerulonephritis (inflammation of part of the kidney) and rheumatic fever—are not due to the direct spread of infection but instead result when the body's immune response to the *Streptococcus* runs amok and damages specific organs.

The tonsils help to form a protective barrier to ward off unwelcome bacteria and viruses that enter the throat.

Most cases of tonsillitis are caused by viruses, particularly the Epstein-Barr (EB) virus and adenovirus. Tonsillitis caused by the EB virus can occur by itself or as part of a full-blown case of infectious mononucleosis ("mono").

Diagnosing tonsillitis is usually straightforward. Patients with this condition complain of a sore throat and typically have fever. When the throat is examined, the tonsils appear red and enlarged, and often they are coated with pus. Occasionally, small purple spots (petechiae) may be present on the roof of the mouth.

Once the diagnosis of tonsillitis is made, the next task is to determine whether or not *Streptococcus* is the culprit. Pinpointing other causes is less important, since bacteria other than strep play a minor role in tonsillitis and there is no effective medication available for the viral causes.

Since doctors often cannot tell if the *Streptococcus* is present by just examining the throat, they frequently must rely on a throat culture. In this technique, a specimen obtained by swabbing an infected throat is "planted" on a plate that is specially designed to grow the *Streptococcus*. Although this test is accurate and relatively simple, it usually takes as long as 24 to 48 hours to confirm the diagnosis. Recently, however, several rapid tests have become available; these give results in about an hour, so that there is no delay in starting antibiotics if strep is identified.

The treatment of tonsillitis depends partly on which organism is causing the problem. Streptococcal infections are treated with antibiotics to relieve the symptoms and prevent complications. Penicillin is generally used, although other drugs, such as erythromycin, are also effective. If the throat culture does not grow strep, it is usually assumed that the infection is due to a virus, and thus an antibiotic is not prescribed.

Regardless of the cause of tonsillitis, a few simple measures can be taken to alleviate the symptoms. Aspirin or acetaminophen (an aspirin substitute) may help reduce fever and relieve the sore throat. Other remedies that often make the throat feel better are ice cream, cool drinks, and lozenges.

Taking Out Tonsils

Tonsils have attracted the eyes and blades of surgeons for over 2,000 years. Even today, after decades of controversy, tonsillectomy (removal of the tonsils)—usually combined with adenoidectomy (removal of the adenoids)—remains the most frequently performed major operation on children in the United States. The crusade to remove tonsils reached its peak early in the 20th century, then gradually lost momentum as skepticism mounted about the purported benefits of the procedure. In recent years, there has been a steady decline in tonsil and adenoid surgery in the United States: between 1969 and 1979, the number of operations to remove tonsils, adenoids, or both fell from over 1,100,000 to about 600,000 per year.

As the number of tonsillectomies has decreased, so has the length of hospitalization for the operation. In the past, most children who had tonsil surgery stayed in the hospital for a few days, but nowadays the majority are discharged within 24 hours. The reason for this trend is mainly economic: fewer hospital days mean lower costs.

Tonsils have attracted the eyes and blades of surgeons for over 2,000 years.

Most tonsillectomies are performed in children with repeated bouts of sore throat, in the expectation that the surgery will prevent further episodes. Yet despite the millions of tonsils that have come and gone, only recently have well-designed scientific studies begun to determine which children truly benefit from surgery.

From a study recently conducted in Pittsburgh, it appears that children with *severe* recurrent throat infection who have their tonsils removed have fewer subsequent sore throats than do such children whose tonsils stay in. To be eligible for the Pittsburgh study, children had to have proven throat infections that were both severe and frequent (for example, seven or more episodes in the preceding year). Therefore, the conclusions from the study can be applied only to children who meet these strict criteria, and not to the average child who has had several sore throats. Equally important, although children who did not have their tonsils out had more subsequent throat infections than the tonsillectomy group had, most of the infections were mild. Thus, despite the potential benefits of tonsillectomy for severely affected children, the majority do quite well even without surgery. □

Exercise
After 50

Terrence Adolph

Some physical changes are an unalterable consequence of growing older, but many are not. Research has demonstrated that about half of the functional decline people experience between the ages of 30 and 70—in stamina, flexibility, and quickness—results directly from physical inactivity. One simple, inexpensive, and enjoyable way to forestall this decline is available to almost everyone—regular exercise.

Exercise improves the quality of people's lives, and recent studies suggest that it may actually prolong life. Yet, according to a 1986 finding of the U.S. Public Health Service, only about 20 percent of adult Americans regularly engage in some form of vigorous physical activity, while 40 percent are basically sedentary.

Even people who have been sedentary for decades can, in most cases, begin regular exercise later in life. They may not be able to keep up with people half their age. But by taking a few precautions and following some com-monsense rules, they can start to reap the physical—and psychological—benefits of fitness.

Effects of Aging

Studies have shown that most people's bodies change with age. In the average person, for each decade after adulthood, the heart's ability to pump blood decreases by about 8 percent. Blood pressure increases, and arteries become narrowed by fatty deposits. (By middle age, the openings of our coronary arteries are nearly one-third smaller than when we were in our 20's.) These changes in the cardiovascular system mean that less oxygen is available to body tissues, which can then do less work. By the time they are 75, men have about 50 percent less oxygen available and women about 30 percent less than when they were 20.

For each decade we live we also lose from 3 to 5 percent of muscle mass. That muscle is often replaced by fatty tissue, so that in order to maintain the same proportion of fat to lean body mass, we must weigh less as we age. Bones become thinner and fracture more easily. And nerve cells age, reducing reaction time and speed of movement.

Delaying the Decline

The physical changes listed above are not entirely inevitable. Research has shown that older people who regularly do even moderate amounts of physical activity can delay these functional declines. Compared to sedentary individuals, they have greater work capacity and a cardiovascular system that provides more oxygen-rich blood to body tissues. Such people have greater muscle strength, stronger bones, less deterioration of joints (and hence less arthritis), quicker reaction times, and a slower conversion rate of lean body mass into fat. They tend to feel more energetic and more self-confident, and they also tend to be less susceptible to depression.

Before You Start

People who want to begin an exercise program after 50 should first see their doctor for a physical examination, to determine their current capabilities and limits. The American Heart Association and the American College of Sports

Medicine recommend that the physical include an exercise stress test, which measures the capacity of the heart and lungs to transport oxygen during physical activity.

The stress test takes about an hour. Several electrodes connected to an electrocardiograph, which records the electrical impulses that trigger the heartbeat, are attached to the patient's chest and arms. For about 15 minutes, the patient performs physical activity—walking on a treadmill or riding a stationary bicycle—designed to achieve a predetermined heart rate, usually near the patient's maximum rate.

The doctor or an assistant takes ECG and blood pressure readings before, during, and after the exercise, the last to detect possible aftereffects of exertion. These readings allow the doctor to recommend a level of exertion that will be appropriate for the individual.

Types of Activities

For conditioning the cardiovascular system, aerobic exercise is best—exercise that involves continuous vigorous activity. Provided the doctor approves, it should be done for a minimum of 30 minutes at least three times a week. But it is not advisable to start at that level. You need to build up to it slowly, perhaps starting with 5 to 10 minutes of exercise at a time.

Aerobic exercises that people over 50 may select include swimming, skating, cycling, brisk walking, and using a rowing machine. Activities involving bouncing or jarring movements that put a great deal of stress on joints—such as vigorous running, jumping rope, or aerobic dancing—should be avoided because there is a relatively higher risk of injury.

A combination of walking and jogging (running slowly) for 30 minutes is a popular and safe form of aerobic exercise. It is best to begin with only brisk walking (3 to 5 miles an hour), then gradually include periods of jogging. Over time, increase the proportion of jogging time. However, bear in mind that jogging more than 20 miles a week does not greatly increase fitness. It does, however, increase the likelihood of injuries, since too much stress is placed on the legs and feet.

Older people can also choose tennis, golf, or horseback riding, although these will not provide the same cardiovascular benefits as the continuous-movement activities. Whatever exercise is chosen, keep a regular schedule, since conditioning can be lost in even a week or two of inactivity.

How Much Is Enough?

Everyone's heart rate should remain within a "target" range during exercise. This range is lower for older than for younger people. To determine the target heart rate, a person over 50 should follow this formula: First, subtract your age from 220; this is your maximum heart rate. Then, find your heart rate while you are at rest by counting the number of pulses at your wrist or neck in 60 seconds. Subtract the resting heart rate from the maximum heart rate, and multiply the resulting number by 0.6 and 0.75. Add the resting rate to each of these numbers and you have the lower and upper limits of your target heart rate. Check your pulse several times as you work out to be sure that you are not exceeding your limit.

While exercising, you should be able to carry on a normal conversation. If you can't, you may be pushing yourself too hard. Also, while you should achieve a mild sweat, a drenching sweat or dizziness, faintness, or nausea could be indications that you are overexerting yourself and should stop exercising or at least slow down. If you feel chest pain or discomfort, stop exercising immediately.

Sleep problems, excessive fatigue, and persistent muscle soreness or joint pain after a workout may also be signs of overexertion. Reduce your level of exercise if such symptoms arise. If any symptoms persist or seem especially severe, see a doctor.

Warm-ups and Cool-downs

Before someone over 50 begins vigorous physical activity, about 10 to 15 minutes of warm-up exercises should be performed. These include stretching exercises and light calisthenics, which increase the blood flow to muscles and raise muscle temperature, both vital for elasticity and the prevention of injuries. Hold a stretched position for at least 10 seconds, relax, and repeat. Avoid bouncing movements, since bouncing tightens rather than relaxes tissues and can lead to muscle pulls and tears.

After exercising, a person over 50 should always cool down with about 10 to 15 minutes of stretching or walking. This prevents possible muscle and joint injuries that result from stopping too suddenly. Also, never take a hot shower or sauna immediately after exercising, since the heat can dilate blood vessels and cause circulatory collapse. Wait at least 10 to 15 minutes before showering, and then take a warm, not a hot, shower.

That Social Instinct

Many health clubs unfortunately either will not or cannot cater to older people. Their staffs may be more attuned to the needs of, and their exercise classes more geared to the capabilities of, a younger clientele. Yet an increasing number of older Americans desire the services that health clubs provide. Group exercise provides social benefits—a chance for making friends. Also, having a regularly scheduled class makes one less likely to skip a workout.

Recently, a number of community organizations have begun to provide group exercise programs geared especially to older people. Check with local YMCA's, YWCA's, community colleges, and senior citizen centers for possible offerings. □

PARKINSON'S DISEASE
New Advances

Hamilton Moses III, M.D.

Parkinson's disease is one of the disorders that is associated with aging. It and such other common afflictions as stroke, arthritis of the spine, and dementia (loss of intellect or memory) contribute to our stereotyped picture of the aged individual: one who is stooped, infirm, tremulous, slow in thought, shaky, and prone to falling. One of the most important tasks the doctor must undertake is to determine the specific cause of these infirmities, should they arise, for each underlying disorder requires a different kind of treatment and has very different implications for the future of the individual and the individual's family.

Parkinson's disease can be treated with a number of medications. Levodopa (commonly called L-dopa) is usually prescribed initially, but a variety of others are used as well. New forms of therapy are also being tried, including surgical implantation of cells from the adrenal gland into the brain.

Symptoms and Effects

Parkinson's disease was first described by James Parkinson, an English physician, in 1817. He observed a "shaking palsy" in some of his patients: tremor in one or more limbs combined with an inability to move at will, or palsy. While there was no actual paralysis, his patients could not initiate movement and felt "frozen." These are essentially the hallmarks of the disease that are recognized

today: tremor (shaking), akinesia (feeling frozen), and rigidity (stiffness). A "pill-rolling" movement of the thumb against the first two fingers is often noted later in the course of the disease. Patients with Parkinson's also have a tendency to fall, which is the major cause of disability as the disease progresses. In addition, we now know that about a quarter of individuals with Parkinson's suffer significant dementia, an equal number suffer from depression, and the two often occur in the same person. Sleep abnormalities are also common and often go unrecognized.

A new therapy being tried for Parkinson's is the implantation of adrenal cells into the brain.

Parkinson's disease affects about 1 million people in the United States and is believed to occur worldwide in all races. Because the population of older individuals is increasing in nearly all developed countries, Parkinson's disease will become more common and important. It is usually recognized in individuals between the ages of 55 and 70. The condition may occur at any age but rarely begins after 75 or before 35. Thanks to modern treatment, an individual who has Parkinson's has a normal life expectancy.

Loss of Brain Cells

The neurological abnormalities of Parkinson's disease are all thought to occur because of a loss of dopamine—a chemical that carries messages between nerve cells in the brain. Most dopamine is produced in a small area of the brain known as the substantia nigra (or black substance). The substantia nigra normally loses some cells with aging. But if about 80 percent of the cells die, the features of Parkinson's become apparent. Unfortunately, doctors do not yet know for certain what causes these cells to die. Much research is currently focused on just this question.

Several years ago it was accidentally discovered that a neurological toxin called MPTP causes a loss of cells in the substantia nigra; this has allowed researchers to do animal experiments that are helping unravel the mystery of Parkinson's disease. MPTP was inadvertently produced through a defective chemical synthesis in an illicit garage-laboratory making synthetic heroin for street sale. It was found that addicts who took the heroin came down with a disorder that closely resembles Parkinson's disease.

Research with MPTP is now under way in many laboratories, and much has been learned about the chemical mechanisms that cause the death of cells in the substantia nigra. A chemical reaction known as oxidation, the reaction that causes iron to rust, is important in the production of MPTP-induced parkinsonism and seems to be important as well in Parkinson's disease itself. Consequently, a large-scale trial of the antioxidant drugs alpha-tocopherol and deprenyl is now under way at 30 centers in the United States and Canada, to learn whether such drugs can forestall the progression of Parkinson's. The trial is expected to take about five years and is particularly exciting because it represents the first attempt to alter the progression of a neurological ailment and not simply treat its symptoms.

Medication

Individuals with Parkinson's disease used to have a shortened life expectancy, but this changed dramatically after L-dopa was approved by the U.S. Food and Drug Administration in 1970. L-dopa can be converted into dopamine by the brain. In the early 1970's its use became common, and most Parkinson's patients were helped greatly.

Unfortunately the limitations of this therapy soon became apparent. As L-dopa and other drugs are used today, most patients do very well for the first three to five years after therapy is begun. Then, a majority of individuals experience one or another side effect that limits therapy. Some develop hallucinations and become confused, while others have wildly erratic abnormal movements, called dyskinesias. Eventually, most patients find L-dopa's effects to be chaotic (the "on-off effect"). For instance, walking is possible one moment and impossible the next.

As a result of these limitations, new drugs have been sought, and many have been tried with mixed success. Today, the physician tries to limit the amount of L-dopa prescribed in the early stages of the disease and to introduce other medications in later stages. These include bromocriptine (brand name, Parlodel) and amantadine (Symmetrel), which enhance the brain's production or utilization of dopamine, and a variety of anti-

cholinergic drugs, which block impulses in a part of the nervous system controlling involuntary muscle action.

The patient, the family, and the physician must work very closely together, because even minor changes in drug schedules (doses and timing) often make an enormous difference. Many centers that specialize in the treatment of Parkinson's rely heavily on specially trained nurses, social workers, and physical therapists in order to provide in-depth counseling, aid with daily activities like cooking, cleaning, and shopping, and monitor the taking of medications for optimum results.

A Role for Surgery?

In the early 1950's neurosurgeons performed several operations to end tremor in patients with Parkinson's disease. Unfortunately, these early attempts were not uniformly successful, and even when they did improve tremor, the other, more limiting features—akinesia and rigidity—were rarely im-

proved. Also, when performed on both sides of the brain, these early surgical procedures led to many serious adverse effects. Because of these limitations, surgery for Parkinson's fell out of favor by the mid-1970's.

More recently work in laboratory animals has suggested that the brain's dopamine deficiency can be corrected by implanting cells taken from other parts of the body or from other sources. In particular, the medulla (inner portion) of the adrenal glands, located above the kidneys, produces small amounts of dopamine as well as other similar chemicals.

In 1982 researchers at the Karolinska Institute in Sweden first implanted adrenal cells into the human brain. In all, four individuals underwent the operation, unfortunately without success. Implants have since been tried in a number of other places, including medical centers in Mexico, China, Cuba, and the United States. Scores of individuals with Parkinson's disease have received implants—of

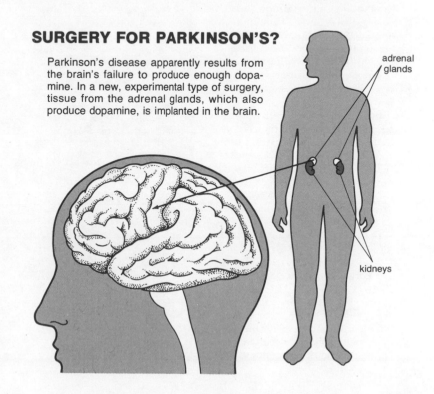

SURGERY FOR PARKINSON'S?

Parkinson's disease apparently results from the brain's failure to produce enough dopamine. In a new, experimental type of surgery, tissue from the adrenal glands, which also produce dopamine, is implanted in the brain.

adrenal glands

kidneys

their own adrenal tissue—over the past year or two.

It is too early to judge the long-term effect of this surgery with any degree of certainty. Some patients do appear to have improved, often dramatically. But as with any new and highly experimental technique, many difficulties have been encountered after surgery. There have been a number of deaths. Some patients have developed serious abnormalities of blood pressure and other body functions; others have developed severe mental problems. It is also not known which patients are most likely to benefit, whether younger or older individuals should be selected for surgery, which anti-parkinsonian drug should be used before and after the operation, and which particular surgical technique is most successful. Much further research in both animals and humans will be necessary before these questions can be answered.

Tissue taken from other sources has also been implanted in animal experiments. The most promising alternative to adrenal cells appears to be brain cells from the substantia nigra of fetuses. In animals, implants of fetal brain tissue have generally been more successful than implants of mature adrenal tissue, though it is not yet known whether this would also be true in humans.

In September 1987, in the first such operations in humans, doctors implanted brain tissue from a spontaneously aborted 13-week-old fetus into one Parkinson's patient, and adrenal tissue from the same fetus into another patient. The operations were performed at La Raza Medical Center in Mexico City by a medical team that had already performed over 20 adrenal-implant operations. It is as yet too early to judge the success of the fetal implants.

Ethical Issues

Many moral and ethical questions have been raised by the use of fetal tissue, the major concern being

that a woman might become pregnant in order to donate (or sell) the fetus's organs. Because rejection of an implant by the body can be minimized by using genetically and immunologically similar tissue, a woman might wish to become pregnant so that she could use fetal tissue herself or provide it to a close relative. Many people find such a notion especially odious. A related, equally unattractive concern is that a black market in organs or tissues might develop.

Lastly, recent advances in cell-culture techniques have allowed fetal tissue to be grown in the laboratory. Such tissue might be very effective in the treatment of Parkinson's disease, as well as other neurological disorders. With the use of these techniques, a single fetus could provide abundant material for many transplants, a notion that gives rise to the serious concerns presented in Aldous Huxley's *Brave New World*, a 1932 novel about a future society

in which human reproduction is a standard laboratory procedure. Brain implantation, as rapidly evolving both in animals and in humans, is bringing us very close to uncharted ethical territory.

Diagnosing Parkinson's

Proper diagnosis is extremely important. Not all stiffness, trembling, and tendency to fall in older people is due to Parkinson's disease. First, several commonly prescribed medications (particularly major tranquilizers) can give rise to temporary parkinsonian symptoms. Once the medications are stopped, these symptoms abate. A form of tremor called essential tremor, which occurs in some families and is more common as one gets older, resembles the tremor of Parkinson's disease, but the two can be distinguished by a thorough medical examination. Multiple small strokes, particularly those associated with high blood pressure, cause generalized rigidity and a tendency to fall, often without overt paralysis, therefore closely resembling Parkinson's disease. In this case, too, a thorough examination—usually including a CT scan or the newer magnetic resonance imaging (MRI)—enables the physician to establish the proper diagnosis.

What to Expect

Once the diagnosis of Parkinson's disease is made, it is very important that the individual and the family be told what to expect. There are a number of excellent sources of information about Parkinson's disease and its allied conditions (see the accompanying box). Medication will be valuable and is ordinarily begun when one or another manifestation of the disease becomes seriously disabling. Since depression is fairly common in all stages of Parkinson's disease, psychotherapy or antidepressant drugs may be necessary and should not be avoided, for often the depression is more seriously disabling than Parkinson's physical effects. □

Giving and Getting Blood

Susan Carleton

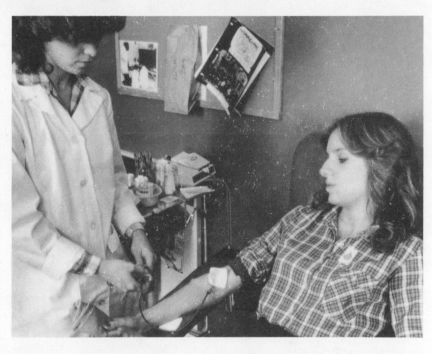

Each year as many as 4 million people in the United States alone receive transfusions of blood or blood products as part of the treatment for a broad range of medical conditions. Transfusions help save the lives of thousands of accident victims yearly. They extend life for cancer patients and people with blood diseases such as sickle-cell anemia, and they allow people with formerly fatal blood-clotting disorders such as hemophilia to live nearly normal lives. Transfusions are vital to patients who may lose large amounts of blood in the course of surgery. It has been estimated that approximately 95 percent of people who reach the age of 72 will at some point receive another person's blood or a product made from blood.

Almost all this blood—about 12 million pints a year in the United States—is donated by volunteers during drives conducted by the American Red Cross, the American Association of Blood Banks, and the Council of Community Blood Centers. In the 1986-1987 fiscal year, the Red Cross took blood from 4 million donors, 85 percent of whom had donated at least once before; as in several previous years, the supply of blood barely met the demand. This chronic near-shortage could be alleviated quickly if more people gave blood. However, fewer than 10 percent of eligible donors actually donate blood.

The low turnout of blood donors has been an especially critical issue since 1985, the year in which blood-collecting facilities were first required to test all donations for antibodies to the virus that causes AIDS. (Antibodies are proteins produced by the immune system in response to a disease-causing agent.) The AIDS virus is transmitted through sexual contact or the exchange of contaminated blood, most commonly when drug users share needles. The AIDS antibody test and two other recently instituted blood tests for a serious but poorly understood form of hepatitis (called non-A, non-B hepatitis) have eliminated a small but significant number of would-be blood donors—from 2 percent in areas where AIDS is fairly uncommon to 10 percent in urban areas with a higher incidence of AIDS infection. Therefore, the need for healthy blood donors is greater than ever.

However, despite repeated appeals and assurances from the Red Cross and blood banks nationwide, a surprisingly large number of people—34 percent, according to a poll commissioned by the American Association of Blood Banks in late 1985—think they can get AIDS from donating blood. Because blood-collection facilities always use sterile, disposable needles and catheters for taking blood from donors, there is absolutely no chance of contracting AIDS while giving blood.

The Question of Transfusions

Before blood donations were routinely screened for AIDS antibodies, a sizable number of people were exposed to the AIDS virus through transfusions. As of March 1988, the U.S. Centers for Disease Control (CDC) reported more than 1,300 cases of AIDS transmitted by transfusions, approximately 2 percent of the total number of AIDS cases.

The CDC also estimated that about 12,000 people in the United States may have been infected by transfusions containing the AIDS virus between 1978, the year before the first definite AIDS cases were reported, and the start of mandatory testing in 1985. Although 12,000 seems like a large number, it is actually only a tiny fraction of the 9 million people living today who received transfusions during the critical period. (The difference between the estimated number of those infected with the virus and the actual number of AIDS cases is quite large because, thus far, only 20-30 percent of people infected with the virus have gone on to develop the disease.)

The test that detects AIDS antibodies in blood is called ELISA (for enzyme-linked immunosorbent assay). Researchers estimate that ELISA is 99 percent accurate in detecting antibodies to the AIDS virus, so it has proven quite effective in keeping the virus out of the blood supply. Blood banks also follow careful procedures to make sure no potentially contaminated blood is cleared for transfusion through human error and to guarantee confidentiality to any donor whose blood is found to contain AIDS antibodies.

All potential blood donors are told before they roll up their sleeves that their donations will be automatically tested for antibodies to the AIDS virus; should a test prove positive, the blood will be discarded and the donor's name added to a confidential registry of individuals who should not give blood. Additionally, donors are told that they will be notified in the event of a positive test.

Once a pint of blood is taken, it is assigned a number that identifies its donor; a sample is then sent to a laboratory at the collection facility for testing. Because the test is so sensitive to antibodies that it occasionally gives a positive result even when AIDS antibodies are not present, two further ELISA tests are performed on the same unit of blood after an initial positive reading. If either test is positive, the blood is discarded; if both are negative, the blood is acceptable. Although all units of blood yielding two positive ELISA tests are deemed infected, a final, more conclusive test is performed to verify the result before the donor is notified. This final test, called Western blot analysis, is more expensive and time-consuming than ELISA. It is used only for final confirmation of AIDS infection.

> **A surprisingly large number of people are under the false impression that it is possible to contract AIDS from donating blood.**

Screening Blood Donors

Although every unit of donated blood is tested for the presence of AIDS antibodies, there is still a small risk that a donor with an early AIDS infection—an infection acquired recently, so that the body has not had time to produce antibodies to the virus—will elude tests. In February 1988 scientists from the CDC and elsewhere reported on 13 people who became infected with the AIDS virus after receiving blood that had been screened as negative. The donations were traced to 7 individuals who now tested positive for the virus; they apparently became infected shortly before donating blood. As a result of the report, the American Association of Blood Banks announced that it was studying new blood screening techniques. The CDC estimates that the chance of a person's receiving blood from a donor with an early AIDS infection that is not detected by current screening tests, and subsequently developing AIDS, is only 1 in 100,000.

Health personnel are also concerned about two viruses that have been discovered that are similar to the virus which causes AIDS. One, not yet shown to cause AIDS in North America, causes an AIDS-like disease in Africa; the other causes a rare form of leukemia. Donated blood is not tested currently for these viruses.

Blood banks have also instituted a program of donor screening to identify individuals who might unknowingly harbor the AIDS virus. Potential donors are screened through questionnaires about activities that might place them at risk for AIDS. These questionnaires are periodically updated as new information about AIDS emerges. At present, these are the groups that screening efforts seek to exclude from blood donation:

• People with clinical evidence of AIDS infection, including symptoms such as unexplained weight loss, blue or purple spots under the skin or on mucous membranes, swollen lymph nodes lasting more than a month, a low-grade fever lasting more than ten days, or a persistent cough.

• Men who have engaged in sex with another man once or more since 1977.

• People who have injected drugs in the past or who currently do so. (Blood banks have refused donations from intravenous drug abusers for many years.)

• Immigrants since 1977 from countries where heterosexual transmission of AIDS is common—for instance, Haiti and Central African nations.

• Hemophiliacs who have received transfusions of human blood products.

• Sexual partners of persons in any of the aforementioned groups.

• Men and women who have engaged in prostitution at any time since 1977.

• People who have been heterosexual partners of prostitutes in the past six months.

Blood-collection agencies have also instituted a procedure designed for individuals who fall into one of these risk categories but give blood because of peer or other social pressures. All donors receive a slip of paper on which they can indicate by checking a box whether their blood should be transfused. Such individuals can also call the blood bank as soon after the donation as possible and indicate that their donations should not be used.

Other Safety Measures

Blood banks also perform several other tests to ensure the safety of donated blood. Every unit of blood is tested immediately after it is drawn to identify to which of

> Healthy people who are to undergo elective surgery are encouraged to set aside a few units of their own blood before the operation.

the eight genetically determined blood groups it belongs (O, A, B, or AB, each of which is either Rh negative or positive). This testing is essential to prevent blood recipients from getting transfusions of blood types incompatible with their own, an error that can lead to serious reactions.

In addition, blood banks screen donations for syphilis, as well as for evidence of the hepatitis B virus. Another test, performed on blood to be transfused to infants and organ-transplant patients, detects antibodies to cytomegalovirus, a virus usually not harmful to adults but with the potential to cause serious illness in patients with weak immune systems.

Two other tests seek to screen out blood that may transmit non-A, non-B hepatitis, the most common transfusion-associated disease. These tests do not detect the viruses responsible for the disease but instead identify factors in the blood that seem to be linked to transmission of the disease. Together, these tests should prevent about 60 percent of transfusion-associated cases.

Blood banks also protect donors who may be too weak to give blood safely. Blood donors generally must be between the ages of 17 and 65, weigh at least 110 pounds, and be in good health. No one can donate blood more often than once every eight weeks; some states limit donors to five donations per year. After giving blood, donors rest for several minutes and are given a snack to prevent dizziness or fainting.

After Collection

Following collection, most donated blood is separated into components: red blood cells, white blood cells, plasma, and platelets (particles essential for clotting). Substances such as clotting factors and certain antibodies may also be isolated for treating specific conditions. Plasma and red blood cells may be frozen and stored, plasma for as long as one year and red cells for as long as three. White cells cannot be frozen and must be used within 24 hours of donation; platelets must be used within five days.

Today, few patients receive transfusions of whole blood. Instead, most receive one or more blood components. Sixty percent of all transfusions are of red blood cells, and more than half of all blood transfused is used in the course of surgery.

If You Need Blood

Hospitals and physicians have adopted a conservative attitude toward transfusion in the past few years, using synthetic compounds rather than human blood products whenever possible and administering blood or blood products only

> Since 1985, all blood donations have been tested for antibodies to the virus that causes AIDS.

when absolutely necessary. With this and other precautions in effect, it is safe to assume that you risk your health more by refusing a transfusion than by receiving one recommended by a doctor.

Of course, if you require blood, you want the safest blood there is; this desire has prompted many people to stockpile a supply of their own blood in the event of need. However, this practice is of limited value for two reasons. One is that blood cannot be stored indefinitely. The other is that in an emergency no one can spare the hour required to locate, thaw, and otherwise prepare a specific unit of blood; it is necessary in such situations to use what is readily available.

On the other hand, if you are planning elective surgery and are generally healthy, it may be a good idea to set aside a few units of your own blood several weeks ahead of time. This practice not only protects you, but it also conserves the blood supply for those who can't plan ahead. Sometimes it is also possible to salvage blood lost during an operation and return it to the patient postoperatively.

Blood-collection officials caution against asking friends or family members to donate blood for you. Health officials say that such donations, known as directed donations, are no safer than the community blood supply and, if widely used, could significantly reduce that supply. Most important, friends and relatives belonging to groups that should not give blood may, if asked for a directed donation, feel pressured to answer screening questions untruthfully and donate blood that may not in fact be safe. □

Children's Ear Infections

David L. Callender, M.D.

The most frequent diagnosis made by doctors who care for children is otitis media, more commonly known as an ear infection. Most children have had at least one ear infection by the time they reach three years of age, and one-third of all three-year-olds have had three or more such infections. Usually, otitis media is treated successfully with antibiotics. Despite the widespread use of antibiotics, however, complications still occur, ranging from varying degrees of hearing loss to severe illnesses like meningitis.

Inside the Ear

To understand ear infections, some knowledge of the ear's anatomy is important. The ear can be divided into three compartments—the external ear, the middle ear, and the inner ear. The external ear consists of the auricle and outer ear canal, which together serve to gather sound. The eardrum, or tympanic membrane, separates the external ear from the middle ear. The middle ear is composed mainly of three small bones (called ossicles), with attached muscles and ligaments; the ossicles connect the eardrum with the inner ear. The inner ear houses the important end organs of hearing that transform the perceived sounds into signals the brain understands and interprets. Normal hearing depends on the unimpaired function of each portion of the ear.

The middle ear—the place where otitis media occurs—and the eardrum serve the vital function of transforming sound waves into vibrations, which are transported to the inner ear for further processing. For the middle ear to work properly, the ossicles must be surrounded by air at about the same pressure as normal atmospheric pressure. Since the eardrum separates the middle ear from the air in the outer ear, air

> **Infants and young children are at the highest risk of developing an acute infection of the middle ear.**

must enter the middle ear from another passage. This passage, known as the eustachian tube, opens at the nasopharynx (the back part of the nose). Blockage of the eustachian tube is believed to play a major role in the development of otitis media.

Types of Ear Infections

When most people think of ear infections in children, they think of an illness that comes on suddenly, characterized by ear pain and fever. That condition is more properly termed *acute* otitis media and signifies a type of infection that usually runs its course over a period of two or three weeks. Acute otitis media is almost always caused by a bacterial infection.

Chronic otitis media is a disease of the middle ear lasting for at least several months. The most common form in children is known as otitis media with effusion, usually abbreviated OME (it is also called serous otitis). This is a condition in which a collection of fluid (an effusion) is present in the middle ear space. OME, unlike an acute ear infection, usually causes no symptoms. It may follow an acute infection or may develop independently. Approximately 25 to 35 percent of children with OME have no previous history of acute ear infections.

Children at High Risk

Infants and young children are at highest risk of developing an acute middle ear infection. The peak prevalence occurs between 6 and 36 months of age; a lesser peak appears between the ages of four and six years.

Age aside, some groups run a higher risk than others of developing single or recurrent acute infections. Boys are affected more commonly than girls. Children with cleft palate and other facial bone abnormalities (including children with Down's syndrome) also have a high incidence.

Causes of Acute Infections

As mentioned previously, acute otitis media is primarily a bacterial disease. Two very common bacteria are responsible for most infections, but a number of other bacteria can be the culprits.

Acute otitis media most often develops during or after a cold, which is a viral infection of the upper airway. Such viral infections cause swelling of the lining of the nose, eustachian tube, and middle ear. The swelling of the tube keeps air from entering or exiting the middle ear. The air that is trapped in the middle ear is resorbed by the body and replaced by fluid. Tiny, disease-causing bacteria, which thrive in a moist environment, make their way up the eustachian tube and set up infection in the collected fluid. This happens more frequently in children than adults because children's eustachian tubes are shorter and more horizontal, allowing the bacteria relatively easy access to the middle ear.

Signs, Symptoms, and Treatment

The typical symptoms of an acute infection are earache, fever, and irritability. Older children also may say they are not hearing well. Some children, though, experience surprisingly little or no pain. Younger children may be only slightly irritable and may have a draining ear. This drainage results from spontaneous perforation, or rupture, of the eardrum. Such perforations may result in only scant discharge and may close by themselves within hours.

> **Quick diagnosis and treatment of ear infections is very important since potentially serious complications can develop.**

These symptoms, combined with a physical examination, are usually the basis for a physician's diagnosis of acute otitis media. Occasionally, however, other tests or procedures may be warranted—including specialized hearing measurements and removal of middle ear fluid for culture (laboratory examination to determine what type of bacteria is present).

Treatment usually begins with antibiotics, given orally, that kill or stop the growth of the bacteria that commonly cause ear infections. The drug most often used today is ampicillin or its similarly acting cousin, amoxicillin (both are types of penicillin). Erythromycin, in combination with sulfa, is a suitable alternative in children who are allergic to penicillin compounds. These drugs can eliminate the infection in the middle ear within three to five days in the majority of cases. Once antibiotics are begun, symptoms disappear rapidly, over 24 to 48 hours. Antibiotics are usually continued for a full ten-day course to prevent recurrences.

Occasionally, a child with an acute infection will continue to have appreciable pain or persistent fever 48 hours after beginning antibiotic therapy. In such cases, the bacteria causing the infection are most likely resistant to the chosen antibiotic; another drug should be substituted and, perhaps, fluid removed from the middle ear for culture. If the infec-

STRUCTURE OF THE EAR

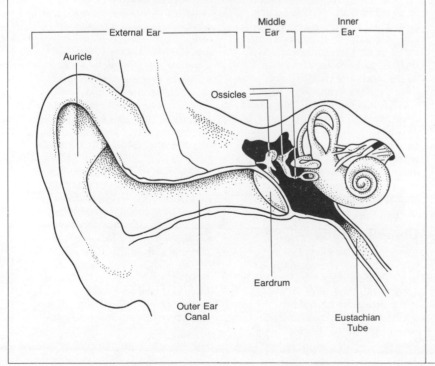

External Ear
Middle Ear
Inner Ear
Auricle
Ossicles
Eardrum
Outer Ear Canal
Eustachian Tube

tion still fails to respond, then (based on the culture results) a different antibiotic can be prescribed that acts specifically against the bacteria found to be causing the infection.

All patients treated for an acute infection should be seen again by the doctor about two weeks after beginning antibiotics. At that time, approximately half will still have appreciable fluid in the middle ear; complete clearing of the fluid may take six weeks or longer. If a child has persistent fluid but no other symptoms, no treatment is necessary. The affected ear should be reexamined in six weeks and periodically thereafter until the fluid is gone. Some children develop OME, which usually requires further treatment.

Recurrent Infections

Some children have recurrent bouts of acute otitis media. Children whose infections are cured completely between episodes may receive standard treatment for acute ear infections. If the bouts are frequent and close together, however, prevention becomes important. The first step is to rule out associated conditions that may predispose the child to otitis media, such as respiratory allergy, a chronic sinus infection, or an immune system problem. A thorough physical examination should be done to rule out abnormalities of the palate and nasopharynx. If none of these conditions is apparent, then measures such as a daily preventive dose of an antibiotic may be tried.

If the preventive antibiotics fail or if the exam indicates that the eustachian tubes are not functioning properly, the doctor may perform a surgical procedure called a myringotomy, making a small incision in the eardrum to drain fluid or pus from it. The slit closes by itself unless the doctor places tiny plastic or metal pressure-equalization tubes into the incision to allow air to enter the middle ear from the outer ear, thus "equalizing" the pressure. This permits any fluid remaining in the middle ear to be cleared, making bacterial infection less likely while the tubes remain in place. They generally fall out on their own after about six months.

Fluid in the Ear

A condition that somewhat overlaps with recurrent acute infections is otitis media with effusion. Since OME usually displays no symptoms, it is usually detected during a routine physical examination and may not be diagnosed for months or even years. Treatment is similar to that for frequent re-

> **If a child suffers frequent bouts of acute ear infections, doctors sometimes prescribe antibiotics as a preventive measure.**

currences of acute infection. In children who have not recently received antibiotics, a ten-day trial may be given with regular follow-up examinations. A once-daily dose of an antibiotic over a prolonged period of time may also cure OME. Other medications, such as decongestants, antihistamines, and steroids, have not been shown to be of value.

When antibiotics fail, placement of pressure-equalization tubes may be advised. Some patients with abnormally large adenoids (the lymph gland tissue at the back of the nose) may have the adenoids surgically removed in an effort to relieve possible eustachian tube obstruction.

Complications

Various complications can occur with acute and chronic otitis media. While further infection rarely occurs with the use of antibiotics, it is possible for bacteria to spread into the inner ear and bones at the base of the skull. Bacteria may then enter the intracranial space through a variety of routes, causing meningitis (inflammation of the membranes around the brain or spinal cord), encephalitis (inflammation of the brain), or a brain abscess. Bacteria may also enter the bloodstream and cause other serious infections. All of these different complications can be life-threatening.

Noninfectious complications include hearing loss, perforation of the eardrum, and destruction of the middle ear structures. Some degree of temporary hearing loss occurs with each episode of acute infection; normal hearing usually returns when the infection is cured. Hearing loss can be prolonged if fluid remains in the middle ear or if the infection has caused thickening and scarring of the eardrum.

Chronic perforations of the eardrum occasionally result from infection. More frequently, the eardrum becomes thin, loses its elasticity, and collapses onto the ossicles of the middle ear, thereby interfering with their functioning. As the eardrum drapes over the bones in the middle ear, pockets and recesses form. Debris may build up in these areas and form what is known as a cholesteatoma, a type of cyst filled with growing skin cells. Cholesteatoma can be extremely destructive and may erode any of the bony structures of the ear and skull base. These complications can lead to permanent hearing loss, but, fortunately, they often are avoidable if early medical care is sought.

One noninfectious complication of middle ear infections that has received much recent attention is the hearing loss accompanying otitis media with effusion. Some degree of hearing loss exists in all patients with OME. Chronic middle ear disease with continuous hearing loss can result in impairment of a child's speech, language, and learning skills. If the child recovers normal hearing, though, most developmental impairments disappear. □

MEASLES
A Preventable Disease

Raymond B. Karasic, M.D.

Measles is not yet vanquished. This often severe illness, occurring most commonly in childhood, remains a serious problem in less developed parts of the world. For more than 20 years it has been quite rare in North America, thanks to the availability of an effective vaccine. But several recent reports suggest that there too measles is resisting eradication, at least partly because of a failure to vaccinate preschool children properly.

Symptoms

Measles is one of the most contagious diseases known: over 90 percent of susceptible individuals exposed to measles will contract it. After exposure to the measles virus, it takes 10 or 11 days for symptoms to develop.

The illness begins with fever, which typically rises to a peak of 103°F to 105°F over four or five days and then quickly subsides. Soon after the fever starts, severe cold symptoms appear, consisting of sneezing, a runny nose, and a harsh cough, all accompanied by conjunctivitis (inflammation of the membrane lining the eyes). These symptoms and signs gradually improve as the person's temperature returns to normal, except for the cough, which usually lasts a few days longer.

The finding that is most helpful in diagnosing measles is the presence of Koplik's spots—small red spots with a raised whitish center that appear on the inside of the cheeks and lips about two days before the onset of the rash, and slowly fade over the next four days. A rash begins on the third or fourth day of the illness. Starting at the forehead and hairline, it gradually travels downward, completing its journey to the feet in about three days. The upper parts of the body—face, neck, trunk, and upper arms—tend to be more heavily covered than the legs. The rash changes over three or four days from bright red to a brownish color, then eventually fades. In some cases, peeling may occur as the rash disappears.

Most children with measles are sick for about a week. Like the fever, the rash and cold symptoms usually reach a peak around the fifth day of the illness, then improve promptly unless a complication arises. Nearly everyone who recovers from measles develops lifelong immunity to the disease.

Complications

Measles is not a trivial disease. Besides making its victims miserable, it can lead to a variety of complications. Middle ear infections are among the most common. Fortunately, once recognized, ear infections usually can be eliminated quickly with antibiotics.

Another common, but more dangerous, complication is pneumonia. This can be caused by the measles virus itself or by bacteria that invade the lungs. Antibiotics are generally used to treat this condition.

Acute encephalitis (inflammation of the brain) occurs in about 1 out of every 1,000 cases and can be devastating. Most experts believe that this complication is caused by direct invasion of the nervous system by the measles virus. Although more than half of those afflicted with encephalitis recover, about 15 percent die, and another 25 percent develop signs of serious brain damage, such as mental retardation or deafness.

An extremely rare but equally serious form of encephalitis resulting from measles is called subacute sclerosing panencephalitis or SSPE. This condition, which begins gradually about seven or so years after a child has had measles, causes progressive deterioration of the nervous system, leading to death within six to nine months once a full-blown case develops.

Diagnosing Measles

Twenty or more years ago—during the heyday of measles—parents and physicians had no trouble recognizing the disease when they saw it. Times have changed. As measles has become less common, fewer young doctors have had extensive experience with it. As a result, it is often overdiagnosed. Although many parents

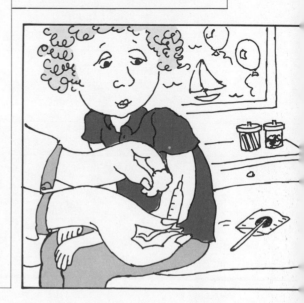

(and some doctors) still think of measles when a child has a fever and rash, most children with these symptoms in fact do not have measles. Even when a rash looks like measles, chances are it is caused by another kind of viral infection, a reaction to a particular medication, or some other condition.

For these reasons, and because of the importance of accurately identifying cases of measles, laboratory tests are usually performed to confirm the diagnosis. In general, this involves obtaining two blood samples from the patient (during and after the illness) and measuring antibodies to the measles virus.

Treatment

However uncomfortable patients with measles may feel, most get better in a week or so. As with the majority of infections caused by viruses, there is no specific medication available to treat measles. Antibiotics are useful only for treating complications, not the disease itself.

Treatment can be provided for symptoms. Most doctors recommend bed rest, especially during the first few days of the illness. Aspirin or an aspirin substitute such as acetaminophen may help reduce the fever. Although cold remedies and cough medicines are often used, they generally are not very effective in relieving the most troublesome symptoms.

Prevention

Vaccination is the key to conquering measles. The vaccine currently used in the United States and Canada consists of a live, attenuated (weakened) virus, which produces immunity to measles without causing the disease. Measles vaccine is generally given together with mumps and rubella vaccines (collectively called MMR vaccine) at age 15 months or soon thereafter; no booster is needed.

The live measles vaccine is safe for most people. Some individuals may experience fever or a rash, typically about five to seven days after vaccination. Certain individuals, however, should not receive measles vaccine, such as those who are pregnant, are markedly ill, are severely allergic to eggs or neomycin (an antibiotic contained in the vaccine), or have seriously weakened immune systems (generally caused by infections or medications).

In addition to its routine use for preventing measles in young children, the vaccine can be given during outbreaks of measles to help contain the spread of the disease. Immunoglobulin (or gamma globulin), a blood product that contains protective antibodies against the measles virus, can also be used during epidemics.

Good News and Bad

Before a vaccine became available, over 400,000 cases of measles were reported annually in the United States and over 30,000 in Canada, and these numbers undoubtedly represented only a fraction of the actual number of cases. Over the 20-year period from 1963 (when a vaccine was first licensed in both countries) to 1983, the incidence of measles fell dramatically, reaching all-time lows of 1,497 U.S. cases and 934 Canadian cases in 1983. For a while, it even appeared that scientists would achieve the remarkable goal of eradicating measles from the United States and Canada by the early 1980's. Alas, it is too early to sound the death knell for measles. In fact, after 1983 the number of reported cases climbed steadily, to a total of 6,282 in the United States and 14,941 in Canada in 1986. And even though in 1987 the number of cases reported in each country fell considerably from the 1986 figures, the 1987 totals were still much higher than the lows reached in 1983.

Why did the campaign to eliminate measles falter? A major reason was the failure to vaccinate children—especially preschoolers—adequately. For example, in the United States, more than one-third of the cases of measles reported in 1986 were clearly preventable, since they occurred in individuals who were not immunized at all. About half of these preventable cases involved preschool children (aged 16 months to 4 years). Making sure that preschoolers get vaccinated is not as easy as it sounds. Most states require that children entering day-care centers and schools be vaccinated for measles. But many parents may wait until then to have their children vaccinated, by which time the children may have already developed the disease. In Canada most provinces do not even require vaccination for entry into the school system.

Nearly 40 percent of U.S. measles cases in 1986 occurred in individuals who reportedly had received vaccine at what has been commonly thought an acceptable age (one year or older). There are a number of possible reasons for these reported vaccine failures. First, the vaccination records may be incorrect—some of the individuals may actually not have been immunized against measles. Second, some children may have been vaccinated too early. Even though the vaccine is over 95 percent effective in children immunized at 15 months or older and has been thought to confer immunity on children as early as 12 months of age, some authorities believe that it may be less effective when given between 12 and 14 months of age. A third possibility is that the immunity resulting from vaccination against measles fades with time, although there is no proof of this.

What Can Be Done

Despite the many obstacles, eliminating measles is a worthy goal, which can be achieved by continuing the effort to immunize all susceptible individuals. Parents, physicians, day-care center directors, and school officials have to work together to ensure that children are protected against measles at the earliest possible age. □

Causes and Treatment of Asthma

Susan K. Pingleton, M.D.
Jacqueline Laks Gorman

Asthma is a common respiratory disease characterized by wheezing, difficulty in breathing, and coughing. The very commonness of asthma may cause some people to underestimate how serious the disease can be. In fact, its severity varies widely. Some people wheeze a bit only when they exercise or have a cold; others suffer periodic attacks—sometimes mild, sometimes more serious—between which they are fine. Still others have breathing difficulties virtually every minute of every day.

While asthma cannot be cured, with treatment, it can be effectively controlled. With proper medication, most patients can suffer few symptoms or attacks and can avoid the emergency room visits and hospitalizations that are often the lot of poorly controlled asthma patients.

Asthma affects 8.6 million people in the United States alone. Almost 3 million of those patients are under the age of 18. The majority of youngsters with asthma—perhaps three-quarters—"outgrow" the condition with time. Many asthma patients first get the disease as adults.

Twitchy Airways

In a person with asthma, the bronchial tubes, the airways leading to the lungs, are hyperreactive, or "twitchy"; they react more than normally to various stimuli. Patients whose asthma seems to have an allergic component or some external cause are said to have extrinsic asthma; this is most often the case with children. Those whose asthma seems to be caused by internal factors—which are not

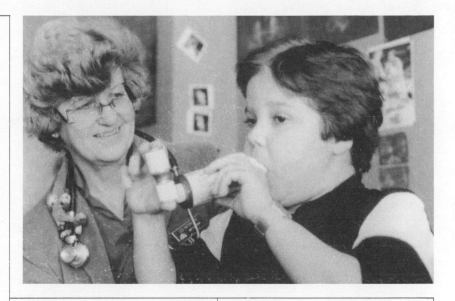

generally known—are said to have intrinsic asthma.

In an adult, a typical asthma attack involves spasm and contraction of the muscles of the bronchial walls, swelling of the bronchial tissues, and the release of excess mucus by the swollen walls. (In children, the only mechanism is likely to be simple muscle contraction.) All of this narrows the airways—a condition called bronchoconstriction. Breathing becomes difficult since the narrowed bronchial tubes permit less fresh air to enter and stale air to leave, and a wheezing sound develops as air forces its way through. Another common symptom is a dry, nonproductive cough caused by the irritated tubes.

None of the things that occur during an attack—the bronchial muscle spasm, swelling of the bronchial tissues, and so on—are lasting. Unlike certain other respiratory diseases, asthma causes no permanent damage if properly controlled.

Common Triggers

No one knows precisely why an asthma patient's airways are hyperreactive; it is possible that there is some sort of dysfunction of the autonomic nervous system, which controls involuntary functions in the body (such as breathing). What is known, however, is that many things can precipitate the disease—or cause specific attacks—in susceptible people.

There is often an overlap in the factors that bring on asthma and also trigger subsequent attacks. For instance, many older asthmatics suffer their first attacks after having a bad upper respiratory infection. For some reason, the viral infection is able to irritate or "singe" the airways in these susceptible people, leading to an onset of asthma. Once they become asthmatic, colds bring on future attacks as well.

Allergies are almost always to blame in children and may be implicated also in younger adults. Common allergens—things that produce allergic responses—are airborne pollen, mold, house dust, and the dander or hair of animals. It is quite common for a child to wheeze around the family dog or cat, and removing the unwitting culprit will often ease the youngster's symptoms. The situation is usually more complicated for most adult asthmatics, in whom the condition is often not related to an allergy.

Exercise or physical exertion can induce an asthma attack in certain patients, as will anything that causes hyperventilation (breathing too hard). In the past, much emphasis was placed on the role of emotional stress in bringing on an asthma attack. It is more than likely that the patient's emotions are not to blame, but that being distressed makes the individual hyperventilate, which in turn causes wheezing, shortness of breath, and other asthma symptoms.

In some asthma sufferers, attacks may be triggered by such things as aspirin, sudden changes in barometric pressure or temperature, or inhaling irritants like smog, paint fumes, cigarette smoke, perfume, spray deodorants, and hair spray. Certain dusts, chemicals, or vapors in the workplace can also irritate the airways. While staying away from these things may not totally prevent attacks, they should certainly be avoided by people who find them irritating.

Treatment Goals

In the past 15 to 20 years, much has been learned about asthma, and new medications have been developed. Yet despite these advances, the mortality rate from asthma has remained largely unchanged. Over 3,800 people in the United States die of asthma each year—a large number of deaths considering that this is a treatable disease.

The number may be so high because many individuals underestimate the potential seriousness of their disease. Doctors can treat asthma attacks of varying severity with the large variety of drugs available today. But when patients reach the most severe stage of asthma—a condition that is called status asthmaticus—their asthma is out of control, and they may no longer respond to medication.

Thus, a key goal of treatment for asthma is to prevent its getting to that severe stage. The therapy philosophy doctors follow is, first, to improve the patient's symptoms and, second, to keep the patient as symptom-free as possible. Patients should take asthma medication not only to make them feel better if they have attacks, but also to diminish the chance of future attacks—which may get worse and worse and more difficult to treat if they keep occurring.

Opening Airways

Bronchodilators are the major class of drugs used to treat asthma. These are substances that widen the airways, reversing the bronchoconstriction and allowing increased air flow.

There are four types of bronchodilators. The most important, called beta-adrenergic drugs, act to widen the airways by their effect on beta receptors, cell structures on the muscles of the bronchial walls. These drugs include metaproterenol (brand name, Alupent), albuterol (Proventil, Ventolin), and isoetharine (Bronkosol). They can be taken orally or inhaled as aerosol sprays.

Aerosol beta-adrenergics are among the most effective treatments for asthma since they act quickly to reverse bronchial narrowing. However, effects usually last only three or four hours, so the aerosols must be taken several times a day. Side effects, which include tremors and shakiness, are usually minor.

ASTHMA: TRUE OR FALSE?

Asthma is not a serious disease.
☐ T ☒ F The severity of asthma varies widely. Some asthma victims wheeze a little when they have a cold, but others have constant trouble breathing. About 3,500 Americans die of asthma each year.

The condition always begins in childhood.
☐ T ☒ F Many asthma sufferers first develop symptoms as adults.

Children may outgrow their asthma.
☒ T ☐ F In about three out of four children with asthma, symptoms eventually disappear.

Asthma can be effectively treated.
☒ T ☐ F Although asthma cannot be cured by medication, it can generally be well controlled.

Over-the-counter drugs are sufficient to control asthma.
☐ T ☒ F All asthma sufferers should be under a doctor's care.

Allergies are the prime cause of asthma.
☐ T ☒ F Allergies are usually the cause in children, but they are not the major cause in adults.

Asthma is a psychosomatic disease.
☐ T ☒ F Emotional stress was once emphasized as a causal factor, but it is now known that emotions are not to blame.

Children with asthma can lead a normal life.
☒ T ☐ F With medication and training to manage their condition, these children can feel well and avoid the stigma of being "different."

Theophylline compounds are the second type of bronchodilators. These drugs—which include aminophylline—work to open the airways by inhibiting certain enzymes that control muscle tone in the bronchial walls. Theophylline can be given only orally or intravenously, and it has a number of side effects, such as nausea and vomiting. It is important that the proper dose be given; blood levels of theophylline must be monitored regularly to make sure that the patient is not taking too little or too much.

In 1987 the drug ipratropium bromide (sold as Atrovent) was approved by the Food and Drug Administration for general use in the United States; it has been available in Canada for a number of years. It opens the airways by blocking the effect of certain nerves. Ipratropium comes in aerosol form and has few side effects.

The last category of bronchodilators—reserved for treating the most severe cases of asthma—are the corticosteroids. Steroids are the most effective therapy for asthma; unfortunately, they have the most severe potential side effects, including diabetes, muscle weakness, cataracts, and osteoporosis.

Steroids can be given in different ways. Prednisone, one of the most common, is given orally or intravenously, but this systemic administration (affecting the entire body) has the greatest number of side effects, particularly over months or years. Other steroids, like beclomethasone (Vanceril) and triamcinolone (Azmacort), can be given via aerosol. Since aerosols reach the lungs directly, much less of the drug is needed, and there are fewer negative effects. Aerosol steroids have been around for only the last 10 to 15 years, and they have been an enormous boon in keeping patients off systemic steroids.

In addition to bronchodilators, some asthma patients—particularly children with allergic asthma—take the drug cromolyn sodium (Intal). Cromolyn does not treat bronchoconstriction; it prevents it. When certain cells in the body called mast cells are incited or triggered by an allergic reaction, they release particles called granules, which are the biochemical beginning of bronchoconstriction. Cromolyn prevents mast cells from releasing granules. The drug is taken using a special device called a spinhaler or, in a more recently available form, is inhaled. Since cromolyn does not widen airways, it should never be taken during an asthma attack.

Inhalers are tricky to use correctly and can pose problems for people who have difficulty timing their inhalation to coincide with the release of the spray. To combat this, devices called spacers have been developed that attach to the inhaler. The patient squeezes the inhaler to discharge the medication into the spacer and then breathes the medicine in from a special mouthpiece at the end of the spacer.

Many asthma patients take a combination of drugs each day to keep them from having symptoms or suffering attacks. Doctors will often begin with aerosol bronchodilators and add theophylline in pill form if the patient is still having trouble. Aerosol steroids may then be added, and if necessary, systemic steroids—which should be used despite the risks if the patient's condition warrants it.

See Your Doctor

Various products are sold over-the-counter for the relief and control of asthma. While they may not be harmful—in fact, many contain in lower doses the same drugs doctors prescribe—physicians have several objections to them. The different tablets and mists, which often contain combinations of drugs, are not tailored to the individual patient's needs. Also, they can provide a false sense of security: being able to buy a pill or spray in any drugstore may cause patients to underestimate the severity of their condition. Anyone with a serious problem like difficulty in breathing should not be engaging in self-medication, but seeking the best professional help possible.

Asthma patients should also consult their doctors when they have an attack, which may indicate that their medication needs to be adjusted. The worst mistake a patient can make is to wait too long to call the doctor: the attack may be much more serious than it initially appears.

Helping Children Cope

Children with asthma have special needs and problems. They may be embarrassed if they have an attack in front of their friends, and the condition can interfere with school and other activities. Having a chronic disease that requires daily doses of medication may make children feel different from their peers and think of themselves as sickly even if their asthma is well controlled. They may resist taking their medication, which only makes them feel worse. In addition, young asthmatics may be quite dependent on their parents.

A number of programs have been developed to combat these problems. The American Lung Association runs Superstuff, a self-help program for elementary school children whose asthma is severe enough to disrupt their lives. Children learn about the disease and how to cope with it. Another successful program, administered by the Asthma and Allergy Foundation of America, is ACT (for Asthma Care Training). The purpose here is to teach children about asthma, with an emphasis on how they can take charge of caring for themselves and play a greater role in managing the disease on their own.

For further information, contact your local chapter of the American Lung Association or the Asthma and Allergy Foundation of America, 1717 Massachusetts Avenue N.W., Suite 305, Washington, D.C. 20036. ☐

SUNGLASSES

Barbara Scherr Trenk

Sunglasses have come a long way since the 1920's, when military aviators began wearing green-tinted lenses to cut high-altitude glare. Later, Hollywood movie stars made sunglasses seem glamorous, and rock stars have recently included "shades" in their contemporary look. Today, sales of sunglasses in the United States alone have passed the $1 billion a year mark.

Dark glasses are often promoted as fashion accessories rather than protective devices, but vision care experts say that sunglasses are important to guard the eyes from both short-term and long-term damage from the sun. Many styles combine a high-fashion look with the recommended amount of protection.

Protection From the Sun

By blocking out visible light, sunglasses can help to avoid squinting and eyestrain, contributing to a feeling of comfort and relaxation in the sun. In addition, sunglasses can prevent the temporary loss of night vision that often occurs after several hours of being in bright sunlight.

Protecting the eyes against the sun's invisible ultraviolet rays is important too, just as sunscreen lotions are needed to protect the skin from such rays. The gritty feeling many people experience in their eyes after a day in the sun is often attributed to the drying effects of the wind. However, it's more likely to be the temporary aftereffect of ultraviolet light that has burned the cornea, the eye's protective outer layer.

There is increasing agreement among vision experts that prolonged exposure to ultraviolet light, in addition to causing short-term discomfort, can do serious long-term damage. It can lead to the formation of cataracts (clouding of the lens of the eye that prevents clear vision), damage to the retina (the part of the eye that receives the visual image), and possibly even eye cancer.

> **Dark glasses are necessary to protect the eyes from the sun's invisible ultraviolet rays, just as sunscreen lotions are needed to protect the skin.**

Screening Out Light

The first choice a consumer might want to make while looking over the sunglasses on display is the color of the lens. Experts advise staying away from such "funglass" colors as blue, pink, or violet when shopping for sun protection. Traditional sunglass colors of gray, green, or brown are more likely to screen out enough visible light to offer protection. Gray is recommended for preserving natural colors in the environment; many people find brown is most effective at screening the glare out of fog.

Unfortunately, few manufacturers provide specific information with the glasses about the amount of visible light that the lenses screen out, and there is no regulation requiring that they do so. In general, if a lens screens out 75 to 80 percent of visible light, it offers sufficient protection for most sun conditions. These are lenses that let you see your eyes fairly well if you look into a mirror in a well-lit room. But skiers and beachgoers should probably choose darker lenses, which screen out 85 percent of visible light. You can barely see your eyes through these lenses in a mirror.

The darkness of the lens has little relationship to the amount of ultraviolet light that is screened out. (In fact, even clear lenses, when specially coated, can protect against most ultraviolet rays.) Don't assume that a dark pair of glasses filtering out visible light offers adequate protection. Actually, when you wear dark glasses, the pupil dilates to allow more visible light in—which may permit the entry of ultraviolet light.

Luckily, an increasing number of manufacturers are labeling their glasses to indicate the amount of ultraviolet light they block. Although there is debate within the medical community as to exactly how much protection against ultraviolet light is essential, many sunglasses are available that will filter out close to 100 percent of these potentially damaging rays.

Other Factors

Although all sunglass lenses sold in the United States must meet federal standards for impact resistance—in fact, this is the only federal standard that affects sunglasses—many people prefer plastic lenses because they are less likely to break than glass. ("Shatter-resistant" does not mean unbreakable or shatter-proof.) Unfortunately, many forms of plastic scratch more easily than glass. It is important to remember that sunglasses are designed only to protect the eyes against the sun. Although they do meet minimal federal standards for impact resistance, they do not meet the impact-resistance standards of more durable industrial safety glasses, designed for use when hammering or working with power tools.

Sunglass lenses should be checked for distortion, experts say, to prevent the headaches or discomfort that can result from poorly made lenses. You can do this by holding the glasses at half an arm's length from your body. Look through one lens at a counter, shelf, or some other horizontal line, and move the glasses up and down. If the line seems to wiggle or move, the lens is distort-

ing your vision. You should try the test with a vertical line like the edge of a sign, moving the glasses from side to side to see if that line wiggles. Finally, find a cross where two lines meet, and rotate the glasses; the lines should remain straight.

While most sunglass wearers still choose standard lens styles, there are a number of options available to meet special needs and preferences. Gradient sunglasses (which are darker on top than on the bottom) can offer a high-fashion look and good eye protection if they're chosen carefully. Some people find they're ideal for driving: the dark top filters the overhead sun, and the lighter lower section makes it easier to see maps and the car's instrument panel. Just be sure the pair you choose screens out ultraviolet light and has a top section dark enough to offer protection from the sun.

Photochromatic lenses change automatically from light to dark when they are exposed to more light. These can be convenient, but they are not recommended for driving. Also, it takes time to "break in" these lenses before they will change color properly, so they're not a good choice to pick up on the way to the beach or a tennis match.

Polarizing sunglasses cut reflected glare, such as from water, pavement, or snow; many people find them useful for boating, driving, or skiing.

Frames play a big part in determining the style—and price—of sunglasses. But they also determine the comfort and durability of your shades, so it's worth the effort to choose carefully. Both the metal hinges and the frame should be smoothly finished all around. Also, the hinges should be firmly attached to the frame and the side pieces. The screw holding the pieces together should be securely in place.

People who wear prescription glasses often find that a pair of custom-made sunglasses is a ne-

cessity, especially if the glasses are worn for driving. Many clip-on lenses (which go over clear glasses) offer good protection from the sun, according to experts, but they can slip off or scratch the lenses of the glasses to which they're attached. □

Sunglasses are essential if you're spending the day on the ski slopes or at the beach, or if you're out for a sail.

The Many Roles of Estrogen

Thomas H. Maugh II, Ph.D.

Cynthia, a 48-year-old vice president at a large manufacturing company, didn't feel like her usual self. At night she would stare at the bedroom ceiling, her heart racing, waves of heat sweeping from her chest to her head, and perspiration flowing from every pore. Daytimes, her moods would change dramatically. Little things her employees did or her husband said would drive her into a frenzy.

Cynthia's problem was not unique. She was simply one of the millions of women experiencing the symptoms of menopause—the "change of life" in which a woman stops menstruating.

Menopause is a natural biological phenomenon that begins affecting most women by the age of 45. The symptoms Cynthia experienced were caused by a slowdown in the body's production of the hormones estrogen and progesterone. When her doctor prescribed doses of synthetic estrogen to relieve the worst of her symptoms, Cynthia was able to function again.

Estrogen and Progesterone

As intimately linked as salt and pepper, estrogen and progesterone play key roles in a woman's body. Estrogen is secreted by the ovaries. It stimulates the growth and development of the uterus at puberty, stimulates changes in breast tissue both at puberty and after childbirth, and thickens the endometrium (the inner lining of the uterus) during the first half of the menstrual cycle.

Progesterone, secreted during the last half of the menstrual cycle, prepares the endometrium to receive the egg released when a woman ovulates. If the egg is fertilized, progesterone secretion continues, preventing further release of eggs from the ovaries.

Oral Contraceptives

Birth control pills containing synthetic estrogen and progesterone work primarily by blocking ovulation. Most oral contraceptives contain both a synthetic estrogen, known as ethinyl estradiol or mestranol, and a synthetic progesterone, called progestogen or progestin. These hormones act together on the pituitary gland, which controls many of the body's hormone-producing glands. The synthetic estrogen suppresses ovulation, and the female body responds by simulating pregnancy. The synthetic progesterone increases the thickness of the cervical mucus, thereby preventing the passage of sperm. Progesterone also promotes menstruation.

An alternative form of the pill, called the mini-pill, contains only synthetic progesterone. It is less effective and is prescribed less often. Sequential forms of the pill, in which each monthly cycle contains 16 estrogen pills followed by 5 estrogen-plus-progesterone pills, were taken off the market because they had serious side effects.

Common side effects of the combined pills are water retention, breast tenderness, and moodiness. Such side effects usually disappear after a few months, but other, more serious ones can persist longer, including depression and a tendency toward elevated blood cholesterol levels. However, doctors do not yet know the significance of the elevated cholesterol levels that are seen to various degrees with different formulations of the pill.

Risks of the Pill

The pill was introduced in the United States in 1960. By the early 1970's, as many as 15 million women in the United States, and perhaps 100 million around the world, were using it. But physicians observed a distressing number of complications associated with these oral contraceptives, especially blood clots, heart attacks, and strokes. Some studies also suggested—erroneously, many scientists now believe—that use of the pill was associated with an increased incidence of breast cancer. By the early 1980's, the number of American women using birth control pills was down to fewer than 7 million, although that number has now rebounded to about 8.5 million.

Further study during the 1970's showed that most serious complications of the pill were associated with the relatively high concentrations of hormones used in early versions. Today's oral contraceptives contain much lower concentrations, and as a result, fewer women suffer these complications.

The U.S. Food and Drug Administration (FDA) now warns that five groups of women should not take the pill: those with a history of blood clots; those with active liver disease; those with a present or previous cancer of the breast or uterus; those who may be pregnant; and those with abnormal vaginal bleeding. Most experts also discourage the use of the pill by women who are beyond the age of 40 and by women who smoke and are beyond the age of 35. Most doctors are also concerned about the continued use of the pill for over ten years.

The Pill and Cancer

Because certain types of breast cancer and other female cancers depend on estrogen for their growth, some scientists feared that the pill might increase the risk of contracting cancer. (One in every 11 women develops breast cancer, an average of 130,000 new cases in the United States per year.) In August 1986, however, scientists released results from the Cancer and Steroid Hormone

Study, in which more than 4,700 women with breast cancer were compared to a similar number of women without the disease. This study found no increased risk of breast cancer associated with the pill.

The results of this study were considered more clear-cut than those of earlier ones because a much larger number of women were polled. Some physicians caution, however, that further studies must be performed because the cancers could arise long after women stopped using the pill.

Findings from the Cancer and Steroid Hormone Study, and many others, also showed that use of the pill is associated with a decreased risk of ovarian and endometrial cancer. The longer a woman used the pill, scientists found, the lower her risk of developing one of these cancers. Moreover, this decreased risk persisted long after use of the pill ceased. The study's authors estimated that over 1,700 cases of ovarian cancer are averted each year by the use of oral contraceptives.

The study also indicated, though, that use of oral contraceptives might be associated with a higher risk of cancer of the cervix. That link is not definitive, however, because the two main risk factors for cervical cancer—first intercourse at an early age and multiple sexual partners—may be

more common among users of the pill.

Estrogen Therapy for Men

Surprisingly, a drug very much like the pill is used for treating prostate cancer in men. The growth of prostate tumors is stimulated by the male hormone testosterone, whose production is also controlled by the pituitary gland. By a complicated pathway, estrogen shuts off the flow of testosterone. Estrogen is used in the therapy of about 75 percent of the 96,000 American men who develop prostate cancer each year. In seven out of every ten patients for whom estrogen is prescribed, life expectancy is extended by months or years and pain is reduced. The chief side effect of estrogen therapy in men is feminization, such as an increase in the size of breasts.

Disorders of Menopause

Millions of women in the United States suffer from the disorders that accompany menopause. In addition to mood swings and hot flashes, these include loss of vaginal elasticity and vaginal irritation or itching.

These problems can be treated by estrogen replacement therapy (ERT), in which women are given medication similar to birth control pills. Most women on ERT report that they have more energy, feel

FACTS ABOUT ESTROGEN

- **Contraception: Most birth control pills contain both synthetic estrogen and progesterone in relatively low doses. The lower concentrations compared to early versions of the pill significantly reduce the risk of serious side effects.**

- **Menopause: Estrogen therapy can relieve mood swings, hot flashes, and other discomforts.**

- **Osteoporosis: Bone loss can be prevented or slowed through estrogen therapy.**

- **Cancer: Over 70,000 American men a year are given estrogen to treat prostate cancer.**

- **Heart Disease: Estrogen therapy may help protect older women from cardiovascular problems.**

> **The symptoms that accompany menopause are caused by a slowdown in the body's production of estrogen and progesterone.**

less depressed, and sleep better than they did previously. Their hot flashes usually disappear, and vaginal changes are typically reversed. Until recently, most patients underwent ERT for one to two years, then were gradually weaned off it; their hot flashes usually did not return. Today, more and more doctors are prescribing ERT for longer periods of time since it seems to have many additional benefits.

Osteoporosis

One problem that postmenopausal women are also prone to develop is osteoporosis, a condition that seems to be related to estrogen deficiency. In osteoporosis, bones become thinner, less dense, more fragile, and therefore vulnerable to fractures. In the United States alone, osteoporosis causes an estimated 1.3 million fractures in the elderly each year, primarily in women, with an estimated annual cost of $10 billion.

Giving older women estrogen—a treatment also referred to as ERT—can prevent osteoporosis or slow bone loss once it has begun. ERT for treatment of osteoporosis, however, must generally be continued indefinitely. A great deal of evidence suggests that loss of bone mass begins anew when estrogen is halted.

In 1984 a conference at the National Institutes of Health called ERT the most effective single therapy for osteoporosis. The conference recommended that ERT be used by all white women whose ovaries had been removed before the age of 50. The conference also urged that ERT be "considered" by all white females who underwent natural menopause. (Black women have greater bone mass and hence run a much lower risk of osteoporosis.) Others at risk for osteoporosis include women with a family history of the disease and those who were treated with steroid drugs for a long period of time.

Physicians have increasingly been turning to estrogen therapy to treat a number of conditions. According to the FDA, in 1986, 20.3 million prescriptions were written for synthetic estrogen, 68 percent of them for treatment of menopausal symptoms. (Another 14 percent were for treatment of ovarian dysfunction in young women, 7 percent for treatment of cancer, and the rest for other uses.)

Help for the Heart

ERT may also help protect women from cardiovascular disease. Many studies have shown that younger women have a much lower risk than men of developing heart disease, but the risk in-

> **Estrogen replacement therapy can prevent osteoporosis or cut bone loss once it has begun.**

creases sharply after menopause. Many scientists now believe that normal levels of estrogen offer a protective effect, and there is hope that ERT will continue this protection.

A major new study of ERT reported in June 1987 indicates that this is the case. Researchers at ten medical schools studied 2,270 women between ages 40 and 69 for nine years. The team, headed by epidemiologist Trudy L. Bush of the Johns Hopkins University School of Hygiene and Public Health, concluded that the risk of cardiovascular disease was three times as high for women not receiving ERT as for those who did receive it.

Side Effects of ERT

ERT does have side effects. About 10 percent of women develop cramps, fluid retention, headache, nausea, swollen breasts, vaginal discharge, and weight gain. These symptoms are frequently so severe that the estrogen dosage must be reduced or eliminated. Furthermore, women given estrogen alone (called unopposed estrogen) run a greater than normal risk of developing gallbladder disease and four to eight times the risk of contracting endometrial cancer.

> **Estrogen may help protect women from cardiovascular disease.**

The risk of endometrial cancer can be reduced to normal if doctors prescribe progestin along with estrogen, which is generally done in ERT. However, some scientists believe that progestin counters the beneficial effects of estrogen on cardiovascular disease, although that has not been studied in depth.

In defense of ERT, Dr. Bush of Johns Hopkins notes that cardiovascular disease is the number-one killer of women and is 14 times as common as endometrial cancer. Furthermore, she says, endometrial cancer is easily detected and readily curable. And in a significant number of women over the age of 45, the uterus has been surgically removed, eliminating the risk of endometrial cancer.

Despite its benefits, ERT is not for everyone. Physicians recommend that it not be administered to women who have or have had endometrial cancer or breast cancer or who have had a stroke, a recent heart attack, or deep vein clotting. □

Discussing Death With Children

Marcia Hartley, M.S.
Carol Murphy, M.S.W.
Michael W. Yogman, M.D.

Talking with children about death is never easy and may make parents uncomfortable. Yet protecting a child from learning about death is not in the child's best interest. In the United States, one out of twenty children loses a parent before reaching the age of ten. Since children who lose a parent are at greater risk for developing behavior problems and depression, many later difficulties can be minimized by helping a child sort out the confusion over the death of a loved one.

Any death a child encounters, including that of a pet, can become an opportunity for both adult and child to share feelings and to learn how to accept and provide emotional support. There is no magical age for understanding death; it is a concept that children must grasp gradually.

Infants and Toddlers

Elizabeth's grandfather died suddenly just after her first birthday. Elizabeth's mother has been very upset ever since. She is sad, is easily distracted, and shows none of her usual cheerfulness when caring for her baby. Elizabeth has been more fretful than usual and not interested in her bottle. She has begun waking at 3:00 A.M. again, asking to be fed. Nap time and bedtime are especially stressful.

As Elizabeth's behavior suggests, while infants and toddlers are unable to understand the meaning of death, they do sense their parents' unhappiness and preoccupation when a death occurs. Parents can minimize their child's upset by maintaining the usual routine as much as possible and spending more time with the child. In addition, every effort should be made to keep the youngster in familiar surroundings (staying at home, sleeping in his/her own crib, playing with the usual toys, and so on).

Preschool Children

Ginny's pet parakeet died while she was away at kindergarten. When Ginny arrived home, her mother explained in simple terms what had happened: "Squeaks isn't flying. He isn't breathing, so he's not just asleep. I'm sorry, Ginny, but Squeaks is dead." Ginny cried for a while. She and her mother planned a funeral, and soon she went outside to play.

The death of a family pet can cause intense personal sadness. Arranging for a pet's burial, saying a few words about the pet before burial, and allowing the child to place a marker on its grave are ways to help a child say good-bye. In this way death can be integrated gradually into the child's experience.

Preschoolers have a short "sadness span," a protective mechanism that allows them to bear the grief to which they are so unaccustomed. At this age children also vacillate between feelings of omnipotence (they, their parents, and teachers are special and somehow immune from death) and feelings of vulnerability (fears of being left alone and of the dark). After a death preschool children may regress to bed-wetting and baby talk for short periods of time. Egocentric and still incapable of understanding external cause-and-effect relationships, preschool children may fantasize and feel

Arranging for a pet's burial can help a child say good-bye.

guilty about whether they contributed to a special person's death. Adults can help to demystify the concept of death by avoiding euphemistic terms such as "passed away" or "gone to sleep." Describing exactly what happened ("Grandpa's heart wore out") will lessen the child's confusion and minimize the tendency to imagine something less natural. It may also dispel fears caused by euphemisms; a child told that Grandpa "went to sleep" or "is away" may be afraid to go bed or to see parents go to work. Similarly, it may be necessary for parents to explain the difference between being "very sick" and having minor illnesses, so that the child is not frightened by the next cold.

School-age Children

Cindy, age seven, was the only girl in a family of four children and had a very special relationship with her father. Suddenly, he died of a heart attack. Cindy's initial reaction was shock and disbelief; she cried very little. She felt so empty. Had she done something to make her father die? She stopped caring about school and started arguing with her brothers much more. She was angry at the doctors for not saving her father. She wanted to ask questions about how he had died, but she had a big lump in her throat. She would find her favorite doll and cry softly so no one would hear her. Only when Cindy at last talked openly with her mother, and they cried together, did she begin to feel less angry. Her mother explained the details of the death, and Cindy no longer felt guilty.

School-age children can understand cause and effect and that death is final. They can use the experiences of others for support. However, they may still feel guilty and blame themselves for the death and may believe that death is violent, contagious, or a punishment. Children who lose a parent

may become isolated from their peers or argumentative, neglect their schoolwork, or have a decreased appetite. They may develop sleep problems and be hesitant to leave home, fearing that another family member will become ill or have a fatal accident.

By age seven children are usually interested in the practical details surrounding a death and funeral, and they may ask questions about the deceased that seem morbid to adults: "What will happen to his body in the ground? Can he feel people walking on it? Is he hungry? How can he be in the ground and in heaven too? Can he see my flowers on his grave?" Listening carefully gives the adult an opportunity to draw out the child's feelings of anger, guilt, and fear and to correct factual distortions before they become too deeply entrenched.

It can be reassuring and constructive to include a child in the rituals surrounding death. Participating in the funeral makes a child feel part of the family and lets the child experience how friends and relatives provide support during a time of stress. What takes place during a funeral should be described in advance, to help the child decide whether or not to participate. An understanding adult should pay close attention to the youngster during the funeral, to sense whether the experience becomes overwhelming and the child needs to leave. If the child has decided not to be included in the funeral, an alternate observance can be created that brings a sense of finality and permits the youngster to gradually integrate happy memories of the deceased into his or her own life.

By age nine or ten children grasp the biological reality of death and its finality and can accept in a matter-of-fact way that they will die sometime. Once the child understands dying more logically, the family can share its beliefs in a discussion of what happens to a person after death. A family with strong religious beliefs might say that the dead person's body is in a special box, while the spirit rests in a place where there is no pain, and that the person is happy now. Other families may choose to explain that the memory and influence of a person who has died can live on forever. Some of these concepts may not be fully understood until adolescence.

Mourning During Adolescence

The headline in the newspaper had been chilling: "Teenage Driver Killed in Fiery Crash." After the last ball game, everyone was celebrating what had been a winning season, but Randy had to leave early and arranged for his best friend, Jeff, to ride home with someone else. While in the car alone, Randy had been hit broadside by another driver who went through a red light. Now Jeff could not forgive himself. If only he had been with Randy, he would have seen the other car and warned Randy in time. How could he face life without Randy? All he wanted now was to die too.

Jeff's parents were excellent listeners and told their son's concerns to the school principal and teachers. The school counselor met with Randy's classmates, and out of their group sessions came the idea of commemorating Randy's life by establishing a memorial park. The project required much planning and cooperation from everyone. A sense of accomplishment helped the students regain control over their lives at a time when they felt powerless to change the original event. They could communicate their feelings about Randy's death more easily through a group task. The big turning point for Jeff was the new headline "Teens Create Memorial Park—Celebrate Friend's Life."

Adolescents experience loss deeply in two phases: acute short-term grief and a longer term of mourning. Grief is a time of turmoil characterized by physical symptoms, as well as anger, sadness, and longing. Jeff had wanted to die and felt guilty to be the survivor. His here-and-now orientation did not initially allow him to think ahead or imagine the gradual resolution of loss. Mourning is a longer healing process that can last from six months to two years or more. The result of mourning should be to say good-bye to the dead person and to resume the neglected areas of one's life. In order for Jeff to say good-bye to Randy, it was important for him to identify with and perpetuate Randy's admirable qualities.

Adolescents experience much the same grieving process as adults: initial shock and disbelief, then anger. This is a dangerous time for adolescents because depression can set in, possibly evoking hopelessness and the desire to die. Any talk of suicide or of wanting to die or go to sleep and never wake up should be taken very seriously by parents and other adults.

Risk taking is also characteristic of adolescents. They often deny their vulnerability and can inadvertently hurt themselves by behaving recklessly. In addition, adolescents may experience physical symptoms such as weight loss, decreased (or increased) appetite, sleep problems, headaches, and stomach pain. Coping skills learned throughout childhood can soften the impact of death at this time. The ability to translate talents and energy into productive activity can also be helpful.

Learning From Pain

Mourning is a long-term process that is tied both to a child's developmental level and to previous experiences. Parents and other concerned adults can help to change a very upsetting experience into one that is integrated in a positive way into a child's emotional life. Since disruption in routine and in consistency of care are disturbing to any child, maintaining ordinary daily activities such as taking walks and reading together are especially important at this time and can facilitate discussion of feelings. There are many good children's books that describe the feelings everyone has at the time of a friend's or relative's death.

Protecting a child from painful emotions may deprive the child of the best means of mastering such an experience. By observing family members crying and talking about the dead person, a child learns how adults experience sorrow. Just as an adult resolves feelings, the child learns that life can continue in a meaningful way after a painful loss. Reassuring a child about death in a positive, sensitive manner can be rewarding for parents too. As a recent book suggests, learning to cope with "necessary losses" is a universal challenge all of us must face. □

> **Children must learn that life can continue in a meaningful way after a painful loss.**

Suggestions for Further Reading

For Children:
KELLER, HOLLY. *Goodbye, Max.* New York, Greenwillow, 1987.
TOBIAS, TOBI. *Petey.* New York, Putnam, 1978.
VIORST, JUDITH. *The Tenth Good Thing About Barney.* New York, Atheneum, 1971.

For Adults:
FAYERWEATHER STREET SCHOOL STAFF. *Kids' Book About Death and Dying,* edited by Eric Rofes. Boston, Little, Brown, 1985.
GROLLMAN, EARL A., ed. *Explaining Death to Children.* Boston, Beacon, 1967.
KUSHNER, HAROLD S. *When Bad Things Happen to Good People.* New York, Schocken, 1981.

GLAUCOMA

Carmen A. Puliafito, M.D.

Glaucoma is the third leading cause of legal blindness in the United States. It affects approximately 2 percent of people over the age of 40. Although glaucoma is most common among the middle-aged and the elderly, it can also strike young adults and, rarely, even children. Many people with glaucoma have no symptoms at all. Routine ophthalmological examinations to detect glaucoma are thus very important, because without treatment, severe and irreversible loss of vision can occur.

Pressure in the Eye

Glaucoma is a disease in which the pressure inside the eye (known as intraocular pressure) is increased. This increased pressure can damage the optic nerve, the sensitive cable of nerve tissue that links the eye with the brain. The optic nerve damage decreases the field of vision.

Vision loss usually begins insidiously. Initially, peripheral vision is slightly reduced—so slightly that the vision loss is usually not noticed by the affected individual. If the intraocular pressure is not treated and remains elevated, optic nerve damage will progress. The central visual field will be affected, with loss of reading and driving vision. Eventually, blindness can occur. Effective treatment can halt the worsening of glaucoma, but it cannot reverse visual damage that has already taken place.

To understand glaucoma, a basic understanding of the physiology of the eye is necessary. The ciliary body, a structure located behind the iris, or colored portion of the eye, constantly produces a fluid called aqueous humor. This fluid travels around the lens of the eye and through the pupil into the front chamber of the eye. There, it is drained from the eye through a sieve-like structure called the trabecular meshwork. In almost every type of glaucoma (there are a number of different types), pressure in the eye is increased because an obstruction blocks the outflow of aqueous fluid through the trabecular meshwork.

Chronic Glaucoma

The most common type of glaucoma is called chronic glaucoma, or open-angle glaucoma. It affects an estimated 2.5 million Americans. People with open-angle glaucoma typically have no symptoms, and without treatment, suffer painless, progressive vision loss. The cause of open-angle glaucoma remains unknown but is related to an anatomic or physiologic abnormality leading to clogging of the trabecular meshwork. Men and women are equally affected, and individuals with diabetes or nearsightedness are at greater risk. Heredity also plays a role: patients with a family history of glaucoma are at greater risk of developing the disease themselves.

Open-angle glaucoma can be detected only by an eye examination—ideally by an ophthalmologist, a medical doctor specializing in medical and surgical treatment of eye disease. One of the most important aspects of preventive eye care is obtaining a complete medical eye examination every year after the age of 40, for the detection of glaucoma as well as other diseases. Testing for glaucoma should be part of every eye exam from adolescence on.

Diagnostic Tests

Several elements of a medical eye examination can detect signs of open-angle glaucoma. The first is tonometry. In this test, the ophthalmologist painlessly and quickly measures the intraocular pressure. Anesthetic drops are placed on the eye, and a small plastic probe (a tonometer) is used to measure the inner pressure by determining how much force is necessary to cause a slight indentation on the outer part of the eye.

A second test is ophthalmoscopy. The doctor uses an ophthalmoscope, an instrument with a special light source, to examine the inside of the eye. Of particular interest are the retina (the light-sensitive tissue that lines the inside of the eye) and the optic nerve. Glaucoma-associated damage to the optic nerve can be directly observed. Instead of having a normal pink color, the optic nerve in a glaucoma patient may be pale. In addition, high pressure may cause the optic disk (where the optic nerve passes through the rear of the eye) to curve outward. This is called cupping and can be seen with an ophthalmoscope.

The third important element of the examination is perimeter testing, or perimetry, a technique for measuring the visual field. In one method, a computer flashes points of light in a bowl-shaped device. Patients indicate when they see the pinpoint flash, usually by pressing a buzzer. This procedure enables doctors to detect early glaucoma-associated vision loss. Moreover, once glaucoma has been diagnosed and treatment begun, perimetry is useful in ensuring that treatment is adequate and that vision loss is not getting worse.

Eye Drops and Other Drugs

A variety of therapies may be used if open-angle glaucoma is diagnosed. Initial treatment almost always involves the use of eye drops containing medications that improve the outflow of fluid through the trabecular meshwork or decrease the production of aqueous fluid.

In the first stages of treatment, the drops usually consist of beta blockers, a class of drugs used widely, in different forms, in a variety of disorders. The most commonly employed beta blockers for glaucoma are timolol (brand name, Timoptic), levobunolol (Betagan), and betaxolol (Betoptic). The drops are typically used once or twice a day. Beta blockers, even in drop form, must be carefully used in patients with certain heart and lung disorders. (The ophthalmologist will obtain information about the patient's general medical condition before prescribing these drugs.)

In addition to the beta blockers, epinephrine and pilocarpine are two other topical medications commonly employed to control open-angle glaucoma. All of these different drops may be used alone or in combination.

If drops do not control pressure adequately, another class of medications called carbonic anhydrase inhibitors can be employed. Examples include acetazolamide (Diamox) and methazolamide (Neptazane). These drugs, given orally, decrease the secretion of aqueous fluid by the ciliary body.

Surgery

When medications cannot reduce pressure adequately, laser surgery or conventional microsurgery are further treatment options. Lasers, first used to treat open-angle glaucoma in 1979, have revolutionized the treatment of this type of glaucoma. In a procedure called argon laser trabeculoplasty, laser light burns small holes in the trabecular meshwork to increase the outflow of fluid. Argon laser trabeculoplasty, which is performed on an outpatient basis with topical anesthesia, is successful in achieving control of intraocular pressure in a high percentage of cases.

With time, however, there is a tendency for the pressure to drift upward. In such cases, a microsurgical procedure may be performed—a glaucoma filtering operation, or trabeculectomy. A small opening is made in the white coat of the eye to create a new, artificial drainage channel that bypasses the trabecular meshwork.

Acute Glaucoma

A less common form of glaucoma is called acute, closed-angle, or narrow-angle glaucoma. It is different from chronic, or open-angle, glaucoma in that eye pressure goes up quickly. The trabecular meshwork becomes acutely blocked because the pupil enlarges too much or too quickly and the iris "bunches up" over the drainage canals.

The symptoms of acute glaucoma include intense pain in and around the eye, severe blurring of vision, and nausea. Acute glaucoma is a medical emergency: if the intraocular pressure is not promptly reduced, there can be severe damage to the optic nerve, and permanent vision loss can result.

Treatment for acute glaucoma usually involves a procedure called laser iridotomy—in which a small hole is burned in the iris, immediately unblocking part of the drainage canals. If the laser surgery is unsuccessful, microsurgery can be used to create an opening in the iris. □

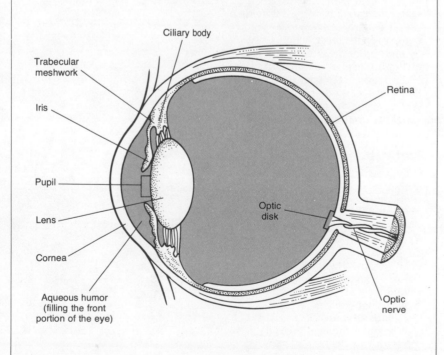

PARTS OF THE EYE

Ciliary body

Trabecular meshwork

Iris

Pupil

Lens

Cornea

Aqueous humor (filling the front portion of the eye)

Retina

Optic disk

Optic nerve

What Are Placebos?

Susan Carleton

According to popular belief, a placebo is a mere sugar pill, a useless pseudo-medication administered to a hypochondriac to soothe some imaginary ill. Medical experts, however, regard placebos and their poorly understood but well-documented powers with considerable respect. Some researchers who study the complex relationships between mental state and physical health suggest that the so-called placebo effect—in which an inert substance or apparently inappropriate treatment causes an actual change in a person's condition—plays a vital role in nearly every aspect of healing.

Moreover, placebos are invaluable in the testing and evaluation of new drugs. In large experiments called clinical trials, researchers gauge how well a medication under study works by comparing its effect, when taken by a group of patients, to the effect of a placebo, identical in taste and appearance, taken by a similar group. (The researchers assessing the patients' responses generally do not know which individuals took which substance.)

Definitions

Why, then, do placebos have such a poor reputation? Part of the problem lies in the very word "placebo," which has carried distinctly negative connotations through much of its history in the English language. In Latin, *placebo* means "I will please," but by the late 14th century, speakers of Middle English were using the word to imply the worst sort of groveling servility. In an early 19th century medical dictionary the term was defined as "any

medicine adapted more to please than benefit the patient."

Today, a placebo is more broadly defined in one standard medical dictionary as an inactive substance given to satisfy an individual's symbolic need for drug therapy or used in controlled scientific studies to determine the effectiveness of medicinal substances. Also, a procedure with no intrinsic therapeutic value that is performed for therapeutic purposes.

Some doctors would go even further and include in the definition any treatment—whether drug or procedure—that does not act specifically against the patient's particular condition. Under this definition, an antibiotic such as tetracycline would be a placebo when taken for a viral illness like a

cold, because antibiotics are ineffective against viruses. Likewise, many other medications used to treat vague and unmeasurable conditions ranging from indigestion to anxiety would be considered placebos.

A Powerful Effect

A broadened concept of placebos has emerged in response to observations made over the past several years showing how powerful and pervasive the placebo effect is. According to some researchers, between 30 and 40 percent of patients with a wide variety of complaints will report improvement during clinical trials after administration of a placebo. Contrary to popular belief, response to a placebo does not indicate that a patient's illness is fabricated. In

Who is getting the real medicine?

fact, the placebo effect appears to be most powerful among patients in considerable discomfort; people experiencing postsurgical pain and acute motion sickness, for example, have shown a high rate of response to placebos. When anxiety accompanies other symptoms, the response rate may be even higher.

Although the placebo effect has been studied most extensively in pain relief, it has been demonstrated in patients suffering from a wide range of conditions or symptoms. In certain studies, placebos have brought about measurable and/or reported improvement in patients suffering from fever, indigestion, depression, Parkinson's disease, diabetes, and angina pectoris (chest pain caused by impaired blood supply to the heart).

The placebo effect may be triggered by the patient's mind—when one is confident that a pill or potion will work, it does—but it is by no means imaginary. Placebos have been shown to alter objective measurements of the severity of numerous conditions. They can lower blood pressure, breathing rate, and heart rate and can decrease the secretion of stomach acid. They can bring about changes in electrocardiograms and alter levels of fats in the blood.

Placebos can have negative effects on the body as well, when that is the type of action expected. People receiving inactive agents in clinical trials have been known to exhibit all sorts of side effects, including skin rashes, heart palpitations, dry mouth, nausea, diarrhea, and drowsiness. Once they stop taking the placebo, the side effects vanish.

Researchers have tried for years to discover whether people who respond to placebos share certain personality traits, such as suggestibility or emotional openness, but these efforts have proved inconclusive. It's possible that everyone is susceptible to some degree, particularly under certain conditions. Placebos seem to work best in hospital rather than outpatient settings, and an injected placebo is more likely to be effective than a pill or elixir.

Why Placebos Work

To some extent a placebo's effectiveness depends on the patient's belief that it is an active medication. Nevertheless, a few investigators studying the placebo effect have demonstrated that some patients will improve even after being told outright that they are being treated with placebos.

These findings suggest that something more than an individual's suggestibility or expectation of

---

While the placebo effect may be triggered by the patient's mind, it is by no means imaginary and can be documented and measured by objective tests.

---

recovery is at work in producing the placebo effect. Many doctors believe that a caring, supportive environment—the essence of the "good bedside manner" that distinguishes the best medical care—makes the difference. It is a truism that sympathetic doctors who have faith in the treatments they prescribe produce the best results for their patients. If this is the case, then the placebo effect is nearly as important in today's therapeutics as it was in the days before antibiotics, insulin, and other mainstays of modern medicine.

Studies of medical treatments that have gone in and out of vogue over the years bolster the idea that the placebo effect plays a large role in healing. Researchers from Harvard Medical School who examined past studies of 13 now-discredited treatments for angina pectoris found that when the treatments were new and popular, they produced high rates of patient response. In time, however, response rates began to decline, leveling off at the 30 to 40 percent rate characteristic of the placebo effect.

Placebos are invaluable in the testing and evaluation of new drugs.

On a more fundamental level, other researchers propose a biochemical basis for the placebo effect, suggesting that the process of taking a placebo—doing something one thinks will help—stimulates the body to produce self-healing substances such as interferon or steroids. Pain researchers have found evidence that a placebo, given to a person in severe discomfort, may trigger the production of endorphins, which are naturally occurring painkillers originating in the brain. A similar mechanism may account for the placebo effect on other symptoms.

Ethical Questions

Some people consider deliberate placebo use ethical in medicine only in the context of clinical trials, in which all participants know that they may be given a placebo rather than the drug under investigation. These observers see as the major ethical stumbling block to widespread placebo use the deception inherent when a doctor prescribes an inactive or ineffective treatment under the pretense that it has been scientifically proven to work.

However, the placebo effect is involved in many physicians' good-faith efforts to help their patients get well, when other forms of therapy seem to be either unavailable or inadequate. Many reputable physicians use placebo therapy in this context since it can cause measurable improvement in the patient. And to the patient, of course, the cause of the improvement isn't what matters; feeling better is. ☐

Understanding Miscarriages

Johanna F. Perlmutter, M.D.

A miscarriage is the loss of a pregnancy before the fetus is capable of surviving outside the mother's womb. With new technological advances in the care of newborns, younger and younger babies are being kept alive. Thankfully, this trend reduces the number of months that a woman needs to be worried about suffering a miscarriage. But it is little consolation to a couple experiencing the pain and grief of a lost pregnancy.

A Common Occurrence

At least 15 percent of all pregnancies end in miscarriage. The number may in fact be much higher; some experts believe that, quite frequently, an egg is fertilized but fertilization does not result in a readily detectable pregnancy. In other words, the miscarriage occurs without the woman realizing that she was pregnant. Miscarriages most often go undetected if a woman tends to have irregular menstrual periods, if she miscarries when her period is only a few days late, or if the miscarriage begins when she expected her period. The cramping and bleeding that may accompany the miscarriage may be taken as signs of a normal period.

Fortunately, it is very rare for a woman to have two or more consecutive pregnancies end in miscarriage. Repeated miscarriages

> It is known that some 15 percent of pregnancies end in miscarriage, but a greater number may not be detected.

occur in fewer than 1 percent of women.

The technical name for a miscarriage is spontaneous abortion. Most miscarriages occur within the first three months of pregnancy (the first trimester), although some occur in the second trimester. A pregnancy that ends during the third trimester is called a premature birth if the baby is born alive or a stillbirth if the child is born dead.

Signs of Miscarrying

Ordinarily, a miscarriage is heralded by vaginal bleeding or spotting and by pain. While some bleeding and cramping are not uncommon in the first trimester and may not be serious, bleeding that gets progressively heavier and is accompanied by increasing pain usually does signal a threatened miscarriage. Half of the women who report bleeding in the first trimester go on to have a miscarriage. But the same figure can be viewed more optimistically: half of the women apparently in danger of suffering a miscarriage go on to deliver a normal, healthy infant.

In the second trimester, bleeding and cramping remain common symptoms of a threatened miscarriage. Because the pregnancy is more advanced, the woman may also be aware of labor-like contractions (rhythmic and progressively more severe cramping) and/or the loss or leaking of clear amniotic fluid. It rarely happens that woman with few symptoms or no symptoms at all will suddenly lose a baby.

A pregnant woman should always report any bleeding to her obstetrician, but it is important to realize that there are many explanations for bleeding during the first trimester. Sometimes it occurs around the time of the first missed period. (Occasionally, this bleeding is so much like regular menstrual flow in appearance that the woman actually thinks it is her period, causing her to miscalculate her expected date of delivery by a month.)

Investigators believe that the implantation of the fertilized egg in the endometrium (the uterine lining) can create some spotting. It is also possible for a woman to start pregnancy with more than one egg fertilized. This could mean that she will have twins or triplets. But not infrequently, one or more of the embryos is absorbed or miscarried, leaving the woman still pregnant but with only one child. If this absorption or miscarriage occurs, it too may be accompanied by some bleeding.

There are also causes for bleeding that are unrelated to pregnancy, such as vaginitis or irritation of the cervix (the mouth of the uterus) from intercourse or polyps (benign growths).

Thus, bleeding alone does not denote a miscarriage. Even the passage of clots, a more ominous sign, does not necessarily mean the pregnancy has ended. However, the passage of tissue usually does signal the loss of the pregnancy. (This material may be difficult for a woman to recognize.)

If the woman had what is called a complete miscarriage, subsequent medical treatment may not be needed. But if she had an incomplete miscarriage, part of the placenta remains in the uterus. This material must be removed by a physician, usually in the hospital. A dilation and curettage (D and C) is done to remove all the tissue. A blood transfusion may be necessary if the woman lost a good deal of blood.

Causes

If a woman is going to have a miscarriage during the first three months, there is very little that can be done to stop it. Put simply, the miscarriage is nature's method of terminating an unsatisfactory pregnancy. For the most part, the products of conception from these ended pregnancies have abnormal chromosome numbers. However, the parents should not automatically assume that there is something genetically wrong with one or both of them. The chromosome abnormalities in the miscarried fetus usually are caused by accidents of cell division, which will generally not recur in future pregnancies.

In a small number of pregnancies, the woman does not produce enough of the hormone progesterone to maintain the pregnancy.

The Early Stages of Pregnancy

Once a month, one of a woman's ovaries releases a ripe egg, in the process called ovulation. The egg is swept into and down one of her two fallopian tubes. The journey through the tube takes several days; at the start of the journey fertilization by the man's sperm occurs. The woman's body is already prepared for pregnancy. Shortly before ovulation, blood vessels in the uterus begin to expand, providing a rich blood supply for the soft, spongy uterine lining (the endometrium)—which will hold the fertilized egg.

The fertilized egg, which is beginning to divide and grow, descends the fallopian tube and advances toward the uterus. It takes seven to ten days after conception for the egg to implant itself in the endometrium. Meanwhile, various hormones are secreted that help form the placenta, which itself produces hormones that help nourish the growing embryo.

Another possibility is that there is an immunological problem, and the woman's body rejects the fetus as "foreign."

At all stages of pregnancy, infections may cause a woman to miscarry. Diabetes and either an underactive or overactive thyroid gland can also be responsible. Some miscarriages occur because the embryo did not implant in the uterus properly.

During the second trimester, some pregnancies are lost because of uterine abnormalities. If the uterus is distorted for any reason, the pregnancy may not be able to proceed properly. A small number of women were exposed to such hormones as DES, or diethylstilbestrol, when their mothers were pregnant with them. (Ironically, DES was given to women from the 1940's through the 1960's in an effort to prevent miscarriages.) So-called DES daughters often have an incompetent (or weak) cervix, which can be the reason for a late pregnancy loss. If the tissues of the cervix are not strong enough, then as the uterus grows and expands, the cervix thins and dilates, and premature contractions expel the contents of the uterus.

Steps to Take

There are no right or wrong answers to the question of what to do if a miscarriage is threatened. If the woman is bleeding, some doctors advise her to go to bed until the bleeding stops. This theoretically makes sense: the uterus contracts and is more irritable when a woman is up and walking around. Actually, bed rest does not appear to alter the course of a pregnancy during the first trimester, although bed rest may be helpful later in the pregnancy.

Should there be a proscription against intercourse? The seminal fluid contains chemicals called prostaglandins, which can potentially affect the pregnancy. There may be some physical trauma to the uterus associated with intercourse. Also, when a woman has an orgasm, the uterus usually contracts. However, although all of this theoretically can adversely affect the pregnancy, in reality it does not appear to play a role in the ultimate outcome of the pregnancy.

In general, in the early stages of pregnancy, there is very little that a woman can do in most cases to alter the course of a threatened miscarriage. If, however, the woman has a hormonal deficiency, she can be given supplemental progesterone, which may help her keep the pregnancy.

In the second trimester of pregnancy, an incompetent cervix can be corrected by placing a stitch around and through the cervix. This procedure, called cerclage—done under an anesthetic—stops the cervix from dilating and thus prevents loss of the pregnancy. (The stitch can be removed when labor begins or when the pregnancy has reached a late enough stage for the baby to be born safely; a cesarean could also be performed.)

Even when it is known early on that the stitch will be needed, the procedure is rarely done before the 14th week of pregnancy because it is prudent to ensure that the pregnancy survives the first trimester before undertaking any surgical procedure.

Preventing Recurrent Miscarriages

Once a woman has had recurrent miscarriages, the chances of her having another miscarriage increase. Among women who have

> If a woman is going to have a miscarriage during the first trimester, there is little that she can do to stop it.

lost two pregnancies, over 30 percent will have another miscarriage. For women who have lost three or more pregnancies, the subsequent miscarriage rate increases to over 45 percent.

For any individual woman, however, figuring out the specific reason she is miscarrying—and how to correct the problem if possible—will determine her chances of having a successful pregnancy in the future. If a specific treatment can be instituted for a treata-

> Only a small percentage of women have two or more consecutive pregnancies end in miscarriage.

ble problem, successful pregnancy rates can rise to 90 percent.

Evaluation to determine why a woman is miscarrying is usually not done until after the second loss. At that time, blood samples from both parents are taken to perform a chromosome analysis. Blood is also examined for evidence of glandular disorders. An X ray can help determine if there are any uterine abnormalities. A biopsy of the endometrium and culture of cells from the cervix are some of the other tests that are performed. Appropriate medical treatment is possible in many cases.

Work is going on to prevent miscarriages caused when the woman's immune system is rejecting the fetus. In the still-experimental treatment, prior to the woman's becoming pregnant again, she is injected with her husband's white blood cells, which set her immune system in motion to protect her future fetus.

The Emotional Impact

A miscarriage can be emotionally devastating to the couple. Many couples refer to the miscarriage as having lost a baby, and indeed, they mourn in a similar manner.

Modern technology has contributed to the intensity and depth of a couple's emotional response.

The use of ultrasound and other sophisticated techniques for looking at and listening to the fetus makes it more real to the prospective parents. Thus, if the fetus is lost, the couple is more likely to feel that an actual child is gone.

The length of the grieving period varies, but most couples go through the same stages. At first, they feel shock, then mood swings and agitation. This is followed by guilt (couples often think the miscarriage occurred because they engaged in intercourse or the woman exercised too strenuously or once had an abortion) and by a sense of loss. Finally, there is acceptance of the loss and a steady lessening of the emotional pain.

When the miscarriage occurs early in the pregnancy, friends and relatives may not be aware of the problem and will therefore be unable to share the couple's distress and give them needed support. The weeks after a miscarriage can be a very lonely time, with the woman feeling much guilt at having been a "failure" and bearing resentment toward other pregnant women. Many couples find it helpful to join a support group made up of others who have had a similar loss.

It may take a year or more for a couple to completely work through the grief. Attempting an-

> The weeks after a miscarriage can be a lonely and difficult time, with the woman feeling guilt at having been a "failure" and bearing resentment toward other pregnant women.

other pregnancy right away does not solve the problem; a couple should deal effectively with their feelings before trying to conceive again. If necessary, outside help should be sought. □

The Debate Over Food Irradiation

Brenda L. Becker

A flyer handed out recently on the streets of New York City began like this: "Did you know that the Food and Drug Administration has approved regulations permitting the irradiation of America's food supply? This means that the foods you and your children eat for the rest of your lives—fresh fruit and vegetables, spices, grains, some meats, canned and packaged foods, restaurant foods, and school lunches—*can be exposed to radioactive waste materials.* Moreover, if the government has its way, you won't even know that your food has been irradiated."

Clearly, as the flyer indicates, there are deep-seated fears about food irradiation, in addition to some ignorance about the facts. The process has been approved by the U.S. Food and Drug Administration (FDA) to kill insects and other pests, prolong shelf life, and retard spoilage. Only certain foods may be irradiated, and tight regulations dictate that irradiated foods (except processed goods with irradiated ingredients) be clearly labeled as such. Irradiation does not make foods radioactive.

The approved doses and uses of food irradiation have been declared safe, after decades of testing, not only by the FDA but by the World Health Organization and the American Medical Association. Proponents of irradiation claim it can replace some dangerous pesticides and help increase world food supplies.

Why then haven't you seen any irradiation labels in your supermarket? Because, despite the potential benefits of irradiation, the U.S. food industry dreads a consumer backlash against irradiated foods and thus far has made almost no use of the process. And in fact, there are just enough lingering legitimate doubts over certain aspects of food irradiation to keep debate percolating for the foreseeable future. Opponents state, for instance, that key questions remain about the safety and nutrient value of irradiated food—not to mention the danger of putting more radioactive material into use in American industry.

It's Nothing New

Ever since World War II food irradiation has been researched by the U.S. Army for possible large-scale use. Hospital patients with suppressed immune systems and astronauts in outer space have been given meals sterilized by irradiation. The process typically involves passing food on a conveyor belt through a sealed, mazelike chamber, where it is bombarded with a form of low-level radiation, usually cobalt-60 gamma rays. By disrupting the electron bonds in molecules, the radiation attacks the genetic structures of organisms on or inside food.

This process, at various doses, can be used to kill insects, molds, or other microorganisms. The simpler the organism, the more radiation is needed to kill it; to kill viruses, which are very primitive, would require doses too high for practical use on food. Processors use the lowest dose effective for the purpose, not only because FDA regulations require it, but because higher doses can affect color and texture in many foods.

The Road to Approval

U.S. regulatory agencies have hardly been hasty in approving food irradiation. It was first permitted in the early 1960's to remove insects from wheat and wheat flour and inhibit sprouting in potatoes. At about this time, approval for irradiating bacon was also granted; it was withdrawn when studies of laboratory animals showed possible adverse effects. It wasn't until some 20 years later that the FDA and U.S. Department of Agriculture drew up guidelines and granted approval for use of irradiation in the following cases: to control *Trichinella spiralis,* the parasitic worm in pork that causes trichinosis (an intestinal and muscle disease); to kill insects in herbs, spices, teas, seeds, and seasonings; and to control insects and slow ripening in fresh fruits and vegetables. Specific dosages— measured in units called grays and kilograys—were permitted for the different foods. (See the chart on page 222 for details.) In Canada the process is permitted (but used on a very limited scale) for potatoes, onions, wheat and wheat flour, and some spices.

Is It Safe?

Safety remains the sticking point, even though food irradiation has been used widely for years in more than 20 countries. A vocal coalition of opponents includes organic food advocates, antinuclear activists, and those who simply question whether research has been adequate to support the FDA's claims that irradiation is truly harmless. Many studies, mostly on laboratory animals, are

221

cited to prove the safety of irradiation, but the validity of some of this research is challenged.

For starters, opponents say, any process should be avoided that will add to the quantity of nuclear material in American towns and dumps. As for irradiated food itself, argument centers on the possibility that irradiation may produce substances that could cause cancer when ingested or cause mutations in the bacteria or insects, making them more dangerous than they were before irradiation.

The molecular action of irradiation does produce by-products called free radicals, which in turn create new chemical substances called radiolytic products (RP's), some of which may be carcinogenic. Normal cooking also creates RP's in many foods. Both cooking and irradiation create such minute quantities of RP's as to be harmless for ordinary consumption, according to irradiation's supporters. However, about 10 percent of the RP's created by irradiation are so-called unique RP's (URP's), found in food only after radioactive exposure. Some scientists claim these URP's are present in insignificant amounts and thus cause no ill effects, and they cite laboratory studies with animals to prove it. Others contend that the animals may not have been fed concentrated enough doses of URP's.

Another aspect of the debate focuses on whether irradiation depletes the vitamin content of some foods—a special concern with foods that will lose vitamins anyway during storage, canning, and cooking. Researchers who have endorsed irradiation concede that it may affect the levels of some vitamins, but no more than other standard processing techniques and not to a degree that would be likely to affect the overall nutritional status for an individual or population.

State of the Art

Is there irradiated food in your future? For now, spices (and just 1 percent of the nation's supply, at that) are the only foods commonly irradiated in the United States. Some careful market testing is under way for other permitted products. The first food likely to be irradiated on a large scale, according to industry insiders, is the Hawaiian papaya. Growers are desperate for an efficient way to rid their crop of pests in order to meet mainland import standards, now that a key postharvest pesticide has been banned.

FDA rules require irradiated foods to be labeled "treated with radiation" or "treated by irradiation," either on the package or, as in the case of fruit, on the bin at point of purchase. In addition, the worldwide irradiation logo (a flower inside a segmented circle) must appear. This rule is in effect at least until early 1988; after that, it may be scaled back to require only the irradiation logo if the symbol is judged to be adequately familiar to the public by then.

Irradiation may also have potential for bringing safer meat to American butcher cases. It can kill trichinosis-causing worms in pork—although thorough cooking does the same thing, and a recently developed test for pork carcasses can quickly determine whether *trichinella* is present. After recent media coverage of salmonella contamination in poultry (a major cause of food poisoning), the Agriculture Department asked the FDA to approve irradiation of chicken to kill salmonella bacteria during packing. No action had been taken on the proposal by the FDA as of early 1988.

Political wrangling between proponents and opponents of irradiation has further slowed the snail's pace of regulatory change. Recent congressional hearings on food irradiation left the debate in limbo. At least one state, Maine, has banned the sale of irradiated foods outright. The irradiation industry, whose business now largely consists of sterilizing non-food items like hospital supplies, is lobbying hard to convince consumers and Congress that the FDA's approval is trustworthy.

Whether irradiated food is a boon or a threat, Americans are not likely to be eating much of it for quite some time. Eventually, consumers will decide for themselves, and the market will respond accordingly. Those who support irradiation point out that microwave ovens provoked similar fears before their widespread acceptance. Meanwhile, no major food producer wants to be first on the bandwagon—although many would like to be second. □

U.S. FOODS APPROVED FOR IRRADIATION

Food	Purpose	Date Approved
Fresh fruits, vegetables	To slow growth and ripening; to control insects	April 1986
Dry/dehydrated herbs, spices, seeds, teas, vegetable seasonings	To kill insects; to control microorganisms	April 1986*
Pork	To control the parasite that causes trichinosis	July 1985
White potatoes	To inhibit sprout development	August 1964
Wheat, wheat flour	To control insects	August 1963

* The irradiation of these products was first approved by the FDA in July 1983; the allowable dosage was increased in April 1986. Source: Adapted from *FDA Consumer*, July/August 1986.

MONOCLONAL ANTIBODIES
Medicine's Powerful New Tool

Thomas H. Maugh II, Ph.D.

Philip Karr, 67, was near death from lymphoma (cancer of the lymphatic system) in 1982 when Stanford University physician Ronald Levy injected him with an experimental substance that Levy hoped would seek out the cancerous cells and kill at least some of them. The treatment with monoclonal antibodies worked much better than even Levy had hoped. The patient's cancer was cured, and he did not suffer nausea, hair loss, or any of the other side effects normally associated with therapy. Five years later, Karr's cancer had not returned and he was enjoying his retirement.

Karr was the first cancer patient to be treated with monoclonal antibodies (MAb's), a remarkable family of guided missile-like proteins that seek out tumors, bacteria, or viruses and target them for destruction by the immune system. His recovery is indicative of the kind of results scientists hope for with MAb's, although such complete success is still achieved only rarely.

Nonetheless, physicians hold high hopes for MAb's in the future, not only for diagnosing and treating cancer, but also for a wide spectrum of other applications. These include preventing rejection of transplants, diagnosing heart disease, and treating multiple sclerosis, as well as performing a plethora of routine laboratory tasks. Many experts consider MAb's the most valuable products of the biotechnology industry, and their sales throughout the world are expected to top $1 billion per year by 1990.

MAb's to the Rescue

Antibodies—proteins produced by specialized white blood cells called B lymphocytes—are the sentries in the human body's defense system. They spot foreign material and bind to it, thereby signaling other components of the immune system to destroy it. Each antibody recognizes only one type or class of invader, but the immune system has the capacity to produce literally millions of different antibodies.

The trick in using antibodies for diagnosis or therapy is to find one B lymphocyte that produces the desired antibody and then to grow

> **Monoclonal antibodies can be crafted to seek out tumors, bacteria, or viruses and target them for destruction by the immune system.**

large quantities of its descendants. Unfortunately, lymphocytes do not grow well outside the body. But in 1975 biologists Georges Köhler and César Milstein found a clever way around this problem.

Köhler and Milstein injected mice with the specific protein, called an antigen, to which they wished to produce antibodies. They then isolated the B lymphocytes that produced the desired antibody. These lymphocytes were fused with cells from a

mouse tumor that grew readily in the laboratory. The resultant hybrid cells, called hybridomas, had the best properties of both parents: they produced a single antibody, and they would grow clones, or exact duplicates, forever in culture (the artificial medium used for the growth of living material). Köhler and Milstein received the 1984 Nobel Prize for physiology or medicine for their work.

Laboratory Tests

The ability of MAb's to bind to one specific molecule in a sea of hundreds or thousands of different chemicals makes them ideal for diagnostic tests. Physicians routinely use them in their offices for determining the concentrations of hormones, vitamins, and therapeutic drugs in blood. They are also used to quickly identify the bacteria causing an infection, a process that formerly took three or more days. By identifying the cause of symptoms immediately, MAb's make it possible for the right antibiotic to be used at once.

Monoclonal antibodies are even more widely used in commercial and research laboratories. Most blood-typing is now done with them, for example, as is the matching of organs destined for transplants. They are also used for such diverse purposes as showing the presence of semen on rape victims and identifying fungal infections on golf-course grasses.

Even the health-conscious consumer uses them. Home tests for colorectal cancer, ovulation, and pregnancy are based on MAb's. According to the U.S. Food and Drug Administration (FDA), well

223

over 200 different MAb's are now being marketed, and at least that many are being used in research applications where approval is not required. By early 1988, only one MAb—a preparation to prevent the rejection of transplanted kidneys—had been licensed by the FDA for use in humans, but that number is expected to grow rapidly. As many as 150 different MAb's are being studied in clinical tests.

Treating Cancer

The greatest interest in MAb's is for the treatment of cancer, and Levy's approach is typical. His group at Stanford selects patients whose cancer cells are studded with an antigen against which the MAb's can be aimed. In a $10,000 process taking 6 to 12 months, cancer cells are removed from each patient and injected into mice to make hybridomas, which produce antibodies custom-tailored to fit the patient's tumor cells.

The next four patients Levy treated after Karr did not respond nearly as well, however. Levy and other physicians soon found two major problems with their approach. The first was that the tu-mor cells had a chameleon-like ability to change their surface antigens, allowing the tumor to continue to flourish. The second was that the immune systems of many cancer patients are weakened by their disease and cannot mount an effective response, even with MAb's. These findings have led researchers into two separate but complementary directions.

One approach, employed by Levy, is to use a mixture, or "cocktail," of MAb's directed against a variety of antigens in the hope that all tumor cells will be targeted. The MAb's are frequently combined with substances such as interferon that stimulate the immune system.

Levy's group has treated several dozen lymphoma patients with such cocktails over the past six years. The treatment typically relieves pain, reduces tumor size, and prolongs life, but it rarely produces a complete remission. Progress has been steady, however, and Levy hopes for better results in the future as researchers gain increased knowledge.

A growing number of researchers are turning to a second alternative—chemically linking MAb's to radioactive isotopes or to poi-sons, to turn the antibodies themselves into killers. The treatment is analogous to using radiation therapy or chemotherapy, but MAb linkage allows all the killing activity of the radiation or drug to be focused on the tumor itself, thereby minimizing side effects.

One of the leaders in this approach is oncologist (cancer specialist) Stanley Order of the Johns Hopkins School of Medicine. Order has been using antibodies that bind to ferritin, an iron-containing molecule that is found in cells from liver tumors but not in healthy cells. The antibodies are chemically attached to molecules of radioactive iodine.

Among the 300 patients Order had treated by the summer of 1987, 7 had complete remissions of their liver tumors, and 48 percent had partial remissions in which the tumors shrank by at least 30 percent. In several of these cases, the tumors shrank enough that they could be removed surgically.

Radioisotope-labeled MAb's are also used for locating and determining the size of tumors. The radiation from the isotopes shows up on sensitive X-ray detectors. Researchers have found that the use of labeled MAb's sometimes permits tumors to be detected earlier than is possible with conventional techniques, thereby improving the odds for successful therapy.

Oncologist Robert W. Baldwin of the Cancer Research Campaign Laboratories in Nottingham, England, has attached anticancer drugs such as methotrexate and doxorubicin to MAb's directed against tumors of the colon. In animals he has found that the MAb-linked drugs are "a bit less effective than the free drugs" but that they have "vastly reduced" such side effects as vomiting and hair loss. Baldwin is now studying the effects of the same agents on humans. Researchers in the United States are testing similar agents against lung tumors and other growths.

Scientists analyze the products of cell cultures that are used to grow monoclonal antibodies.

Other researchers are linking MAb's to poisons such as ricin, a protein obtained from castor beans. Ricin is so potent that one molecule is enough to kill a cell. (When used in MAb's, the ricin affects only cancer cells, not healthy ones.) In the summer of 1987, scientists from Xoma Corporation of Berkeley, Calif., reported encouraging preliminary results using this technique to treat malignant melanoma, a frequently fatal form of skin cancer. Xoma has

Home tests for colorectal cancer, ovulation, and pregnancy are based on monoclonal antibodies.

also begun testing the technique against colorectal cancer, while scientists from Cetus Corporation in Emeryville, Calif., are using similar antibodies to treat breast cancer and ovarian cancer.

An Obstacle

One major problem exists with MAb therapy for cancer and many other diseases. Humans rapidly build up antibodies against the MAb's themselves because they are made from mouse cells and therefore recognized as foreign by the immune system. As a result, only one course of treatment, typically lasting about six weeks, is normally possible. After that, additional MAb's are destroyed by the body before they can have any therapeutic effect. Recipients often also suffer from fever, chills, tremors, shortness of breath, and nausea. Scientists thus far have had only limited success in making hybridomas from human cells, although work is proceeding.

For Successful Transplants

Preventing rejection by the body of organ or tissue transplants is an-

other major use of MAb's. In June 1986 the FDA approved for the first time the marketing of an MAb designed for use in humans. The antibody—called muromonab-CD3 (marketed as Orthoclone OKT3) and manufactured by Ortho Pharmaceutical Corporation of Raritan, N.J.—helps prevent rejection of kidney transplants by binding to specialized lymphocytes that attack the kidney during a rejection episode. In a major national trial, researchers found a 94 percent success rate in halting acute rejection with muromonab-CD3, compared to a success rate of only 75 percent with conventional antirejection therapy. The antibody is now being used experimentally to halt rejection of other types of transplants, including the liver and pancreas.

In July 1987 researchers at Stanford announced a breakthrough that could have major implications for people with diabetes whose bodies cannot produce enough insulin. Dr. C. Garrison Fathman developed a new way to transport insulin-producing cells from one strain of mouse into another. Normally, such cells are rejected quickly. But instead of waiting for a rejection episode, Fathman injected the mice at the time of the cell transplant with an MAb that triggered the destruction of 95 percent of T helper lymphocytes, the type of white blood cells that initiate rejection. When the mice's immune systems later made new T helper lymphocytes, the T cells did not recognize the transplanted cells as foreign. The transplants survived for the rest of the animals' lives without any further drug treatment. Fathman predicted that the technique could be tried in humans within five years.

The Immune System

Antibodies similar to those used to block rejection may also be used to combat autoimmune diseases, in which the immune system attacks the body's own tissues. Neurologists at Harvard University and Columbia University have

demonstrated in laboratory animals that MAb's directed against certain T lymphocytes can halt the progression of a disease similar to multiple sclerosis, which is an autoimmune disorder. They began testing the effects of MAb's on multiple sclerosis in humans in 1986 but abandoned the project early in 1987 when the patients developed severe allergies to the mouse antibodies.

Immunology specialist David Wofsy of the University of California at San Francisco has had success in treating research animals for systemic lupus erythematosus (a connective-tissue disease that can affect the entire body) and rheumatoid arthritis, which are also autoimmune diseases.

Experts predict that monoclonal antibodies could become the single most frequently used agent in the diagnosis and treatment of disease.

Wofsy, the Columbia and Harvard researchers, and others are now trying to develop human hybridomas that will produce similar antibodies, in order to overcome the allergic reactions to the mouse proteins.

Other scientists are developing MAb's that can detect the onset of transplant rejection, measure the extent of damage incurred in a heart attack, break down blood clots, neutralize toxins produced by infectious bacteria, and even prevent the viral infections that cause the common cold. Within the next decade, experts predict, monoclonal antibodies could become the single most frequently used agents for diagnosing and treating disease. □

ROOT CANAL

Andrew W. Krieger, D.D.S., M.P.H.

Anthropologists analyzing the tooth of a 3rd century B.C. soldier have concluded that the man had had a form of root canal treatment. Although it was a primitive attempt, this example of treating a tooth's infected core serves to remind us of the ancient origins of both toothache and attempts to remedy it. Toothaches are still with us, but the quest for a pain-free existence has been made easier with the development of modern root canal treatment.

A Tooth Attacked

Infection of a tooth was explained by the ancients as caused by worms living inside the tooth or evil spirits expressing their displeasure. Bacteria are our modern-day equivalent.

An intact tooth will coexist in harmony with the bacteria present in the environment. But a tooth damaged by decay, accidental injury, or the ravages of periodontal (gum) disease can be susceptible to bacterial infection. Such an infection will often damage the pulp inside a tooth—the soft tissue, containing nerves, arteries, and veins. Some pulp tissue is contained in the tooth's pulp chamber, located in the crown (the visible portion of a tooth, above the gum line). Pulp is also found in the root canal, or inside of the root (the portion of a tooth located below the gum line). Canines and incisors (the eye teeth and front teeth) have only one root; other teeth have two or more.

Damaged pulp will often cause a tooth to have prolonged sensitivity to heat or cold. There is frequently generalized soreness, especially upon biting. Various degrees of swelling and foul-tasting saliva may be present. In some cases, no pain is felt, while in other cases there may be a great deal of pain.

If the tooth is not treated, the infection will get worse and will spread down the root canal and out into the surrounding bone and tissues of the jaw. This is known as a dental abscess. An untreated infection of this kind can spread beyond the jawbone, into the face or neck, causing serious and painful swelling. As the abscess worsens, the prognosis for the tooth becomes worse.

One of two choices must be made when the pulp is irreversibly damaged: saving the tooth through root canal or extracting it. Prior to the early 1900's extraction was the accepted practice, but now every effort is made to save affected teeth.

Treatment

The goal of root canal (or endodontic) treatment is to remove the infected pulp and prevent future infection within the tooth. Toward that end, the root canals must be identified and measured, canals and pulp chamber thoroughly cleaned, and the canals filled.

An X ray is taken to allow the dentist to visualize the root anatomy and obtain diagnostic information. Once the number of canals and their exact shapes have been determined, treatment is begun.

Local anesthesia is usually required. The tooth is then isolated with a rubber dam, a sheet of rubber covering the inside of the mouth, with an opening for the tooth to be worked on.

An opening is made in the crown of the tooth with a high-speed drill, and the diseased pulp chamber and root canals are

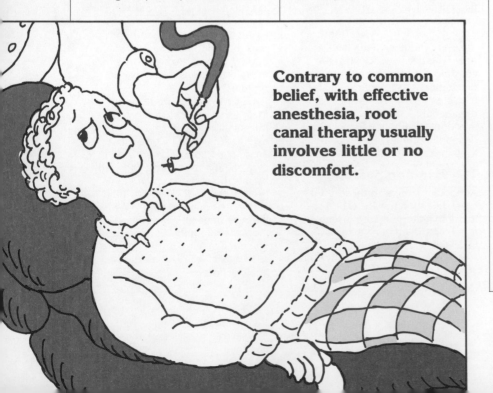

Contrary to common belief, with effective anesthesia, root canal therapy usually involves little or no discomfort.

cleaned. The canals are also enlarged and given a smooth, regular shape, so that they can easily be filled. Very small and delicate pointed instruments called files are used. Some dentists are using ultrasonic equipment to clean and shape the area, and experiments are under way using lasers.

The cleaning and shaping may involve several visits to the dentist because of the difficult technical procedures involved. A tooth with more than one root is likely to take longer to treat. Also, it may take time to eliminate the infection, for which antibiotics may be prescribed. A temporary filling is placed in the opening between appointments.

Once all of the canals are completely clean and infection-free, they must be filled and sealed, most commonly with a rubber compound called gutta-percha. Bacteria is unable to enter the filled and sealed canals.

Finally, the opening in the tooth is closed with a filling or covered with an artificial crown—a protective cap, generally made of porcelain, that is sometimes supported by a post placed in the tooth.

Questions Patients Have

Does root canal treatment hurt? No. Contrary to common belief, with effective anesthesia, root canal therapy usually involves little or no discomfort. Often, patients are in severe pain when they need root canal work and feel immediate relief from pain when treatment is begun. There may be some posttreatment soreness that can be readily controlled with analgesics.

The reputation root canal has as the most painful of dental procedures is probably based on the severe pain that sometimes accompanies an untreated abscess or on perceptions carried over from earlier eras.

Is the tooth dead after root canal treatment? No, an endodontically treated tooth, although pulpless, is alive, nourished by surrounding tissues.

AN INFECTED TOOTH

Crown

Root

Abscess

Decay

Pulp Chamber

Pulp in pulp chamber and root canal

Root Canal

How long will such a tooth last? With proper restoration and care, such a tooth may last a lifetime. Regular brushing and flossing and periodic dental checkups continue to be necessary.

What complications, if any, are associated with endodontic therapy? Some teeth have root canals with accessory, or side, canals that are not fully accessible to the dentist. Severely curved roots or very thin canals may also be partially inaccessible. Therefore, it is sometimes impossible to eliminate all of the infection with conventional therapy. More advanced techniques may be required, such as a procedure—done with local anesthesia—in which a small opening is made in the gum, enabling the dentist to locate the end of the root and remove the infected material.

Who can do root canal therapy? All dentists receive training in endodontics and are qualified to perform root canal work. The dental specialists called endodontists have additional training in the procedure. There are currently about 2,000 endodontists practicing in the United States, treating patients, referred by general dentists, who have complicated cases requiring specialized care. Many general dentists prefer to refer all root canal patients to endodontists.

Other Endodontic Services

Endodontists also are specialists in diagnosing and relieving oral pain and in treating teeth damaged in accidents. An injury to a young tooth may cause development of the tooth to stop; endodontists perform a procedure called apexification to save such teeth, placing a substance inside the root canal system that stimulates the root to grow again. It is even possible for an endodontist to replant a tooth that has been knocked out. Endodontists can also restore the natural color of a tooth by bleaching it in the case of a tooth discolored by an infection, trauma, or drugs such as the antibiotic tetracycline. □

227

Caring for an Alzheimer's Patient

Sharon Begley

In a patient with Alzheimer's disease, the last thing to go—after memory, after speech, after the ability to control even the most basic bodily functions—is the smile. In the families of these incurably ill victims, it is the first. Alzheimer's comes to dominate and even ruin the lives of patients' families no less than it claims the victims' own.

For years little attention was given to the impact of this devastating disease on the family—especially the spouse, but also children, siblings, and grandchildren. But within the past five years the problem has increasingly been recognized. Part of the reason is sheer numbers. Alzheimer's disease afflicts an estimated 2 million to 4 million Americans, according to a 1987 report by the congressional Office of Technology Assessment. This number is expected to double by the year 2000 and quintuple by 2040 as the baby boomers grow older and life expectancy increases. Already, says Representative John Dingell (D, Mich.), "there is probably no family in America that has escaped the unending problems of Alzheimer's and the other diseases causing dementia."

A more tragic reason for the growing attention paid to the families of Alzheimer's patients is the well-publicized case of Roswell Gilbert. In 1985, when the Florida man was 76, he shot and killed his 73-year-old wife, Emily, who had Alzheimer's. Gilbert said that he could not stand to see her suffer from the senile dementia that was tearing her away from him. For months he had been patiently and single-handedly bathing and dressing her, applying her makeup, telling her uncounted numbers of times each day who she was, where she was, what day it was. When Gilbert could no longer care for his wife, he said, he could not bear to send "my beautiful Em" to a nursing home. He was convicted of first-degree murder.

A 24-Hour Task

Although Gilbert's case is extreme, it illustrates many of the problems faced by people caring for a relative with Alzheimer's. Often, these caregivers are themselves elderly and thus not up to the 24-hour task. Taking care of such a patient is like caring for a sick child who gets only worse, never better. The analogy is apt, for re-

> **Despite the physical and emotional cost, most families keep Alzheimer's patients at home for as long as possible.**

cent research indicates that Alzheimer's patients lose mental abilities in the reverse order that babies acquire them. The loss of memory, especially short-term memory, is the best-known symptom of the disease, but other failings mirror the gains that children make as they age. Patients become disoriented in time and space, often getting lost and being wakeful and active at night. They undergo personality changes, at times becoming agitated, irritated, and confused as a result of their mem-

ory loss and inability to function. Patients eventually can no longer put words together. They forget the faces of those closest to them. In the last stages of the disorder, they cannot walk, sit up, or control bodily functions. The disease claims the lives of 120,000 people in the United States every year.

A patient, however, can live with the disease for 5 to 20 years, so the burden on the caregiver is extraordinary. A major problem is simply the loss of sleep. Anxiety and the patient's day-night reversal conspire to deprive the caregiver of much-needed rest. But the caregiver's problems do not end with fatigue. According to a recent study by the Duke University Center for Aging, primary caregivers of Alzheimer's patients experienced a 22 percent increase in the use of prescription drugs to relieve tension, depression, and sleep disorders. Some 28 percent of these caregivers reported increased alcohol consumption.

Keeping Patients Home

Despite the physical and emotional cost, most families keep Alzheimer's patients at home for as long as possible. They resist sending their loved ones to nursing homes, many of which have poor reputations when it comes to Alzheimer's. Until recently, there were few facilities staffed and equipped to handle the special needs of these patients. Many nursing homes overmedicated them or even kept them physically constrained—tied to a chair, for instance—to keep them from wandering.

Still, more than half of the Alzheimer's victims in the United States are in nursing homes, and not necessarily because the family has grown emotionally or physically unable to provide the bulk of their care. Rather, it is often a matter of economics. Medicare, the government's health insurance program for those over age 65, does not cover nonmedical care, either at home or in a nursing home. Medicaid, the joint federal-state health insurance program for the poor, pays for nursing homes but not for less expensive home care or day care that may be sufficient for Alzheimer's patients, at least in the disease's early stages. Thus, according to the Office of Technology Assessment study, families have "financial incentives to place the patients in nursing homes." Even semiskilled home care can easily cost $7 to $10 an hour. If help is hired for 30 hours each week, it can cost a family some $15,000 a year, for which they will not be reimbursed. The average nursing home costs $22,000 annually, but medicaid may foot the bill.

Although almost all of those who suffer from Alzheimer's require institutionalization in the later stages of the disease, researchers, family support groups, and community social welfare agencies offer advice on ways to postpone sending the patient to a nursing home. In many cases, they also offer services that will enable the family to keep the victim at home a while longer.

Experts advise families, first, not to expect too much from the patient. Take one day at a time, and treat the patient as an adult even if behavior is childish. Don't lash out in anger, and understand that repeated questions about where something is or what day it is are not meant to annoy; rather, the patient truly cannot remember having asked the question before, much less remember the answer.

On a more practical level, family caregivers may need to use fire-retardant bedding, since patients can forget they are smoking. Remove hazards from the medi-

cine cabinet and from cupboards as one would for a child; an 80-year-old Alzheimer's patient is as likely to swallow a bottle of pills or drink from a bottle of cleanser as is a three-year-old.

Turn down the hot water heater if possible, for patients can burn themselves if they forget which faucet they turned or which faucet is for hot water. Buy irons that shut off automatically. Install locks on both room and house doors; dementia patients tend to wander, especially at night. Finally, to lessen the patient's confusion and anxiety, keep clutter and excitement to a minimum, use calendars clearly showing the day of the week, and post message boards to remind the patient of daily routines. Put up signs with pictures to explain the function and operation of previously familiar household appliances and to

give directions for finding once common destinations. (For additional tips on caring for an Alzheimer's patient, see the box on page 230.)

Even with the best intentions, the most devoted spouse, son, or daughter will need breaks from caring for the full-time needs of the Alzheimer's patient. The availability of such relief has greatly increased. Many adult day care centers have sprung up to take care of such patients, although the majority admit only those patients who are still in the early enough stages of the illness so that they can walk and take responsibility for their physical needs. Day care centers offer crafts, programs, exercises, and group games, giving patients both mental and physical stimulation and a chance to socialize. Meanwhile, the caregiver is provided

Posting simple instructions around the house helps to remind the patient of basic day-to-day routines.

Coping at Home

Various measures can be taken to ease the difficulties of caring for an Alzheimer's patient.

- Maintain as normal a routine as possible. Change can be confusing and disruptive.

- Keep discussions with the patient as simple as possible; stick to only one topic at a time.

- Don't invite more than one or two visitors at a time.

- Keep telling the patient what is going on: "Now we are going to set the table, and then we will eat dinner."

- Provide easy tasks for the patient to do, like watering plants or folding laundry.

- Do not give patients open-ended choices. Instead of saying, "What would you like to eat?" say, "Would you like an apple or a pear?"

- Label items around the house, and post simple instructions on household appliances. If the patient cannot read, use pictures.

- Write lists and reminders for the patient.

- Post a calendar on which the days are clearly checked off.

- Lock up all drugs and potentially hazardous substances.

- To minimize the chance of accidents, turn down the hot water heater and buy an iron that shuts off automatically.

- Install hard-to-reach locks on doors.

- To protect against injury during episodes of night wandering, use nightlights and install gates on stairways.

- In case the patient gets lost, provide an ID bracelet with name, address, and the words "memory impaired."

with time to run errands, see friends, or just spend a couple of hours alone.

In-home respite programs are available as well. In one such project, in Portland, Ore., trained care providers visit patients' homes, at which time family members can leave for a few hours. The same person visits regularly, in time gaining the acceptance of the patient.

Homes and Hospices

When institutionalization can no longer be avoided, the family has many more choices today than it did just a few years ago. Some nursing homes now have special segregated units where patients are permitted to deviate from the institution's usual routine. Alzheimer's patients may be allowed to stay in bed during the day, for instance, and are not forced to participate in general group activities. They are not even forced to change out of their nightclothes in the morning. Some of the segregated units tolerate "inappropriate behavior," such as wandering about (under supervision). Such units may well come into more widespread use: according to the Office of Technology Assessment, most caregivers are middle-aged daughters, but with women increasingly joining the work force, fewer and fewer will be free to take care of elderly parents.

A more novel approach to caring for the senile dementia patient in the last stages of the disease is the hospice. These institutions are dedicated to making terminally ill patients as comfortable as possible. Hospices can be free-standing or based in a hospital or may provide care in the patient's home. They generally do not use such devices as feeding tubes and, unlike nursing homes, do not transfer dying patients to a regular hospital ward, where intensive efforts may be made to prolong the patient's life. More and more hospices are beginning to accept people in the final stages of Alzheimer's.

Seeking Support

Behind the tragedy of Alzheimer's lies one godsend for the patients and their families: a proliferation of private and governmental organizations to provide support. In 1985, New York City opened the first governmental referral service for Alzheimer's patients. The service's trained staff can offer advice ranging from lists of qualified nursing homes to how to obtain medicaid. In addition, there are more than 170 chapters across the United States of the private Alzheimer's Disease and Related Disorders Association. These offices, too, can advise families on where to seek help in caring for the dementia patient. They can provide lists of nursing homes qualified to care for Alzheimer's patients, advice to family members acting as home caregivers, and referrals to day care centers that offer respite care.

The association's chapters also sponsor support groups for family members; participants in these discussion groups share their problems and air their concerns, offer practical suggestions, and provide both moral and physical support. Information on local chapters and support groups can be obtained from the national headquarters of the Alzheimer's Disease and Related Disorders Association, 70 East Lake Street, Chicago, Ill. 60601 (phone number: 1-800-621-0379). Chapters of the Alzheimer Society of Canada also sponsor support groups for family members; consult local telephone directories for information on contacting them.

As with many diseases, notably AIDS, the pendulum of concern over Alzheimer's has swung from indifference to near obsession. It is important to remember, therefore, that only 5 to 7 percent of people over the age of 65 contract Alzheimer's disease. These reassuring odds in no way diminish the problems of the families of Alzheimer's patients. But the increasing availability of extensive support services can. □

Facts About HMO'S

Barbara Schen Trenk

A health maintenance organization is a healthcare plan that not only covers the cost of medical care—it actually provides it. HMO members pay a preset, fixed fee. They get their healthcare from doctors and other health professionals who are either employed by the HMO or are part of a panel that works with it. Whether that is a problem or a benefit is a matter of debate among both consumers and the medical community. But what few people debate is that this form of medical care delivery has become widespread in the United States. (The Canadian healthcare system is markedly different, with all citizens covered by health insurance plans paid for by the provincial and federal governments.)

The First HMO

The history of what are now known as health maintenance organizations began in the 1930's,

when Dr. Sidney R. Garfield, a young Los Angeles surgeon, established a prepayment medical plan for workers on a construction project in the Southern California desert. Payments of 5¢ per day were collected from workers, entitling them to medical care by Dr. Garfield's group.

Eventually, Dr. Garfield began similar plans for other construction workers. In 1938 he set up a group practice prepayment plan in eastern Washington state, where industrialist Henry J. Kaiser's construction crews were working on the Grand Coulee Dam. First the plan cared for just the construction workers; later, dependents were covered as well.

Dr. Garfield's health plan eventually became known as the Kaiser Permanente Medical Care Program, operated by the Kaiser Foundation Health Plan. Today there are 5.2 million members in 16 states, and the plan has over 6,000 full-time physicians and

52,500 nonphysician employees. As Kaiser grew, other prepaid health plans were begun, including the Group Health Cooperative of Puget Sound, in Washington state, and the Health Insurance Plan of Greater New York, both begun in the 1940's. HIP was established by Mayor Fiorello La Guardia for New York City employees, but private employers may now also purchase HIP for employee health insurance coverage, and individuals may join HIP as well.

Cost Concerns

The pioneering Kaiser Permanente remains the largest group practice prepayment health plan in the United States, but it is by no means alone in the field. In 1973 a healthcare cost-conscious U.S. Congress passed the Health Maintenance Organization Act, encouraging the growth of prepaid group care. The law set quality standards for HMO's, made start-

231

up funds available to many new ones, struck down some state restrictions on health maintenance organizations, and required that many employers make an HMO option available to their workers as part of an overall fringe benefit program.

In 1985 new federal regulations enabled medicare subscribers to join HMO's, with the government's medical fund footing much of the bill. And some states have contracted with HMO's to serve patients on medicaid (the government health insurance program for the poor).

> **A major reason for the growth of HMO's in recent years is the escalating cost of medical care and the health insurance that covers that care.**

As of early 1988, nearly 30 million people were enrolled in some 700 health maintenance organizations throughout the United States. (This was a startling jump from 1976, when 6 million were enrolled in 175 HMO's.) Many of these HMO's are nonprofit organizations, but some are profit-making enterprises. A number of major health insurers have added HMO's to their health coverage options. Traditional fee-for-service insurers that have entered the HMO market include the nonprofit Blue Cross and Blue Shield plans and such private, profit-making firms as Metropolitan Life, Prudential, and CIGNA.

There are several different kinds of health maintenance organizations; often they operate in the same geographic area and may be in fierce competition with one another for members of large employee groups or unions. Some HMO's are actually hybrid health coverage plans, offering insurance

to reimburse non-HMO medical costs.

Many HMO's provide services at one or more health centers, through physicians and other healthcare personnel who are employees of the HMO. Sometimes groups of physicians form health maintenance organizations, or a network of physician groups may contract with an HMO to care for its members. An individual, or independent, practice association (IPA) is made up of physicians who practice out of their own offices and have agreed to care for members of an HMO.

Some of the larger HMO's have their own hospitals; others contract with area institutions for in-patient services. Some have a full range of specialists within the HMO; others may refer patients to specialists when such services are required, picking up the tab through an agreement between the HMO and the physician.

One important reason for the growth of HMO's in recent years is the high cost of medical care, and thus of health insurance that covers that care. Large employers are particularly concerned about the cost of insurance because they may be footing the premium bill (or at least most of it) for thousands of people. Individuals, of course, are directly affected by high healthcare costs, even those who have health insurance. Their plans may have a high deductible before bills are paid, or may pay only a portion of the total bill, or may not cover such prevention-related services as periodic check-ups, well-child visits, or immunizations.

The monthly cost of HMO membership—whether paid for by an employer or an individual—is often the same or somewhat lower than standard health insurance premiums. But an HMO patient's out-of-pocket costs for a visit to the doctor or a hospital stay are likely to be low or nonexistent (although many plans are raising their prices and premiums somewhat). One way in which the

cost of care is kept down at most HMO's is by having primary care doctors act as "gatekeepers," often deciding what treatment a patient gets and whether a visit to a specialist is necessary. HMO advocates say that because pre-paid health plans emphasize preventive medical care, their members use fewer services than they would in traditional fee-for-service medicine.

Shopping Around

The person interested in considering an HMO will want to begin "shopping" by finding out which plans are available in the area. When an employer provides health insurance, the benefits coordinator or personnel director should be able to provide information. Many employers have brochures comparing the benefits of HMO's and other insurance plans offered by the company and may hold meetings where representatives of different kinds of health coverage can describe the benefits of their option.

> **Some HMO's offer members a wide range of services, including clinics to stop smoking and weight reduction groups.**

For people whose jobs do not provide HMO or other health benefits, information resources include county medical societies, health departments, or public libraries. There may be a listing of health maintenance organizations in the yellow pages as well.

If an HMO is available, the next step is to decide whether this kind of healthcare coverage is right for your family. To accomplish this, you may have to explore the costs and benefits of several competing HMO's.

The best way to gather information on an HMO is to call the membership department and request a packet of printed materials. (An employer-sponsored HMO will probably distribute these materials to eligible workers.) The packet should include a copy of the member handbook, a map showing where service centers or participating physicians are located, and a list of staff or participating physicians, including information about their specialties, training, and credentials, such as board certification. Find out whether there's an open house for prospective members, or ask to make an appointment to see the facility (if there is one) and ask questions. If health coverage is provided through an employer or union benefit program, be sure you're getting information on the program that is available to you; the same HMO may have several options or customized packages for different groups.

Among the first questions you'll want answered is whether you will save money or spend more by switching to an HMO. What are the premiums, and are there any deductibles? Are fees charged when you see a doctor? If so, what are they?

This information must be weighed, of course, against whether you'll receive more services or fewer than your health insurance plan now covers. Some HMO's offer stop smoking clinics, weight reduction groups, discounts on health club memberships, and exercise classes. If you'll take advantage of these services, they are a plus. Some plans offer dental and/or vision care services. You'll want to know how comprehensive these offerings are, since some plans provide fairly limited care. Is orthodontic treatment included? How about new glasses? Are prescription drugs covered? What about mental health services, and to what extent? And what is the policy on second opinions?

Another important consideration is convenience. Will the health-care providers in the HMO be in more or less convenient locations than the physicians and others you now see? Will you have to travel farther? Is public transportation or adequate parking nearby? And will the HMO's services be available during more or fewer convenient hours than your current care-givers offer? What about weekend and nighttime coverage? How long must you wait for an appointment with a primary care physician or a specialist?

If you're considering joining an HMO, it is very important to find out whether a plan meets the particular needs of your family.

Find out which hospital the HMO uses most often. Is this the hospital you would probably go to anyway, or is it one you would prefer not to use?

You should find out how the HMO handles healthcare benefits for members who spend substantial amounts of time away from home. This is important not only when you travel on business or vacation but also for children who are away at summer camp or school and for retired people who may spend part of the year in the Northeast and the winter months in Florida or Arizona.

It is impossible to predict the kinds of medical care anyone will need in the future, but you can at least find out whether you're comfortable with the way the HMO treats the known medical problems of your family. Are allergy injections given at convenient times? How available is a cardiologist? A podiatrist? Young couples may want to know about maternity care. US HealthCare offers a home-care program for new mothers that has undoubtedly sent many women home from the hospital with fewer worries about caring for a newborn.

Of course, the answers to all these questions must be compared to the evaluation you give the medical care you now receive. Do you spend much money out-of-pocket, or are most healthcare costs reimbursed by your current insurance company? Can you conveniently see most of your physicians, or do you have to travel long distances and settle for appointments at inconvenient times?

Are you happy with the doctors who are now caring for you and your family? Would joining an HMO mean losing the services of care-givers with whom you are comfortable? If so, the savings may not be worth the disadvantage of making the change. You should also consider the fact that critics of the HMO system contend that if a plan doctor is receiving a set fee per patient, it may be in the doctor's financial interest to provide less thorough care.

It's important to find out what to do if you join an HMO and you're not happy. How much notice must be given before withdrawing from the health plan? How do you regain your previous health coverage? And what is the grievance system at the HMO if you have a complaint about the service? How difficult is it to switch doctors within the HMO if you do not develop a good rapport with the first one? And what happens if the HMO goes out of business—a situation that does occur?

Some people are not comfortable with the idea of prepaid healthcare, preferring the fee-for-service method of paying and wider choice of doctors. Many doctors prefer to practice without the umbrella of an HMO. There are, of course, both patients and physicians who have left HMO's because they were not happy there. But the large number of Americans who have chosen this system for their healthcare seems to reflect at least a reasonable level of satisfaction. ☐

Curing Bed-wetting

Nathan H. Azrin, Ph.D.
Michael A. Azrin, M.D.
Victoria A. Besalel, Ph.D.

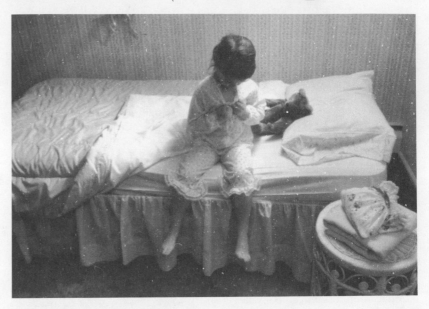

Bed-wetting, involuntary nighttime urination occurring beyond the age at which bladder control is expected, is a fairly common problem, and a frequently frustrating one for both parents and child. Bed-wetting (or nocturnal enuresis) occurs most often, though certainly not exclusively, in younger children, and it is twice as common in boys as in girls.

Parents often consider a child's bed-wetting an indication of laziness and react by punishing the child. Some parents see bed-wetting as an indication of an emotional problem and consequently overindulge their child. Still other parents view the problem as a developmental stage that the child will grow out of; these parents become indifferent to the problem, though it may persist for years. For the child, bed-wetting can cause shame and embarrassment. But with current medical knowledge and treatments, there is no need for punishment, indifference, or overindulgence on the part of the parents and mental anguish in the child.

In girls full bladder control is usually achieved by age five, and in boys, by age six. Therefore, although toddlers and preschoolers may be essentially toilet trained, at least during the day, wetting the bed at night will occur in about three-quarters of two-year-olds, one-half of three-year-olds, and one-fifth of five-year-olds. Brief regressions to wetting the bed in a toilet-trained child may also occur during stressful times—for instance, when a new baby comes home from the hospital. If enuresis persists beyond the age of five or six, it becomes a diagnosable condition.

Among those children still wetting the bed at age five, about 15 percent will spontaneously stop doing so in each succeeding year. Nevertheless, 1 to 3 percent of children will still have the problem at the age of 20.

Contributing Factors

There is clearly a family tendency to enuresis; the likelihood of developing the problem is directly related to the number of close relatives with a similar history. If both parents were bed wetters, about three-quarters of their children will have the problem.

It was previously believed that deep sleep contributed to bed-wetting, but studies of sleep habits have shown that enuretic episodes occur at random during the different stages of sleep. Also, it was once believed that enuresis was caused by psychological problems. It is now believed that any increase in emotional difficulties in this group is an effect of enuresis and its stigma and not the cause of the enuresis.

Medical Causes

While the vast majority of children with enuresis do not have an identifiable medical problem or urologic abnormality, a number of disorders can cause or contribute to bed-wetting. These problems can be readily detected by a physician through routine examination and testing.

Urinary tract infections may result in bed-wetting. Screening for such infections can be done through urine analysis and culture. Various diseases that may cause enuresis need to be ruled out. These include conditions that cause larger volumes of urine to be excreted, such as diabetes or sickle-cell diseases (inherited disorders of the red blood cells); diseases that result in the blockage of urine flow, in fecal impaction, or in irritation of the vagina or genital area; and perhaps even food allergies, which may produce irritation of the bladder.

Certain neurological problems, such as spinal cord lesions and brain damage, can result in enuresis. Mental retardation or developmental delay is also associated with enuresis.

For the vast majority of bed wetters, no medical or urologic cause can be identified. In such cases the bed-wetting is called functional enuresis.

Drug Treatment

When no underlying medical problem can be identified, effective medical treatment for bed-wetting consists mainly of drug therapy. Of the large number of drugs that have been tried, the oral antidepressant drug imipramine (sold under the brand name Tofranil) has been shown to be effective in stopping bed-wetting and is the only drug approved for this use by the U.S. Food and Drug Administration. Imipramine is initially effective in as many as three-quarters of patients. However, this rate of effectiveness drops to less than one-half after only two weeks of therapy. Long-term cures are seen in only about one-quarter of patients. Thus, although there is often initial improvement, some patients do not respond to the medication at all, others become tolerant to the effects, and enuresis often recurs when the drug is discontinued.

How imipramine acts is unclear. Its effect on bed-wetting does not seem to be clearly related to its antidepressant effect because the anti-enuretic response usually occurs in the first week of use, whereas the antidepressant effect in general takes longer and requires higher doses. Nor does the effect seem to be achieved by causing increasing wakefulness. Rather, it is thought that imipramine works primarily by acting on the muscles of the bladder.

The side effects of imipramine are infrequent but can include dry mouth, dry eyes, changes in sleep and personality, and gastrointestinal symptoms. Overdoses can cause seizures, stupor, respiratory depression, high or low blood pressure, irregular heartbeat, or congestive heart failure and can be fatal. In some instances the child has taken large doses in an effort to hasten progress. This must be prevented.

Antispasmodic drugs like oxybutinin (Ditropan) inhibit the muscular activity involved in urination. Although results with these drugs are generally disappointing, they may be helpful in some cases. But they often have side effects, such as drowsiness, nausea, and constipation.

A possible future addition to the medical arsenal against enuresis is a drug called desmopressin (brand name, DDAVP), which is used in treating certain forms of diabetes and hemophilia. It prevents bed-wetting by causing fluid retention. It rapidly ends bed-wetting, but enuresis resumes as soon as the patient stops taking the drug. The side effects have not yet been fully documented. The drug may be most valuable for occasional overnight visits away from home.

Parents and children must be fully informed of the possible dangers of anti-enuretic drugs. Because of the high relapse rate and the possible side effects of medications, restraint should be exercised in their use; they should be avoided in children under age six.

Behavior Therapy

Three types of behavior therapy have been tried for bed-wetting. The first suggests as a plausible cause of bed-wetting that the child's bladder has not developed a sufficient capacity. Treatment thus consists of rewarding the child to delay daytime urination so as to build up the functional bladder capacity. Clinical tests have shown this simple method to be slightly beneficial.

In 1938 researchers first developed and tested a method of alerting the sleeping child and parents at the moment of bed-wetting. A thin pad containing a circuit sensitive to urine is placed on the mattress and sounds an alarm as soon as the child begins to urinate, causing the child to awaken. Eventually, the child will either wake up when there is an urge to urinate, or, more commonly, will remain asleep and not wet the bed. This method has been found to be about 80 percent effective in extensive clinical tests. About 20 percent of those cured by this method suffer a relapse after they stop using the apparatus, but retraining with the circuit and alarm usually eliminates the problem again.

The third treatment, called the dry-bed method, was developed more recently. Its proponents see bed-wetting as a deficiency in learning that requires special training and motivation to correct. Indeed, this method was initially developed for severely retarded people for whom alternative treatments were not effective. The child is taught to be more aware of bladder sensations, to take responsibility for the episodes by remaking the bed, to learn to retain the urine during the day or night for progressively longer periods, and to practice leaving the bed to go to the toilet when bladder urges arise. Extensive rewards are used for partial successes, to increase motivation. Clinical tests show that the method is more effective than either the bladder-capacity or the urine-alarm method. Bed-wetting is almost entirely decreased, and relapses are fewer and are almost always treated successfully by reinstating the training briefly. The bladder-training, urine-alarm, and dry-bed procedures may be used concurrently for increased effectiveness. □

Suggestions for Further Reading

AZRIN, NATHAN H., and VICTORIA A. BE-SALEL. *A Parent's Guide to Bedwetting Control: A Step by Step Method.* New York, Pocket Books, 1981.

AZRIN, NATHAN H., and RICHARD M. FOXX. *Toilet Training in Less Than a Day.* New York, Pocket Books, 1976.

FOXX, RICHARD M., and NATHAN H. AZRIN. *Toilet Training the Retarded: A Rapid Program for Day and Nighttime Independent Toileting.* Champaign, Ill., Research Press, 1973.

HEPATITIS

Rowen K. Zetterman, M.D.

Hepatitis (or more precisely, acute viral hepatitis) is a generalized infection that mainly affects liver cells. The cells are damaged either directly by one of several viruses or by the body's immune reaction to the virus.

The two most common types of viral hepatitis are hepatitis A (originally called infectious hepatitis) and hepatitis B (originally serum hepatitis). The terms infectious and serum hepatitis were replaced because they had misleading implications, since both illnesses can be spread by person-to-person contact. When diagnostic blood tests became available for hepatitis A and hepatitis B, it was obvious there were patients with hepatitis that was neither hepatitis A nor hepatitis B. These patients were, therefore, said to have non-A, non-B (nAnB) hepatitis. Recently, another form of the disease—called hepatitis D or delta hepatitis—has been identified.

Why the hepatitis viruses damage the liver is unclear. Some may directly injure liver cells (nAnB and D), while others (A and B) may indirectly lead to the destruction of liver cells when the immune system becomes activated to rid the body of the virus. As the virus reproduces in liver cells, part of its surface coat may be incorporated into the cell membranes. Then, as lymphocytes (white blood cells) become activated against the hepatitis virus, they also see the liver cell membranes as abnormal. The lymphocytes destroy the liver cells while also destroying the virus.

Symptoms and Complications

Patients with hepatitis may have mild symptoms that go unnoticed or are simply thought of as the "flu," or they may be so ill from life-threatening destruction of liver cells that they go into a coma. In a typical case, the patient experiences nausea, loss of appetite, vomiting, weakness, and tiredness. The person may develop jaundice (yellow eyes or skin), darkening of the urine, or light-colored stools. For most patients, symptoms last one to six weeks. Then they disappear, and the individual makes a complete recovery. Fortunately, liver cells can regenerate.

When more than 60 percent of liver cells are destroyed, however, fulminant hepatitis can occur. Patients with fulminant hepatitis

There is no definite therapy for hepatitis beyond resting in bed, drinking lots of fluids, and eating enough food.

may go into a coma. Death from fulminant hepatitis may be caused by brain swelling (edema) or such complications as bleeding or infection.

Hospitalization for hepatitis is usually not required unless the patient is very sick. If there are concerns about the cause or severity of hepatitis, a liver biopsy can be performed by putting a needle into the liver and withdrawing a specimen to examine under the microscope for damage to liver cells. This is not usually done in the typical viral hepatitis patient.

While hepatitis symptoms may be mild, some hepatitis B patients can suffer life-threatening complications.

Although most patients recover from viral hepatitis, some develop chronic hepatitis. Chronic hepatitis is a condition of continuing infection and/or liver cell damage that may lead, for some patients, to the scarring of the liver called cirrhosis. In cirrhosis, the liver is distorted by fibrous scars that interfere with its functioning. If this disruption is severe, death can result. Not all patients with chronic hepatitis progress to severe liver damage.

At present, there is no definite therapy for acute viral hepatitis other than bed rest and adequate fluid and food intake.

Hepatitis A

Infection of susceptible people with the hepatitis A virus will lead to illness between 15 to 50 days following exposure. This interval is called the incubation period. (People who have previously contracted hepatitis A are immune to the disease, and no longer susceptible.)

The hepatitis A virus reproduces in the liver cells, subsequently enters the intestines, and is eliminated in the feces. Contamination of water or food by infected feces can lead to ingestion of the virus. Shellfish in contaminated water may also pick up the virus and transmit hepatitis A when eaten. Conditions of poor sanitation and crowding contribute to transmission. As a consequence, hepatitis A is more common in lower socioeconomic areas and developing countries.

Most cases are isolated, and a source may not be evident. Rarely, an epidemic may occur where an individual with acute hepatitis A is shedding virus in the stool and fails to adequately wash contaminated hands. If such an individual prepares uncooked food for many people (a restaurant worker, for example), a hepatitis A outbreak may occur.

Day-care centers may be another place for transmission when the children in attendance are in diapers. Contamination of the children's hands by feces and subsequent handling of toys may lead to transmission of the virus, especially if other children put the toys into their mouths. In families, intimate contact and sharing of utensils and dishes may promote infection; however, adequate dish and hand washing can prevent intrafamily spread.

Hepatitis A is generally mild and often unrecognized as a hepatitis illness. Rarely, the illness can be severe and lead to fulminant hepatitis. Some patients may take weeks to recover; however, no patients have been reported to develop chronic hepatitis from hepatitis A.

Vaccines for prevention of hepatitis A are being developed, though none are yet available. If a person is intimately exposed to a patient with hepatitis A or ingests contaminated food or water, an intramuscular injection of gamma globulin (immune serum globulin) may prevent or reduce the severity of infection. Gamma globulin is

the part of human blood containing protein molecules called antibodies. The antibodies can bind to a virus, rendering it inactive and also making the virus a target for other parts of the immune system. A gamma globulin injection is not usually required for casual contact.

Hepatitis B

Hepatitis B can cause illness 30 to 180 days following exposure. It is often transmitted by blood transfusion or sharing of contaminated needles; however, it can also be transmitted by direct person-to-person contact. Hepatitis B virus is not transmitted by feces; rather, the virus is in the blood and most secretions of the body. Intimate contact with one of these, such as saliva, may allow the virus to enter the recipient's body through breaks in the mucous membranes or skin. Transmission may occur

---

Vaccination for hepatitis B is recommended for such high-risk groups as dentists, nurses, and drug addicts.

---

through sexual intercourse, sharing of contaminated articles (a toothbrush, for example), or other intimate contact. Sporadic cases without an obvious source occur as well. Hepatitis B may also be transmitted from an infected mother to her offspring shortly after birth. The mother must either have acute viral hepatitis B or be an infectious carrier of the virus at the time of delivery.

In the United States hepatitis B is the most common cause of viral hepatitis with obvious symptoms. The illness is generally mild. However, it can also lead to fulminant hepatitis, and 5 to 10 percent of patients have continuing liver damage (chronic hepatitis).

In some patients the immune system fails to completely kill the virus, and these people become carriers. They can be identified by test results showing a portion of the virus in the blood more than six months after initial infection. Some carriers remain infectious for long periods of time. Hepatitis B virus can also cause liver cancer.

Vaccines have been developed for hepatitis B and are recommended for such high-risk groups as newborns of infected mothers, family members of carriers, people in high-risk occupations (for example, oral surgeons, dentists, some physicians, and nurses), homosexuals, prisoners, and drug addicts. For those with direct or needlestick exposure to hepatitis B, a form of gamma globulin called hyperimmune B immunoglobulin, which has a large amount of hepatitis B antibody, can be given.

Non-A, non-B Hepatitis

To date, the viruses responsible for non-A, non-B hepatitis have not been identified. Studies of patients and epidemics suggest there are three viruses, known as long-incubation, short-incubation, and enterically transmitted. A diagnosis of nAnB hepatitis is made when the patient has symptoms of hepatitis, but blood tests show no evidence of infection with either the hepatitis A or B virus.

Long-incubation nAnB hepatitis has an incubation period of 30 to 180 days and can be transmitted in blood or other body fluids as hepatitis B is. The virus is the most common cause of hepatitis occurring from transfusion, accounting for 95 percent of all cases. It can also occur in isolated cases where there has been no previous blood exposure. From 10 to 42 percent of patients may become carriers of the virus. However, the lack of a specific blood test makes identification of carriers difficult.

Long-incubation nAnB hepatitis is generally a mild illness with typical symptoms of viral hepatitis. It

can also cause fulminant or chronic hepatitis and may be associated with liver cancer. At present, no vaccine or proven treatment is available.

Short-incubation nAnB hepatitis has an incubation period of 7 to 50 days and is usually associated with transfusion of blood clotting factor concentrates isolated from the blood of many donors. Hemophiliacs and others with bleeding disorders who require transfusion of factor concentrates are at greatest risk. Short-incubation nAnB hepatitis is usually self-limited, though chronic hepatitis may occur. It also appears that some patients may develop multiple acute episodes of viral hepatitis when repeatedly exposed to the

Two Common Types of Hepatitis

Hepatitis A
How acquired: Consuming contaminated food or water; intimate contact with an infected person; putting a contaminated object (fork, glass, another child's toy) in the mouth.
Incubation period: 15-50 days.
Symptoms: Loss of appetite, nausea and vomiting, fatigue, jaundice—lasting 1-6 weeks.
Risk of complications: Low.
Vaccine available: No. A gamma globulin injection after exposure may prevent or reduce the severity of illness.
Treatment: Bed rest, plenty of fluids, adequate food intake.

Hepatitis B
How acquired: Receiving contaminated blood or blood products; sharing a contaminated needle or syringe; intimate contact; may be transmitted from mother to child shortly after birth.
Incubation period: 30-180 days.
Symptoms: Same as for hepatitis A.
Risk of complications: 5-10 percent of patients develop chronic hepatitis; may lead to liver cancer.
Vaccine available: Yes; recommended for high-risk groups such as family members of carriers, drug addicts, some healthcare workers. A type of gamma globulin may be given after exposure.
Treatment: Same as for hepatitis A.

virus. No vaccine or treatment method is available.

Enterically transmitted nAnB hepatitis is similar in epidemiology to hepatitis A. Transmission appears to be by fecal-oral means, and large-scale outbreaks have occurred following water contamination. Typical acute viral hepatitis symptoms occur, though some groups seem particularly at risk for fulminant hepatitis. In one outbreak fulminant hepatitis deaths occurred in 10 percent of pregnant women who became ill with enterically transmitted nAnB hepatitis. It is unclear whether chronic hepatitis occurs following infections. Patients do develop antibodies to the virus. Gamma globulin harvested from these people can provide postexposure protection for exposed patients. To date, no outbreaks of enterically transmitted nAnB have been identified in the United States, though isolated cases following initial exposure in another country have occurred.

Hepatitis D

Hepatitis D is an unusual infectious agent. Sometimes called the delta agent, it is apparently an incomplete virus that requires the simultaneous presence of the hepatitis B virus to infect liver cells. Hepatitis D utilizes the surface coat of the B virus to coat itself. Although similar viruses are observed in plants, this is the first such human virus identified. Infection with hepatitis D increases the probability that someone who is also infected with hepatitis B will develop fulminant hepatitis or cirrhosis.

Transmission appears to be by blood and other body fluids. Blood tests that detect antibodies to hepatitis D are available to aid in diagnosis of the disease.

Although no method of treatment for hepatitis D is available, prevention of hepatitis B through vaccination or administration of hyperimmune B immunoglobulin should also protect a person from hepatitis D. ☐

HEALTH AND
MEDICAL NEWS

Aging and the Aged

Paying for Long-term Care • Abuse of the Elderly • Aging and Increased Suicide Risk • New Treatments for Depression

Long-term Care Insurance

Alternative methods of paying for nursing home stays are receiving increased attention as the American population ages. Many insurance companies are beginning to offer plans that include long-term care coverage, partly because few employee or retirement benefit packages include such insurance.

This type of coverage is likely to become more common since the population of the United States is aging. There are now 28 million people aged 65 or over, representing 12 percent of the population. By the year 2030 the proportion of people aged 65 or older will exceed 20 percent. Some older people become limited in their ability to perform basic daily activities (bathing, dressing, using the toilet, feeding themselves, cooking, or shopping). If they have no family members or close friends to assume these tasks, these individuals frequently need to be placed in nursing homes. Currently, 5 percent of the U.S. population over the age of 64 resides in nursing homes, with the percentage rising to 20 percent for those aged 80 or older. With dramatic increases anticipated in the number of people surviving to very old ages, the number of nursing home residents is expected to rise proportionately.

Since nursing home stays cost from $20,000 to $40,000 a year, few people can afford them for extended periods of time. Medicare, the federal health insurance program for the aged and disabled, does not pay for extended nursing home care, nor is that care completely covered by the "catastrophic coverage" legislation introduced in Congress in 1987, or by insurance policies to supplement medicare, such as medigap. Payment, then, becomes the responsibility of the individual or of medicaid, the government health program for the poor, if the individual is impoverished. Those elderly who are not impoverished must look to other sources of financial assistance if they need to stay in a nursing home and want to protect their lifetime savings.

Anyone interested in buying long-term care insurance should be aware of several pitfalls with these policies. First, the costs of such policies vary widely and will be higher for people who are older or have underlying medical conditions. Second, the cost of such insurance—which can be more than $100 per month—must be carefully weighed against the chance that long-term care will ever be needed. The difficulty here is that catastrophes such as a broken hip or a stroke are hard to predict. People must essentially decide whether their families would be able to care for them in such an event. An individual with no surviving spouse or heirs may be less concerned with drains on savings for medical expenses and so may have little interest in paying for long-term care insurance.

Other variables to examine when considering long-term care insurance include whether or not home care is covered (often an enviable alternative to nursing home care), what restrictions on eligibility exist, what deductibles are required, and the length of coverage available.

Elder Abuse

Despite the devotion demonstrated by many families toward their dependent elderly relatives, abuse of the elderly is a serious and frequently unrecognized problem. It affects approximately 1 out of every 25 older Americans. Elder abuse is reported in only 1 out of 5 cases (compared with 1 out of 3 cases of child abuse). Funds devoted to protective services for the elderly amount to one-tenth of those spent on child abuse, despite the fact that elder abuse represents 40 percent of all cases of abuse.

Elder abuse may be so seldom reported because its victims often deny problems for fear of abandonment or retribution. Healthcare workers may often fail to react to even the most obvious signs of abuse. This "inattention" by healthcare workers, although usually not deliberate, may stem from fears of confronting family members who are the sole support for many elderly patients and from a lack of knowledge concerning abuse of the elderly.

People at risk for abuse include those aged 75 and older, females, people who have suffered from multiple physical and/or mental impairments for several years, and those who are without financial resources. The abuser is a relative in almost all cases and has a 75 percent likelihood of living with the victim.

Abuse of the elderly may be physical, sexual, or psychological. Passive neglect, however, is most frequent and often manifests itself as malnutrition, poor personal hygiene, and improper administration of medications or treatments.

There are many causes of elder abuse, including the stresses inherent in caring for severely disabled and dependent relatives and mental disturbances in the abuser. Although most states have enacted legislation to protect the elderly from abuse, the scope of such legislation remains highly variable and often lacks the necessary clout to ensure effective intervention in abuse cases.

Suicide and the Elderly

The elderly have the highest suicide rate of all age groups in the United States. This is an unappreciated problem. Youthful suicides are more numerous because of the larger number of young people in the United States, but an elderly person is at higher risk of a suicide death, with rates peaking at age 80.

Variable rates. Researchers have noted that the risk of suicide in the elderly is not uniform across the population. White males 75 to 84 years of age have the highest suicide rate of any group in the United States, with 45.5 deaths per 100,000 people a year. This rate contrasts sharply with the rate for white females of the same age (5.7 deaths per 100,000 a year) and for nonwhite males and females of the same age (11.2 and 2.6 per 100,000, respectively).

Possible causes. A number of factors may contribute to the alarming suicide rate in the elderly. Depression, thought to be a major factor in all suicides, is made worse in the elderly by chronic diseases and subsequent disability. Social isolation and the recent loss of a spouse are also strongly associated with the risk of suicide in the elderly, especially in elderly men.

Living in a continuing-care community is a welcome alternative for many elderly people who might otherwise be forced to enter a nursing home. The residents of a Pomona, Calif., community (at right) have unlimited access to the facility's nursing home at no extra cost should they require medical care. Another alternative is living at home but spending the day at an adult center (left, a neighborhood facility in San Francisco).

Poverty that is of recent onset and not a lifelong condition is also associated with increased suicide risk. While drug and alcohol use are prevalent among youthful suicide victims, they are less likely to be involved in elderly suicides.

White males seem particularly vulnerable to the effects of losses—such as loss of economic resources, social prestige, and self-esteem—perhaps because their expectations of such societal rewards are higher than for women or minorities. In addition, many non-whites in the United States tend to hold the elderly in higher esteem and to accept the consequences of aging better than do whites.

In contrast to youthful suicides, elderly suicides are preceded by few warning signals. Older persons also have a higher suicide success rate than younger people; in the elderly 1 out of 4 suicide attempts results in death, compared with 1 out of 20 in the young.

Confounding the data on elderly suicides is the fact that many suicides may be attributed to disease or accidents. Families may be embarrassed and may try to disguise the suicide. Physicians may be more inclined to attribute death in older people to natural causes or to an accident, when in fact the cause may sometimes be an overdose, the failure to take a needed medication, or an intentional car crash.

Elderly people die of many things; suicide is only the tenth leading cause of death in the elderly. Nonetheless, it remains a senseless and preventable waste of life. If timely recognition of the elderly at risk of suicide can be made by alert families and healthcare workers, and appropriate intervention taken, important strides will have been made.

Treating Depression

Because older adults often have a variety of medical problems, treating them for depression can be especially difficult. Two newly rediscovered treatments—an antidepressant medication and electroconvulsive therapy—may work more quickly and with fewer side effects than standard therapies.

Standard antidepressant drugs may induce a plethora of side effects, including the inability to urinate, oversedation, confusion, and serious heart rhythm disturbances. In addition, standard drugs have a very gradual effect, with patients continuing to be depressed for weeks or even months after therapy is begun. This delay in effect can be life threatening if, for instance, a patient is refusing to eat.

The first newly rediscovered treatment is the drug methylphenidate (sold under the brand name Ritalin). Methylphenidate can be used in low doses, with very rapid and dramatic improvements in alertness, appetite, and mood. This has been shown to be particularly important and effective in cancer patients and other medically ill depressed individuals who are essentially starving because of lack of appetite. Despite potential side effects, including heart rhythm disorders, methylphenidate has been shown to be safe for the elderly when prescribed in small doses by a physician familiar with its use.

Electroconvulsive therapy, or ECT, was so misused and received such bad publicity from the 1950's to the 1970's that many psychiatrists discontinued its use altogether. This represented a therapeutic setback in the treatment of severe depression, in that, when used cautiously and appropriately, ECT can provide dramatic improvements. General anesthesia and powerful muscle relaxants are now used during ECT to eliminate any outward signs of a seizure during treatment. In addition, the anesthesiologist carefully controls the patient's breathing to prevent injury from lack of oxygen. These improvements, as well as recent technical advances such as the development of a machine that can give the equivalent of four treatments in a single session, make ECT not only much safer than it was 20 years ago but also more effective.

Depressed patients treated with ECT or methylphenidate respond much more rapidly than do patients treated with the usual antidepressant medications. These two methods of therapy are now important alternatives for the treatment of elderly patients whose medical conditions prevent the use of the standard therapies or in whom it is necessary to rapidly lift depressive symptoms in order to preserve life.

See also the Spotlight on Health articles Caring for an Alzheimer's Patient *and* Exercise After 50.

Paul R. Katz, M.D.
Teresa P. Chau, M.D.

Arthritis and Rheumatism

Anticancer Drug Helpful • Fatigue and Rheumatoid Arthritis • The Role of Education and Exercise • Inflammation of the Gut and Ankylosing Spondylitis

Methotrexate Therapy

Interest continues to grow in the use of methotrexate, the well-known anticancer drug, for treatment of rheumatoid arthritis, one of the most common types of arthritis. Rheumatoid arthritis is a disorder of the immune system; why this system sometimes malfunctions and causes chronic inflammation of the joints is not known. While aspirin and the nonsteroidal anti-inflammatory drugs can modify the symptoms of inflammation (pain, heat, swelling, and stiffness), they frequently are ineffective in stopping the inflammatory process itself. So-called second-line agents, such as antimalarial drugs, gold salts, and penicillamine (a derivative of penicillin), do modify the inflammatory process, but the symptoms may not improve for several months.

Methotrexate had been found to be beneficial in treating psoriasis (a common skin disorder) and rheumatoid arthritis in the early 1950's. However, it was only in the late 1970's and early 1980's, with increased medical understanding of arthritic inflammation, that doctors again became widely interested in using it for treating the latter disease. Methotrexate is now recommended for this purpose by the American College of Physicians, and while it hasn't yet been approved specifically for rheumatoid arthritis by the U.S. Food and Drug Administration, physicians are legally entitled to prescribe it for this disorder. With the informed consent of patients, many rheumatologists are doing so for cases that have proven resistant to other treatments.

Like azathioprine, another anticancer drug that has been used to treat rheumatoid arthritis, methotrexate is an immunosuppressant; that is, it inhibits the functioning of the immune system. Only a fraction of the dosage of methotrexate used for treating cancer is required in the treatment of rheumatoid arthritis. As a result, relatively few arthritis patients experience serious side effects.

Since patients frequently show a positive response to methotrexate as early as the first month of administration, its usefulness may be assessed sooner than that of the more traditional second-line treatments for rheumatoid arthritis. Although true remission from the disease is rare, results from short-term studies of methotrexate therapy show a 26 percent decline in the number of inflamed joints and a 30 percent reduction in overall pain. A recent study comparing methotrexate therapy with gold therapy found that the former was equally effective and produced less toxic side effects over a six-month period.

The oral dosage schedule for methotrexate in rheumatoid arthritis, adapted from that used in psoriasis, is three doses per week, with these doses taken over a 24-hour period, at 12-hour intervals. A few studies have shown the drug to be equally effective when taken in a single larger weekly dose. Some physicians prefer weekly intramuscular injections to ensure that their patients are taking the drug and to make it easier to monitor side effects. Occasionally, switching from the oral to the intramuscular dosage route has improved responsiveness, presumably because of better absorption.

Methotrexate treatment has to be discontinued in about one-third of patients because of side effects, which commonly include gastrointestinal problems, mouth ulcers, anemia, decreased counts of white blood cells and platelets, and loss of hair. The side effects sometimes respond to a lowering of the dosage and are usually reversible. Life-threatening complications from methotrexate are rare, occurring in less than 1 percent of treated cases. These include liver damage, bone marrow suppression (which results in a decline in the production of new blood cells), and inflammation of the lungs. Because fetal abnormalities are known to be associated with its use, methotrexate is not prescribed for women who may become pregnant. It is also more dangerous in patients with abnormal kidney function, and it is used with caution in the elderly.

Judging from the experience of its use in psoriasis, there is a long-term risk of liver cirrhosis in 3-5 percent of patients on methotrexate therapy. Liver biopsy is recommended for patients after two years on the drug, and monthly monitoring of blood counts and liver function is advisable. Alcoholism, diabetes, and obesity have been identified as significant risk factors for this complication. Patients who consume more than 14 ounces of 100-proof liquor or the equivalent on a weekly basis should not have the drug prescribed for them.

Disrupted Sleep Patterns

In addition to pain, stiffness, and limitation of mobility, patients suffering from active rheumatoid arthritis frequently complain of fatigue. Previously, doctors thought this symptom reflected a secondary response to inflammation. But a recent study that assessed the quality and amount of sleep in patients with rheumatoid arthritis, as compared with people without the disease, found that the patients experienced more frequent disruption of normal sleep patterns, even though they were not aware of such disruption upon awakening. These findings were similar to the abnormalities found in patients with fibromyalgia (nonjoint rheumatism), who also experience fatigue as a prominent symptom.

Education and Exercise

Helping patients cope physically and psychologically with the restrictions of chronic arthritis remains an important part of treatment of the disease, and a novel approach to this task, termed Educize, has been found to benefit people with rheumatoid arthritis. In the study that produced this finding, conducted at Evanston Hospital in Evanston, Ill., three groups of patients were compared. One group participated in a standard Arthritis Self-Help course, which fosters mutual support for adjustment to the physical and emotional effects of having arthritis. A second group participated in an exercise program consisting of low-impact aerobic dance. In addition to this exercise, the third, or Educize, group also participated in classes that focused on improving patients' skill in solving physical problems posed by their arthritis rather than just increasing their knowledge of the disease. The Educize group experienced the most significant overall benefits, including a decrease in pain and depression and an increase in physical activity and general psychological well-being. This study confirmed that patients with rheumatoid arthritis can benefit from a structured exercise program and that the effects of such a program are measurably greater when it is coupled with education to instill a "can do" attitude.

Ankylosing Spondylitis

Recent research has suggested that arthritis of the knees and hips may sometimes result from gastrointestinal disorders. Arthritis is known to be a possible complication of inflammatory bowel disorders, such as Crohn's disease and ulcerative colitis, and of certain diarrheal infections. Recent studies have found unsuspected inflammation of the gut in certain patients with ankylosing spondylitis, a chronic, progressive arthritis of the spine that most commonly affects men and that usually leads to deformity. The patients suffered from arthritis of their peripheral joints (knees and hips) in addition to back pain due to spinal involvement.

When biopsies were obtained from the small intestine of each patient where it connects with the colon, abnormalities similar to those found in Crohn's disease were present even though the patients did not have gastrointestinal symptoms. Subsequent biopsies were found to be normal if the arthritis symptoms had improved. These findings suggested that the peripheral arthritis characteristic of ankylosing spondylitis may be related to abnormalities in the gut. The arthritis may be an immune reaction either to foreign proteins absorbed from the patient's diet or to normal gut microbes.

Sulfasalazine, a sulfa drug used to treat inflammatory bowel disease, has also been found to be beneficial in treating rheumatoid arthritis, and recently its effectiveness has been tested in patients with ankylosing spondylitis and a related disorder known as reactive arthritis. Improvement was found in a majority of the patients treated, and there were few side effects.

M. E. Csuka, M.D.

Bioethics

Refusing Treatment for the Dying • Do-not-resuscitate Law • Transplanting Fetal Tissue and Infants' Organs • Ongoing Debate Over Surrogate Motherhood

Treatment for the Dying

Guidelines on termination of treatment. The most comprehensive guidelines ever developed for forgoing life-sustaining treatment of dying patients were published in September 1987 by the Hastings Center, a New York medical ethics research institute. The "Guidelines on the Termination of Life-Sustaining Treatment and the Care of the Dying" were the result of a 2½-year study by a group of 20 specialists in the fields of health, law, and ethics. The guidelines built on previous documents, such as a 1983 report by the President's Commission for the Study of Ethical Problems in Medicine and Biomedical and Behavioral Research, which addressed ethical issues but did not offer specific guidelines. Though they do not have the force of law, the Hastings Center guidelines are likely to influence healthcare administrators in designing related policies for their institutions.

The guidelines are based upon a growing national consensus that the patient or the patient's representative has the right to refuse or to stop any life-sustaining treatment, including medication and artificially administered food and water. This broadened notion of "treatment" has sparked particular disagreement, especially concerning the inclusion of feeding in the scope of medical treatment.

A more general issue addressed by the report, one that will surely be an area of continuing debate as the costs of healthcare increase, is whether financial considerations should affect decisions to terminate treatment of the dying. Although the guidelines state that there is currently no economic justification for rationing life-sustaining care for those near death, policymakers may wish to develop policies to limit wasteful or costly practices. According to the guidelines, patients themselves should determine which treatments are "costworthy," but society must assure them that their decisions need not be affected by their ability to pay for the costs of care. Currently, tens of millions of underinsured and uninsured Americans have no such assurances. The guidelines attribute this prob-

Mary Beth Whitehead-Gould, who lost her legal battle to keep "Baby M," the daughter she bore under contract, won a partial victory when her parental rights were restored and the contract she signed was declared illegal by the New Jersey Supreme Court in February 1988. Whitehead-Gould, shown at right at a press conference after the court decision, was established as the child's legal mother, although the father retained custody. In an ongoing Michigan case, a court awarded surrogate Laurie Yates (above, with her husband) temporary custody of the twins she bore under contract.

lem partly to lack of consensus about the meaning of costworthy medical care. Without such agreement, it is very difficult to decide what level of care is decent, adequate, and can be available to all.

The case of Nancy Ellen Jobes. In June 1987 the New Jersey Supreme Court ruled that the wishes of a patient or a patient's surrogate take priority over the policies of medical institutions in cases involving a patient's refusal to accept life-sustaining treatment. The ruling cleared the way for the family of Nancy Ellen Jobes to have feeding tubes removed from the comatose woman, a move the family had been urging since 1985.

In 1980, Jobes, 4½ months pregnant, was injured in an automobile accident. Her unborn child died and had to be surgically removed. During the operation, Jobes sustained a severe loss of oxygen and blood flow to the brain. She never regained consciousness, settling into a persistent vegetative state,

a condition in which a person has no awareness but continues essential biological functions, including respiration. Jobes, in a nursing home, was fed through a tube inserted in a surgically created opening near her small intestine.

Jobes's condition resembled that of Karen Ann Quinlan, another New Jersey resident whose family in 1976 won the right to have her removed from a respirator. After the respirator was disconnected, Quinlan, like Jobes, breathed on her own. (She was cared for in a nursing home until her death in 1985.) But unlike Quinlan's family, who only wanted life-support systems disconnected, Jobes's family wanted to discontinue the artificial feeding and asked the nursing home to remove the tube. The nursing home refused, stating that such an action would result in Jobes's death and would constitute euthanasia.

The case was taken to the New Jersey Supreme Court, which found itself challenged by a variety of conflicting considerations: Jobes's right to determine the course of her treatment, but her inability to do so; her family's role as surrogate decision maker; the nursing home's right to establish its own policies; and society's concern with protecting the interests of those who are gravely ill, difficult though it may be to determine those interests. Underlying all these issues was a conceptual question that permeated the debate: Should artificial feeding be considered a form of therapy, or is feeding a substantially different kind of activity that cannot ethically be denied?

As is usual in such cases, the court addressed the question of how the right representatives of incompetent patients should be chosen, since Jobes's actual wishes could not be determined. It concluded that treatment decisions could be made by close family members, close friends, or, if none were available, by a guardian. So long as these decisions are made "in good faith," they have much the same force as if they were made by the patient. The court also ruled that the nursing home could not refuse to participate in the removal of feeding tubes, especially since it did not inform the Jobes family of its policy until the request for removal of the feeding tube was made. The court observed that it was highly unlikely now

A problem in medical ethics was raised when Brenda and Michael Winner decided to carry to term their baby that would be born missing most of its brain—an always fatal condition—in the hope that its organs could be used for transplants.

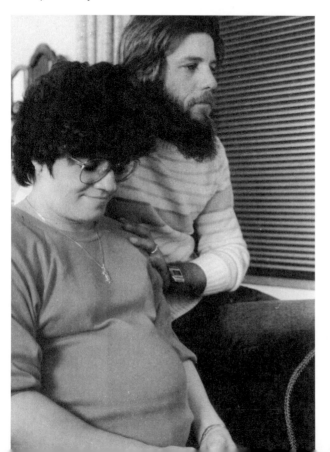

that another nursing home would accept her. Thus, the court ruled that Jobes's "right to self-determination" must be respected.

The nursing home appealed the decision to a federal court. The appeal failed, and the Jobes family removed Nancy to a hospital that had agreed to cooperate with them. Jobes's feeding tube was removed, and she died on August 7, 1987, at the age of 32.

Do-not-resuscitate law. In August 1987, New York Governor Mario Cuomo signed the first law in the United States requiring that hospitals and nursing homes withhold emergency cardiopulmonary resuscitation from patients who refuse it. Patients can in advance decide, or appoint someone to decide for them should they become incompetent, not to undergo emergency resuscitation efforts. The law also requires medical institutions to establish rules, under guidelines set by the New York State Health Department, for issuing so-called do-not-resuscitate orders for terminally ill patients.

Under the new law, do-not-resuscitate orders can be issued in medical institutions if resuscitation would probably be unsuccessful and merely prolong the dying process. If the patient or previously designated representative cannot give verbal or written permission, the decision on issuing the order may be made by two physicians or a court. The law grants criminal and civil immunity to physicians and other healthcare professionals who carry out do-not-resuscitate orders according to the procedures specified.

The New York law is different from the so-called living will legislation that has been passed (as of early 1988) by 38 other states and the District of Columbia. Those laws refer to patients who have expressed in writing their wishes to be or not to be kept alive by artificial means should they become terminally ill and unable to direct their own care. The do-not-resuscitate law relates to all patients for whom resuscitation decisions must be made. But both forms of legislation are based on the ethical principle that people's right to self-determination should be respected even when they are no longer capable of insisting upon it. The New York law takes this principle a step further by requiring that a patient's decision to delegate medical authority to a proxy be respected as well.

Using Fetal Cells

A promising new treatment for Parkinson's disease raises troubling questions about the ethics of using cells taken from fetuses.

Recent research. In 1987 public curiosity about a new surgical treatment for neurological disorders was sparked by word that former heavyweight boxing champion Muhammad Ali went to Mexico to investigate a potential therapy for his Parkinson's-like symptoms. The treatment involves transplanting cells from the adrenal glands (located above the kidneys) into the brains of people suffering from Parkinson's disease, whose symptoms include shaking, stiffness, and an inability to move at will. Doctors hope that the new brain transplant technique may also help people with other neurological problems. So far, dozens of patients throughout the world have received brain grafts of their own adrenal tissue. Operations have taken place in the United States as well, though at this early stage there is much uncertainty and disagreement about the technique's prospective effectiveness.

Adrenal gland cells produce dopamine, a chemical that carries messages between brain cells. In the case of Parkinson's disease, dopamine is lost as the brain ages. The adrenal cells are implanted in a nerve junction in the brain that controls movement. The cells are then expected to produce sufficient amounts of dopamine to alleviate the disease's symptoms.

This raises no special ethical problems, but in late 1987, Mexican and Swedish researchers began using fetal brain tissue rather than adrenal cells, because it holds the promise of greatly improving the results of the surgery. Fetal cells grow more quickly than adult cells, and tissue from a fetus is more adaptable. If the difference turns out to be dramatic, the ethical question of the widespread use of fetal material will have to be faced.

Ethical concerns. With the promise of medical benefits from using fetal tissue, critics worry that a fetus may be produced only in order to be destroyed and its body parts harvested for the benefit of another. This prospect aggravates the concern that some women may be paid to become pregnant and then electively abort an organ-providing fetus. Further, limiting donations to fetuses that are known to have been aborted for reasons other than donation may not yield the more developed fetal tissue that may be most useful in the techniques, since most elective abortions take place in the first four months of pregnancy.

Whether or not human fetuses are considered persons, should even very primitive forms of human life be conceived only to be sacrificed for the sake of those now living who suffer from diseases? Should payment for fetal donors be permitted? If not, does the good that may be done for many patients outweigh the risk of promoting a lucrative black market in fetal tissue? Should society permit the supposed exploitation of disadvantaged women who may wish to use their reproductive capacities to produce fetal donors, or is this simply a matter of reproductive freedom? The debate has just begun, and the more promising the results of the research using fetal tissue, the more lively this debate is likely to be.

See also the Spotlight on Health article PARKINSON'S DISEASE: NEW ADVANCES.

Anencephalic Babies

A slightly different ethical concern was highlighted in late 1987 by the case of a California couple who decided to carry their unborn anencephalic baby (missing most of its brain) to term in the hope that its organs could be used for transplants. The baby was stillborn and its organs unfit for transplantation, but the case raised the question of whether it is ethical to keep such babies artificially alive only so their organs can be used to treat other patients. In October 1987 an anencephalic baby girl's heart was donated to a newborn boy with a fatal heart defect at California's Loma Linda Medical Center.

Although anencephalic babies lack most of their brains, they do have brain stems, which sometimes allow them to survive for a few days, breathing on their own. Since organs are not removed from donors until the donors are declared legally dead, such babies pose special problems for doctors in deciding when death actually occurs. Under most state laws, death occurs when all brain activity stops. But if doctors wait until the brain stems of anencephalic babies stop functioning, their organs often will not have received enough oxygen to leave them suitable for transplants. Some hospitals have established policies for these babies, declaring death to occur when they stop breathing on their own. The infants are placed on respirators, which are disconnected at set intervals until spontaneous breathing stops. The babies' organs can then be donated. If brain activity is still detected after seven days, life support is removed and the baby allowed to die naturally.

Aborting Multiple Fetuses

The advance of technology has created yet another ethical dilemma in the ongoing abortion debate. Doctors are now able to perform selective abortions in the case of multiple pregnancies. When a woman is carrying so many fetuses that she is highly unlikely to carry them to term, or when a woman decides that she is unprepared to rear so many children, doctors, with the use of ultrasound techniques, can abort some of the fetuses while leaving others intact to grow to maturity.

Most cases of multiple pregnancy involve women who have taken fertility drugs or have had several embryos implanted during in vitro fertilization (commonly done, since most embryos usually do not survive). While some doctors think that a woman has the right to determine whether to carry a pregnancy to term and that physicians are not the ones to decide how many fetuses a woman should carry, others question where to draw the line. Some do consider it ethical to perform a pregnancy reduction if there is no chance all the fetuses would survive. But what about reducing quadruplets to twins? Is this any different from reducing twins to a single child or from aborting a single fetus? Since no published data is available on the dangers of such pregnancy reductions, some doctors insist that women cannot make an informed choice regarding them.

Surrogate Motherhood Controversy

In February 1988 the New Jersey Supreme Court ruled that surrogate motherhood contracts involving payment for the service were illegal because they violate the state's law that prohibits payment for adoption. The court also established the surrogate as the child's legal mother. The decision, legally binding only in New Jersey, was the first to come from a state's highest court in a case involving a surrogate's efforts to keep a child.

The case involved Mary Beth Whitehead-Gould, the surrogate mother who in March 1987 lost her first legal effort to keep the daughter she bore in 1986 under a contractual agreement. She appealed the ruling. The Supreme Court in 1988 upheld the earlier decision awarding custody to the child's father, William Stern, and his wife, Elizabeth, but it restored Whitehead-Gould's parental rights. The court determined that a mother's parental rights could be terminated only if she proved unfit to rear the child because of abandonment or neglect or if she willingly gave up her child to an approved state adoption agency. The court ruled against allowing Elizabeth Stern to adopt the child, known as Baby M. After a subsequent hearing, Whitehead-Gould was awarded broad visitation rights with the child.

The stability of Whitehead-Gould's relationship with her first husband had been a major issue in the 1987 New Jersey Superior Court trial. Whitehead-Gould and her husband, Richard, announced in August 1987 that they had separated, which she said was a result of the exceptional stress placed on their marriage by the publicity surrounding her case. They were divorced in November, after it became public that Mary Beth was pregnant by another man, Dean Gould, whom she subsequently married.

The New Jersey decision most likely will serve as a guide for state legislatures and judges now debating the surrogacy issue. That state courts have found no standard means of treating disputed surrogate motherhood cases was demonstrated in Michigan. On September 15, 1987, Laurie Ellen Yates won the right to retain temporary custody of twins she bore under contract, though the father and his wife were permitted to visit the children twice a week. The decision to award temporary custody is normally an important, albeit preliminary, step in awarding permanent custody of children. The Michigan court's ruling contrasts with that in the Whitehead-Gould case, in which the New Jersey court gave temporary custody to the contracting father. A final decision on behalf of Yates would effectively throw out the contract she signed. The trial was scheduled to begin in April 1988.

Part of the reason for this unsettled legal situation is the absence of precedent or legislation that could help guide the courts. Many state legislatures are considering a response, though the proposals vary widely, as do the relevant laws already adopted in Nevada and Louisiana. Nevada specifies that surrogacy is exempt from the ban on payment for adoption, and Louisiana that contracts for paid surrogacy are unenforceable. Of state laws pending in early 1988, five would prohibit the entire practice, seven would prohibit paid surrogacy, and three would allow highly regulated unpaid surrogacy.

Minors and Abortion

Should minors seeking elective abortions be required to consult their parents or a judge? As of early 1988, 10 states required only parental notification, but 13 states went further and mandated parental or judicial consent prior to abortion. In many states these laws are not being enforced because they are being challenged in the courts. Proponents of the laws argue that minors require adult guidance in such an important decision, while opponents cite the constitutionally protected right to abortion and the burdens placed on teenagers.

A U.S. Court of Appeals in August 1987 struck down a 1981 Minnesota law requiring women under 18 years of age to notify their parents or obtain judicial approval on the grounds that the law did more to damage than to promote "family integrity." Evidence was presented showing a large increase in the birthrate among 15- and 16-year-olds after the law took effect. Opponents of the law claimed that this was due to teenagers' fears of consulting parents. Opponents also argued that since those teenagers who chose the judicial consent option almost always received permission, they should not have been burdened with travel over long distances to see a judge. The state has petitioned for a rehearing before the full Court of Appeals.

But the resolution of that case and several others in litigation could be influenced by developments regarding a similar statute in Illinois, which required that a minor notify both parents 24 hours before an abortion. In December 1987 the U.S. Supreme Court, by splitting its vote evenly, in effect reaffirmed a lower court's decision that the requirement of notifying parents was constitutional but that specifying a time period for notification was not. The State of Illinois appealed for a rehearing before the Supreme Court, but the appeal was denied.

See also the feature article THE PROBLEM OF TEENAGE PREGNANCY.   JONATHAN D. MORENO, PH.D.

Blood and Lymphatic System

Purer Blood Clotting Factor for Hemophilia • Preventing Complications of Chemotherapy • Sickle-Cell Trait Linked With Death From Exercise

Safer Treatment for Hemophilia

Among the products of the biotechnology industry to become available in 1987 was a new form of factor VIII, the blood clotting protein essential for the treatment of hemophilia. Use of this purer form of factor VIII, produced using monoclonal antibodies, may virtually eliminate the possibility of a hemophiliac's contracting a blood-borne disease such as AIDS or hepatitis from factor VIII treatment.

In most people, the body produces enough factor VIII to enable the blood to clot normally. But in hemophilia, the body does not make the protein or else produces too little of it. The disease is inherited, and almost all its victims are males. About 1 in every 10,000 boys born in the United States has hemophilia. Affected individuals bleed excessively after minor injury. Bleeding into the joints results in permanent, sometimes crippling, joint damage. Bleeding may threaten the patient's life if it occurs in the brain or gastrointestinal tract.

Most of the factor VIII used in the prevention and treatment of bleeding in hemophiliacs is obtained from donated blood. Since the beginning of the AIDS epidemic over 10,000 hemophilia patients have been infected with the virus that causes AIDS. Fortunately, the chances of such infection had already dropped very substantially in the past few years. Since March 1985, all donated blood in the United States has been screened for the presence of antibodies to the AIDS virus (donated blood is also tested for evidence of hepatitis); in addition, the concentrated clotting factor is now pasteurized to kill the AIDS virus. Use of the new factor VIII should remove even the small re-

maining risk. The source of the factor VIII is still blood donations, but the new product is made by filtering monoclonal antibodies (MAb's) through the blood. The MAb's used are special proteins that attach only to factor VIII and pull it out of the blood, providing a purer form of the substance.

The new factor VIII was approved for general use in October 1987 by the U.S. Food and Drug Administration. Sold under the brand name Monoclate, the substance is manufactured by Armour Pharmaceuticals Company of Kankakee, Ill. The main drawback of Monoclate is its price: at a cost of as much as $25,000 a year, it is many times more expensive than the previously available factor VIII.

Preventing Chemotherapy Complications

Genetic engineering techniques are being used to produce a substance that may counter some harmful effects of anticancer drugs. In general, the drugs used in cancer chemotherapy are a double-edged sword for thousands of patients, providing lifesaving treatments yet resulting in serious complications and side effects. One complication caused by almost all anticancer drugs is the suppression of white blood cell and platelet production. White blood cells are critical in the prevention and control of infection, and patients who have inadequate numbers of such cells are susceptible to serious, often life-threatening infections. Platelets are important in the prevention and control of bleeding, and patients who have inadequate numbers of platelets often bleed in the stomach, the intestines, or even the brain. The tendency of anticancer drugs to suppress the production of white blood cells and platelets thus limits the doses that can be administered—limiting the effectiveness of therapy.

A potent blood hormone capable of increasing the production of white cells and platelets is known as colony stimulating factor, named after its ability, in laboratory experiments, to stimulate the growth of blood cell colonies. Researchers have known about this substance for many years, but it has been available in only minute amounts for laboratory purposes. Recently, production of large quantities of pure colony stimulating factor has been possible because of what is known as recombinant DNA technology.

This highly sophisticated method of manufacturing various substances turns genetically modified bacteria or other microorganisms into tiny drug factories. A human gene is inserted into the bacteria's own genes, and the microorganism then produces whatever protein that specific gene codes for. After years of painstaking research, scientists have isolated the specific human genes that control the production of numerous hormones and other regulatory proteins and have

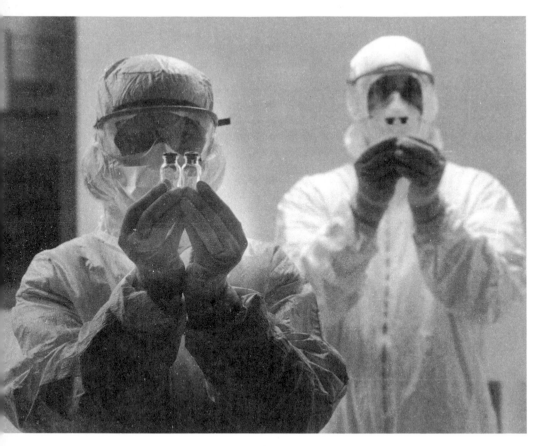

Technicians at the Armour Pharmaceuticals plant in Kankakee, Ill., check vials of a new and purer form of factor VIII, a blood clotting protein used in the treatment of hemophilia. The procedure used to make the improved drug— filtering monoclonal antibodies through donated blood— virtually eliminates any chance that a hemophiliac will contract AIDS, hepatitis, or other blood-borne diseases from the product.

successfully modified bacteria to produce and release large quantities of these important substances. The mixture is then purified, removing all bacteria, foreign substances, and unwanted products, and the pure product is ready for human use.

The colony stimulating factor produced through genetic engineering has been used experimentally in cancer patients receiving chemotherapy (as of early 1988 the substance had not been approved by the Food and Drug Administration for general use). In these studies, colony stimulating factor resulted in increased numbers of white blood cells and platelets. Cancer specialists are optimistic that this substance will eventually allow larger, more effective doses of anti-cancer drugs to be given, with fewer side effects— thus improving the overall safety and effectiveness of available medications.

Sickle-Cell Trait

In September 1987 researchers from the Walter Reed Army Institute of Research reported that otherwise healthy young black men with the sickle-cell trait in their blood were at significantly increased risk of sudden death during extreme physical exertion. The reseachers studied the records of deaths among the 2.1 million U.S. military recruits who went through basic training from 1977 to 1981.

The sickle-cell trait is hereditary and occurs most commonly among blacks (about 8 percent of blacks in the United States have it). People with the trait have inherited from one parent a gene for an abnormal type of hemoglobin, the substance in the red blood cells that carries oxygen. These people are generally not made ill by the condition (in contrast to those who inherit the gene from both parents and develop sickle-cell anemia).

Of 62 deaths from natural causes among recruits during the period that records were studied, 40 occurred suddenly during strenuous exercise. Of those 40 people, 13 (all of them black) had the sickle-cell trait. The researchers noted, however, that "civilian activities are seldom as [physically] stressful as basic military training." Although some people in extremely strenuous occupations may be at greater risk, most people with the sickle-cell trait should have no difficulty performing routine daily tasks.

See also the feature article AIDS UPDATE *and the* Spotlight on Health *articles* GIVING AND GETTING BLOOD, HEPATITIS, *and* MONOCLONAL ANTIBODIES: MEDICINE'S POWERFUL NEW TOOL.

J. DONALD TEMPLE, M.D.

Brain and Nervous System

*Conference on Dementia •
Immunological Therapies for
Myasthenia Gravis and Multiple
Sclerosis • Surgery for Epilepsy*

Conference on Dementia

In July 1987 the U.S. National Institutes of Health convened a 12-member panel of experts to assess the current state of knowledge about dementia and the diseases causing it. Specialists in neurology, psychiatry, geriatric medicine, and other fields attempted to answer questions on what dementia is, which of its causes can be readily arrested or reversed, and how the initial evaluation and diagnosis should be made.

What is dementia? The panel in its consensus statement termed dementia a clinical state with many different causes, characterized by decline from a previously attained intellectual level. Though dementia occurs at all ages, the panel found the highest rate in individuals over 75. As the population ages, dementia and other age-related disorders are expected to become more common. A mild decline in intellectual ability and, particularly, memory occurs as a part of normal aging, and it is not always possible to distinguish the early stages of true dementia from the changes brought about by normal aging.

Almost every patient with dementia can be treated, the panel said. Although the mental decline is often permanent, the past practice of many doctors telling patients that their dementia was beyond help was described as seriously mistaken.

Causes of dementia. The panel concluded that nearly 80 percent of dementia cases are caused by two irreversible disorders: Alzheimer's disease (which involves the loss of nerve cells and the development of tangled protein clusters in the brain) and multi-infarct dementia (where a series of strokes destroys parts of the brain). The remaining 20 percent are the result of a variety of conditions—including severe depression, reactions to prescription drugs, stroke, heart attack, brain tumors, infections such as syphilis and AIDS, chronic alcoholism, drug abuse, and nutritional deficiencies. Many of these conditions can be treated, and the dementias they cause can be arrested or reversed if treatment is begun promptly.

Evaluation and testing. The committee said that proper identification of the cause of an individual's dementia was critical in managing the disease and urged doctors to take the time needed to make their own detailed diagnosis of such patients. This should include a thorough physical examination, complete medical history, and—when necessary—neurologic tests and brief, standardized tests of mental status.

Gathering a patient's history often requires the doctor to conduct interviews with the individual's family and friends. The family background is especially important if members of earlier generations also had dementia. A genetic cause of Alzheimer's disease is widely suspected, but estimates of the cases accounted for by genetic factors vary from 20 percent to 80 percent. The panel heard evidence suggesting that the lower figure is probably more accurate, which should be reassuring to family members of Alzheimer's patients.

No single test can establish the presence of dementia, the panel said. The speakers stressed that dementia is defined by changes in a patient's behavior and that there is no substitute for a doctor's expertise in judging such symptoms. However, a number of basic diagnostic tests—including complete blood cell count, urinalysis, electrocardiogram, and tests of thyroid gland functioning—were recommended for patients with a new onset of dementia. In addition, some imaging devices and other laboratory tests can be helpful in diagnosing specific dementias. These devices include computerized tomography (CT, or CAT, scanning), a sophisticated X-ray technique, and magnetic resonance imaging, which is sensitive in discovering small, unsuspected strokes and atrophy (shrinkage) of parts of the brain. Positron emission tomography, which measures blood flow in specific regions of the brain, may prove valuable in predicting the occurrence of Alzheimer's disease and other similar disorders such as Huntington's disease in individuals with family members who have been afflicted.

Future research priorities. The most important priority identified by the committee was distinguishing more accurately the changes of normal aging from those of dementia. A number of long-term studies on this problem are currently under way in the United States and in Europe. The panel also agreed on the need to perform more autopsies to further research. Most of the primary diseases causing dementia can be diagnosed with absolute certainty only after death, and it is important to correlate findings during life with those obtained at autopsy. Unfortunately, because of a decline in the number of autopsies performed, such correlations are very difficult to make. In Denmark and Sweden, where the rates of autopsies performed are higher, such studies on dementia are more frequently carried out. Several important findings have been made, in particular that stroke may be a relatively more common cause of dementia than previously thought.

Immunological Therapies

Several reports were released in 1987 suggesting that certain nervous system diseases can be treated using drugs that alter the body's immune response. Normally, the immune system serves to protect the individual against foreign substances like bacteria, viruses, and parasites. In certain diseases, though, the immune system goes awry. For reasons that are not known, the nervous system is particularly vulnerable to immunological mischief—when an immune attack is triggered against a neurological structure.

Myasthenia gravis. New treatments are being found for myasthenia gravis, a disorder involving the nerves and muscles that occurs in both children and adults. Characterized by muscle weakness, it may at times be localized to the muscles of the eyes, causing droopy lids and double vision. But most often, it affects the entire body—producing fatigue, difficulty walking or ascending stairs, and, eventually, difficulty in breathing because of weakness of the chest and diaphragm. Myasthenia gravis is caused by an antibody (a protein formed by the immune system) in the blood that affixes to the junctions of nerves and muscles, preventing the normal electrical activity by which signals are transferred there.

Medications that prolong electrical activity at these neuromuscular junctions have been used successfully to treat myasthenia gravis for many years. More recently, plasmapheresis—an experimental "blood cleaning" technique for removing antibodies from the blood—has been used successfully to provide short-term relief. Corticosteroids, drugs that suppress the immune system throughout the body, have also been used. However, they have a number of serious side effects. The drug cyclosporine (brand name, Sandimmune)—first used to inhibit the immune system's rejection of transplanted organs—has now been shown to effect long-term suppression of myasthenia with relatively few side effects. However, as with all powerful immunological agents, cyclosporine must be used cautiously.

Multiple sclerosis. Encouraging work has gone on with new drugs to treat multiple sclerosis, a disease of the brain and spinal cord that also seems to be caused by an attack of the immune system. In this disorder, myelin (the insulating sheath around nerve fibers) is destroyed, apparently by the immune system. This loss of myelin brings about a slowdown in the transmission of neural messages and eventually results in paralysis, double vision, dizziness, loss of coordination, and sometimes blindness. The disease most often occurs between the ages of 20 and 40, at a time when people are most productive. Its course is quite unpredictable. Many people have one or two attacks and remain well or are only minimally affected. Others become increasingly incapacitated from repeated attacks, while still others have few acute attacks but undergo chronic, progressive deterioration over many years.

Numerous medications have been used during the past 20 years in an attempt to prevent acute exacerbations of multiple sclerosis and to alter its course in patients with the chronic, progressive form. None has been uniformly successful. Recently, though, researchers at the University of Rochester found that human beta-interferon (an immune-modulating substance formed by the body) was helpful when injected into the spinal fluid of patients with the relapsing-remitting form of multiple sclerosis. Side effects were minor, and the number of acute attacks decreased over a period of months. Earlier attempts at injecting interferon directly into a vein—a simpler approach—were also of value but not as dramatically so.

In the chronic, progressive variety of multiple sclerosis, two drugs were used in combination—corticotropin (ACTH), a pituitary gland hormone, and cyclophosphamide (sold as Cytoxan, or Neosar), a cancer drug. Treatment was found to be of value in slowing progression of the disease. However, there were major adverse side effects, and not all patients were helped. Additional trials will be necessary before these treatments can be generally recommended.

Related disorders. Clinical trials are also under way in a number of other neurological disorders thought to have an immune basis. These include amyotrophic lateral sclerosis (Lou Gehrig's disease), which causes progressive weakness and loss of muscle bulk in middle and late life, and the Guillain-Barré syndrome, which causes reversible paralysis.

Surgery for Epilepsy

It may become possible to greatly decrease the number of seizures that an epilepsy patient suffers by performing surgery on the brain. The crucial step is determining the site of the abnormal epileptic activity.

Epilepsy is characterized by recurrent seizures that result from an abnormal or excessive discharge of electrical signals by nerve cells in the brain. The discharge may be caused by injury to the brain, a brain tumor, a stroke, very high fever, poisoning, a chemical imbalance, or some congenital defect. Often, no cause is found. While most epileptics can be treated successfully with one or more medications, enabling them to lead nearly normal lives, about 10 percent continue to have seizures despite taking high doses of medication or suffer major side effects from the drugs, limiting their usefulness. When the site of the abnormal electrical discharge can be localized, it may be possible to remove the affected area surgically to decrease the number of seizures.

Routine electroencephalography—an electrical recording of brain-wave patterns—is made on the scalp and can only localize activity to a general area of the brain. Much more precise information can be obtained by actually recording on the surface of the brain itself. By doing so, epilepsy specialists can closely define an area to be removed and, more importantly, can guide the surgeon so that normally functioning areas will not be removed, thus minimizing the risk of neurologic injury. In the procedure, an operation is performed where a plastic grid is inserted on the surface of the brain, allowing recordings to be made at 100 or more locations over a period of days. During that time the patient remains closely monitored in an intensive care unit. The electrical signals are processed by computer so that areas of abnormal activity can be recognized and accurately mapped and the part of the brain originating the activity can be pinpointed.

Newer techniques may avoid the need to implant a recording grid. There is, for example, a method called magnetoencephalography, in which a sensitive device records the magnetic field that surrounds the brain, allowing the electrical activity to be charted. At present, these new techniques are not yet sufficiently developed to be clinically useful. Patient and doctor alike can anticipate much medical progress as these noninvasive devices become more refined.

See also the Spotlight on Health articles CARING FOR AN ALZHEIMER'S PATIENT *and* PARKINSON'S DISEASE: NEW ADVANCES. HAMILTON MOSES III, M.D.

Cancer

Questioning Progress Against Cancer • Emphasis on Early Detection and Prevention • Link Between Breast Cancer and Drinking • Cancers Resulting From Successful Treatment

Assessing Progress

Industrialist Armand Hammer, chairman of the U.S. President's Cancer Panel, referred to a March 1987 General Accounting Office report on cancer survival

as "a prime example of bureaucratic gobbledygook." His comments reflected the feelings of many experts in the field who felt that the report was too pessimistic. Although the GAO, a congressional investigative agency, concluded that progress has been made against cancer over the last 30 years, the report questioned the reliability of data showing improved survival-rates, since other factors such as earlier detection and changes in the way data are compiled make it difficult to clearly define the amount of progress. More patients are cured or have their lives extended by current treatment, but the major gains have been in the less common forms of cancer, especially in those that affect young people. Progress in treating older patients and the more common cancers, including those of the lung, breast, and colon, has occurred more slowly. This further supports the need for prevention or early detection.

Another major difficulty with assessing progress is related to the long delay between the initiation of research studies and the application of their results in the clinical setting. As so accurately stressed by Benno Schmidt, the first chairman of the President's Cancer Panel, we are just now seeing the results of work begun after the National Cancer Act of 1971. The ultimate role of therapeutic agents such as interferons, interleukins, and blood cell growth factors in treatment is yet to be determined.

The American Cancer Society estimated that in 1987, 965,000 Americans would develop cancer and half as many, or 483,000 people, would die of cancer. The National Cancer Institute (NCI) has set an ambitious goal to halve the cancer death rate by the year 2000; a recent Louis Harris poll of biomedical scientists yielded predictions that by the year 2000, two out of three patients with cancer will be cured. To accomplish these goals, research to improve treatment of early and advanced cancers must continue. But the emphasis in research is shifting to the areas of prevention and early detection, which require a great deal of public education and also require that patients assume a major role in their own healthcare.

Prevention and Early Detection

The National Cancer Institute's effort to halve the cancer death rate by the year 2000 will focus on three key areas: a reduction in smoking, changes in diet, and increased use of methods of early detection of cancers of the breast and cervix.

Tobacco. Smoking is a major cause of lung cancer and, along with other forms of tobacco abuse, is associated with cancers of the larynx, mouth, esophagus, pancreas, and bladder. Smoking is estimated to be responsible for approximately 130,000 cancer deaths a year in the United States. The NCI goal is to reduce the percentage of adults who smoke from the current level of more than 25 percent to 15 percent or less by the year 2000. (*See also the feature article* LUNG CANCER: PREVENTION AND TREATMENT.)

Fat in the diet. According to the NCI, about one-third of U.S. cancers are thought to be linked to diet. The strongest association is between increased dietary fat and a greater incidence of colon cancer; a lower fat intake and an increased fiber intake appear to lessen the risk of this type of cancer. A similar though weaker association between fat intake and breast cancer has been suggested, but this hypothesis remains controversial. The NCI goal includes a reduction in the proportion of fat in the total U.S. caloric intake from 38 percent at present to 30 percent and an increase in individual fiber intake from approximately 12 grams a day to 30 grams a day by the year 2000. (*See also the feature article* FACTS ABOUT FAT.)

Testing for women. In addition to these preventive measures, the NCI goal will depend upon intensified screening programs for cancers of the breast and cervix. Early detection increases the probability that these cancers can be cured.

In the 1980's, the majority of women aged 20 or older have a Pap test performed at least once every three years to screen for cervical cancer. The goal for the year 2000 is to increase the utilization of the Pap test from 79 percent to 90 percent in women aged 20 to 39 and from 57 percent to 80 percent in women aged 40 to 70.

Frequent screening for breast cancer is extremely important because a woman's chance of survival is greatly increased if the cancer is detected early; half of all breast cancers spread beyond the breast before they are discovered. At present only about 45 percent of women aged 50 to 70 have their breasts examined by a physician each year, and only 15 percent of those who should have a mammogram (breast X ray) each year actually do. Cancer experts hope that by the year 2000 at leat 80 percent of these women will have annual breast exams and mammograms. The American Cancer Society suggests that women have an initial mammogram between the ages of 35 and 39 and that the exam be repeated at least every two years until the age of 50, after which annual mammography is recommended.

Improved techniques have reduced the radiation exposure from X rays and, therefore, the cancer risk from recurrent exams. Although this reduced risk should encourage greater utilization of mammography, a major obstacle continues to be cost. Current efforts to reduce the cost of mammography and to have medicare, medicaid, and insurance companies cover this cost may have a major impact on the use of this technique for early detection.

Women may now be more likely to have mammo-grams because of the highly publicized recent experience of First Lady Nancy Reagan, whose breast cancer was detected in an early (and most likely curable) stage. In October 1987, as part of a routine checkup, a mammogram revealed a small lesion in Mrs. Reagan's left breast. After a biopsy showed it to be malignant, Mrs. Reagan underwent a modified radical mastectomy, in which the breast and underlying tissue were removed. Because the cancer was detected at an early stage, before it had spread to other tissue, many medical experts considered Mrs. Reagan's prognosis excellent.

Possible Causes of Cancer

Identifying the causes of cancer is important for successful preventive care and early detection programs. Several recent studies have tried to find links between specific cancers and possible chemical, environmental, and dietary factors.

Alcohol and breast cancer. Two studies published in May 1987 in *The New England Journal of Medicine* found an association between alcohol consumption and breast cancer. One of the studies found no increased risk in women who averaged fewer than three drinks a week; women who consumed three to nine drinks a week had a 30 percent higher risk, and those who consumed more than nine drinks a week had a 60 percent higher risk. (A drink is commonly defined as a beverage containing the amount of alcohol found in 1¼ ounces of 80 to 90 proof liquor, 5 ounces of wine, or 12 ounces of beer.) The other study found an excess risk of breast cancer with any amount of alcohol intake, the increase in risk ranging from 40 percent for women who have less than one drink a week to 100 percent for those who have more than three drinks a week. The increase in risk was most remarkable among younger women. The exact cause of this possible association between alcohol intake and breast cancer is unknown; possible explanations include the direct effects of alcohol on breast tissue and the changes alcohol may cause in other bodily functions, such as hormone production, that may then affect breast tissue. The results of the two 1987 studies were called into question in March 1988 by another study, presented to an American Cancer Society seminar, that found no association between alcohol and breast cancer.

Obesity. Preliminary results of studies of a possible association between obesity and the more common cancers of men and women show limited evidence of an increased risk. In women there are suggestions of an increased risk of cancer of the uterus, or womb, and possibly of breast cancer in postmenopausal women; there is no evidence of an increase in other cancers in men or women.

Pesticides and herbicides. A study reported by the University of Southern California found that children in homes where pesticides are used have a greater than threefold increased risk of acute leukemia; when garden sprays are used, the risk is over sixfold. A 1986 report had showed a sixfold increase in lymphatic cancer among Kansas farmers who used herbicides, especially those who had direct exposure to the chemicals, such as from failure to use protective clothing.

Distressing news also came in September 1987 from the Veterans Adminstration. A study that examined the causes of death of Vietnam veterans showed much higher death rates from lung cancer (58 percent higher) and lymphatic cancer (110 percent higher) among Marine veterans who had served in Vietnam than among Marines who had not served there. The reasons for these differences are not known, but exposure to the herbicide Agent Orange or other environmental factors are suspected. Higher death rates from other cancers were not found, nor were greater numbers of cancer deaths noted in Vietnam veterans who served in the Army, possibly because they were primarily located in different parts of Vietnam.

Second cancers from treatment. The risk of a new cancer developing from the successful therapy for another cancer is becoming an important problem for cancer experts. Although this problem reflects the increasing ability of medical science to cure the initial cancers, there is growing concern about long-term hazards of treatment, especially in patients with potentially curable cancers. A study of long-term survivors of Hodgkin's disease (a form of lymphatic cancer) presented to the American Society of Clinical Oncology in May 1987 found an 18 percent risk of a second primary cancer in patients who survived the treatment of their initial cancer for 15 years. (A primary cancer is one that originates at a new body site, rather than one that spreads from an existing cancer.) While the incidence of leukemia was greatest in the first five years after therapy, the risk of developing non-Hodgkin's lymphatic cancer and solid tumors (most frequently lung cancer) was greatest between 10 and 15 years after initial treatment. Many of the solid tumors developed in areas that had been treated with radiation.

In a similar study published in September 1987, researchers from the National Cancer Institute identified an increased risk of bone cancers in children treated for a variety of cancers with radiation therapy with or without chemotherapy (drugs). Radiation therapy alone was associated with a greater than twofold increase in bone cancer, and the risk was proportional to the amount of radiation received. The addition of chemotherapy with a class of drugs known as alkylating agents further increased this risk. Many studies currently under way are attempting to develop effective treatment programs with minimal long-term hazards, especially in patients with potentially curable cancers such as Hodgkin's disease and many childhood cancers.

Mechanisms of Development

The mechanisms by which most cancers develop remain poorly defined, but recent progress in the definition and understanding of genetic or chromosomal

First Lady Nancy Reagan greets well-wishers after surgery for breast cancer. Mrs. Reagan's modified radical mastectomy served to draw public attention to the high rate of breast cancer among American women and the potential benefits of regular mammograms.

cancers of the breast and lung, and in children with neuroblastoma (a cancer of the nervous system), when specific proto-oncogenes are present. Ongoing research to further understand proto-oncogenes will not only increase our knowledge of cancer development and prognosis but may also identify these genetic areas as potential targets for prevention, early detection, or treatment of cancer.

Lymphokines

Lymphokines, products of activated or stimulated lymphocytes (a type of white blood cell), are becoming more important in the treatment of malignant diseases. Examples of lymphokines include the interferons, interleukins, tumor necrosis factor, and colony-stimulating factors, which stimulate normal blood cell production by the bone marrow. Recent advances in genetic engineering have made possible the production of large amounts of these substances for widespread research and clinical use. Alpha-interferon is now in clinical use for the treatment of hairy-cell leukemia, a rare cancer of white blood cells, and is under investigation for several other cancers.

Interleukin-2. The lymphokine that has received the most attention in the past few years has been interleukin-2 (IL-2). This agent activates lymphocytes to become lymphokine-activated killer (LAK) cells, which kill cancer cells. But the enthusiasm of the scientific community following early results of IL-2 trials, and the extensive media coverage of these developments, led to great and somewhat unrealistic expectations from the public. More recently, in an editorial in the *Journal of the American Medical Association*, Dr. Charles Moertel, a renowned cancer researcher, questioned the value of further studies of IL-2 because of the high cost and serious side effects of the therapy, which has shown modest effectiveness in early trials. Although few, if any, experts would argue that this therapy is still experimental and is not ready for general use, many feel its effectiveness is sufficient to justify further clinical trials. Researchers from the National Cancer Institute and elsewhere have reported continued progress and less toxicity in recent treatment programs.

Colony-stimulating factors. Recent studies of colony-stimulating factors have suggested that these lymphokines may become important components of cancer treatment in the near future. At present the amount of cancer drugs (chemotherapy) that can be given to a patient is limited by their toxicity to normal cells. The most frequent problem with cancer drugs is that they suppress the functioning of bone marrow, resulting in decreased levels of red blood cells (oxygen-carrying cells), white blood cells (infection-fighting cells), and platelets (cells necessary for normal blood

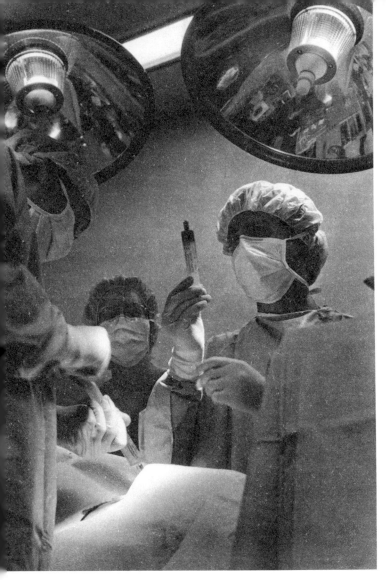

As treatment of cancer patients by bone marrow transplants continues to expand, one focus is increasing the number of potential donors. Here a medical team draws bone marrow from a donor's pelvic bones.

abnormalities associated with cancer provides insight into the origins of cancer development. Proto-oncogenes (oncogenes are genes that cause cancer) are areas of normal genetic material (portions of chromosomes) that probably have a function in normal cell growth or maturation. However, when these proto-oncogenes are altered or activated to become oncogenes by an appropriate stimulus, they generate proteins that can cause abnormal cell growth or cancer. Possible stimuli that "turn on" proto-oncogenes include certain viruses, radiation, chemicals, and other known carcinogens. Specific proto-oncogenes have been identified in association with several human cancers, including leukemia, lymphatic cancer, and cancers of the breast, colon, and lung. Recent studies have also shown a poor prognosis in certain clotting). These lowered blood cell levels lead to serious complications, including potentially fatal infections and bleeding. The recent development of genetically engineered colony-stimulating factors may eliminate or reduce this problem with cancer drugs and therefore allow for more effective therapy. If these factors are successful in stimulating the growth of normal blood cells (especially white blood cells and platelets), larger and possibly more effective doses of cancer-killing agents can be safely administered. These growth agents may also be useful in stimulating earlier recovery of blood cell production after bone marrow transplants and in stimulating the immune systems of patients with AIDS (acquired immune deficiency syndrome). But their utility in blood cell malignancies may be limited, since there is evidence that the factors may also stimulate the production of cancerous blood cells in diseases such as leukemia.

Bone Marrow Transplants

Research to make bone marrow transplants available to greater numbers of people continues in many cancer centers. This procedure was once used only for patients with an identical twin but is now available to a much larger group of patients. The use of bone marrow from closely matched relatives has become an accepted therapy for selected patients with leukemia, most of whom would otherwise be incurable. Current trials are focusing on the use of the patient's own marrow, marrow from a partially matched relative, or marrow from an unrelated matched donor, and studies also continue to explore the value of bone marrow transplants in patients with malignancies other than leukemia.   BAYARD L. POWELL, M.D.

Digestive System

New Cause for Ulcers Suspected • Injections Halt Bleeding • Gastric Bubble Fails to Work • Does Peanut Butter Cause Cancer? • Gallstones Treated With Shock Waves

Bacteria May Cause Ulcers

A recently discovered bacterium, *Campylobacter pylori*, may cause gastritis and ulcers. Gastritis, inflammation of the lining of the stomach, may occur alone or with a tiny sore—a peptic ulcer—in the stomach or uppermost part of the small intestine. Each year millions of Americans develop nausea, vomiting, or abdominal pain as a result of gastritis or peptic ulcer disease. In many instances an underlying cause is readily identified, for example, the ingestion of alcohol, aspirin, or some other stomach irritant. In other instances, however, no obvious cause is apparent.

A recent Canadian study found *C. pylori* in the stomach linings of 7 of 10 children with gastritis without a known underlying cause. The bacterium was not present, however, in 8 children in whom the cause of the gastritis was known. Moreover, the bacterium was not present in the stomachs of any of 49 children without gastritis. Reports of similar findings in adults also suggest a relationship between the organism and gastritis and ulcers. The bacterium has been found in the stomachs of only 20 percent of healthy adults but in up to 93 percent of people with ulcers of the upper small intestine and 70 percent of stomach ulcer patients.

There is considerable controversy about the role of *C. pylori* in the production of gastritis and peptic ulcers. Some researchers, who agree that there is an association of the bacterium with inflamed stomach linings, believe the organism does not cause the inflammation. They suggest that it grows preferentially in an already inflamed area. Further investigation needs to be done to establish a role for *C. pylori* in gastritis and peptic ulcers.

If such a role is confirmed, this could alter the currently accepted treatment for these two conditions. Some researchers suggest that patients with gastritis or peptic ulcers who have not responded to conventional therapy may be candidates for treatment with a combination of an antibiotic and a bismuth compound, such as bismuth subsalicylate (sold by the brand name Pepto-Bismol).

Injections Halt Bleeding

Bleeding in the upper gastrointestinal tract—esophagus, stomach, or upper part of the small intestine—is a common and serious problem. It may be caused by an ulcer, dilated blood vessels, or various other conditions. One out of ten patients admitted to the hospital with acute bleeding of this type dies. Researchers looking for ways to stop gastrointestinal bleeding without resorting to surgery now believe that injection of alcohol or epinephrine (adrenaline) is a simple, safe, and effective form of treatment.

In a recent study injections of ethanol—drinking alcohol—initially controlled bleeding in 68 of 72 patients with upper gastrointestinal bleeding. Five of the 68 patients subsequently started bleeding again. To determine the cause and location of bleeding, the patients were given a mild sedative and a flexible fiber-optic tube called an endoscope was passed through the mouth into the stomach. The endoscope permits direct observation of the lining of the upper gastrointestinal tract. Once the site was located, a needle at the end of a long tube was passed through a channel in the endoscope and three or four injections of ethanol were made around the bleeding site. This resulted in clotting of the blood vessels. No deaths occurred during the study.

Epinephrine causes constriction of blood vessels. Another study indicated that injections of epinephrine into the site of actively bleeding peptic ulcers caused cessation of bleeding in all 37 patients treated. Five patients, however, subsequently started bleeding again, and three of them required surgery.

Other methods used to stop upper gastrointestinal bleeding include electrocoagulation and laser photocoagulation. Both of these techniques have had varying success. These methods require more elaborate equipment and training than injection of alcohol or epinephrine does.

Gastric Bubble Ineffective

There were more adverse findings about the Gastric Bubble, the device approved in 1985 by the U.S. Food and Drug Administration for use as an aid in weight reduction. The Gastric Bubble is a small balloon introduced into the stomach through a tube. When blown up, it is supposed to make the patient feel full and therefore eat less. After serious side effects developed in a number of early users, the manufacturer recommended in 1986 that the bubble be used for no more than three months (the original recommendation was four) and only in patients with life-threatening obesity. Now, researchers indicate the bubble is not effective in promoting weight loss.

In one recent study involving 21 patients who were 25 to 110 percent over their ideal weight, the bubble was compared to a "sham" treatment for promoting weight loss. In the sham, a tube was inserted into the patient's stomach, just as in the real treatment, but no bubble was introduced. During the six-month study period, all patients received Gastric Bubbles for three months and sham for three months. For the entire six-month period, the patients were also placed on 1,000-calorie diets and given dietary counseling. At the conclusion of the study no significant difference in weight loss was found between bubble and sham. Participants lost almost 12 pounds, on average, during each three-month period. Based on these results the researchers questioned the role of the bubble in weight reduction. Several other recent studies have also questioned the effectiveness of the Gastric Bubble in promoting weight loss in obese people.

Peanut Butter and Cancer

As of January 8, 1988, California included aflatoxin in its list of chemicals known to cause cancer. Aflatoxin is a chemical commonly found in peanut butter.

Aflatoxin is produced by the fungus *Aspergillus flavus*, which grows on raw peanuts and other foods. Aflatoxin is highly toxic to the liver of most animals and has been linked to human liver cancer in Africa and Asia. Although there is no direct evidence that aflatoxin causes human liver cancer, studies from Africa and Asia reveal a close correlation between the amount of food contamination and the frequency of liver cancer. Areas in which aflatoxin is found in high concentrations in foods have a high frequency of cancer.

The mold that produces aflatoxin occurs naturally in peanuts and other foods, but the amount of aflatoxin is increased significantly if raw food has been improperly stored. The mold grows best in a warm, moist climate, typical of the regions where peanuts are grown and where the raw peanuts are stored.

Some experts believe that for Americans the risk of developing liver cancer from eating peanut butter is low. They point out that peanut butter is tested after it is manufactured and is discarded if the amount of aflatoxin is above the allowable level of 20 parts per billion established by the U.S. Food and Drug Administration. The average level of aflatoxin in peanut butter is about 2 parts per billion.

The role of aflatoxin in producing liver cancer in humans is unclear in any case because in most instances people developing this form of cancer are also infected with the hepatitis B virus, which is known to cause liver cancer. It is possible that aflatoxin acting with the virus results in cancer.

Gallstones Treated With Shock Waves

About 22 million Americans have gallstones, and half a million of them undergo surgery for this problem each year. Researchers now report that surgery may no longer be necessary for some of them. Lithotripsy, a technique employing shock waves to break the stones, has been shown to be an effective treatment for some gallstones.

Lithotriptors, or stone crushers, were initially developed in West Germany in 1980 to crush kidney stones. The technique employs repetitive shock waves of high energy to fragment stones. The first lithotriptors required partial immersion of the patient in a water bath following the administration of a general or spinal anesthetic. While the patient was in the water bath, between 500 and 1,500 shock waves were applied to the stones over one to two hours.

A newer version of the lithotriptor has been used in Europe and Canada to treat 600 gallstone patients without serious complications. This device does not require a water bath. Instead, a water-filled cushion in which shock waves are produced is placed against the abdomen. The shock waves pass through the tissues of the body, in the same manner as in the water bath, striking the stones and causing them to fragment. Since the newer technique produces little or no pain, a general anesthetic is not required, as it may be with the earlier lithotriptors that used water baths. However, an injection of a pain killer is administered.

The U.S. Food and Drug Administration has approved testing of the new device on 600 gallstone patients at ten medical centers in the United States. The tests, to begin in 1988, are designed to evaluate the safety and effectiveness of the device and to determine which gallstone patients might benefit from this form of treatment.

In the study, after shock waves are used to fragment the stones, some of the patients will also be treated with bile acids, such as a combination of cheno-deoxycholic acid (Chenix) and ursodeoxycholic acid, to dissolve the fragments. The latter drug has not been approved for routine clinical use in the United States. The inclusion of the bile acids for some of the patients in the study is intended to determine whether it is necessary to dissolve the stone fragments or whether the fragments will simply pass out of the body without causing problems.

See also the feature article PROTECTION FROM FOOD POISONING *and the Spotlight on Health article* DEALING WITH HEARTBURN.   DANIEL PELOT, M.D.

Drug Abuse

AIDS Among Intravenous Drug Users • Drug Testing in the Workplace • Treatment Programs and Reimbursement

AIDS

The single topic that dominated the drug abuse field in 1987 was AIDS. While the rapid spread of the AIDS virus in the gay population has been well documented and publicized, the seriousness of the AIDS threat to intravenous (IV) drug users, and through them to the general population, has become increasingly evident.

Recent reports from substance-abuse treatment programs in New York City indicate that in some programs as many as 80 percent of intravenous drug users applying for treatment are infected with the AIDS virus. This extremely high rate of infection is probably not found in any other American city at this time, but all figures indicate that the proportion of IV drug users who are infected is rising everywhere. For example, in Philadelphia one center found that 7.1 percent of IV drug users screened in 1986 tested positive for the virus, but that 14.5 percent of those screened in the first half of 1987 tested positive. Sample figures from San Francisco indicate that from 1986 to 1987 the proportion testing positive increased from 12 percent to 20 percent. These rapid increases in the rate of infection appear to be primarily caused by the practice of sharing needles. Almost all intravenous drug users admit to this practice, which provides a very rapid means for the transmission of the AIDS virus among this population.

Public health authorities have become extremely concerned with the rise in AIDS-virus infection among IV drug users for two reasons. First, it has resulted in more actual AIDS cases, with the attendant social, economic, and human costs. (A particularly tragic aspect of this situation is the infection of an unborn child by a drug-using mother. An increasing number of such cases was reported in 1987, especially in large cities such as New York.) Second, because IV drug users are primarily heterosexual, they may become vehicles for spread of the virus to nongay, nondrug-using persons via sexual contact.

The spread of AIDS among addicts has been studied intensely, and additional research is being solicited by the National Institute of Mental Health and the National Institute on Drug Abuse. Many efforts are also being made to prevent IV drug users from engaging in "high-risk" behavior that may spread the virus further, including sharing needles and having sexual intercourse without condoms. Unfortunately, public health authorities do not yet know the most effective means of changing such behavior in drug users. Educational techniques promoting public health are not highly successful even among "mainstream" members of society. Most intravenous drug users are outside the mainstream, and as a result, they are even more difficult to reach through the use of traditional educational methods.

Unfortunately, the results of studies now in progress will not be available for several years. This means that the pace of research may not keep up with the clinical realities and that the discovery of a meaningful way to reduce high-risk behavior may occur only after a very large number of IV drug users have been infected with the virus.

See also the feature article AIDS UPDATE.

Drugs in the Workplace

A second major issue, drugs in the workplace, has been increasingly recognized as a serious problem. A national uproar ensued in January 1987 when an Amtrak train collided with three Conrail freight locomotives near Baltimore and caused an accident that left 16 persons dead and 175 injured. The engineer and brakeman of the Conrail caravan were found to have detectable levels of illicit drugs in their blood and urine. This accident led to efforts on many levels to implement policies that could prevent such incidents from occurring in the future.

Many employers have been requiring workers to undergo urine tests for illicit drugs as part of their preemployment physical examination, after an accident on the job, or as part of an examination following any other behavior that leads a supervisor to suspect drug use. These requirements have caused debate but have generally been accepted, provided the screening laboratory is accurate and the administrative responses to a positive test have been agreed upon previously by management and labor.

In February 1988, however, a U.S. appeals court ruled unconstitutional a federal requirement that all railroad workers on trains involved in accidents or rule violations undergo blood or urine tests; the court said there must be other grounds to suspect drug or alcohol use. In general, management proposals for random tests on employees who show no outward signs of drug use have been vigorously contested in court by many labor unions on the grounds that they constitute an unlawful search. Some of the most

notable cases have resulted from President Ronald Reagan's September 1986 executive order and subsequent congressional legislation mandating drug testing of over a million federal workers—air traffic controllers, Treasury Department employees, and U.S. Army civilian guards, among them.

At present, the government has won more cases than it has lost, but many legal battles are in progress, and it is difficult to predict the eventual practices and policies that will result. One possible outcome is that employers may gain the right to use random urine testing in situations where grave harm to the public could stem from a worker's drug abuse. Examples of such workers might be air traffic controllers, operators of public transportation, and law enforcement officers. In late 1987, Congress enacted a law requiring drug testing of new recruits entering the armed forces, beginning in June 1988. In March 1988 the Transportation Department proposed a wide-ranging drug testing program for over 500,000 airline workers, including pilots, flight attendants, and mechanics.

Employee Assistance Programs

Another aspect of the debate about the use of urine testing has been the development of programs to assist employees in overcoming their drug abuse. Some of the most successful programs appear to have resulted from combining clear administrative sanctions against drug use with regular monitoring of employees' behavior and effective assistance to those found to be using drugs. A great number of these programs have been developed over the last 20 years to deal with

The deadliest crash in Amtrak history occurred in early 1987 when an Amtrak passenger train collided with three Conrail freight locomotives near Baltimore, leaving 16 dead and 175 injured. The engineer and brakeman of the Conrail caravan were found to have used illicit drugs. The engineer later pleaded guilty to one count of manslaughter.

alcohol problems, and authorities are now trying to broaden the scope of such treatment to include abuse of drugs, especially cocaine. Some of these programs are run by unions, some by management, and others by outside agencies. There is considerable variety in the policies and treatments used. Much effort appears to be going into educating supervisors and employee assistance counselors in how to identify and counsel drug-abusing workers and into developing more standardized ways of dealing with these problems. This area of expertise is extremely complex, as it covers employees who perform a wide range of services. Several agencies, including the National Institute on Drug Abuse, are attempting to develop training methods for use by industry and labor in setting up sound employee assistance programs.

Reimbursement for Drug Abuse Treatment

Another area of interest in the drug abuse field is the development of cost-effective treatment. Twenty years ago, when current U.S. problems with drug abuse were beginning to emerge, little help for abusers was available. The methadone programs for heroin addicts that subsequently developed in many large cities were some of the first large-scale public services in the field, but they were not appropriate for abusers of other substances and were aimed primarily at the large numbers of poor inner-city addicts. The 1980's have seen increased pressure from consumer groups and labor unions for insurance coverage of substance-abuse treatment.

Correspondingly, there has been a vast expansion in the number of residential treatment programs aimed at drug users with health insurance. These programs have greatly improved the availability of treatment, but they have also increased the costs to health insurers. In fact, treatment of substance abuse has been one of the most rapidly rising items in the U.S. healthcare budget. This development probably relates to the fact that most health insurance has been set up to pay only for inpatient treatment, and thus those who wanted to treat drug abuse have had little choice but to do so on this basis. However, the rising cost of inpatient care has led many insurers to examine its cost-effectiveness, especially in comparison with outpatient care.

Publicly based treatment programs that have focused on outpatients for reasons of cost have shown that many drug abusers can do very well with this less expensive intervention. For example, an individual found to be using cocaine only intermittently is placed in an intensive outpatient setting involving regular therapy combined with urine testing, rather than a more expensive 21-day inpatient program.

Nonresidential programs are being examined by several insurance companies with an eye toward identifying those types of patients who can be treated safely and effectively as outpatients. If guidelines for such treatment are developed, and if they are translated into reimbursement policies, the coming years may see a significant expansion of outpatient programs for substance abuse.
GEORGE E. WOODY, M.D.
A. THOMAS MCLELLAN, PH.D.
CHARLES P. O'BRIEN, M.D., PH.D.

Ears, Nose, and Throat

New Ear Implants • Light and Voice • Fewer Overnights After Tonsil Removal • Nose Reconstruction • Creating New Skin

Ear Implants

Researchers continue to develop new cochlear and other implants for the hearing-impaired and to study which devices are best for which circumstances. Cochlear implants are electrical devices surgically inserted into the inner ear that directly stimulate the auditory nerve leading to the brain. A key question under study is whether there is an advantage to stimulating with multiple electrodes rather than just one.

Surgical restoration of hearing with implants is also possible when there are disruptions of the hammer, anvil, and stirrup. These three tiny bones of the middle ear conduct sound vibrations from the eardrum to the inner ear. One promising new replacement for these bones is made of glass ceramic.

Some people with "conductive" hearing loss in both ears but with good nerve function in at least one may benefit from the Xomed Audiant Bone Conductor, approved in 1987 by the U.S. Food and Drug Administration. A tiny magnetic disk is implanted in the skull behind the ear, and a miniaturized external sound processor is held in place over the implant by another magnet. (An earlier system used a larger processor worn on the body.) The processor picks up sound and sends the vibrations to the disk, which transmits them through bone to the inner ear.

Implants also appear to be a possible solution in some cases of Ménière's disease. This condition is a

261

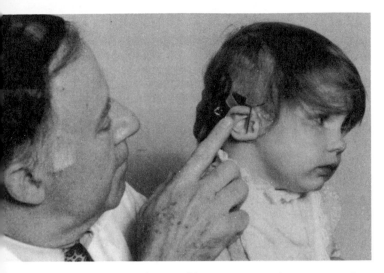

Her inner ear damaged by meningitis, this young patient has received the latest "bionic ear," which enables her to hear by stimulating her auditory nerve with electric impulses. Called a cochlear implant, the device reverses what is called sensorineural deafness.

relatively common disorder of the inner ear that is characterized by fluctuating hearing loss, tinnitus (ringing in the ear), pressure in the ear, and severe attacks of vertigo. The underlying problem is believed to be an overaccumulation of one of the fluids of the inner ear. For cases that cannot be eased by medication, there appears to be great promise in reducing the symptoms by implanting a tiny valve in the inner ear. The valve can be used to remove excess fluid.

Light Makes Contributions to Voice

The larynx, or voice box, is a structure vital for human communication. Recently, novel applications of the technology of light have been used to correct problems in the larynx.

One application relates to chronic hoarseness. The hoarseness may be due to vocal-cord polyps (thickenings of the covering of the vocal cord due to irritation), vocal-cord weakness or paralysis, nodules on the vocal cord, or cancer. These are relatively easy to diagnose. Sometimes, however, the vocal cords appear to move normally, yet the voice is still not satisfactory. This type of hoarseness may be due to stiffness or subtle abnormalities of vocal cord motion, which can now be detected by laryngeal stroboscopy.

Stroboscopy involves flashing a light very quickly, over and over. When the flashes are close to the frequency of vibration of a moving object, the motion appears to slow down. Keeping the rate of flashing slightly different from the rate of the vocal cord shows the undulating motion of the cord with each vibration. Changes in the normal pattern of vibration can then be easily detected. Such changes can explain hoarseness caused by a vocal cord that otherwise appears normal. Once this information is obtained, medical therapy can be directed toward its correction. The whole examination can be recorded on videotape for later study and review. Professional voice users, such as opera singers, can also study the videotape and gain insight into any vocal problems they may have.

The use of the laser in medicine has made great strides in recent years. Otolaryngologists use the laser in many parts of their specialty, but nowhere has it found greater application than in operations on the larynx. For example, vocal-cord growths can be removed bloodlessly without a cutting instrument having to touch the tissue directly. Small cancers of the vocal cord formerly were treated with radiation therapy. Now, some are amenable to removal by use of a laser without much alteration in vocal quality. This type of surgery can in certain cases avoid the use of radiation, which can lead to complications such as dryness and scarring of the vocal cord.

Shorter Hospital Stays for Tonsillectomy

Removal of the tonsils and adenoids is one of the most commonly performed operations in the United States today. Physicians long preferred to keep patients in the hospital for one night after the operation to watch for postoperative complications, such as bleeding or airway obstruction. In an effort to reduce costs, however, many insurance companies no longer pay for a hospital stay after the operation. There is evidence that this policy may be justified. A recent study of over 1,000 patients at a large teaching hospital showed that complications are unlikely to occur if the patient has done well for about ten hours after surgery.

New Approach to Nose Reconstruction

A recent technique facilitates plastic surgery on the nose, particularly in cases where there is a complex deformity or serious injury. Formerly, "rhinoplasty" was performed from the inside of the nose with the surgeon working through the nostrils. This limited the surgeon's ability to visualize the nasal cartilage and bones. The new technique allows the soft tissue and skin to be lifted off the outside of the nose, giving the surgeon an excellent view of the bone and cartilage structure. In addition to incisions inside the nose, a small incision is made along the junction of the nose and lip. Although this results in a small external scar, the scar is barely visible.

Expanding the Skin

Techniques are improving for major reconstruction operations that require moving skin and soft tissue from one area of the body to another to repair a defect. Surgeons report refinements in graft and flap procedures, notably in the use of tissue expanders. In a graft the tissue to be moved is totally separated from the body. With a flap, the substitute tissue is left partially attached to its original site and rotated into its new position. A flap has the advantage of keeping intact the blood supply from its site of origin. But sometimes not enough skin is available for a flap. For example, additional tissue may be required for certain types of reconstruction of the throat or jaw when these areas have to be removed because of cancer. Additional skin can be "created" by stretching the skin over the proposed flap with the use of a tissue expander. This is a plastic bag placed underneath the skin. It can be progressively inflated with fluid over a period of several weeks. As the plastic bag gets larger, it stretches the overlying skin and makes more tissue available for transfer.

See also the Spotlight on Health article CHILDREN'S EAR INFECTIONS.

CHARLES P. KIMMELMAN, M.D.

BRITAIN'S STUFFED-NOSE VACATIONERS

No one would willingly catch cold on vacation—that is, no one except a visitor to the Common Cold Unit in Salisbury, England. Housed in a World War II hospital (originally built to handle epidemics that never happened), the Harvard Hospital virology laboratory uses volunteers—30 at a time for ten-day intervals—to study how cold viruses are transmitted and to test anticold medicines. Since 1946, CCU scientists have studied the effectiveness of vitamin C, zinc, and interferon, and the effects of wetness, coldness, personality, and kissing on some 20,000 subjects.

A few days after volunteers arrive, they receive a "virus challenge," which may be either a harmless saline wash or a solution containing a live cold virus dripped into their noses. Volunteers are expected to record their temperatures daily, save any used tissues, take a psychological test, and stay at least 30 feet away from all other guests except their roommates. In some cases they will take experimental drugs for cold prevention, symptom relief, or cure.

In exchange for acting as research subjects, guests at the CCU get free room and board, about $3 a day in pocket money, and ten days of peace and quiet. The center is equipped with television, games, a library, and plenty of room to roam or bicycle outdoors. Because of the isolation, idyllic setting, and reasonable cost (the CCU even pays the round-trip fare from London to Salisbury), the center has become a popular holiday spot for harried homemakers, students preparing for exams, the unemployed, and even newlyweds.

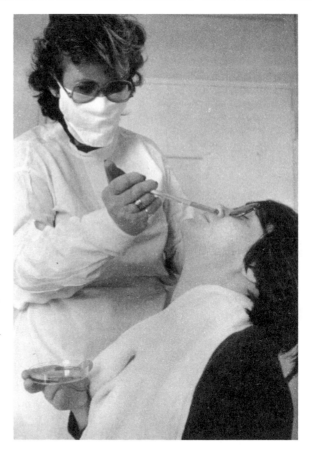

In spite of the abundance of cold viruses on the premises, the center reports that a volunteer's chance of becoming infected during the ten-day stay is only between 1 in 5 and 1 in 3—a statistic cheering to the human guinea pigs but discouraging to researchers. According to CCU virologists, the work could go a lot faster if more subjects would catch cold.

Environment and Health

Risks of Radiation • Air Pollution Standard Redefined • Report on Acid Rain • Treaty to Protect the Ozone Layer

Health Risks of Radiation

How dangerous is radiation to the human body? Several reappraisals of this question that were made public during 1987 all concluded that some fundamental health risks from radiation are greater than previously believed. Two of the studies presented new information about the health hazard of radon, a naturally occurring radioactive gas that can accumulate in houses and other enclosed spaces. Much of what scientists know about the effects of radiation in the human body is built on the over 40 years of study of survivors of the atomic bomb attacks on the Japanese cities of Hiroshima and Nagasaki in 1945. Another of the 1987 reports made public the first results of a reappraisal of this information; these also suggested that radiation was far more likely to cause cancer than scientists had thought.

NCRP radiation study. According to a new study by the National Council on Radiation Protection and Measurements (NCRP), the average American's annual radiation dose is 360 millirem (or, in the preferred unit of measurement, 3.6 millisieverts). This is almost twice the amount estimated previously, and inclusion of radon encountered in the home and other enclosed spaces acounts for virtually the entire increase. Since the NCRP's figures represent the average dose for the entire population, individuals' exposures vary considerably. The total radiation dose can be divided into six categories, as follows:

1. Natural sources make by far the largest contribution to the total dose. In this category is radon from soil and rock, which alone accounts for 55 percent of the total. Other natural sources, accounting for 27 percent, include cosmic radiation from space and naturally radioactive substances within the body.

2. The NCRP estimated that 1.7 million Americans are exposed to radiation at work, of whom about 900,000 receive measurable doses. For the latter group the annual average dose from work is about the same as that from natural radiation. Spread over the

entire population, however, the dose from this source of radiation accounts for only 0.3 percent of the total. Fields in which workers are exposed to radiation include medicine, oil drilling, and uranium mining.

3. Nuclear power plants—including what is called the nuclear fuel cycle, from mining to waste disposal—account for another 0.1 percent, although this figure is of course higher for persons living near such plants. Possible radiation from decommissioning of nuclear plants is not included. The largest component is from uranium mining and milling.

4. Various consumer products, including smoke detectors, cigarettes, and X-ray devices used to inspect luggage, contribute 3 percent of the total dose. Building materials and the domestic water supply are other potentially large contributors in this category, since they may give off radon that accumulates in closed areas.

5. Medical diagnosis and treatment, including X rays and various nuclear medical procedures, make up 15 percent of the total dose. Doses from dental procedures are so low that they are no longer included. The NCRP noted that older people undergo more medical examinations than others, so that calculation of the average dose for the population perhaps should include correction factors for age and possibly sex (there are more women than men in the older population). Three procedures account for more than half of the collective dose from X-ray examinations—lumbar spine, upper gastrointestinal, and barium enema exams. Among nuclear medical procedures, bone, cardiovascular, and brain scans make up 60 percent of the collective dose of radiation.

6. Other sources of radiation include transportation of radioactive materials, operation of research reactors, activities of governmental weapons and research facilities, and fallout from testing of nuclear weapons. The nonradioactive mineral extraction industry—aluminum, copper, lead, and zinc—is also included in this category. Even for nearby individuals, the average dose from these sources is extremely small; the average dose for the entire population is smaller still.

Fallout affects the entire population but is no longer a significant radiation source. Most components of fallout already have lost most of their radioactivity through decay over time. However, people will continue to experience one component of fallout, carbon-14, for many additional generations.

New radon study. People exposed over their lifetimes to concentrated amounts of radon are 1½ times as likely to die from lung cancer as people not so exposed, according to a three-year study by a committee of the National Research Council, a part of the National Academy of Sciences. Its conclusions were based on epidemiological studies of uranium miners in the United States and Canada and metal miners in

Sweden, which were then extended to the general population. The new study estimated an additional 350 deaths from lung cancer for every 1 million people exposed to concentrated amounts of radon. This figure is 2½ times more than a 1984 estimate by the NCRP, but it is less than half the excess mortality estimated in a 1980 study by the same National Research Council committee.

The new report comes at a time when there has been increasing evidence that radon-222 is accumulating in houses and other enclosed areas in large portions of the United States. Radon's radioactivity is in the form of alpha particles, which can lodge in the lungs. Over several years' time, the radon decays to form other radioactive substances, stimulating the formation of cancer cells in the body.

The risk of lung cancer increases with the length of exposure to radon, the committee stated, but decreases over time when the person is no longer exposed to the higher level of the gas. On the average, a man exposed to concentrated amounts of radon over a lifetime will lose one-half year from his lifespan; a woman will lose about one-quarter of a year.

The study found that the people most at risk of lung cancer are cigarette smokers who are also exposed to radon; their risk is at least ten times that of non-smokers exposed to the gas. (Only about 15 percent of all lung cancers occur among nonsmokers.) Besides the radon, these people receive radioactive substances from the inhaled tobacco smoke. Radioactive particles from both sources lodge in the lungs, creating an increased risk of lung cancer that the members of the committee said is calculated by multiplying the risk from radon by the risk from smoking.

The committee's calculations of excess lung cancers and increased risk were based on a lifetime exposure to the equivalent of one Working Level Month (WLM) per year of radon's radioactivity. For comparison, the present federal limit for occupational exposure to radon is 4 WLM per year (four times the exposure assessed in the study). The WLM is a unit devised to measure the radiation exposure of underground miners, who typically work about 170 hours (or 21 eight-hour days) per month. One WLM is defined as exposure to a specific level of radon radioactivity (100 picocuries per liter of air) for 170 hours. Exposure to that level of radon 24 hours a day for a month, or 720 hours, is equal to 4.2 WLM. If someone stays at home 12 hours a day in such an environment, the exposure is 2.1 WLM per year.

Atomic bomb survivors study. Atomic bomb victims in Hiroshima are showing larger increases in cancer rates than expected, and an investigation has revealed that they were subject to less radiation and from a different mixture of radiation types than was earlier believed. Since smaller amounts of radiation

are associated with the cancer rates, this finding may mean that the risk of cancer from radiation is twice that previously supposed, or even greater. These are the results of a preliminary report by the Radiation Effects Research Foundation in Hiroshima, which has been studying survivors in both Hiroshima and Nagasaki since shortly after the end of World War II. Results in Nagasaki are closer to what were expected.

Through reexamination of data from a postwar simulation of the Hiroshima bomb, the researchers found that much of the radiation previously thought to be from neutrons actually came from gamma rays. The error was made, in part, because the bomb was dropped in the relatively humid atmosphere of the port city of Hiroshima, while the simulation was conducted at a desert site in Nevada. Moisture absorbs neutrons, so that far less neutron radiation reached the ground in Hiroshima than in Nevada.

The distinction is important for human health because each type of radiation interacts differently with living tissue. Neutrons have a much higher relative biological effectiveness than gamma rays, meaning that they are many times more effective in causing cancer. So in reality, the people at Hiroshima received lower doses of radiation than previously believed. Therefore, the doses that they actually received create a much greater cancer risk than had been thought.

Further research is now under way into the significance of these findings, both for the bomb survivors and for the health of general populations around the world. An important part of this study will focus on creating the most precise mathematical model possible of the effect of each type of radiation on the human body and specific organs.

Air Pollution

In 1987 an important and controversial report by a federal task force concluded that acid rain is not a significant health problem in the United States. In another significant development, the U.S. Environmental Protection Agency (EPA) completed the first comprehensive revisions of the way air pollution is measured since the Clean Air Act was enacted in 1970. These changes will form the basis for determining the priorities for cleaning U.S. air, the length of time the cleanup will take, and how cleanup funds will be spent.

Acid rain. In its 1987 interim report, the National Acid Precipitation Assessment Program said that acid rain—defined as precipitation at a pH lower than 5.65—is not yet a major threat to the U.S. environment, to agricultural crops, or to human health. The only possible health risk, the report stated, is to people who are especially sensitive to pollution and those

265

with chronic health problems. However, the study concluded, sulfur-based pollution does contribute to degradation of the air's visibility and clarity.

Many health and environmental experts in the United States and Canada disagree with the conclusion that acid rain does not harm human health. On the contrary, they believe that the pollutants in acid rain are a major cause of asthma and bronchitis in children, can harm adults who have emphysema and heart disease, and pose a risk during pregnancy. One expert called these pollutants the third most important cause of lung disease, after active and passive smoking. In addition, critics point out that when acid rain enters the earth's water supply, it can carry along toxic heavy metals that enter the food chain, posing an additional health risk.

Acid rain is formed when certain air pollutants that are naturally quite acidic mix with water formed in clouds. Acidity and alkalinity are measured by pH, a scale ranging from 0 to 14. The more acidic a substance is, the lower its pH, from 7 to 0. Distilled water is neither acidic nor alkaline and has a pH of 7. Normal (unpolluted) rainwater is slightly acidic, having a pH of 5.65. Each whole number on the pH scale from 7 to 0 registers acidity ten times greater than the number above it, so that a substance with a pH of 3 is ten times as acidic as one with a pH of 4. Because of air pollution, much of the rain, snow, and fog now experienced in the United States and Canada has a pH ranging from about 4.0 to 3.0 or below. In other words, precipitation in many parts of North America is between 10 and 100 times as acidic as normal rainfall.

The pollutants in acid rain are oxides of nitrogen and sulfur that are released into the environment from the burning of fuels, mainly coal from power plants and other large industrial sources and gasoline from automobiles. These oxides occur in the form of very small particles less than 2.0 micrometers in diameter. (One micrometer is a millionth of a meter.) When combined with moisture in the air, they become nitric acid and sulfuric acid.

Fine particles of sulfur-based pollution originate primarily in the Ohio River Valley and are carried to the East Coast of the United States and into Canada by prevailing winds. They are much less prevalent in the West. Canada also produces sulfur-based pollution; some of this enters the United States, but the amount is much smaller than that Canada receives from the United States.

Nitrogen-based pollutants often result from auto emissions, and they are especially prevalent in the western portions of the United States. Ozone, an unstable form of oxygen created when nitrogen oxides and various other substances react with sunlight, also contributes to the formation of acid rain. Concentra-

tions of ozone in the lower atmosphere—where it is a pollutant—are highest along the East Coast and in southern California. High concentrations of ozone and of nitrogen and sulfur oxides often occur together during periods of stagnant air.

Measuring harmful pollutants. The new standard for air pollution measurement that was adopted by the EPA is based on the concentration of smaller particles, which are more damaging to health. For many decades, the standard EPA measure of air pollution had been the total amount of pollution particles in the air, a figure referred to as total suspended particulates. This figure includes particles as small as 0.1 micrometer in diameter and as large as 25-45 micrometers. However, scientific research has made clear that different sized particles have different effects on the human body. Air pollutants harm the body when they lodge in the lungs, reducing their ability to function. Essentially, the larger particles breathed in through the nose are filtered out before they reach the lungs. It is the smaller particles that pass through the early filtering process and end up in the lungs.

In determining limits to air pollution, the problem is to determine exactly which sized particles do most of the damage and then to give them the most weight

Lee Thomas of the U.S. Environmental Protection Agency (left) points to a chart showing the process by which certain chemicals, used in plastic foams and as aerosol-can propellants, deplete the ozone layer, allowing harmful ultraviolet rays to penetrate. At right, scientists, in Antarctica to study a growing hole in the ozone shield, survey the rugged landscape.

in measuring pollution levels. In 1987 the EPA determined that particles 10 micrometers and smaller are the major health hazard. Its new standard for pollution measurement replaces total suspended particulates with what is called PM_{10}, which represents this limited-size range. The new 1987 rule sets the maximum average concentration of PM_{10} for a 24-hour period, not to be exceeded more than once a year, at 150 micrograms per cubic meter. The new annual standard is an average PM_{10} concentration of 50 micrograms per cubic meter. Individual states are to enforce the new regulation, under implementation plans that must be approved by the EPA. Timetables for compliance by urban, suburban, and rural areas will differ depending on an area's likelihood of compliance (for instance, severely polluted areas will be given more time). The specific method of air sampling used to measure compliance will depend on the characteristics of an area's air.

Not all scientists think that PM_{10} is the most accurate standard for measuring pollutants harmful to human health. In recent years, various scientists have suggested that the most harmful range of particulates is 0.1-1.0 micrometers, and certainly below 5.0 micrometers.

The EPA reasoned that recent studies show particles 6-10 micrometers in diameter can enter the lungs, especially in children and some adults who breathe partially or entirely through the mouth. Also, fine particles—less than 2.5 micrometers in diameter—comprise 40-70 percent of PM_{10}, depending on geography, so this portion is taken into account. The amount of fine particles in the air over a wide region affects visibility, climatic change, and acidity of precipitation, and the EPA is considering adopting another standard specifically for fine particles to address these problems, though the agency has not mentioned associated health effects as such.

Protecting the Ozone Layer

The first international agreement to protect the ozone layer of the upper atmosphere, which serves as a shield against cosmic ultraviolet radiation that can cause skin cancer, was signed in 1987. In addition, scientists confirmed in laboratory tests that chlorine is the cause of the current thinning of the ozone shield and of the growing "hole" that has been observed each polar spring for the last five years in the portion of the ozone layer over Antarctica.

The Montreal treaty. For more than a decade, it has been known that the thin layer of ozone high in the stratosphere is vulnerable to destruction by a class of chemicals composed of chlorine, fluorine, and carbon and known as chlorofluorocarbons (CFC's). As a result, the United States and Canada in 1978 outlawed the use of CFC's as aerosol-can propellants. CFC's remain a multibillion-dollar industry worldwide, however, used in plastic foams and as refrigerants and solvents, as well as propellants in some countries.

In September 1987, 23 nations signed a treaty in Montreal agreeing to reduce their use of CFC's over the next decade. Before taking effect in 1989, the treaty must be ratified by at least 11 industrialized nations representing at least two-thirds of the world's consumption of CFC's. The United Nations, which sponsored the treaty, expects the necessary ratifications to be obtained.

After the treaty takes effect, industrialized countries approving it are to restrict their domestic use of CFC's to their 1986 level of consumption and limit their production to a 10 percent increase over the 1986 level. By 1994 they must reduce their consumption to 80 percent of the 1986 figure and production to 90 percent. And by 1999, use must drop to 50 percent of the 1986 level and production to 60 percent. Consumption of halons, another class of chemicals damaging to ozone, must be frozen at 1986 levels by 1994. The production levels for CFC's were set slightly higher than consumption levels in order to allow the industrialized nations to continue producing CFC's for use by developing countries, which were allowed to increase their consumption for economic reasons. The EPA announced plans to issue rules to comply with the treaty, which the U.S. Senate ratified in March 1988.

Further research. Also in 1987, scientists at two California research facilities independently reproduced the process by which the ozone layer is reduced. Stratospheric clouds are composed principally of a mixture of ice and nitric acid, at temperatures of around 180°K (−93°C). When chlorine-containing molecules like CFC's react with the ice-nitric acid clouds, two-atom molecules of chlorine gas are released. The chlorine then reacts with sunlight, and the two atoms separate, each reacting with a molecule of ozone, which consists of three atoms of oxygen. The chlorine combines with one oxygen atom to form chlorine monoxide, leaving the other two in the form of conventional oxygen. Since ozone is inherently unstable, it is always in the process of forming and being destroyed. The presence of chlorine speeds up the process of destruction.

Scientists have also learned that the ozone layer is not uniform around the world and is concentrated at the poles. There is always some seasonal fluctuation in its thickness, but the change is greatest over the Antarctic during its springtime because of heavy clouds formed during the winter, extreme cold, and the angle of the sun. Recent investigations have found that levels of chlorine compounds are many times higher over the Antarctic than expected from past research. Scientists also believe that the total amount of ozone in the layer may be decreasing by 0.5-1 percent per year. Each 10 percent decrease in ozone can account for a 20-500 percent increase in the amount of radiation coming into the atmosphere.

Early in 1988 the National Oceanic and Atmospheric Administration announced the start of an expedition to the Arctic to investigate reports of depleted stratospheric ozone over that region. And in March 1988 a study by the National Aeronautics and Space Administration indicated that there had been significant ozone depletion over the Northern Hemisphere. The study also concluded that ozone loss in the Southern Hemisphere, while most acute in the springtime over Antarctica, occurred at other times of the year as well and over a wider area.

Industry actions. In January 1988 the American Telephone and Telegraph Company and a small company announced the development of a substitute for CFC-113, which is widely used for cleaning electronic equipment and accounts for about 17 percent of annual CFC production worldwide. The new compound, considered environmentally safe and competitive in cost with CFC-113, is expected eventually to greatly reduce the use of CFC-113. In March 1988, E. I. du Pont de Nemours & Company, the largest producer of CFC's worldwide, announced that it would phase out production of the chemicals.

See also the feature article LUNG CANCER: PREVENTION AND TREATMENT.

ELLEN THRO

Eyes

Genetic Test for Cancer • New Types of Contact Lenses • Laser Surgery for Nearsightedness • Long-term Study of Cancer Treatment

Cancer Test

Researchers at the Massachusetts Eye and Ear Infirmary in Boston have developed a genetic test to identify children at risk of developing the hereditary form of retinoblastoma, an eye cancer that affects young children, usually under age five. Approximately 200 children in the United States develop retinoblastoma each year, and 30 percent of these patients have the inherited form. The latter patients also are at increased risk for other cancers, especially osteosarcoma, a form of bone cancer.

Currently, children from families with a history of hereditary retinoblastoma must be examined under anesthesia every three months during the first five years of their lives. The new genetic test, which is based on a blood sample, will allow such examinations to be limited to children who test positive and will permit early, vision-saving treatment. Retinoblastoma may be treated by radiation, cryotherapy (freezing), lasers, or removal of the affected eye.

Contact Lens Advances

In July 1987 the U.S. Food and Drug Administration approved routine clinical use of the first soft contact lenses that block ultraviolet (UV) light while permitting transmission of visible light. The lenses, made by the Cooper Companies, were approved for both daily wear (in which the lenses are removed each night) and extended wear (in which they are worn continuously for several days). The effect of UV light on the eyes remains controversial, but there is evidence that it may be associated with the development of cataracts and age-related macular degeneration (deterioration of the central part of the retina). In recent years UV-shielding compounds have been included in eyeglasses and in artificial lenses implanted in the eye following cataract surgery, and the availability of UV-blocking soft contact lenses represents the latest development in this trend.

Another product that has been awaited for several years—disposable contact lenses—reached the marketplace in early 1988. These lenses, manufactured by the Vistakon subsidiary of Johnson & Johnson, are designed to be disposed of after as little as one week's wear and replaced with a fresh, sterile pair. Disposable contact lenses, particularly if designed for extended wear, have a number of potential advantages. First, frequent changes of lenses eliminate the long-term buildup of chemical deposits and subsequent risks to the health of the cornea, the clear outer surface of the eye. Disposable extended-wear lenses also provide the easiest system of lens care, eliminating the need for cleaning and disinfecting procedures and probably decreasing the risk of corneal infection associated with contact lenses. Vistakon in early 1988 was test marketing the lenses in Florida and California before releasing them nationwide.

See also the Health and Medical News article MEDICAL TECHNOLOGY.

Laser Surgery for Nearsightedness

During 1987, research intensified into the potential use of lasers for surgery to correct refractive errors (conditions such as myopia, or nearsightedness, and hyperopia, or farsightedness). The laser that shows the most promise for this application is the excimer laser, a high-power source of ultraviolet radiation. Experiments performed in the early 1970's showed that excimer laser radiation could perform extremely precise etching of polymer films, etching a pattern with tolerances of a thousandth of an inch. Some ophthalmologists then recognized that the excimer laser might be useful for extremely precise surgery on the cornea. Most of the optical power of the eye is derived from the corneal shape; therefore, if the shape is altered surgically, it is possible that optical defects—for instance, myopia—may be corrected.

Specifically, the excimer laser may be useful in an automated version of radial keratotomy, a surgical procedure in which four to eight slits are made in the edge of the cornea (like the spokes of a wheel) to flatten its surface and correct myopia. Some ophthalmologists believe that the use of the excimer laser will improve this procedure by making the surgery more controlled and predictable. The excimer laser may also be usable to lathe a permanent "contact lens" into the corneal surface; that is, tissue can be removed by the laser in such a controlled way that a contact-lens-like correction can be etched into the cornea. Although this is an exciting possibility, many technical obstacles—for instance, controlling the cornea's healing response—must be overcome before the technique could be used routinely in humans.

Choroidal Melanoma Treatment

An international study has begun to compare the relative effectiveness of two forms of therapy—radiation and removal of the eye—for the most frequent type of eye cancer, choroidal melanoma. These tumors, which arise from tissue within the eye, are uncommon, with 1,500 cases diagnosed annually in the United States. Treatment of them is particularly important since they may not only disturb vision but also spread outside the eye and threaten the patient's life. The traditional treatment for choroidal melanoma has been removal of the eye, a procedure referred to as enucleation. Over the past ten years, however, the value of enucleation in reducing the spread of the melanoma to other body tissues has been seriously questioned. Other treatment techniques—in particular, radiation using locally applied radioactive material (plaques) or tightly focused beams of charged particles generated by cyclotrons—have been used to treat thousands of patients.

To resolve this controversy, the U.S. National Eye Institute is sponsoring the Collaborative Ocular Melanoma Study, whose primary goal is to establish whether enucleation or radiation plaque treatment is most effective in ensuring cancer-free survival in patients. Ongoing recruitment for the study is being conducted at 32 medical centers in the United States and Canada. Patients who meet the eligibility criteria will be randomly assigned to one of the two treatment groups and will be followed for ten years after treatment. Because of the large number of patients required for statistically significant calculations, the relative rarity of the tumor, and the fact that tumor spread may occur five or more years following initial diagnosis, it is anticipated that the results of this study will not be available for another decade.

Improving Eye Examinations

During 1987, a West German optics company introduced a commercial version of the scanning laser ophthalmoscope. This device uses a low-intensity laser to sweep rapidly across the retina, creating images of the back of the eye that can be viewed on a television monitor. High-resolution images of the eye's interior are produced without dilating the pupils with drops or shining bright lights into the eye. The increased comfort for the patient allows the physician to examine the eye for longer periods of time than the three or four minutes possible with conventional ophthalmoscopes. The scanning laser ophthalmoscope is expected to improve early diagnosis and treatment of a number of retinal diseases, including diabetic retinopathy and age-related macular degeneration. Images obtained from it can be recorded on videotape for later viewing and analysis, or they can be digitally recorded, permitting computer-assisted reconstruction and study. It is hoped that the new device can also help provide information useful in designing laser treatment for retinal disorders.

Drug for River Blindness

Progress in the treatment of onchocerciasis, or "river blindness," a parasitic eye disease that affects an estimated 17.5 million people worldwide, was made in 1987 with the release of a new and highly effective drug, ivermectin (Mectizan). Onchocerciasis is a public health and socioeconomic problem of great magnitude in many tropical countries, particularly in Africa, and it appears to be spreading in Latin America. It primarily affects people in rural areas, especially in remote places. The parasitic worm that causes it is carried by blackflies, which are often found along the banks of tropical rivers, hence the term river blindness.

Humans are infected with the worm, *Onchocerca volvulus*, after being bitten by infected blackflies. The adult worms produce millions of larval microfilariae in patients, causing severe itching, disfiguring skin lesions, and a variety of eye lesions that eventually produce the feared blindness. The World Health Organization estimates that the total number of people at risk of contracting onchocerciasis is 85.5 million and that approximately 340,000 people are totally blind as a result of the disease. On the basis of the last figure, it can be estimated that 1 million people worldwide have suffered a significant loss of vision, leading to at least partial disability, as a result of onchocerciasis.

Ivermectin, which was developed by Merck Sharp & Dohme Research Laboratories, rapidly eliminates the parasites from the eyes and skin after a single oral dose, with minimal side effects. Prior to its development, the antiparasite drugs available all produced significant side effects that limited their widespread use. The World Health Organization feels that retreatment with ivermectin at intervals of 6 to 18 months will probably be the ideal schedule in areas with endemic disease transmission.

Merck, as part of a unique collaborative program with the World Health Organization, will donate ivermectin for use by qualified treatment programs throughout the world.

See also the Spotlight on Health articles GLAUCOMA *and* SUNGLASSES.

CARMEN A. PULIAFITO, M.D.

Genetics and Genetic Engineering

Detecting Down's With Ultrasound • Identifying Genes That Cause Birth Defects • A Crash Program to Map the Genes? • Genetic Fingerprinting Comes to the United States

Prenatal Screening

Intensive research continues on the prenatal detection of disorders caused by abnormalities among the tens of thousands of genes on the 23 pairs of human chromosomes. Recent developments included a simpler way of recognizing Down's syndrome, while questions were raised about the accuracy of one method of testing for genetic defects.

Detecting Down's syndrome. New findings on the use of ultrasound to reveal signs of Down's syndrome suggest that the technique may be effective in the second trimester (roughly from 13 to 24 weeks) of pregnancy. Down's syndrome affects as many as 2 out of every 100 live births and is caused by an extra copy of chromosome 21. Children born with Down's syndrome, once known as mongolism, are mentally retarded.

In November 1987 physicians at Harvard Medical School reported that when a fetus is viewed by ultrasound, the genetic defect is revealed by two telltale signs: thighbones that are slightly shorter than normal and an extra roll of skin on the back of the neck. If these signs are present, the researchers said, the mother should undergo amniocentesis to confirm the diagnosis of Down's syndrome. In amniocentesis doctors search for genetic defects in fetal cells from the amniotic fluid surrounding the fetus.

CVS accuracy questioned. The increasingly popular method of prenatal screening called chorionic villus sampling, or CVS, may be less accurate than physicians believe, according to researchers from the University of Amsterdam. In CVS, fetal cells are obtained from chorionic villi, small hairlike projections from the membrane surrounding the fetus that are formed early in pregnancy. CVS can be performed as early as 8 weeks into pregnancy, whereas amniocentesis is usually performed at 16 weeks. However, CVS may be slightly more dangerous than amniocentesis, which leads to a miscarriage in 0.5 percent of the procedures performed.

The Dutch physicians reported that in 15 out of 500 pregnancies, CVS indicated the presence of a genetic defect when there was none. But some experts assert that inaccuracies could be reduced by more thorough testing. The villi have three layers of cells. Usually the second layer is used because results can be obtained in a day or two. Using cells from the third (innermost) layer requires a week or longer but is apparently more accurate.

New Products

The U.S. Food and Drug Administration approved a fifth genetically engineered product for marketing in 1987. The four products previously approved were human insulin, human growth hormone, interferon, and a hepatitis B vaccine. The agency also authorized two companies to begin human tests of a genetically engineered vaccine against AIDS (acquired immune deficiency syndrome).

TPA. The new product approved by the FDA in 1987 was tissue plasminogen activator. It also gained approval in Canada. An enzyme that dissolves the blood clots that cause heart attacks, TPA can save lives and minimize heart damage if it is administered to victims within six hours after an attack. In the United States about 1.5 million people a year have heart attacks, and about a third of them die. Many analysts believe TPA will be the best-selling genetically engineered pharmaceutical of the century and will give its manufacturer, Genentech, Inc., of South San Francisco, Calif., a dominant position in the industry. However, the retail price of a single dose of TPA is about $2,000.

According to a March 1987 report from the congressional Office of Technology Assessment, at least 80 enzymes, hormones, proteins, and other biological agents were being studied by the biotechnology industry for use in humans. Among those expected to be approved soon were erythropoietin, a kidney hormone that stimulates the production of red blood cells and may be useful in treating anemia, and atrial hormone (also known as atrial natriuretic factor, or ANF), a heart hormone that lowers blood pressure.

AIDS vaccines. In August 1987 the FDA gave permission for the first U.S. trials in humans of a potential vaccine against AIDS. The vaccine, manufactured by MicroGeneSys, Inc., of West Haven, Conn., is composed of proteins that are the same as proteins found on the surface of the AIDS virus but are produced by genetic engineering in a virus (baculovirus) that normally infects insects. It was hoped that the proteins would cause the body's immune system to make antibodies against the AIDS virus. The tests began in September at the National Institute of Allergies and Infectious Diseases.

In November the FDA approved tests of a second potential vaccine, produced by a subsidiary of the Bristol-Myers Company based in Seattle. That vaccine was prepared by inserting genes coding for an AIDS surface protein into the vaccinia virus, a well-known, relatively safe virus used for smallpox vaccinations. The idea was that once it was in the body the virus would produce the AIDS proteins, thereby stimulating an immune reaction. The human trials were to be conducted at the Pacific Medical Center in Seattle. The initial tests for both potential vaccines were designed to determine their safety and whether they prompt the body to produce antibodies. Most experts caution, however, that it will be years before an AIDS vaccine will be in general use.

Tourette's Syndrome

A wide range of behavioral disorders may be caused by the genetic defect responsible for the neurological disease known as Tourette's syndrome, according to researchers from the City of Hope National Medical Center in Los Angeles. The best-known symptoms of Tourette's are the compulsive shouting of obscenities and tics—repetitive movements such as eye blinking or finger tapping. But the new results indicate that many individuals who do not display these symptoms may also suffer from the syndrome. The gene responsible for Tourette's syndrome is surprisingly common, occurring in 1 of every 83 people. The researchers said that the defect could also cause hyperactivity, conduct problems, stuttering, dyslexia, panic attacks, phobias, depression, sleep problems, compulsive behavior, and mania.

The most important result of this discovery may be a recognition that individuals with the genetic defect who have these related disorders should not necessarily be treated with psychotherapy alone, as is now often done. Because the syndrome results from a chemical imbalance in the forebrain, the researchers said, psychotherapy will not be effective unless it is accompanied by drug therapy to relieve the imbalance. Moreover, the drug therapy must take into account the presence of the genetic defect. One of the most common disorders in children with Tourette's syndrome is hyperactivity. A hyperactive student can't sit still, can't concentrate, can't follow through on assignments, and shouts things out in class. Hyperactivity is often treated with low doses of amphetamines, but those drugs, when given to a child with Tourette's, may worsen the tics and other symptoms.

The Search for Defective Genes

Scientists reported more progress in identifying genetic "signposts" of inherited diseases through a genetic engineering technique introduced in the past few years. Using specialized proteins called restriction enzymes, researchers break each of the 46 human chromosomes into shorter segments and separate them by length. By studying families with a history of a particular disease, they are often able to identify genetic markers—strands of DNA (deoxyribonucleic acid) of characteristic length—associated with the disease. These genetic markers can then be used in amniocentesis or CVS to identify fetuses that have the defective gene. They also point the way to identification of the defective gene itself.

Neurofibromatosis. Researchers at Harvard Medical School and Massachusetts General Hospital in Boston and at the University of Utah in Salt Lake City independently reported in May 1987 that they had identified on chromosome 17 the approximate location of the gene that causes von Recklinghausen's neurofibromatosis. This is the condition commonly known as elephant man's disease, after a celebrated case in

19th-century England, which served as the basis for a popular stage play and film in recent years. The disease's effects actually range from benign lumps or discolorations on the skin to nerve-cell tumors called neurofibromas that can severely disfigure the patient. The disease occurs in 1 of every 4,000 live births and affects about 100,000 Americans. Researchers speculated that success in identifying the gene itself could lead to improved treatment for the disease or even to a cure.

A few months after the von Recklinghausen's discovery, a team headed by the Boston researchers reported that it had found on chromosome 22 genetic markers for bilateral acoustic neurofibromatosis, a rarer form of the disease that occurs in 1 of every 50,000 births. It is characterized by multiple tumors of the cranial and spinal nerves, which produce deafness, balance disorders, and paralysis. Some evidence indicates that the gene involved normally oversees the production of a substance that suppresses growth of tumors in the brain and nervous system. Isolation of the gene might thus lead to therapy for many types of neural tumors.

Gaucher's disease. In March 1987 researchers at the U.S. National Institute of Mental Health reported that they had identified a gene defect associated with a form of Gaucher's disease that can kill children in infancy. Gaucher's disease is caused by deficiency of an enzyme that normally breaks down a certain type of fat. In the enzyme's absence, the fat builds up in the victim's cells, causing complications that include enlargement of the spleen and liver, as well as bone deterioration. In a few cases, neurological disorders may result as well. The nervous system is not affected in the most common form of the disease, which occurs notably among Jews of Eastern European, or Ashkenazic, origin—including as many as 20,000 Americans. The newly identified defect in the gene for the enzyme was linked with forms of Gaucher's disease involving the nervous system. The most severe form is normally fatal by the age of 2½. Identification of the defect may eventually help doctors predict which patients with Gaucher's will develop neurologic symptoms, and may contribute to the development of genetic therapy for the disease.

Cancer. The discovery of evidence of a gene defect that may contribute to the development of colon cancer, the second most deadly type of cancer in the United States, was reported in August 1987 by a group of British researchers. The team studied 13 families with familial adenomatous polyposis, or FAP, a rare hereditary condition that strikes 1 in 10,000 individuals and often leads to colon cancer. In the disease, the large intestine is carpeted with hundreds of small growths called polyps. The British researchers found that the gene for the condition is on chromosome 5.

Genetic Crime Solving

Genetic fingerprinting performed by Leicester University geneticist Alec Jeffreys (right) led to the release of one suspect and the identification of the man who raped and murdered two teenage girls near London. The family of one of the girls—Lynda Mann (inset)—is shown above.

In related work they studied cells from 45 people with ordinary colon cancer. It was found that in more than 20 percent of the cases the cancer cells were missing portions of chromosome 5—from the same general area where the FAP gene was thought to be. Apparently, the gene in the missing segment of chromosome 5 somehow protects against colon cancer. The researchers suggested that a faulty FAP gene may play a role in some cases of noninherited colon cancer, as well as in the rarer familial form. Scientists hope that an understanding of how the gene works may lead to new therapies for cancer.

The biggest cancer killer is lung cancer, which each year accounts for more than 130,000 deaths in the United States and more than 11,000 deaths in Canada. In December 1987 a team of Dutch and British researchers reported identifying a genetic defect that appears in all major types of lung cancer. The defect involves the absence of both copies of a gene on chromosome 3 that seems to protect individuals against cancer development.

See also the feature article LUNG CANCER: PREVENTION AND TREATMENT.

Mapping the Genes

In order to speed the search for the causes of human diseases, many biologists have been pushing for the creation of a mammoth project, known as the Human Genome Initiative, that would lead to the identification of each of the 3 billion individual chemicals that make up the genes in a set of human chromosomes—the human genome. The project could involve hundreds of scientists and technicians working for 10 to 20 years and, by some estimates, could cost as much as $3 billion.

But the cost and time would be well worth it, proponents argue. The knowledge gained, they say, could lead to new insights into, and perhaps cures for, the estimated 3,500 inherited diseases. It might also provide new information about such diseases as cancer, heart disease, and diabetes, which are all thought to involve a genetic predisposition.

The U.S. Department of Energy took a step toward the initiative in September 1987 when it ordered three of its eight labs to accelerate their preliminary work on the project. The labs in Berkeley and Livermore, Calif., are breaking down individual human chromosomes into smaller fragments—a process called genetic mapping—as a first step toward identifying each chemical, while the lab at Los Alamos, N.M., is developing new instruments and computer techniques for carrying out the actual identification of each chemical. The massive genome project was strongly endorsed by a National Academy of Sciences committee in February 1988.

Genetic Fingerprints

The same technology used for identifying genetic markers for disease can also be used for unequivocal identification of individuals. The technique is already being used widely in Britain for identifying suspects in crimes and for establishing familial relationships in immigration and paternity cases. It was first used in the United States in 1987.

In genetic fingerprinting, DNA from any type of cell—such as cells in sperm, blood, or hair—is broken down with restriction enzymes and separated by length. The result is a pattern of DNA fragments of characteristic sizes. This pattern, like fingerprints, is unique for every individual, but similarities can be used to establish family relationships.

In 1987 police in three small villages near London used the technique to identify the man who raped and murdered two teenaged girls. Genetic fingerprinting established that the crimes had been committed by the same man and led to the release of a youth who had been charged with one of the murders. Police then called upon all young men in the area to submit cell samples for analysis. The suspect was caught in September when he tried to get a friend to submit specimens for him.

In November a jury in Orlando, Fla., convicted a man in a rape case in which genetic fingerprinting was the only evidence tying him to the crime. The man was later convicted of another rape, again on the basis of his DNA fingerprint. The technique is also expected to find wide use in paternity testing.

See also the Spotlight on Health article MONOCLONAL ANTIBODIES: MEDICINE'S POWERFUL NEW TOOL.

THOMAS H. MAUGH II, PH.D.

Glands and Metabolism

Somatostatin: Potent New Hormone Treatment • Possible New Oral Contraceptive

Treatment With Somatostatin

A new preparation of the hormone somatostatin has been successfully used to treat a variety of conditions associated with tumors throughout the body. These tumors cause excess amounts of other hormones to be secreted—excesses that the somatostatin preparation can suppress.

Somatostatin was originally discovered in the hypothalamus, an area of the brain that produces several hormones that regulate the pituitary gland—which, in turn, secretes various hormones that act upon glands throughout the body. One of somatostatin's effects is to inhibit the pituitary gland from secreting two hormones—growth hormone and thyroid stimulating hormone. Somatostatin is also found in and acts upon other parts of the body. In the pancreas, it has the unique ability to inhibit the secretion of both insulin and glucagon, which lower and raise blood sugar levels, respectively. In the gastrointestinal tract, somatostatin can directly and indirectly inhibit aspects of digestion and absorption.

Until now, somatostatin could not be used therapeutically because it has an extremely short duration of action, only several minutes. Recently, however, a long-acting somatostatin analogue (synthetic equivalent) called SMS 201-995 was created. It has been extensively studied in the treatment of various conditions associated with endocrine tumors.

Treating acromegaly. SMS 201-995 has been used to treat acromegaly, a disease in which a pituitary tumor causes excess production of growth hormone; effects include enlarged internal organs, oversized hands and feet, and coarsened facial features. The synthetic somatostatin is injected under the skin, and a single injection can inhibit growth hormone secretion for 6 to 12 hours. Many patients whose acromegaly was incompletely treated by other means (for instance, if the pituitary tumor could not be completely removed surgically) have been successfully treated with SMS 201-995, with minimal side effects. Some patients have been successfully giving themselves injections for several months.

Controlling gastrointestinal conditions. SMS 201-995 has also been used in patients with certain hormone-secreting gastrointestinal tumors. These tumors secrete insulin (causing prolonged states of low blood sugar), gastrin (causing excessive acid production in the stomach and peptic ulcers), or hormones that cause intractable diarrhea.

The best therapy for most of these tumors is surgical removal. Sometimes, however, the tumors cannot be completely removed, and patients may have persistent, disabling symptoms. SMS 201-995 injections have been shown to be effective therapy for many such patients. The excess production of the problematic hormones can be suppressed and symptoms relieved by the somatostatin analogue.

Taming overactive thyroids. Finally, there is a rare pituitary tumor that secretes excess thyroid stimulating hormone and thereby causes overactive thyroid glands. This condition—called hyperthyroidism—causes a general speeding-up of the body's chemical processes; the results include anxiety, shakiness, rapid and irregular heartbeat, and weight loss. Hyperthyroidism has many other possible causes, and it usually can be treated with medication, radioactive iodine, or surgery. However, these forms of therapy are ineffective in the rare cases of hyperthyroidism caused by a pituitary tumor that secretes excess thyroid stimulating hormone. The pituitary tumor in these patients often is large and cannot be completely removed surgically. However, injections of SMS 201-995 can suppress secretion of thyroid stimulating hormone and alleviate the symptoms of hyperthyroidism. Side effects have been minimal.

New Contraceptive

Work is proceeding on a potential new contraceptive drug known as RU 486. RU 486 blocks the action of the hormone progesterone. This hormone is normally secreted by the ovaries in the latter half of the menstrual cycle and helps prepare the wall of the uterus so that a fertilized egg can become implanted there. But if something interferes with the action of progesterone, menstruation occurs (that is, the lining of the uterus is sloughed off). Exactly how RU 486 acts against progesterone is not known. But by doing so, it presumably prevents any fertilized egg from becoming implanted—thus preventing what doctors would define as pregnancy. (Those who consider pregnancy to begin with fertilization would characterize RU 486 as an abortion agent, and its development for contraceptive use in the United States is opposed by anti-abortion groups.)

In a 1987 study, a single oral dose of RU 486 was given to normal young female volunteers once a month. RU 486 consistently induced menstruation within 72 hours after its administration. The women were then given an injection of a hormone (human chorionic gonadotropin) that normally prevents menstruation during pregnancy. They still menstruated despite the hormone injection. There were no side effects reported.

For those not opposed to RU 486 on moral grounds, its advantages are obvious: it could serve as a once-a-month contraceptive pill, free of the side effects of currently available birth control pills. A key disadvantage is less obvious: the timing of the administration of RU 486 is critical. In the 1987 study, daily blood tests were performed to verify the day of ovulation (the production of an egg by the ovary) and the day on which RU 486 should be given. Women with irregular menstrual cycles would not be good candidates for this contraceptive. It should also be kept in mind that studies thus far are preliminary, and the long-term safety and effectiveness of RU 486 remain to be determined.

Although the greatest potential of RU 486 may be as a contraceptive, a 1986 study indicated it could also be used in the first weeks after implantation to terminate an early pregnancy—thus serving as what everyone would consider an abortion pill.

See also the Spotlight on Health article THE MANY ROLES OF ESTROGEN.

MERVILLE C. MARSHALL, JR., M.D.

Government Policies and Programs

UNITED STATES

Meeting Rising Healthcare Costs • Continuing Debate Over Abortion Funding • New Regulations for Experimental Drugs • Increased AIDS Funding

Controlling Medical Costs

Government efforts to control the rising costs of medical care continued in 1987 and into 1988 at both the federal and state levels. Late in 1987, last-minute budget negotiations between U.S. President Ronald Reagan and congressional leaders cut medicare spending by $2.1 billion for the 1988 fiscal year (October 1, 1987, to September 30, 1988) and by $3.8 billion for the 1989 fiscal year. However, medicaid spending was increased as a result of the budget negotiations by $44 million for the 1988 fiscal year and by a total of $633 million over three years.

Hospital reimbursement. Hospitals found that the budgetary shoe that medicare cost-control procedures imposed on them was beginning to pinch. (Medicare is the federal health insurance program for the elderly and disabled.) In 1983 the government began reimbursing hospitals with a flat fee for each patient, based on that patient's diagnosis and regardless of length of stay. Early in 1988 the inspector general of the Department of Health and Human Services released a report that showed that the average profit margins for hospitals from treating medicare patients in fiscal

year 1987 had fallen from 14.4 percent for the previous fiscal year to 9.6 percent. The higher profits in earlier years had been used to justify the medicare reimbursement restraints instituted in 1983. Medicare payments total about 40 percent of the revenue that hospitals receive from treating patients.

This announcement followed soon after other dismaying news for hospitals. In late 1987 the budget agreement between the president and Congress significantly limited increases in hospital reimbursement under medicare. One of the most difficult issues in the lengthy 1987 budget negotiations was to determine what the equitable rates of reimbursement should be for two types of hospitals with special problems. The first type consists of large urban hospitals with a high proportion of low-income patients without private insurance, who force these hospitals to absorb charges not reimbursed through medicare or other government programs. The second type consists of rural hospitals with higher per patient costs because of lower rural population density and the need to provide a wide range of services in isolated areas served by only one hospital. The solution was to provide complicated changes in the reimbursement formula. Through March 31, 1988, medicare hospital reimbursement was limited to a net rate increase of 0.4 percent over the fiscal 1987 level. Effective April 1, 1988, and continuing until September 30, 1988, hospitals in metropolitan areas with populations of more than 1 million were limited to a 1.5 percent medicare reimbursement increase; rural hospitals would get a 3.0 percent increase; and all other hospitals, a 1.0 percent increase.

The administration and congressional budget negotiators reached agreement on budgets not only for fiscal year 1988 but also for fiscal year 1989, which begins on October 1, 1988. Thus, the budget legislation limited medicare reimbursement to hospitals in fiscal 1989 to the following rate increases, which are below the anticipated inflation rate: 2 percent for large metropolitan hospitals, 1.5 percent for rural hospitals, and 2.5 percent for other hospitals.

Payments to physicians. Medicare reimbursement to physicians was cut as part of the 1987 budget agreement. Through March 31, 1988, physicians' reimbursement was reduced by 2.3 percent from 1987 levels—the amount stipulated in the automatic Gramm-Rudman budget cuts passed by Congress a few years ago. From April 1 through September 30, 1988, participating physicians (those who accept what medicare pays as payment in full for their services) got an increase of 3.6 percent for primary care services, such as office and home visits, and an increase of 1.0 percent for all other services. Nonparticipating physicians were limited to an increase of 3.1 percent for primary care services and 0.5 percent for all other services.

For fiscal year 1989, participating physicians got an increase of 3.0 percent for primary care services and 1.0 percent for other services. Nonparticipating physicians were given reimbursement rates 0.5 percent below the rates for participating physicians.

In addition, starting April 1, 1988, an across-the-board reduction was imposed on payments to physicians for 12 procedures that the Department of Health and Human Services determined were overpriced. For these procedures, a sliding scale reduction of up to 15 percent was also authorized for any charge that exceeds 85 percent of the weighted national average for that procedure. These procedures include coronary artery bypass surgery, hip replacements, cataract surgery, and pacemaker surgery.

Social security premiums. Beginning January 1, 1988, social security recipients began paying a higher premium for physicians' services, outpatient clinics, and home healthcare, which are covered under Part B of medicare. President Reagan had proposed the increase in the premium in September 1987. The increase was considered excessive by many members of Congress. The premium is paid through deductions from social security checks.

Legislation dating back to the early 1980's required that these premiums cover 25 percent of the cost of Part B of medicare. The late 1987 budget agreement extended through 1989 the requirement that the premium increase be sufficient to cover 25 percent of the program costs but also directed that premium increases not be allowed to cause the total social security checks of the 31 million disabled and elderly recipients in the United States to drop from one year to the next. The 1988 premium is $24.80 a month, which is an increase of 38.5 percent over the 1987 level of $17.90 a month.

Medicaid. Not all of the health provisions in the budget legislation were cost reductions. The medicaid program, which provides health benefits primarily to low-income people, received a $44 million increase in fiscal 1988. The budget agreement continued the policy of recent years of encouraging states to expand participation in the medicaid program. The federal government provides matching funds for medicaid varying from equal amounts to three times the amounts provided by the states. The newly expanded medicaid program is intended to encourage states to offer coverage to pregnant women and to infants who are in families not participating in public assistance programs but who have relatively low incomes. The budget legislation contained two provisions with this objective. First, states have the option, starting on July 1, 1988, to offer medicaid coverage to pregnant women and to infants up to one year of age in families with incomes below 185 percent of the federal poverty level. Second, also on July 1, 1988, states have the option to provide medicaid protection to all children in families with incomes above the state-determined level for benefits under the Aid to Families With Dependent Children (AFDC) program but below the federal poverty level.

In March 1988 the Reagan administration issued a new regulation, scheduled to take effect April 8, that was expected to increase the cost of nursing home care for many medicaid recipients who have other sources of income. Under the current system, medicaid recipients can deduct from their income, before determining what share they will pay for their nursing home care, the cost of certain medical expenses such as eyeglasses and hearing aids. The new rule allows states to cut back or eliminate these deductions, so that patients would wind up paying more for their nursing home care while the federal and state governments would pay less.

States take action. In 1987 public hospitals expressed concern about the increasing yearly losses they sustain from treating the millions of Americans without either private insurance or government health benefits. The House Ways and Means Committee heard testimony that in 1985 hospitals across the country incurred losses of $7.4 billion from providing care to patients who either could not or did not pay their bills. This amount was more than double the amount in 1980. The American Hospital Association testified that hospitals were having difficulty covering these losses by charging more to patients with private insurance and those who pay their own bills. The hospital spokespeople urged Congress and the states to assume a greater share of the costs of treating poor patients.

Some states began attempts to extend health coverage to the estimated 37 million Americans without private insurance or access to government programs. This approach had been spearheaded by Hawaii, which for 13 years has required employers to provide health insurance. In 1987, Massachusetts Governor Michael S. Dukakis proposed that employers in his state be required to provide health insurance for workers and that the state provide insurance for the unemployed. This measure was still pending in the Massachusetts legislature as of early 1988, but other states enacted more limited laws. Oregon began selling health insurance to small firms and providing businesses a state tax credit of up to $50 a month per worker. Arizona offered to sell to small employers the insurance program that covers the poor under the medicaid program operated by that state. Michigan began to sell health insurance to people who leave public assistance for jobs that do not provide health insurance. The state of Washington began a pilot program to sell subsidized health insurance to families with incomes at or below 200 percent of the federal

Opponents of abortion marched in Washington, D.C., in January 1988 to protest the 15th anniversary of the Supreme Court decision that legalized abortion in the United States. President Ronald Reagan told demonstrators he would push for new antiabortion regulations; however, a federal judge prohibited enforcement of the regulations when pro-choice advocates challenged them in court.

poverty level, which means families of four that earn up to $22,400 a year.

One unusual response to high medical costs came from the state of Nevada, some of whose hospitals have the highest profits and highest treatment charges of any hospitals in the United States. Legislation enacted in June 1987 forced three investor-owned hospitals in Las Vegas to reduce by 15 percent their actual revenue from patients whose bills are not paid by government programs—that is, revenue from health insurers or from patients who pay their own bills. Less stringent provisions applied to other hospitals in Nevada with lower profit margins.

Family Planning

The controversy continues over whether federal funds should be used to finance abortions, even indirectly. In February 1987, Secretary of Health and Human Services Otis R. Bowen issued an order to his department's field organizations directing them to review family planning grants to ensure that "no family planning program of which abortion or abortion-related activities" is a part would be eligible for federal family planning funds.

For some proponents of the right-to-life movement in the Reagan administration, Bowen's directive did not go far enough. In July, Bowen fired Jo Ann Gasper, a deputy assistant secretary of HHS, after she refused to renew funding for several family planning agencies affiliated with Planned Parenthood, saying that they advocated abortion. The department said that in doing so Gasper had exceeded the statutory authority granted by Congress in its 1970 Public Health Service Act, which established the government's family planning program. That act had never been interpreted to allow denial of federal funds to an organization, such as Planned Parenthood, that performs abortions with nonfederal funds. The restriction had always been that federal funds could not be used for that purpose. Gasper claimed that she was only carrying out the Reagan administration's antiabortion policies.

Later that same month, it became clear that controversy over this issue would continue. At a White House meeting of antiabortionists, President Reagan proposed new regulations that would prohibit family planning clinics that receive federal funds from offering abortion counseling, referring pregnant women to abortion services, or even discussing abortion as an option. (Under current law, clinics receiving federal funds may offer abortion counseling or perform actual abortions, but private funds are used to do so.) Immediately, pro-choice advocates announced that they would go to court if these regulations were issued, seeking to get them overturned as a violation of the constitutional right to freedom of speech.

Reagan again pushed the new antiabortion regulations in January 1988 in remarks broadcast over loudspeakers to some 50,000 abortion opponents assembled in Washington, D.C., to protest the 15th anniversary of the U.S. Supreme Court ruling in *Roe* v. *Wade*, which legalized abortion. Shortly thereafter, HHS issued the new rules, to go into effect March 3. However, in February, in a case brought by Planned Parenthood and other groups, a federal district judge in Colorado temporarily blocked the enforcement of the regulations, finding them unconstitutional because they were an "unduly burdensome interference with a woman's freedom to decide whether to terminate her pregnancy." The same month a New York judge temporarily banned enforcement of the regulations in that state.

Finally, on the day the regulations were to take effect, a federal judge in Boston issued an injunction permanently prohibiting their enforcement "anywhere within the United States." The Reagan administration appealed the ruling.

Regulation of New Drugs

The drug approval procedures of the U.S. Food and Drug Administration came under considerable fire during 1987. Federal law requires elaborate testing of any new drug, so as to avoid tragedies such as occurred a quarter of a century ago when thousands of infants were born deformed because their mothers had taken an inadequately tested drug, thalidomide, during pregnancy. These procedures follow a strict and lengthy progression from test-tube experiments, to tests on animals, and finally to clinical tests in humans. Fewer than 20 percent of the drugs tested are eventually approved for commercial sale. The dilemma is that individuals faced with terminal illnesses want immediate access to a potentially lifesaving drug, even if it has not been fully tested and approved by the FDA.

A major factor in this controversy had been the furor over the drug zidovudine, formerly known as azidothymidine, or AZT, which is used to treat AIDS. Even though the testing and the FDA's approval to market the drug took less than two years and was the fastest any drug ever received such approval, AIDS activists considered this too long a period. In September 1987 the state of California established its own AIDS drug testing approval program, independent of the FDA procedures. A previous California law allowed drug manufacturers to apply for state approval to test and sell drugs without adhering to federal regulations as long as the drugs were manufactured and distributed only in California. The new law directs the state to take advantage of this little-used ability to develop experimental AIDS drugs and provides funds for that purpose.

In May 1987 the FDA issued regulations designed to make experimental drugs more widely available to greater numbers of patients with serious or life-threatening conditions. Drugs could be made available at earlier stages in the testing process if preliminary tests showed promise and if no other treatment exists. The FDA would also allow more manufacturers to charge for experimental drugs (they could be sold at cost), thereby giving companies an incentive to make products available.

Battling AIDS

The growing AIDS epidemic, which has already claimed over 31,000 lives in the United States, continued to receive major attention in government policies. Despite the budgetary stringency, Congress before adjourning in December 1987 doubled the funding for AIDS. An overall appropriation of $932 million for AIDS research, education, and training for fiscal 1988 was approved. The largest amount, $448 million, went to the National Institutes of Health, primarily for research. The Centers for Disease Control in Atlanta received $305 million for education and preventive activities. The third major allocation was $112 million to the Alcohol, Drug Abuse, and Mental Health Administration, primarily for drug abuse programs to prevent the transmission of AIDS through contaminated needles. Other funds went for training healthcare personnel and for renovating long-term care facilities for AIDS patients.

In March 1987 the Supreme Court extended the protection against discrimination granted in federal law to persons with contagious diseases. By a 7-2 vote, the Court held that the prohibition of discrimination against the handicapped by employers, schools, and others receiving federal funds includes persons with contagious diseases. Although the case involved a Florida teacher who had been fired because she had tuberculosis, the Court's decision strongly suggests that the ruling applies to AIDS victims.

See also the feature article AIDS UPDATE.

JAMES A. ROTHERHAM

CANADA
Supreme Court Issues Ruling on Abortion • Drug Patent Bill Is Passed • New Steps to Combat AIDS • No-Smoking Rules for Federal Employees

Abortion Law Struck Down

In January 1988 the Supreme Court ruled that Canada's restrictive abortion law was unconstitutional and interfered with a woman's right to the control of her body. The 5 to 2 ruling removed the offense of abortion from the criminal code, making abortion a matter between a woman and her doctor.

Canada's previous abortion law, passed in 1969, allowed for abortions only at accredited hospitals and only after a hospital committee had decided by a majority vote that the pregnancy was a threat to the "life or health" of the woman. Critics charged that that law was unfair, since some areas, including the entire province of Prince Edward Island, did not have a single authorized hospital for abortions. They also charged that the approval process caused delays that were distressing and often dangerous for the women involved. About 60,000 legal abortions are performed each year in Canada.

The ruling vindicated Dr. Henry Morgentaler, who had performed an estimated 20,000 abortions in defiance of the 1969 law. Since 1970, he had been tried and acquitted four times on abortion charges, though he also spent ten months in jail after an appeals court overturned the first acquittal. When an Ontario ap-

Tried four times for openly performing abortions, Dr. Henry Morgentaler won his appeal before the Supreme Court in Ottawa in January 1988, effectively legalizing abortion in Canada.

peals court overturned the fourth acquittal, Morgentaler appealed the decision to the Supreme Court, which based its 1988 decision on the 1982 Charter of Rights and Freedoms.

Antiabortion activists vowed to press for new laws restricting abortion, and the legal struggle over the issue was expected to continue for years. Several of the Supreme Court justices who voted to overturn the 1969 law indicated in their written decisions that they would accept some legal restrictions on abortion in the later stages of pregnancy. (Such a policy would be similar to that authorized by the 1973 *Roe* v. *Wade* decision of the U.S. Supreme Court, which essentially allows unrestricted access to abortion in the first three months of pregnancy but permits states to regulate it thereafter.) The individual provinces could also impose abortion regulations, treating the issue as a health concern, not a criminal one. The health minister for British Columbia, for example, announced after the Supreme Court decision that the provincial medical plan would pay only for abortions approved by committees at accredited hospitals—the same conditions required by the 1969 law. But such regulations and any new federal laws undoubtedly would face further challenges in court.

Passage of Drug Patent Law

A historic showdown between the House of Commons and the Senate threatened enactment of Canada's long-awaited new drug patent legislation, which arrived in the upper chamber in May after passing its third reading in the House. (To become law, a bill must pass three readings in the House and receive Senate approval.) But finally, after more than six months, three Senate votes, and two House rejections of attempted Senate revisions, the Senate passed the controversial bill, which gives ten-year Canadian patent protection to products of multinational drug manufacturers. The tally was 27 to 3, with 32 abstentions.

Despite intense Senate scrutiny, in the end the Conservative government's original version of the bill passed largely intact. Senate demands, all rejected by the House, included giving the drug companies only four-year instead of ten-year patent protection, making them legally bound by promises to invest $1.4 billion in Canada in the next ten years, and withdrawing all patent protection from firms that don't maintain investment. Just before the opposition Liberals finally let the bill pass in mid-November—with all but three of their senators abstaining from the vote—they called for a free conference, a procedure not used since 1947, in which three or more representatives of each chamber would work out a compromise. But the government staunchly refused to adopt all but minor changes and loudly rebuked the delaying tactics

Members of the AIDS Committee of Toronto, financed in part by the Canadian government, meet to prepare pamphlets on safe sex for distribution in gay bars, restaurants, and bookstores.

of the nonelected chamber, which had not killed a bill since the 1940's.

Efforts to enact the bill began in 1984 after 15 years of free-for-all legislation that allowed makers of generic drugs to copy and sell brand name products by simply paying a 4 percent royalty on the net selling price to wholesalers and retailers. Changing the 1969 law was strongly opposed by New Democrats, Liberals, generic drug makers, and consumer groups, who maintain the new law will cause drug prices to rise dramatically and hurt consumers, especially the poor. The bill had been the subject of hard lobbying by the drug companies and the Pharmaceutical Manufacturers Association.

Combating AIDS

Preventing the spread of AIDS (acquired immune deficiency syndrome) took on greater urgency across Canada in 1987, the year the number of reported cases nationally surpassed 1,000. The federal government gave $3.7 million (Canadian dollars used throughout) to the Canadian Public Health Association to create four television advertisements, three of which were rejected in March 1987 by a committee representing 20 private stations. The committee thought that the ads' direct message—"Sex with different partners is risky. You've got to avoid it or use a condom for protection"—promoted promiscuity. The federally

funded Canadian Broadcasting Corporation accepted all of the ads, running them even in prime time.

Other public education efforts were started in earnest in 1987. Ontario, Quebec, and British Columbia, the provinces with the vast majority of reported AIDS cases in Canada, announced plans to create sex education programs in their high schools, with Quebec committing $2 million to the cause. Ontario made AIDS education mandatory for grades 7 through 13 and pledged $12.5 million over two years to improve and coordinate provincial AIDS prevention efforts.

The federal government took steps to protect the staff and employees of its diplomatic missions and employees and inmates in penitentiaries. Medical kits containing sterile first aid equipment, including syringes and a blood substitute, were sent to Canadian embassies in certain Third World countries where federal officials worry about inadequate sanitation and procedures for testing blood. Plans also got under way for a joint Canada-U.S. project to supply embassy staff in such countries with blood from North America should an emergency transfusion be needed. In prisons, staff members were given disposable resuscitation equipment, gloves, and gowns for use when dealing with prisoners with AIDS. Policy guidelines for handling such prisoners were issued, saying that they should not be treated differently from other inmates unless necessary for medical reasons.

See also the feature article AIDS UPDATE.

Curbs on Smoking

Federal employees had to stop smoking at their desks October 1. The sweeping rule affects about 30 percent of the 200,000 public servants, who now must move to designated areas to light up. The crackdown was one step in the federal government's plan for a total smoking ban in the public service by January 1, 1989. Effective December 9, the government also banned smoking on Canadian airline flights of two hours or less within North America. The new regulation, which could affect 65 percent of all flights in Canada, provides fines of up to $5,000 for passengers who smoke and $25,000 for airlines that allow them to. Proposed legislation to ban all forms of tobacco advertising by January 1, 1989, is being vigorously opposed by the tobacco industry, which launched an $800,000 publicity campaign protesting the plan.

Fighting Drug and Alcohol Abuse

In May 1987 the federal government launched a $210 million, five-year program to curb drug abuse. The department of Health and Welfare announced the wide-ranging plan, which involves fighting the problem through public education, treatment and rehabilitation, law enforcement, and research. The government said statistics show that more than 1 million Canadians used marijuana and 16 million used alcohol in one year, that nearly 200,000 used cocaine, and that drug importing and trafficking increased significantly between 1984 and 1985. Among other measures, the department pledged to update Canada's drug laws, to provide more personnel and equipment to customs drug squads and the Royal Canadian Mounted Police, and to revise the Criminal Code so that police would have the power to trace and seize the profits of drug dealers.

Reimbursing Physicians

Following a 1986 boycott of nonemergency patients from Quebec by Ontario orthopedic surgeons, the reimbursement of doctors who treat out-of-province patients became a divisive issue for the federal, Quebec, and Ontario governments. At the center of the dispute was the fact that in violation of the Canada Health Act, the Quebec government was not reimbursing Ontario doctors as much for treating Quebec patients as the doctors were paid by their own province for treating Ontario patients. In some cases, an Ontario doctor received 35 percent less for a Quebec patient than for an Ontario patient. The problem was most acute in Ottawa, where some 16,000 Quebec patients are treated each year. In May 1987 the Quebec government pledged $8.9 million for new

medical services, which would stem the tide into Ontario by half. But Ontario doctors still demanded that the federal government step in to enforce the Canada Health Act.

LYNNE COHEN

Health Personnel and Facilities

Changing Healthcare System • Cutting Costs • Hospital Shutdowns and Professional Shortages • Future for Doctors

Changes in the System

The U.S. healthcare system is undergoing a revolution. Healthcare is increasingly being delivered in new places, with new rules governing the care that is given and how that care is financed. Despite the dramatic changes that have taken place over the past few years, doctors and hospitals remain the key players. But their role is precarious, for they are also prime targets for budget cutters and others concerned about the continuing escalation in the cost of healthcare. In their ceaseless efforts to curb the cost of medical care—in 1987 consuming 11.2 percent of the U.S. gross national product—both public and private payers have increased their scrutiny and control over how medicine is practiced and what it costs, challenging the autonomy and authority the key players have traditionally enjoyed.

Role of doctors. In response, doctors and hospitals have become increasingly competitive and creative just to stay in business. Doctors who once practiced alone and charged patients what they could afford now belong to groups that provide care for a fixed fee or offer discounts to large insurance groups. The American Medical Association estimates that at least 40 percent of the 550,000 physicians in the United States have some type of affiliation with at least one such group—whether a health maintenance organization (HMO), preferred practice (or provider) organization (PPO), or independent (or individual) practice association (IPA).

Today's doctors advertise and market as never before, emphasizing convenience as well as service. Offices and clinics are located near shopping malls;

hours are adjusted to meet the needs and schedules of working patients; walk-in clinics offer round-the-clock care without waits or appointments. In some areas, doctors once again make house calls.

Doctors are also branching out. Procedures like cataract surgery, once hospital staples, are performed routinely on an outpatient basis. And at least 5 percent of the nation's doctors now dispense the medications they prescribe, a controversial practice defended by those who dispense drugs as a convenience and service to their patients.

Role of hospitals. Hospitals, too, have turned to new and different ways of doing business. Confronted with declining occupancy, which translates into declining revenues, hospitals are actively seeking more staff doctors as a way to bring in more patients. Where they once relied on image to fill beds and assure revenues, hospitals now market such extra services as fitness clubs and classes, gourmet meals, a homelike ambience, long-term care, and programs for alcoholism, drug addiction, sports medicine, weight reduction, and other special problems. They have established neighborhood "doc-in-the-box" clinics for cash customers who want quick, convenient advice on colds, cuts, and other simple medical problems, and they have set up "800" telephone numbers and referral services to help patients find a doctor.

Continued growth. Such changes are symptoms—signs of correction within a system that literally became the victim of its own success. Sparked by spectacular technological advances and a philosophy that strove to provide care to all, the U.S. healthcare system swelled into a $458 billion industry by 1986, continuing to outpace the economy as a whole. The healthcare system is now one of the largest employers in the United States.

So far the system has continued to grow despite efforts to rein in expenditures. Experts anticipate that growth will continue as new technology is developed, as the population ages, and as the number of people suffering from AIDS places increased demands on the system. By 1990 healthcare is expected to account for 12 percent of the U.S. gross national product; by the year 2000, 15 percent.

Cutting Costs

To date, the most radical change in the healthcare system took place in 1983, when the U.S. government's medicare program for the elderly and disabled began paying hospitals a fixed fee for each patient according to diagnosis, instead of paying whatever the hospital charged and regardless of the length of stay. At the same time, some private insurers began to require preadmission approval and second opinions for non-emergency surgery.

The result was fewer hospitalizations, with patients who were admitted discharged more quickly. Overall hospital occupancy rates dropped from a high of 76 percent in 1983 to 63 percent in 1987. With tighter reimbursement controls, many hospitals have found it difficult to come up with resources to pay for uninsured and indigent patients and have refused nonpaying patients or "dumped" them into public hospitals, further straining that already overburdened system. (Another result of efforts to discourage patients from entering the hospital was a sharp increase in the use of outpatient facilities—at a higher cost than healthcare analysts had anticipated.)

As Congress has checked growth in medicare reimbursement rates in an effort to control costs, hospitals have been faced with steady inflation in the prices of goods and services they purchase. At some point, U.S. hospital officials warn, the fat will be gone and the cost cutting will affect both the quality of care and people's access to it.

In some parts of the United States, cost cutting has already affected the availability of healthcare. Faced with impossible deficits, many of the nation's large public hospitals are in precarious financial condition, and increasing numbers of small rural hospitals have been forced to close. In 1985, 61 rural hospitals closed; in 1986 the number was 71, 59 of which had fewer than 100 beds.

Personnel: Shortages and Stress

Adding to hospital woes is a growing shortage of medical personnel. An American Hospital Association survey found that the number of openings for nurses had doubled between 1985 and 1986, prompting hospitals to boost salaries and offer bonuses, flexible shifts, and other special inducements. The government predicts that by the year 2000 the United States will need an additional 1.2 million registered nurses, but enrollment in basic education programs for nurses has declined dramatically, by more than 20 percent from 1983 to 1986.

The shortage is not confined to nurses or to any geographic area. Hospitals nationwide are experiencing shortages of rehabilitation professionals, radiologists, pharmacists, laboratory technicians, and home-care workers. Many of these healthcare personnel have been drawn away from hospital-based work by the growth of ambulatory care and the greater number of freestanding facilities.

Doctors: Less money, more work. To date, doctors appear to be having an easier time than hospitals, but that may be only superficial. Doctors say they may be making more, but they are working harder and enjoying their work less. The average annual physician's income (before taxes and after expenses) rose to $119,500 in 1986, up 6.5 percent from 1985. But that figure conceals a range of average incomes within specialities that runs from $80,300 for family practitioners to $162,400 for surgeons and $168,000 for radiologists. According to the American Medical Association, one-quarter of the nation's physicians make less than $70,000 a year.

The annual average salary also obscures the fact that, according to the American Medical Association, the average doctor worked harder to earn that income in 1986, spending 52.2 hours per week on patient care, up an hour from the previous year. Physicians performed an average of 3.5 surgical procedures a week, compared with 3 the year before. The number of office visits a week rose to 75.7, continuing a trend that began when medicare changed the way hospitals are paid.

Efforts to Control Spending

Like hospitals, doctors are now subject to increased second-guessing and outside scrutiny that many of them believe threatens both their autonomy and their ability to make independent decisions for individual patients, paving the way for standardized "cookbook" medicine. Caught in a classic double bind, doctors are confronted on one side with insurers and third-party payers questioning whether each test or procedure is really necessary and on the other with the threat of malpractice if a diagnosis is missed or an indicated test or procedure is not performed.

It is clear that physicians are the next major target of efforts to control health spending. Significant changes will be made in the way physicians are paid in the next few years. For doctors who treat medicare

Confronted with a reduced number of patients and declining revenues, hospitals have started to advertise a variety of hotel-like amenities.

ROBOT ON CALL

The newest employee at Danbury Hospital in Connecticut doesn't need a lunch break, medical benefits, or even a paycheck. Roscoe is a 3-foot-tall robot, created by Transitions Research Corporation, that will fetch and carry patient meal trays, laboratory specimens, and supplies. He was acquired by the hospital as an experimental solution to a high staff vacancy rate, especially among nurses and dietary aides.

Steered by a TRC worker during his first six probationary months on the job, Roscoe will eventually have an on-board video screen and keyboard to receive commands. By the end of 1988 he will navigate the 450-bed community hospital alone using computer programs and sensors (rather than following a wire or painted line on the floor, as less sophisticated automated vehicles do). He will summon the elevator with an infrared signal.

Although affectionately named by the dietary staff and painted with green candy-stripes, Roscoe is not intended to be a mascot or pet, nor does he have humanoid features such as arms or a head. He will not enter patient rooms or perform any tasks beyond the lowest of drudgery; his primary purpose will be that of a self-propelled delivery cart. (Just in case, however, TRC technicians *may* program Roscoe to greet people he meets in the hall.)

patients, Congress and the executive branch are considering various options, including fixed fees for each diagnosis and a predetermined annual fee for providing care for each patient. Changes in the way doctors are paid are also being driven by efforts within the profession to balance the existing pay inequities between the doctors who are technicians—surgeons, radiologists, and anesthesiologists—and those, like internists, pediatricians, and family practitioners, who rely on so-called cognitive skills.

Medicare statistics suggest that some physicians may be bolstering incomes by increasing volume of services, both with increased visits and additional testing. To control volume, medicare is also contemplating financial incentives for patients who select from a panel of "preferred providers" who practice conservative medicine. Medicare would pay more of a patient's bill from an approved doctor—one who makes efforts to eliminate unnecessary office visits and procedures.

Too Many Doctors?

Such changes are taking a toll. In many parts of the United States, the well-publicized "doctor glut" has cut into patient loads and forced younger doctors to join HMO's and other groups simply to survive. Escalating malpractice premiums have caused mass exodus in some specialities, such as obstetrics and gynecology, where one in eight doctors has stopped delivering babies. Though no systematic study has been made, more and more doctors seem to be retiring early or switching to administrative positions.

The difficulties also have had an impact on medical school enrollment, which declined in 1987 for the sixth consecutive year; 15,927 were admitted, a drop from the 1981 high of 16,600. (The number of applicants has also declined.) At the same time, the costs of a medical education have steadily risen so that the average doctor completes education $30,000 to $80,000 in debt. As student loans have become scarcer, minority and lower income student enrollment has also dropped, prompting fears that medical school in the future will be limited to the affluent.

Ironically, a number of experts have started to question the widely held belief that the United States is producing more physicians than it can afford. They reason that there will be increased demands on physicians as a result of an aging population (which tends to be sicker and require more intensive and expensive care); the unmet healthcare needs of the poor, the homeless, and chronically mentally ill; and the AIDS epidemic. At the same time, some experts warn that overall physician productivity could be reduced by growing numbers of women in the field (many of whom take time off for childbearing and child rearing), a trend toward practice styles with predictable hours (which are favored by younger doctors), and early retirement.

See also the Spotlight on Health articles How to Select a Doctor *and* Facts About HMO's.

MARY HAGER

Heart and Circulatory System

Aspirin and the Risk of Heart Attack • Drugs to Dissolve Blood Clots • New Research on Balloon Therapy • Lowering Blood Cholesterol Levels

Lifesaving Effects of Aspirin

In January 1988 the results of a nationwide survey provided evidence that aspirin taken every other day can significantly reduce the risk of heart attack in healthy individuals. Studies in recent years have shown that a person who has suffered one heart attack can reduce the risk of a second attack by taking aspirin, but until now no research had shown that aspirin could be useful in preventing first heart attacks among the general male population.

For nearly five years, researchers monitored more than 22,000 male physicians between the ages of 40 and 84. Those selected for study were reported to be health-conscious and in excellent health, with no previous history of heart disease or stroke. Half took

a placebo (a harmless, inactive pill) every other day, and half took a buffered aspirin. (None of the doctors knew which substance they were taking.) Among the physicians taking the placebo, 189 suffered heart attacks, 18 of them fatal; among the physicians taking aspirin, only 104 suffered heart attacks, 5 of them fatal. The results were considered so dramatic that the study was halted years before it was scheduled to end so that the information could be reported.

Although the results of this investigation are exciting, it should be noted that the overall incidence of heart disease was much lower than expected in all of the men studied—including those who did not take aspirin. This finding to some extent suggests that merely controlling risk factors for cardiovascular disease, as these health-conscious physicians did, can produce a lower risk of heart attack.

Aspirin thins the blood by blocking the action of platelets, which are the particles in the blood that cause clots to form. (Tylenol and other similar painkillers contain acetaminophen instead of aspirin and so do not have this effect.) Heart attacks occur when a clot forms in a blood vessel nourishing the heart; if the vessel is already narrowed by atherosclerosis, the clot may totally block the vessel, cutting off the blood supply to the heart.

Doctors caution that not everyone should start taking aspirin every other day. Aspirin is a powerful drug and has potential side effects, including stomach distress, internal bleeding, and ringing in the ears. It also could increase the risk of a certain type of often fatal stroke for some people, since, if the ability of the blood to clot is decreased too much, hemorrhaging (bleeding) in the brain could result. Moreover, aspirin does not eliminate the risks posed by atherosclerosis, cigarette smoking, and high blood pressure. Decisions about taking aspirin regularly should be made by individuals in consultation with their doctors.

Dissolving Blood Clots

In November 1987 the U.S. Food and Drug Administration approved a new drug—called tissue plasminogen activator—that dissolves the blood clots that often cause acute heart attacks. (The drug was approved for use in Canada at the same time.) The same month, the agency also approved a new usage for streptokinase, a drug that had previously received approval for use in dissolving blood clots. Both drugs will offer cardiac care centers and hospital emergency rooms greater options in treating people in the hours immediately after a heart attack. In the United States, about 1.5 million people suffer heart attacks each year, and about one-third of them die. About 95 percent of those heart attacks are caused by blood clots that plug arteries.

In a major study of male American physicians, subjects who took an aspirin every other day had significantly fewer first heart attacks. Here, Bufferin tablets—the brand of aspirin used in the study—are mass-produced.

Tissue plasminogen activator. The first product of the biotechnology industry with a major potential market, tissue plasminogen activator (TPA) is an enzyme naturally produced in the body in very small amounts. Through genetic engineering techniques, the product's manufacturer, Genentech, Inc., of South San Francisco, produces large amounts of the enzyme in the cells of mammals. When administered intravenously (injected into a vein) within six hours after a heart attack, TPA quickly restores blood flow and thus can minimize damage to the heart and save lives. Sold under the brand name Activase, a single dose costs between $2,000 and $2,500. Pharmaceutical industry analysts expect TPA to become the most widely used product developed through genetic engineering techniques.

Streptokinase. Sold under the brand names Streptase and Kabikinase, streptokinase had been approved previously to treat heart attacks only when injected directly into the heart through a catheter—something that could be done only in special cardiac catheterization laboratories. The new approval allows the drug to be injected intravenously. Studies show that its greatest effectiveness occurs if injected within three hours of an attack.

Comparisons of the two. In trials conducted in 1985 at the National Heart, Lung, and Blood Institute, TPA proved nearly twice as effective as streptokinase in dissolving clots. However, a single dose of TPA also costs about ten times a single dose of streptokinase. (In March 1988 the Reagan administration decided to deny medicare payments to hospitals that

287

use TPA to treat heart attack patients—a move apparently caused in part by the high cost of the drug.) Both TPA and streptokinase are more effective when given as soon as possible after a heart attack, making it very important for people to go to the hospital as soon as they are aware of their symptoms. Both drugs also have certain limitations. Although higher doses of the drugs dilate a larger percentage of blocked arteries, serious and sometimes fatal bleeding becomes more common as well. However, at the dosage recommended by the manufacturers, the drugs cause bleeding in only a very small percentage of patients. Another problem is that the arteries of 15 percent of the patients treated with the drugs become obstructed again because of recurrent clot formation. Newer drugs are being developed and tested to overcome these limitations.

More on Cholesterol

About 20 million Americans have blood cholesterol levels that place them at high risk for developing coronary heart disease, the leading cause of death in the United States. In 1987, one U.S. government agency urged all adult Americans to be tested regularly for blood cholesterol levels, while another approved a drug to help lower those levels. Research showed that lower levels can reduce fatty deposits in the arteries and that an anticholesterol drug reduces the risk of heart attack.

New drug approved. In September 1987 the U.S. Food and Drug Administration approved a powerful new cholesterol-lowering drug called lovastatin (sold under the brand name Mevacor). The drug was found to reduce total blood cholesterol levels by up to 34 percent. In addition, it reduced blood levels of the harmful form of cholesterol known as low-density lipoprotein, which clogs arteries, by up to 39 percent in some patients. The drug either does not affect the blood levels of the beneficial form of cholesterol known as high-density lipoprotein, which helps remove cholesterol from the blood, or it raises these levels slightly.

Lovastatin works by inhibiting the action of an enzyme that is necessary for the liver to make cholesterol. About 70 percent of the cholesterol in the body is produced by the liver. When it cannot manufacture enough cholesterol, the liver takes it from the blood, lowering levels there.

Less likely to cause the annoying side effects that most other cholesterol-lowering drugs cause, such as flushing and indigestion, lovastatin seems to work best when combined with a low-fat, low-cholesterol diet. Doctors caution that cholesterol-fighting drugs should be taken only as a last resort, after changes in weight, diet, and exercise have failed to reduce a person's blood cholesterol levels. Possible long-term side effects of lovastatin are not known for certain; there is some evidence that long-term use may contribute to liver injury and possibly to cataract formation. The drug must be taken for life: if it is stopped, cholesterol levels rise.

Reducing heart attacks with anticholesterol drugs. In November 1987 researchers released a study demonstrating for the first time that a popular cholesterol-lowering drug reduces the incidence of heart attack in men who have high levels of cholesterol in their blood. In a five-year study of 4,000 men in Finland, the drug gemfibrozil (sold under the brand name Lopid) was found to raise blood levels of beneficial high-density lipoproteins while reducing the levels of dangerous low-density lipoproteins. The men in the study who took gemfibrozil had one-third fewer heart attacks than the men who took a placebo. Although the effectiveness of gemfibrozil in lowering blood cholesterol levels is not nearly as dramatic as lovastatin (they work in completely different ways), its side effects are mild and it is known to be safe for long-term use.

Reducing fatty deposits. Doctors have known for a long time that lowering blood cholesterol can delay or possibly prevent the development of coronary heart disease. But in June 1987 scientists from the University of Southern California reported evidence showing for the first time that greatly reducing blood cholesterol levels can actually reverse the accumulation of the fatty deposits that clog coronary arteries and can cause heart attacks.

The USC study involved approximately 160 non-smoking men who had clogged arteries and had undergone coronary bypass surgery. Half of the men were placed on a low-fat, low-cholesterol diet and were given the anticholesterol drug colestipol hydrochloride for two years. The other half of the group received placebos and were placed on a less restricted diet. After two years, those in the placebo group showed little change. But those in the treatment group showed a 43 percent reduction in the level of low-density lipoproteins that clog arteries, as well as a 37 percent increase in the beneficial high-density lipoproteins. One out of six of those patients had a shrinkage in the size of the fatty deposits lining their arteries.

Testing urged. The National Heart, Lung, and Blood Institute published a report in 1987 calling for all Americans, 20 years of age or older, to have their blood cholesterol checked at least once every five years. A cholesterol level lower than 200 milligrams for each deciliter of blood was considered desirable, a cholesterol level from 200 to 239 mg/dl was considered borderline, and a level of 240 mg/dl or more was considered high risk. The report cautioned, however, that many labs are inaccurate, so that having results confirmed by more than one test might yield more definite measurements.

Specific recommendations were made for patients based on their cholesterol levels. Those with levels lower than 200 mg/dl should do nothing except have the test repeated every five years. People with levels of 200 to 239 mg/dl should follow a cholesterol-lowering diet and have the level rechecked every year. People at high risk, with levels of 240 mg/dl or more, should also adopt low-fat, low-cholesterol diets. In addition, they should undergo further testing to determine their level of low-density lipoproteins. If these levels are high and remain so even if people follow a prudent diet, anticholesterol drugs may need to be prescribed.

See also the feature article FACTS ABOUT FAT.

Balloon Therapy

A major study released in September 1987 found that emergency balloon angioplasty, used in the hours immediately following a heart attack and after tissue plasminogen activator had already been given to dissolve the blood clot, provided little added benefit to patients over elective angioplasty performed in the days following the heart attack.

Balloon angioplasty, also called percutaneous transluminal coronary angioplasty, involves inserting a small catheter with a deflated balloon attached to its tip into a blood vessel. The tube is guided by X ray through the bloodstream to the point in the coronary artery where severe narrowing has occurred. The balloon is then inflated, opening the artery.

The study concluded that immediate balloon angioplasty was unnecessary once TPA had been administered. A common problem with angioplasty is that the obstructed blood vessels often become clogged again. The researchers showed that the rates of renarrowing of the blood vessels were about the same for each of two groups of patients, one that had the emergency angioplasty right after the heart attack and one that had elective angioplasty in the days following the heart attack.

The use of elective angioplasty as a preventive—in people with narrowed coronary arteries who have not had a heart attack—continues to increase. Researchers explored innovative new techniques to improve the success of the procedure. The major limitation of angioplasty has been its high failure rate: up to 30 percent of all dilated arteries renarrow within six months. Many of these failures require another balloon angioplasty or bypass surgery.

A possible solution was suggested in 1987 by Swiss and French researchers. After opening the narrowed artery with the balloon, these doctors placed an expandable stainless steel mesh device in the dilated area of the arteries of 25 patients. Although 10 percent of the arteries became blocked again because of serious clot formation, the other 90 percent remained open during a year of follow-up study. This approach, although still experimental, is the first to reduce successfully the otherwise significant problem of renarrowing of dilated blood vessels.

Drugs for Heart Problems

Enalapril. Swedish researchers reported in June 1987 that people with "weak hearts," or congestive heart failure, live longer when given drugs that dilate their blood vessels. These drugs, known as vasodilators, work by lowering the pressure exerted by blood vessel walls, thereby widening the vessels and allowing the heart to pump blood more easily through them. The drugs were known to improve patient's symptoms, but until recently it was not clear that they also prolonged life. The Swedish researchers studied approximately 250 patients. Half were given placebos and half the vasodilator enalapril (Vasotec) for an average of about six months. Over that time the mortality rate for those taking enalapril was reduced by 40 percent. The results of this study were similar to those of a 1986 Veterans Administration trial that treated congestive heart failure with a combination of the drugs hydralazine and isosorbide dinitrate. About 200,000 people in the United States die each year from congestive heart failure.

Nitroglycerin. Used by heart patients for more than 100 years, nitroglycerin dilates blood vessels in the body, helping people with narrowed coronary arteries. However, many patients who are exposed to nitroglycerin over a long period of time develop tolerance to it. Too much exposure to the drug will lessen its effectiveness in the body. Scientists have discovered that if a patient gives the body a break with a drug-free interval, nitroglycerin retains its potency. Using nitroglycerin for only 12 to 20 hours a day is more effective than taking it all day.

Patients who use a 24-hour nitroglycerin patch, which attaches to the skin and allows the drug to be absorbed into the bloodstream through the skin, may benefit from removing it after 12 to 16 hours in order to allow a "wash-out" period. Other drugs that dilate the coronary arteries and prevent angina, such as the class of medications called calcium blockers, may be used during the period of time when the nitroglycerin patch is removed. Calcium blockers have not as yet been shown to require this respite to maintain daily effectiveness.

See also the feature article HYPERTENSION: THE SILENT KILLER.

BRUCE D. CHARASH, M.D.
JEFFREY FISHER, M.D.

Kidneys and Urinary System

*Early Warning of Kidney Stones •
AIDS-Associated Kidney Disease •
Drugs to Prevent Progressive Kidney
Failure • Faster and More Efficient
Dialysis*

Children and Kidney Stones

A tendency to form kidney stones may begin very early in life, according to a series of recent studies of children with hematuria, or the presence of red blood cells in the urine. This condition is one of the hallmarks of kidney disease, and when it is observed in children, doctors have traditionally focused their diagnostic concern on local injury or irritation, a urinary tract infection, a form of glomerulonephritis (inflammation of the glomeruli, the tufts of capillaries where blood coming into the kidneys is filtered), or a considerably rarer possibility such as malignancy. But the recent studies have revealed that up to a third of children with hematuria may have renal (kidney) bleeding caused by hypercalciuria—an abnormally high concentration of calcium in the urine. This condition is a well-recognized antecedent of kidney stones in adults.

In a study at the University of Tennessee, 23 of 83 children (28 percent) with hematuria and without evidence of urinary tract infection or glomerulonephritis were found to have hypercalciuria. Similar proportions were found in studies in São Paulo, Brazil, and Cleveland. Research to determine the cause of the hypercalciuria has revealed an abnormally high gastrointestinal absorption of calcium in some patients, while others have a "renal leak" abnormality, in which the kidney is unable to reabsorb calcium that it filters out of the blood.

A number of children with hypercalciuria go on to develop kidney stones. Prevention of this complication can be facilitated by increasing the child's fluid intake, in order to increase the volume of urine and thus dilute urinary calcium, and by restricting dietary intake of milk products in those children with very high calcium absorption from the digestive system. The use of thiazide diuretic drugs, which lower urinary excretion of calcium, is usually reserved for children with demonstrated stone formation.

The new research indicates a need to measure urinary calcium excretion in all children with unexplained hematuria.

AIDS-Associated Kidney Disease

As clinical experience in the care of patients with AIDS (acquired immune deficiency syndrome) grows, a characteristic form of kidney disease is being observed in many patients that has been termed AIDS-associated nephropathy. In contrast to the transient, reversible forms of kidney impairment that AIDS patients develop as side effects of antibiotic therapy or as a consequence of AIDS-related infections and their complications, AIDS-associated nephropathy is characterized by a progressive, irreversible course of kidney failure.

Increased loss of protein in the urine is usually the first sign of the condition. As this loss, called proteinuria, increases in quantity, protein concentration in the blood plasma diminishes, and edema, or generalized swelling of the body, develops as a consequence. At the same time, the functioning of the kidneys diminishes, and kidney failure rapidly develops. In some patients, this loss of kidney function is frequently accompanied by progressive weight loss that does not respond to treatment; in such cases survival is measured in months. Biopsy or autopsy examination of kidney tissue reveals a scarring process that obliterates normal capillaries of the glomeruli.

The risk factors associated with the development of AIDS appear to play a major role in determining the frequency of AIDS-associated nephropathy. Its occurrence is highest in intravenous drug users and considerably lower, or even rare at some medical centers, among homosexual men, the other major group at high risk for AIDS. However, it occurs in Haitian patients without other identified risk factors, as well as in infants and children with AIDS transmitted through birth.

Of particular interest is the relationship of AIDS-associated nephropathy to heroin nephropathy, a form of scarring glomerulonephritis that is associated with intravenous drug use and usually progresses to end-stage kidney disease. Heroin nephropathy has been reported primarily in black males. Researchers are continuing to investigate whether latent infection with the virus that causes AIDS may be an underlying common denominator in cases of heroin nephropathy, as well as what other factors may be contributing to these severe forms of kidney disease.

Therapy for Kidney Failure

A number of related new medications now in clinical use appear to slow the progressive loss of kidney function in patients with chronic kidney failure, which can be caused by a variety of underlying diseases. According to a theory proposed several years ago, the site of action of this beneficial effect is the nephrons, the approximately 1 million tiny units that perform the filtering and excretory work of the kidney. When some nephrons are lost in the early stages of kidney disease, this theory holds, their work load is "shifted" to the remaining healthy nephrons by increasing the flow of blood through them.

This "hyperfiltration" of the remaining nephrons, according to the theory, leads to an increased flow of protein across the walls of the glomerular capillaries, which has an injurious effect, ultimately leading to scarring and obliteration of the nephron unit. In a spiraling cycle of damage, other nephrons that are still functioning are then subjected to even greater hyperfiltration. Reducing the amount of protein in the diet has been found, by researchers in various studies, to decrease this hyperfiltration and to slow progressive kidney failure.

The new drugs, which are believed to produce the same effect by a different mechanism, are in the family of medications called angiotensin-converting enzyme (ACE) inhibitors. Specifically, they inhibit the action of the enzyme that converts angiotensin I, a protein found in blood plasma, to angiotensin II, a powerful constrictor of small blood vessels (arterioles); thus, they help to keep these vessels open. The ACE inhibitors enalapril (brand name, Vasotec) and captopril (Capoten) are widely used to treat high blood pressure. Their particular effectiveness for patients with chronic progressive kidney disease appears to be their inhibition of angiotensin II's effect on the arteriole that leads out of each glomerulus. By keeping these vessels open, the ACE inhibitors reduce blood pressure within the glomerulus and thus reduce hyperfiltration and the resulting damage to nephrons. Studies in laboratory animals show that ACE inhibitors are considerably more effective in preventing the loss of kidney function than other types of drugs that lower blood pressure.

Clinical trials of ACE inhibitors thus far have shown that they slow the progression of kidney impairment in three groups of patients: people whose loss of kidney function is a complication of a type of high blood pressure, people with kidney impairment due to diabetes, and people with moderate to severe kidney impairment from other causes. The drugs have also been shown to reduce urinary protein loss in patients with a variety of other kidney diseases. These studies demonstrate the potential of both nutritional and drug therapy, alone or in combination, to alter the course of progressive kidney disease and perhaps delay, or even prevent, the need for dialysis or a kidney transplant.

Rapid, High-efficiency Dialysis

Dialysis, required three times a week by patients whose kidney function is so severely impaired as to be life-threatening, can now be done more quickly and efficiently. Early dialysis units, used for filtering the patient's blood and returning it after removal of accumulated waste and excess fluid, took as long as 12 hours. Standard treatment programs now require only 4 to 6 hours, and a series of developments shows promise of reducing these sessions to 3 hours for most patients and even to near 2 hours for some, with fewer uncomfortable side effects.

The goals of dialysis—normalizing patients' blood chemistries and maintaining their weight by removal of accumulated fluid—can now be accomplished more rapidly thanks to three measures: (1) more efficient transfer of dissolved substances into and out of the blood, through the use of dialyzing units with higher blood flow rates and larger surface areas made up of more highly permeable membranes, (2) carefully controlled faster rates of filtration for fluid removal, and (3) the use of a bicarbonate buffering system to maintain the bland alkalinity of the fluid surrounding the blood and hence of the blood itself. Although the bicarbonate system is more cumbersome than the widely used acetate buffer, it reduces blood pressure fall and muscle cramps in many patients. Experience with rapid, high-efficiency bicarbonate dialysis in a number of medical centers throughout the United States for over three years indicates no increase in complications or decrease in survival rates with this system.

MARVIN FORLAND, M.D.

Medical Technology

Pacemaker for Rapid Heartbeat • Opening Clogged Arteries With Laser Heat • Contact Lenses That Turn Brown Eyes Blue

New Pacemaker

Everything from a new elastic bandage to an artificial heart goes through the U.S. Food and Drug Administration's approval process for devices, a screening that the agency believes will keep unsafe products from harming members of the public. Recent FDA approvals for marketing included, in early 1987, a computerized pacemaker for slowing abnormally rapid heartbeat, or tachycardia. Whereas conventional artificial pacemakers speed up and regulate a slow heart rate, the Intertach antitachycardia pulse generator prevents the heart from racing wildly when abnormal contraction signals occur in the heart's upper chambers. Intermedics, Inc., the Texas firm that manufactures the pacemaker, had had a premarketing approval from the FDA for two years to test the device in humans.

In its milder forms tachycardia can cause a person to feel weak, faint, and short of breath; dizziness and a loss of consciousness may be experienced. In its more severe forms tachycardia can be fatal. The condition is usually treated with drugs, but medication is not effective for about 400,000 American heart patients with tachycardia. The FDA estimates that the new implantable pacemaker could prevent from 10,000 to 20,000 deaths a year.

The Intertach pulse generator is a small device—about the size of a pocket watch and weighing an ounce and a half. Implanting the device requires relatively simple surgery, usually lasting about 90 minutes. While the patient is under a local anesthetic, the heart surgeon makes a small incision in the upper right or left side of the chest. The pulse generator is placed in a "pocket" formed under the skin, and a wire from the device is threaded through a large vein and into the heart.

The interior of the tiny pacemaker contains a sophisticated computer that uses up to four criteria to determine when the patient has an accelerated heartbeat that the device should attempt to correct. The computer will, of course, look for the presence of a rapid heart rate. But it may also check to see how sudden the onset of the high rate is, how stable the rate is, and how long it is sustained. The computer is programmed to try different combinations of electric pulses until it finds the right one to slow the rapid heartbeat. The next time an episode of tachycardia occurs, the pacemaker will use the successful combination of signals first. At the same time that the device controls the heartbeat, the computer is storing information on how severe the tachycardia is and how frequently it occurs. With the help of a "telemetry" device for receiving coded signals, the doctor can retrieve this information when the patient comes in for the next checkup.

Laser Probe for Clogged Arteries

The FDA in 1987 for the first time gave marketing approval to a laser device for treating blood vessel

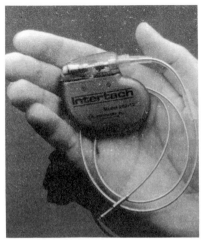

A new type of implantable pacemaker, Intertach (below), uses a tiny computer to slow down heart rate during periods of abnormally rapid and possibly fatal heartbeat, called tachycardia. Richard Martin (left) was on the Intermedics, Inc., team that developed the device.

disorders. Developed by Trimedyne, Inc., of Santa Ana, Calif., the device features a fiber-optic probe with a metal tip heated by an argon laser. It was approved for use, with a technique called balloon angioplasty, in leg arteries.

Blood vessels that are clogged with fatty material can sometimes be cleared with balloon angioplasty, a method that is cheaper and less risky than surgery. To perform the procedure, a doctor threads a small uninflated balloon into the narrowed area; the balloon is then inflated, thereby enlarging the opening. Occasionally, however, vessels are blocked by hard, calcified obstructions that the balloon probe cannot pass through. The new probe can. Moreover, the laser probe can clear an obstructed area as long as 8 inches, while the balloon works best in very short obstructed areas.

To use the laser probe, the physician makes a small incision, inserts the probe into an artery, and then advances it to the site of the obstruction. The argon laser is turned on, and within two seconds the metal tip of the probe heats up to about 750 degrees Fahrenheit. It is pushed gently through the blockage with a continuous back-and-forth motion that minimizes the heat exposure of any one segment of the artery wall. (There is no danger of the laser beam burning a hole in the artery wall, since the laser is used only to heat the metal tip.) It takes an average of 23 seconds to get through totally blocked vessels. After an opening is made, the laser is turned off; within five seconds the metal tip is cool enough for the probe to be removed. The hole made by the probe is very narrow—only a few hundredths of an inch—and a balloon is inserted to widen the opening. The manufacturer hopes that the next generation of laser probes will cut a wider opening, so that, eventually, the balloon will not be needed.

For now, the laser probe can be used only for total blockages in leg arteries and for a painful cramping condition known as intermittent claudication that is caused by obstructed leg arteries. People with this condition have circulatory problems that can lead to gangrene and may require amputation of the affected limb.

How well the device works can be seen in a group of 70 patients with blocked leg arteries that could not be treated with surgery or balloon angioplasty. Laser probe treatment (followed by balloon angioplasty) was successful in 42 of these high-risk patients, who were left with no significant blockages. The 42 were still healthy when checked a year later.

Researchers are investigating whether a laser probe would be a safe and effective means of clearing blocked coronary arteries. Depending on the results of this research, the device may well prove to have even wider applications in the future.

Genetics played no part in creating these blue eyes. Durasoft contact lenses, which are colored with opaque dot patterns rather than tints, can make even the darkest eyes appear blue, green, or aqua.

Lenses That Change Eye Color

Contact lenses that let the user actually change the apparent color of the iris (the colored part of the eye) were approved by the FDA in late 1986. The Durasoft 3 Colors hydrophilic contact lens, manufactured by Wesley-Jessen of Chicago, can be worn for extended periods. Tinted contact lenses were already on the market, but they could merely enhance the color of light eyes—making, say, green eyes more green or turning gray eyes blue. The Durasofts can change the color of dark eyes; they are able to turn brown eyes blue—or aqua or green.

Durasofts can alter eye color because they use not a tint but an opaque color. This is applied to the outside surface of the lens in a striated, dot-matrix pattern that is ring shaped, like an iris. Some of the user's natural eye color shows through in the clear spaces between the dots, creating a blend that gives the visual effect of a natural iris. Since the area in the center of the lens covering the pupil is left uncolored, vision remains clear. The new lenses are 55 percent water and allow more than twice as much oxygen to permeate as daily-wear lenses. Consequently, Durasofts can be worn for up to 30 days. They are also durable and tear-resistant.

The new lenses can be worn by people who simply want to change their eye color, as well as by those who need vision enhancement. The company said that in the nearly two years of clinical testing that preceded FDA approval there were virtually no adverse effects. Some doctors note, however, that since the Durasofts have opaque color, they should be centered perfectly on the eye to leave the pupil clear. Moreover, since the pupils will naturally expand (dilate) when a user goes out into the dark, a halo of color may then be seen by the wearer, which requires getting used to.

See also the Health and Medical News article EYES.

VIRGINIA COWART

Medications and Drugs

Clot-dissolving Drugs for Heart Attack Victims • New Antibiotics • Improving Chemotherapy and Combating Its Side Effects • Potent New Anesthetic

Cardiovascular Drugs

Two new medications—one for preventing heart attacks and the other for treating them—are among the most important recent advances in drug therapy.

Blood clot dissolvers. In late 1987 a product of recombinant DNA technology, or genetic engineering, received approval from the U.S. Food and Drug Administration (FDA) and the Canadian government for use in treating heart attacks. Called tissue plasminogen activator (or TPA), the drug acts by dissolving blood clots that completely block coronary arteries, the cause of most of the 1.5 million heart attacks that occur in the United States each year.

Injected into a vein as soon as possible after a patient complains of chest pain, TPA (brand name, Activase) works quickly to restore blood flow to areas of heart muscle that are being deprived of oxygen. This limits the degree of muscle damage and helps prevent such complications as congestive heart failure and heart rhythm irregularities.

TPA is a natural part of the body's complex system for keeping circulating blood free of clots. However, the amounts produced naturally are too small to dissolve a large artery-clogging clot. To obtain enough TPA to treat an ongoing heart attack, scientists insert the human gene for making this substance into cells obtained from the ovaries of hamsters. These cells then manufacture the substance in large enough amounts for intravenous use in heart attacks.

Bleeding occurs less often with TPA than with previously available clot-dissolving drugs. This is because it acts mainly on the clot within the coronary artery rather than on substances circulating in the blood that are essential for clotting. Nonetheless, care is required to avoid causing hemorrhage in patients who are at high risk of developing bleeding episodes (for example, people who recently have undergone major surgery or suffered a stroke or severe injury).

Another clot-dissolving drug, streptokinase (brand names, Streptase and Kabikinase), had been approved by the FDA to treat heart attacks only when injected directly into a blocked coronary artery. This required transporting the patient to a hospital having a special cardiac catheterization laboratory. In late 1987 the drug was also approved for infusion into a vein in massive amounts, a procedure that is easier and quicker to carry out than injection into a coronary artery.

The time saved by infusing streptokinase intravenously in an ambulance or emergency room can be life-saving. In one large clinical trial, 41 percent of patients survived when they received streptokinase intravenously within one hour after first complaining of chest pains. The survival rate of those treated within three hours was 23 percent; only 17 percent lived when treatment was not begun until between three and six hours after the first symptoms appeared.

Lowering cholesterol. The first of a new class of medications for reducing high blood cholesterol levels received FDA approval in 1987. Called lovastatin (brand name, Mevacor), the new drug proved much more effective in studies than any of the medications previously available for lowering elevated levels of low-density lipoprotein (LDL) cholesterol. This form of blood-borne cholesterol is considered most responsible for causing hardening of coronary arteries and subsequent heart attacks. Lovastatin may also modestly raise the blood level of high-density lipoprotein (HDL) cholesterol, which can actually remove cholesterol from artery walls and keep fatty deposits from forming there.

An enzyme inhibitor, lovastatin acts by blocking activity of the main liver enzyme involved in making 70 percent of the cholesterol produced by the body. The resulting low liver-cell cholesterol content stimulates an increase in cell surface receptors that then pull circulating LDL-cholesterol particles out of the bloodstream. A drop of up to 39 percent in the level of this artery-damaging cholesterol in the blood occurs when lovastatin is taken daily together with a diet low in fat and cholesterol.

Most patients tolerate lovastatin much better than other commonly employed anticholesterol medications. Most side effects are minor and transient.

A powerful new cholesterol-lowering drug called lovastatin was approved by the U.S. Food and Drug Administration. Various medications are available to reduce blood cholesterol levels, but lovastatin—sold under the brand name Mevacor—belongs to a new and different class of drugs and is better tolerated by most people than some of the other agents. Above, members of the research team at Merck & Company who developed lovastatin.

However, there is a possibility that long-term use might lead to liver damage or to cataract formation.

See also the feature article FACTS ABOUT FAT.

Blood pressure medications. A new drug called guanfacine (Tenex) became available for use in patients with mild to moderate high blood pressure (hypertension) that fails to come down far enough when patients are first treated with only a diuretic antihypertensive medication. When guanfacine is added to the diuretic, it often helps bring pressure back to normal. Since it produces a prolonged pressure-reducing effect, most patients need to take it only once a day.

Guanfacine is the most recent addition to a class of antihypertensive medications that act on the brain's blood pressure control center. Its action lessens the outflow of nerve impulses that raise blood pressure by constricting small arteries.

Side effects include drowsiness, dizziness, and fatigue, so patients starting treatment are advised not to drive or do other tasks that require great mental alertness. They are also warned not to stop taking guanfacine without consulting their physician, as discontinuing the drug suddenly can lead to an abrupt rise in blood pressure. However, this reaction occurs less often and is less severe than with previously available antihypertensive drugs of this type, and guanfacine is also better tolerated than those drugs.

Verapamil, a so-called calcium channel blocker used originally to treat heartbeat irregularities and angina pectoris, is now available in a long-acting form for use in cases of mild to moderate high blood pressure (the brand names are Calan SR and Isoptin SR). These tablets generally need to be taken only once daily, in the morning, to keep pressure at a low level. The most common side effect of verapamil is constipation. More serious side effects are uncommon.

See also the feature article HYPERTENSION: THE SILENT KILLER.

Drugs for heartbeat irregularities. The newly available drug esmolol (Brevibloc), an ultrashort-acting medication in the class of drugs called beta blockers, is said to be safer for use in acute cardiac emergencies than other compounds of this class. Beta blockers interrupt heart-stimulating impulses and also affect the functioning of other organs. When infused into a vein of a patient having a postoperative rapid heartbeat attack, esmolol quickly slows the heart rate. It is especially useful for patients who have just had bypass surgery or heart-valve replacements.

Because esmolol is rapidly eliminated from the body, it is much less likely to cause the adverse effects of such long-acting drugs as propranolol (Inderal), the prototype beta-blocking drug; these effects can include an excessively slow heart rate or even heart failure. Another advantage of esmolol over propranolol is that the new drug acts fairly selectively on the heart and has relatively little effect on the lungs. This selectivity helps to keep patients with asthma or other respiratory diseases from developing drug-induced narrowing of the air passages. The most common side effect of esmolol is a drop in blood pressure.

A new drug for treating heart rhythm disturbances that originate in the ventricles, the heart's main pumping chambers, received FDA approval. Called encainide (Enkaid), the drug is useful mainly for patients suffering from prolonged episodes of rapid irregular ventricular beats (sustained ventricular tachycardia). In such cases, treatment is best begun in a hospital, where the patient's cardiac responses can be closely watched. Encainide, like all other drugs for irregular heart rhythm, can sometimes cause new or worsened heartbeat abnormalities in patients with serious organic heart disease. For this reason oral doses are raised only very gradually to levels that produce the desired therapeutic effect.

Among the advantages claimed for encainide is its ability to control the heart's rate and rhythm in patients who had not responded to other heart rhythm regulating drugs. It is also said to cause less frequent side effects than quinidine, the oldest and still most commonly prescribed drug of this class (brand names include Duraquin, Quinaglute, and Quinalan). The number of patients who have discontinued encainide because they could not tolerate its adverse effects is lower than for any of the other drugs introduced in recent years for control of heart rhythm irregularities. However, encainide does cause dizziness, headache, and blurred vision in a small minority of patients.

Help for hemophilia patients. Tranexamic acid (brand name, Cyklokapron) received FDA approval for use by hemophilia patients who have to undergo dental surgery. Administered orally or intravenously before, during, and after tooth extractions, the drug prevents or reduces the risk of bleeding from tooth sockets. It keeps the protective clots that are formed in injured gum tissues from being dissolved by anticlotting substances in the blood.

Tranexamic acid is taken in tablet form several times daily beginning on the day before oral surgery and continuing for two to eight days. Patients unable to take it by mouth receive several intravenous injections each day. Because tranexamic acid binds to local blood clots for long periods, patients need to take it less often and in lower doses than the only other available synthetic substance for keeping clots from dissolving—a medication called aminocaproic acid (brand name, Amicar). Both these drugs lessen the need for intravenous administration of natural anticlotting-factor concentrates obtained from human blood—thereby reducing the risk that the hepatitis B virus or perhaps even the AIDS virus might be transmitted to hemophilia patients.

Tranexamic acid causes few side effects. Loose stools and, occasionally, diarrhea are the most common complaints, but these problems can be minimized if the physician reduces the drug's dosage.

Infection Fighters

The FDA approved for general use the antibiotic aztreonam (Azactam). It is the first of a new subclass (monobactams) of what are called beta-lactam antibiotics. Its main difference from other beta-lactams, such as the penicillins and cephalosporins, is that it strikes specifically against aerobic gram-negative bacteria (microbes that require oxygen and fail to take on a blue color when exposed to Gram's stain in the laboratory). These bacteria are responsible for many serious infections, including those that people tend to pick up in hospitals. Unlike many other beta-lactam antibiotics, aztreonam is not destroyed by enzymes that gram-negative organisms often secrete. It also does not stimulate bacteria to make these enzymes, production of which can result in the development of drug-resistant bacterial strains.

Aztreonam is effective for treating urinary tract infections and the blood infections (septicemia) that occur when bacteria spread from the kidneys and elsewhere to the bloodstream. It is also useful against hard-to-treat pneumonias caused by the bacterium *Klebsiella pneumoniae* and by strains of *Pseudomonas aeruginosa*. In addition, infections within the abdomen, of female reproductive organs, and of the skin often respond to treatment with this antibiotic.

Aztreonam is much safer than the other antibiotics (called aminoglycosides) that have been the main weapon against serious gram-negative infections; there is no risk that it will induce kidney damage or deafness. And unlike broad-spectrum cephalosporins and penicillins, aztreonam does not tend to eliminate normal intestinal microbes that help protect the intestines from illness-causing gram-negative bacteria.

Unasyn is the brand name of a new injectable

product that contains the bacteria-killing antibiotic ampicillin in combination with sulbactam, a penicillin derivative that has only limited antibacterial activity when given alone. However, sulbactam has the ability to inactivate antibiotic-destroying enzymes that have made many kinds of bacteria resistant to treatment with ampicillin alone. Thus, the addition of sulbactam to ampicillin dramatically restores ampicillin's ability to kill numerous strains of previously resistant illness-causing bacteria.

Unasyn, when used to treat infections within the abdomen, eradicated over 90 percent of the causative bacteria. It was as effective as, and much safer than, other available drugs for curing abdominal abscesses, bile duct and gallbladder infections, and peritonitis (a dangerous disorder marked by inflammation of the lining of the abdominal cavity). Similarly, the ampicillin-sulbactam combination cured over 90 percent of women with pelvic inflammatory disease and other gynecological infections. Most skin and soft tissue infections caused by certain strains of *Staphylococcus* and *Streptococcus* bacteria were also cured or improved.

The new drug ciprofloxacin (brand name, Cipro) kills many different kinds of bacteria and can be taken by mouth to treat various types of infection. It is rapidly absorbed and reaches effective levels (which are long-lasting) in most of the body's organs and tissues. While this drug is especially useful for treating urinary tract infections, it is also effective for gastrointestinal, respiratory, skin, and bone infections. Ciprofloxacin attacks the bacteria that cause traveler's diarrhea and cures this annoying disorder in about one day. In osteomyelitis, a chronic bone disease, long-term use of the drug has proved effective for wiping out strains of bacteria that are often resistant to antibiotics.

Ciprofloxacin is generally well tolerated, but some patients complain of gastrointestinal upsets. Occasional dizziness or lightheadedness may also occur, affecting a person's ability to drive. Because young laboratory animals given the drug have developed joint damage, ciprofloxacin is not recommended for young children or pregnant women. Thus, while ciprofloxacin can be employed for treating male patients with pencillin-resistant gonorrhea, its use for this purpose in women of childbearing age is generally not advisable.

Clofazimine (Lamprene), a drug developed close to 20 years ago for treating leprosy (Hansen's disease), finally received FDA approval. It is taken at first in combination with one or two other antileprosy medications. The purpose of this multiple drug therapy is to prevent the emergence of drug-resistant strains of Hansen's bacilli, the hard-to-eradicate bacteria found in large numbers in leprosy patients' skin lumps,

or nodules. Strains that have become resistant to dapsone, the first drug proved effective for treating leprosy, remain responsive to clofazimine.

After three years of combined drug therapy, patients may be able to continue on clofazimine alone, in low daily oral doses. Patients who suffer a sudden acute inflammatory flare-up (called erythema nodosum) can be given double the ordinary dose for a brief period, together with certain steroids. This therapy often causes the reaction to subside before irreversible nerve damage occurs and the painful red swellings cause skin to break down and ulcerate. (However, to avoid a toxic effect, the clofazimine dosage has to be quickly tapered down.)

The earliest and most common adverse effect of this drug is the appearance of pink to brownish-black skin discoloration. The skin also becomes dry, scaly, and itchy. Close to half of the patients treated with clofazimine complain of abdominal pain, nausea, and vomiting. They must be closely monitored by a physician for signs of bowel obstruction caused by accumulation of clofazimine crystals in the lining of the large intestine and in abdominal lymph nodes. Leprosy patients who persist with their treatment in spite of side effects can be cured of this mutilating infectious disease.

Hormone Treatments

A highly purified form of the hormone known as FSH (follicle-stimulating hormone) was approved by the FDA to induce ovulation in women with polycystic ovarian disease (PCOD). Women with this disorder are infertile and also tend to be obese and hairy. They produce an overabundance of another hormone—luteinizing hormone, or LH—and are relatively deficient in FSH. This imbalance keeps them from ovulating.

The new product—urofollitropin (brand name, Metrodin)—is extracted from the urine of postmenopausal women. It contains more than 75 times as much FSH as LH. This makes it more suitable for stimulating ovulation in PCOD patients than menotropins (Pergonal), the standard ovarian stimulant for treating infertility, which contains equal quantities of FSH and LH.

The purified FSH product is first injected, in carefully individualized doses, for 7 to 12 days. When tests indicate that the injections have produced the desired effect, a single injection is given of the hormone called human chorionic gonadotropin. This combination therapy has produced ovulation in 88 percent of treated PCOD patients, and it has resulted in pregnancies in 30 percent. The treatment can lead to multiple births.

A synthetic form of the human hormone calcitonin

is now available as Cibacalcin, an injectable product for treating Paget's disease. This is a bone disorder that can cause pain, deformity, and fractures. Like the previously available salmon calcitonin, the new product regulates human calcium and bone metabolism, and thereby helps to heal local bone lesions (damaged areas) and bring about formation of more normal, less weak bone. It also relieves the severe pain that occurs when deformed vertebrae press on nerves.

Because the chemical makeup of synthetic human calcitonin is identical with that of the hormone produced by the body, the patient's immune system does not react to it as it does to salmon calcitonin, which can stimulate production of antibodies that neutralize its therapeutic action. In fact, patients who have become resistant to salmon calcitonin respond favorably when they receive human calcitonin. Another advantage is that allergic reactions do not seem to occur with human calcitonin.

The most common adverse reactions to calcitonin are transient nausea and flushing of the face and hands soon after the injection. These and other symptoms are said to be minimized by making the daily injection at bedtime. In addition, many patients find that drug-induced side effects tend to diminish with continued treatment.

Emphysema Drug

The drug Prolastin was approved by the FDA for use in treating a rare form of emphysema. A purified form of the naturally occurring substance alpha$_1$ proteinase inhibitor, Prolastin is recommended as replacement therapy in patients with a hereditary deficiency of this lung tissue-protecting protein. Administered intravenously once a week, Prolastin protects the delicate lining of the patient's lower respiratory tract from the destructive action of an enzyme released by certain inflammatory cells. It works best to slow the progress of emphysema when given in the early stage of the disease.

Adverse reactions are relatively few, mild, and transient. For example, fever sometimes develops in the first 12 hours after an injection, but temperature drops to normal within 24 hours. However, because Prolastin is obtained from plasma pooled from many blood donors, precautions are required to avoid transmission of viral infections. One of these precautions is giving patients hepatitis B vaccine before they start Prolastin treatment. The chances of the AIDS virus being transmitted are considered extremely small; not only is each unit of plasma tested for antibodies to the virus, but the extracted Prolastin is heated to a high temperature for at least ten hours in order to kill virus particles.

Treating Cancer

Etoposide (VePesid), a drug initially approved by the FDA for treating cancer of the testicles that had spread to other sites in the body, has also received approval for use against a kind of lung cancer called small-cell carcinoma, which tends to spread (metastasize) very rapidly. This drug is now available in a soft gelatin capsule that can be easily swallowed. Enough is absorbed to produce levels in the blood half as high as those reached with intravenous injections. Taken alone in oral doses twice as high as the IV dose, etoposide shows clear-cut antitumor activity. When added to a combination of three other drugs used to treat small-cell lung cancer, etoposide has helped bring about an increase in the length of beneficial effects and in survival time. (*See also the feature article* LUNG CANCER: PREVENTION AND TREATMENT.)

The most serious adverse effect of etoposide is bone marrow damage, which leads to a drop in white and red blood cells and in platelets (the small circulating particles that play an important role in setting off blood clotting). Baldness has been observed in up to two-thirds of treated patients, but the hair grows back when etoposide treatment is terminated. Nausea and vomiting commonly occur but can be controlled with antinausea medications.

A new drug for controlling the nausea and vomiting caused by cancer chemotherapy was also approved by the FDA. Called nabilone (brand name, Cesamet), it is a close chemical relative of the main active ingredient in marijuana. It is meant for use only after other drugs have failed to control chemotherapy side effects, and it must not be used for nausea and vomiting that has any other cause. The reason for these restrictions is that nabilone can produce serious mental disturbances in some patients.

The most common side effects of the recommended low doses are drowsiness, dizziness, and mouth dryness. However, some patients may have a marijuana-like "high" or develop such conditions as confusion and disorientation, swift swings in mood ranging from elation to depression, and—most dangerously—hallucinations and other symptoms of toxic psychosis. Because of nabilone's potential for producing such psychiatric reactions, it is best given in a hospital. People who are allowed to take a few days' supply of nabilone capsules home should be observed by a responsible person.

A genetically engineered form of interleukin-2, a substance made in small amounts by the body's immune system, is now available in larger quantities from the U.S. National Cancer Institute for research purposes. This substance, one of a class of immune system stimulants called lymphokines, received limited FDA approval for use in cancer research centers to treat two types of cancer—the rapidly spreading skin cancer called malignant melanoma and widespread (metastatic) kidney cell cancer.

Employed in a complex experimental procedure, interleukin-2 seems to stimulate the growth of special white blood cells and make them more effective for fighting far-advanced cancers. These so-called lymphokine-activated killer cells seek out and attack cancer cells when injected into the patient's bloodstream along with additional doses of interleukin-2.

This type of immunotherapy can cause severe adverse reactions. A few patients have even died after developing circulatory difficulties marked by a buildup of fluid in the lungs, a drop in blood pressure, and heartbeat irregularities. Other patients show signs of abnormal liver and kidney function and suffer fever, anemia, and gastrointestinal problems. Still others experience such psychiatric effects as disorientation and paranoid delusions. Doctors now conducting new clinical trials hope to reduce the side effects of interleukin-2 by using carefully controlled lower doses.

Anti-inflammatory Drugs

A sterile solution of a nonsteroidal anti-inflammatory drug, flurbiprofen (brand name, Ocufen), was approved by the FDA for use before surgery for a cataract, a condition in which the eye's lens becomes too cloudy to let light pass through. One drop is placed in the eye about every half hour beginning two hours before surgery. This helps to keep the pupil, the opening in the center of the eye's colored area, from growing smaller during the operation and limiting the surgeon's ability to see that the clouded lens and surrounding tissue have been completely removed. The only side effect of applying flurbiprofen eye drops is a brief stinging or burning sensation, but its use may somewhat delay healing of the eye wound.

Alclometasone (brand name, Aclovate), a synthetic steroid available as a cream or ointment, was approved by the FDA to relieve inflammation and itching associated with various skin disorders, including eczema and psoriasis. The medication is usually massaged gently into the skin two or three times a day. However, to treat areas damaged by deep-seated skin conditions, the affected parts are covered—for up to four days—with a thick layer of the product, a light gauze dressing, and a piece of pliable plastic film. This keeps the medication in contact with the hard-to-penetrate skin lesions. Alclometasone does not tend to cause the serious local reactions or suppression of adrenal gland function sometimes seen after application of more potent steroids. The new drug has proved relatively safe even when applied to the thin, delicate skin of children. However, parents of youngsters who need diaper area treatment are advised not to put tight-fitting diapers or plastic pants on their child, as this could lead to the steroid's being absorbed into the bloodstream.

Drug for Anesthesia

The drug alfentanil (Alfenta), a potent new narcotic recently approved for use in the United States and Canada, has properties that make it especially valuable as an anesthetic during short but painful surgical procedures. Administered intravenously in low doses, along with an intravenous sleep-producing barbiturate and inhalation of a mixture of nitrous oxide and oxygen, alfentanil produces very rapid loss of consciousness. However, its effects wear off in 5 to 7 minutes unless additional doses are injected, so that individuals having outpatient surgery tend to recover consciousness quickly and soon become alert enough to leave the hospital.

Alfentanil can also be injected in much higher doses for longer operations. In such cases, its use in preparing the patient allows a ventilation tube to be passed into the windpipe without setting off an alarming rise in blood pressure and heart rate. The drug solution can then be infused into a vein continuously at rates that the anesthetist can adjust precisely to the patient's needs (an inhalation anesthetic is also administered). The most common adverse reactions to large doses of alfentanil are a reduction in the rate and depth of breathing and a tendency for skeletal muscles to become rigid.

MORTON J. RODMAN, PH.D.

Mental Health

Genetic Marker for Manic-Depression • AIDS and Mental Health • The Effects of Stress and Mood on the Immune System • New Research on Eating Disorders • Care of the Homeless

The Genetics of Manic-Depression

The techniques of modern molecular biology are being applied not only to the treatment of cancer and viral diseases but even to the diagnosis, if not the treatment, of psychiatric diseases. In perhaps the major mental health finding of 1987, researchers identified a segment of the 11th chromosome that seems to be involved in the development of manic-depression, a disorder characterized by extreme mood shifts. The presumed genetic marker—a section of DNA that lies so close to a defective gene that it is inherited along with it— was the first discovered for a mental illness.

Doctors have long known that it is very common for someone with manic-depression to have a parent, grandparent, aunt, or uncle with the disease. The new findings came from a study of members of the Amish population of Pennsylvania who had manic-depression. The Amish community was studied because their tradition of intermarrying allows researchers to track genetic diseases, since individuals with relatively similar genetic profiles marry and reproduce, allowing even rare recessive genes to be expressed relatively frequently.

The discovery of a possible genetic marker for manic-depression is exciting, since it holds open the possibility of identifying a specific physiological abnormality that may cause the disease. However, the actual defective gene remains to be identified, and other researchers as of yet have been unable to duplicate the finding of the marker using other populations of manic-depressive patients. Even were the finding to be confirmed, it would not necessarily provide new means of treatment for the disease, although it might offer the possibility of prenatal diagnosis, so that parents would know whether an unborn child would develop the disease. The use of such knowledge prior to birth, of course, poses major ethical questions. Nonetheless, the research holds promise for advancing the understanding of the genetic basis of manic-depression and other psychiatric diseases such as schizophrenia.

Drug Treatments

Anxiety disorders. There have been in recent years some modifications in the treatment of anxiety disorders. One new drug, buspirone (sold under the brand name BuSpar), approved by the U.S. Food and Drug Administration in late 1986, differs chemically from the other common antianxiety agents such as chlordiazepoxide (Librium), diazepam (Valium), and alprazolam (Xanax). Buspirone has the advantage of not producing sedation or drowsiness, which is a major and sometimes troubling side effect of many of the standard antianxiety agents. It can cause dizziness in some patients, however.

A drug that is used to control disturbances in heart rhythm, propranolol (also sold as Inderal) has been used for the treatment of certain kinds of anxiety, especially performance anxiety. It seems to work by reducing the physical state of arousal that is often associated with anxiety.

Panic disorder. Studies over the past several years have shown that antidepressant medications—such as imipramine (also sold as Tofranil) and the class of drugs called monoamine oxidase inhibitors—can be useful in treating certain types of panic disorders. These are acute anxiety states in which people suddenly feel an increase of heart rate and shortness of breath and become acutely uncomfortable and fearful that they will die, although there is no physiological reason to suspect that death could occur. These panic states have been treated effectively with antianxiety drugs, especially alprazolam, but there is evidence that antidepressant medications are also effective.

Obsessive-compulsive disorder. There has been progress in the search for medications to treat obses-

A possible genetic marker for manic-depression was identified through a study of Pennsylvania Amish patients living in a tightly knit community with easily traceable ancestors.

sive-compulsive disorder, a rare but debilitating condition in which individuals find themselves obsessed with thoughts that produce anxiety and compelled to take some action to relieve the anxiety. Examples of obsessive-compulsive behavior include spending hours washing one's hands out of a fear of contamination or taking many hours to leave one's home or apartment because of checking and rechecking whether the gas and electrical appliances are turned off. Obsessive-compulsive individuals tend to have very rigid thought patterns. Such patients have had only limited results at best with psychotherapy, which primarily uses behavioral techniques to provide reinforcement to the patients for preventing their typical response to an obsessional thought.

Three new drugs that affect brain levels of serotonin, a neurotransmitter (a chemical that carries messages in the brain), have shown some promise in treating this disorder. Two of the drugs are currently experimental—clomipramine, an antidepressant, and fluvoxamine. The third drug, fluoxetine (brand name, Prozac), was approved by the FDA in late 1987. The drugs cause moderate improvement in obsessive-compulsive behavior as well as depression and anxiety. These new drugs, along with the currently used antidepressant trazodone (Desyrel), may work by altering the way some nerve cells in the brain respond to serotonin. The medications both raise levels of this chemical at the synapse (the junction between cells) and block receptors for it.

Psychiatric Aspects of AIDS

As the AIDS epidemic has spread, psychiatric interest in its prevention and treatment has intensified. There is encouraging evidence that knowledge about the spread of AIDS has affected sexual practices in the homosexual community, resulting in a decreased rate of spread within that community. While the prevalence of the disease in the heterosexual community in the United States is still comparatively low, the fears of the spread are understandably high.

The fear people have of contagious diseases is a problem that has long afflicted patients with cancers that cannot possibly be spread by physical contact. It is a more serious psychosocial problem for people who have been infected by the human immunodeficiency virus that causes AIDS or who have actually developed AIDS or AIDS-related complex (ARC), a less severe form of the disease. While casual contact with such people is not dangerous, contact with blood products and sexual contact is, and contact of all sorts understandably arouses anxiety in friends, family, healthcare workers, and the public at large. Support and research programs for AIDS patients and their families are being established. In the meantime,

schools, hospitals, and other public facilities are being forced to balance the rights and needs of patients infected with the virus against the safety and fears of the general public. The fact that the rate of infection is much higher among groups often viewed by society as deviants—intravenous drug abusers, homosexuals, and prostitutes—only complicates public attitudes towards AIDS patients and the medical treatment they receive.

At this point, education seems to be the main weapon in the fight against AIDS. This involves informing people about ways of minimizing the risk of acquiring the virus—such as by reducing the number of sexual contacts, using a condom during sexual intercourse, and avoiding intravenous drug use. From a mental health point of view, a certain amount of anxiety over AIDS is beneficial in that it may help people make necessary changes in their behavior to reduce the risk of a life-threatening infection. However, extremes of anxiety require professional attention. Some people fail to be reassured that they do not have AIDS even if they have repeated negative blood tests for the disease. Others fearfully avoid situations in which there is no realistic danger that they will be exposed to the virus.

The psychiatric problems of those who have contracted AIDS fall into two categories. The first is purely psychological. Individuals who have the disease, and those who perceive themselves to be at risk of developing it, are understandably anxious and depressed. This is complicated, of course, by the fear and social isolation they encounter. The second type of psychiatric problem is physiological: 30 to 40 percent of AIDS patients suffer some impairment in brain function. This may be the result of an infection of the nervous tissue by a parasite such as toxoplasma, which often develops as the body's ability to fight disease is reduced, or directly the result of infection of the brain by the human immunodeficiency virus itself, a condition called viral encephalitis. These individuals are not primarily anxious but rather may become disoriented and comparatively unresponsive, with poor memory and concentration. There is no specific treatment for these kinds of disorders. But careful assessment and appropriate supervision can be very helpful to those individuals who become unable to make decisions for themselves.

See also the feature article AIDS UPDATE.

Stress, Mood, and Immune Function

There is accumulating evidence that stresses such as the loss of a spouse and psychiatric conditions such as depression can influence the functioning of the immune system, with the obvious implication that people suffering such maladies may be more vulnerable to disease. There is considerable evidence that people who have lost their husbands or wives are more vulnerable to a variety of illnesses in the first year after the loss. Some are expectable, such as alcohol-related diseases, but others are harder to explain, such as cancer.

Researchers have found evidence that depressed patients have reduced activity of lymphocytes, cells in the blood and bone marrow that play a special role in the body's immunity. While some studies show that more routine factors, such as poor diet and sleep problems, may account for any observed differences in immune system function, other studies provide substantial evidence that depressed patients have high levels of certain hormones, such as cortisol. When a cortisol-like drug is given to healthy people, their bodies reduce their production of cortisol; however, this is not true for many depressed patients, whose cortisol levels are not reduced. Cortisol tends to suppress certain aspects of immune function. Thus, chronically higher cortisol levels would tend to have a suppressing effect on immune cell activity. While much research remains to be done, there is growing interest in the idea that psychological and social stresses and changes in mood may have a systematic effect on the body's ability to fight disease.

Even the animal research in this area is not clear-cut, however. For example, while acute stresses tend to reduce immune function in animals, chronic stress actually tends to increase it. The animals seem to adapt to the stress and mobilize bodily resources to fight it. It is certainly too early to draw any simple conclusions about the relationship between stress and the ability to fight disease.

New Findings on Bulimia

Eating disorders continue to be an area of considerable psychiatric research. Recent studies that have examined eating behavior in these disorders demonstrate an interesting phenomenon regarding victims of bulimia—patients with the binge/purge syndrome, who alternate between compulsive eating and self-induced vomiting and abuse of laxatives.

Researchers found that habitual dieters of normal weight and bulimics have certain disorders of eating behavior in common. They tend to have a poorly modulated response to the normal sensation of hunger. They alternate between periods of starvation, in which they ignore hunger signals, and periods of excessive eating, in which they ignore satiety, or the satisfaction of hunger. In addition, dieters often rationalize that once they have broken a diet, they might as well let themselves go, and bulimia victims often feel themselves unable to control the impulse to continue eating. Bulimia victims also respond to a sense of fullness by

actually eating more, whereas normal eaters eat less as they ingest more food and start to feel full. Thus, people who eat normally seem to have a high psychological sensitivity to the physical signals of hunger and satiation, whereas chronic dieters and bulimics have in common an insensitivity to both hunger and satiety, resulting in repeated cycles of starvation and overeating.

Researchers in eating disorders have found further evidence that certain antidepressants such as imipramine are quite effective in treating bulimia. This suggests that eating behavior may be regulated by certain brain neurotransmitter systems, especially those involving serotonin. On the other hand, some researchers studying treatments for eating disorders have compared behavioral therapy, designed to reinforce improved patterns of eating, with antidepressants and found both treatments equally effective. Similarly, recent studies have shown comparable effectiveness of antidepressants and psychotherapy in the treatment of depression.

Posttraumatic Stress Disorder

There has been growing interest in the psychological aftermath of trauma, and a number of theories have emerged to account for the symptoms of what is now called posttraumatic stress disorder. One major theory proposes that extreme stimulation, such as that experienced by soldiers in combat and victims of violent crimes or natural disasters, causes a change in the way the brain processes perception and experience. In essence, the brain decreases its sensitivity to perception, perhaps by secreting greater amounts of substances called endogenous opiates, or endorphins; these substances reduce the perception of pain. (The situation is somewhat analogous to putting your hands over your ears after hearing a loud explosion.) This may lead to loss of pleasure in ordinary activities, since normal stimuli would be perceived as less noticeable and less important than they ordinarily would. The theory holds that people become overly sensitive to subsequent events that are reminiscent of the trauma, since it was originally associated with extreme overstimulation.

Other theories have suggested that a kind of dissociated state occurs during the traumatic event. Many individuals subjected to traumatic experiences have unusual psychological reactions. Rape victims may experience themselves floating above their own bodies, feeling sorry for the person who is being assaulted below. Victims of car accidents often feel no pain until hours later, despite being seriously injured. To these victims, remembering the event means reliving it, so they frequently tend to turn it off. They thus shift back and forth between periods of intensely reliving frightening events and acting as though they never happened. This leaves them feeling fragmented. The task for therapists is to help these people tolerate their painful memories and cease to live and experience events in a fragmented, divided fashion.

Multiple personality disorder (commonly known as a split personality) is now thought to be an extreme form of posttraumatic stress disorder. The overwhelming majority of these individuals repeatedly experienced extremes of physical and sexual trauma in childhood. They seem to develop a syndrome in which they experience themselves not as one individual but as a series of people, with different identities and characteristics, some of whom seem to specialize in absorbing physical abuse without experiencing extreme fear and pain.

The Homeless Mentally Ill

New York City has been the focus of a broad debate regarding the care of the homeless mentally ill. The large number of such people on the streets of New York, coupled with the murder of a number of innocent people on the Staten Island Ferry in the summer of 1986 by a recently released psychiatric patient, put a great deal of pressure on Mayor Edward Koch to provide better services.

The problem in New York highlighted the perception around the United States that in many ways the social experiment in deinstitutionalization has been a failure. Under deinstitutionalization, patients were released from long-term care in state hospitals and were supposed to come under the care of community programs. The policy in general has failed, despite the fact that it may be best to treat psychiatric patients as close to home as possible and that more powerful and effective psychiatric medications and greater sophistication in the use of psychosocial support have allowed many patients to function with some degree of supervised independence.

The problem has been twofold. First, patient "dumping" has placed patients who have spent many years in state hospitals and have lost connections with their families and communities back into strange communities where they are unwelcome and where they often become the victims of criminals and official neglect. Second, we have never adopted sufficient resources to compensate for the loss of supervised care the patients had in state hospitals. Tremendous community pressure has now been building for locked facilities to take these patients out of the inner-city areas, yet the state hospital facilities that still exist are overwhelmed. Thus, whenever even seriously impaired psychiatric patients are admitted to acute care hospitals, finding appropriate long-term care facilities for them is a significant problem.

Joyce Brown (in white hat) is taken to court in New York City, where she challenged the city's right to hospitalize her against her will. Brown was the first person detained under New York City guidelines to remove mentally ill homeless people from the streets. She was eventually released.

New York City has opted to provide more long-term care beds, although mental health practitioners there argue that the number of beds planned comes nowhere near to meeting the needs. Just a few of the more disturbed and/or potentially violent patients monopolize expensive inpatient facilities, leaving the care of the majority of psychiatric patients little improved. Furthermore, New York has changed the criteria for involuntary admission to hospital beds, adding the inability to care for oneself to the criterion of being a danger to oneself or to others by reason of mental illness. This means that patients who pose no threat of suicide or harm to others may still be detained if, in the judgment of a mental health worker, they are unable to provide for their own personal needs. This change will further tax the limited capacity of inpatient facilities.

The first person picked up off the streets under the new New York City guidelines, in October 1987, was Joyce Brown. The city claimed that she was suffering from chronic schizophrenia. With the help of New York Civil Liberties Union lawyers, Brown (who called herself Billie Boggs) challenged the city's right to detain her in the hospital. After a number of court decisions, she was released in January 1988 following a ruling that she could not be treated with antipsychotic drugs against her will. She entered a residence for formerly homeless women.

Revised Psychiatric Manual

The American Psychiatric Association has refined the diagnostic categories that form the basis of psychiatric treatment decisions. The third edition of the *Diagnostic and Statistical Manual of Mental Disorders (DSM-III)* was published in 1980. It was much more precise in terms of the criteria for selecting a diagnosis than the previous editions, but this very precision naturally led to disagreements about some of the specified disorders. Therefore, the APA published a revision in 1987, the *DSM-III-R.*

Among the changes made, a category was added for the flashback state that may occur in individuals who have in the past taken hallucinogenic drugs like LSD. The definition of drug dependence was broadened to include a variety of interpersonal and social problems related to the misuse of drugs. The new diagnostic manual also indicates that a patient's having one or more serious diagnoses, such as schizophrenia or major depression, does not rule out the possibility that the patient can also have another diagnosis, such as anxiety disorder. The category *egodystonic homosexuality* was dropped. This category essentially referred to homosexuality that was not accepted by the person. The committee that revised the diagnostic criteria recognized that most homosexuals go through a period during which they are uncomfortable about their sexual orientation. There remains a category of sexual disorder for individuals who find their sexual orientation aversive.

Three controversial diagnoses were included in an appendix, which meant that they were not considered standard diagnoses and needed further study. The first such diagnosis, called late luteal phase dysphoric disorder, is more commonly known as premenstrual syndrome (PMS). The second is self-defeating personality disorder, commonly known as masochism. Both of these diagnoses were felt to lend themselves to misuse, particularly to discrimination against women, and were therefore considered in need of further research. The third diagnosis, sadistic personality disorder, was felt to be a relevant category but, again, dangerous because it could be easily confused with simple cruelty and misused when legal responsibility was being considered. The *DSM-III-R* is an attempt to answer some of the problems observed in the *DSM-III*, to provide specific and reliable criteria for psychiatric diagnosis, and to facilitate psychiatric research and treatment.

See also the Spotlight on Health article WHAT IS AUTISM? DAVID SPIEGEL, M.D.

Nutrition and Diet

Preventing Adult Diseases During Childhood • Are All Calcium Pills the Same? • Obesity and Metabolism • Nutrition Before Pregnancy

Children's Diets and Disease

Attention has focused recently on how the diets consumed by children could either contribute to or prevent some common adult diseases.

Atherosclerosis. At what age should people start following the "healthy heart" diet? The answer to this question has become somewhat controversial in recent years. The relationship between diet and coronary artery disease has long been in the spotlight, with the realization that a diet high in fat and cholesterol can lead to atherosclerosis—fatty deposits building up in and sometimes narrowing the blood vessels. The focus now has shifted to the age at which a low-fat, low-cholesterol diet should be started.

The debate began a few years ago when a consensus conference was held by the National Heart, Lung and Blood Institute. The consensus committee examined the data and concluded that at the age of two years it is desirable to begin children on a diet consisting of less than 30 percent of total calories as fat (divided equally among saturated, monounsaturated, and polyunsaturated fat) and less than 300 milligrams per day of cholesterol. These conclusions were reached on the basis of evidence that the antecedents of coronary artery disease begin early in life. For example, young American soldiers killed during the Korean war and Vietnam war showed evidence in an alarmingly large number of cases of "fatty streaks" within their coronary arteries. Such streaks of fat along the arterial walls are considered by some to be the earliest sign of atherosclerosis, which can lead to a heart attack.

Shortly after the publication of the report by the consensus committee, the American Academy of Pediatrics issued a report put out by its own Committee on Nutrition, concluding that the data currently available did not justify those recommendations. The American Academy of Pediatrics committee instead recommended that dietary changes not be made until after adolescence. The committee noted that breast milk and infant formula are very high in fat (about 50 percent of total calories) and that breast milk and cow's milk are very high in cholesterol. Yet despite

Obesity at an early age can become a lifelong problem: A child who is significantly overweight at age three has an 80 percent chance of being an obese adult.

this, an infant's blood shows no accumulation of cholesterol. In addition, the committee felt that there were no data demonstrating that a low-fat, low-cholesterol diet would adequately support normal growth and development in a child. For example, myelination (the depositing of myelin, a fat-containing insulation around nerve sheaths) is not complete until about age five. The changes that occur during adolescence, particularly in girls, are associated with the depositing of large amounts of body fat (in the abdominal wall, over the hips, and in the buttocks and thighs), and the hormonal changes in both sexes may involve changes in fat metabolism. Thus, two prestigious groups of scientists, beginning with the same data, have reached very different conclusions and, based on these conclusions, have made very different recommendations.

My own position, based on present knowledge, falls somewhere in between the extremes of these two recommendations. Certainly if we are interested in *preventing* atherosclerosis, the earlier we start the better. However, starting a low-fat, low-cholesterol diet too early could subtly affect normal growth and development. My particular concern is that some parents will go well beyond the National Heart, Lung and Blood Institute's recommendations and limit fat and cholesterol intake to very low levels (using only skim dairy products, fruits, vegetables, and grains). Such a diet could supply too little fat and cholesterol to support adequate myelin deposits. Moreover, reducing fat to very low levels could cause other problems, including deficiencies of essential fatty acids and of fat-soluble vitamins. It might be better to institute such a diet after age five, when myelination is complete. It is also at this time that most children

begin to consume a diet similar to that consumed by adults. In addition, the amount of milk consumed by children often drops at this age, as calories are available from a greater variety of foods. Thus, giving a child low-fat dairy products will still allow adequate fat to be supplied from the rest of the diet.

Calories. Perhaps more important from the standpoint of preventing adult disease is the issue of avoiding childhood obesity. Again, the question is at what age dietary intervention is appropriate to prevent obesity. Here the data continue to accumulate, and the answer is much clearer. Studies have shown that a child who is obese (120 percent of ideal weight) at age three has a 60 to 80 percent chance of being an obese adult. Hence, if we wish to reduce the risk of adult obesity, we must seek to prevent childhood obesity before age three. This does not mean that caloric restrictions should be instituted in all young children. Nor does it mean that any special diet has to be instituted. What it does mean is that young children whose rate of weight gain is too rapid (as plotted on standard height/weight curves) should have their caloric intake reduced while at the same time they are given a varied diet so as to ensure an adequate supply of all needed nutrients. One good way to do this—for a child over 18 months who is gaining weight too quickly—is to reduce somewhat the amount of dietary fat. Just changing from whole milk to 2 percent milk can reduce the number of calories significantly. Such a change will have the added benefit of bringing down the total fat intake, which in itself may be beneficial.

Osteoporosis. Consuming enough calcium prior to adulthood may help reduce the risk of osteoporosis, a condition (more common in women) in which bones become thin, brittle, and susceptible to fracture. Some thinning of the bones occurs as part of the aging process. The risk of osteoporosis is inversely related to a woman's bone mass before this thinning starts: the greater her bone mass, the lower her risk for osteoporosis. Bone mass reaches its maximum by the end of adolescence, with very little increase thereafter—meaning that any dietary intervention designed to increase bone mass must occur during the growing years. Thus, it is during the childhood and adolescent years that particular attention must be paid to dietary calcium intake. It may be that consuming a diet with sufficient calcium during the growing years is much more important in lowering a woman's risk for osteoporosis than taking calcium supplements later on.

Hypertension. Hypertension (high blood pressure) is present in 30 to 40 percent of adult Americans. Although it is much rarer among children, there is a growing body of evidence that some of its antecedents may begin in childhood. Currently, it is believed that some people are prone to hypertension if they consume a diet that is high in sodium. Most Americans, including older children and adolescents, consume such a diet. Two aspects of this high intake of sodium by children may be important in the development of hypertension in adults. The first is that a number of studies have demonstrated that a preference for salt (the main source of sodium) is learned. Thus, a child exposed to a high-sodium diet will "learn" to prefer foods that have a salty taste and, hence, prefer such foods as an adult. The second aspect is that in animal experiments the longer the exposure to a high-sodium diet, the greater the chance of inducing hypertension. If this is true in humans, it would suggest that some children consuming a high-sodium diet may be increasing their risk for adult hypertension.

Are All Calcium Pills Alike?

New research indicates that some types of calcium pills do not dissolve in the body, which means that the calcium is not absorbed. Women taking such calcium supplements to help prevent osteoporosis might well be wasting their time and money.

Scientists have known for a long time that the absorption of any mineral by the body depends to a large degree on the chemical form in which the nutrient reaches the absorbing surfaces of the gastrointestinal tract. Recent evidence has shown that the best calcium absorption occurs from calcium citrate (particularly in older individuals). Good absorption also occurs with calcium carbonate, which is used in some antacid tablets. In contrast, certain other forms of calcium, such as calcium phosphate, are poorly absorbed.

Recently, an important study examined the physical properties of the tablets used for calcium supplementation. Regardless of its chemical form, if the calcium tablet does not disintegrate and dissolve before it reaches the site of absorption, the calcium will not be absorbed. The United States Pharmacopeia, a nonprofit group, sets standards for how fast a drug in tablet form must disintegrate and dissolve. By these standards, a tablet should totally disintegrate and be 75 percent dissolved in 30 minutes. Since calcium is considered a nutrient rather than a drug, no such standards have been set for calcium tablets. However, when over 80 commercially available calcium tablets were evaluated, more than half did not meet the minimum standards set for drug-containing tablets. In many cases less than 5 percent of the tablet dissolved in 30 minutes. When we consider the millions of Americans taking calcium supplements, these data are alarming. As a result, the U.S. Food and Drug Administration began a study to examine this problem in detail.

The study on calcium supplements has even more ramifications. Some research has shown that calcium supplementation does not prevent or improve certain conditions, but this research may not be valid if the calcium tablet consumed did not dissolve. How can consumers taking calcium supplements protect themselves? A simple test can tell you if the pill you take is likely to dissolve in your intestines. Place a calcium tablet in six ounces of ordinary vinegar (white distilled vinegar is recommended because it is cheapest) for 30 minutes, stirring it occasionally; high-quality tablets will disintegrate within that period of time.

Obesity Linked to Metabolism

Two studies released in February 1988 provided evidence that some people become obese not because they eat too much but because their bodies burn calories too slowly. The research also suggested that some people inherit the tendency toward obesity.

One study focused on Pima Indians in Arizona, a population prone to obesity. The researchers measured how many calories each of 95 people burned up while at rest in a 24-hour period. The subjects were then followed for two years. Those subjects with low energy expenditures (fewer calories burned) were four times as likely to have gained considerable weight as those with high energy expenditures. The researchers also found that similar metabolic rates occurred in families, indicating that the tendency to become obese may be inherited.

The second study, done in Britain, involved 6 babies born to thin mothers and 12 born to overweight mothers. One year after birth none of the babies in the first group was overweight, while half of those in

IS THERE SOMETHING FISHY IN YOUR SEAFOOD SALAD?

It tastes like crab meat (or shrimp or lobster) but, increasingly, it may be surimi, a highly processed, fish-based food developed in Japan and introduced in the United States about ten years ago. Marketed largely as an affordable shellfish substitute, surimi is made from bland whitefish that is skinned, boned, minced, washed, laced with salt or sugar as a stabilizer, and frozen solid. When it is thawed and reduced to a paste, any number of flavors, dyes, and texture agents may be added, depending on the desired taste and appearance of the final product.

Most surimi consumed in the United States is served by restaurants and carry-out food establishments in seafood salads and stir-fried dishes, sometimes combined with bits of unprocessed fish or shellfish. Several fast food chains have developed menu items based on surimi. Frozen fish entrees containing surimi have also begun showing up in supermarkets.

Nutritionally, surimi is high in protein and low in fat and cholesterol, although some protein and other nutrients are lost in the processing. It is also very high in sodium and, of course, has various chemical additives.

Americans consumed 48,000 metric tons of surimi in 1986, but many people may not know what they were eating. According to the U.S. Food and Drug Administration, if surimi is sup-

posed to represent a specific food, such as crab, it must be labeled imitation. If, however, the product is called something like Sea-Legs Salad or Neptune Salad, the word imitation need not be used, since surimi is made from real fish. For those who want the authentic—and presumably more expensive—thing, a close reading of the ingredients list or an inquiry to the vendor may be in order.

the second group were. When the babies were three months old, before any were overweight, the researchers measured how much energy each expended over a seven-day period. The babies who became overweight by age one expended almost 21 percent less energy than did the other babies.

The studies do not discount the possibility that some people with normal metabolic rates gain weight simply because they eat too much. However, some obese people may eat no more than other people and must exercise and diet constantly in their difficult battle to maintain a normal weight.

Nutrition Before Pregnancy

Today there is little doubt that the quantity and quality of a pregnant woman's diet is extremely important in ensuring the best possible outcome of pregnancy. A number of prestigious scientific and medical organizations, including the American College of Obstetricians and Gynecologists and the National Academy of Science's National Research Council, have recommended that for the normal woman a minimum of 25 pounds should be gained during pregnancy. In addition, there are specific dietary recommendations for pregnant women that take into account the increased demand for most nutrients.

In March 1987 a conference was held at the University of Maryland under the auspices of the March of Dimes Birth Defects Foundation to discuss nutrition before pregnancy. More and more women today are carefully planning their pregnancies, and many are consulting physicians and other health professionals about measures they might take before becoming pregnant to ensure a smooth course and optimum outcome. The conference was designed to identify the nutritional needs of a woman planning to become pregnant and the measures necessary to meet these needs. Although all of the participants agreed that a great deal of research was necessary in this area,

Ideal Weights for Women

The Metropolitan Life Insurance Company in 1983 issued weight standards. The weights listed below are for women age 25-59 of small, medium, or large frame. All weights include 3 pounds for clothing, and heights include shoes with 1-inch heels.

Height	Small	Medium	Large
4'10"	102-111	109-121	118-131
4'11"	103-113	111-123	120-134
5' 0"	104-115	113-126	122-137
5' 1"	106-118	115-129	125-140
5' 2"	108-121	118-132	128-143
5' 3"	111-124	121-135	131-147
5" 4"	114-127	124-138	134-151
5' 5"	117-130	127-141	137-155
5' 6"	120-133	130-144	140-159
5' 7"	123-136	133-147	143-163
5' 8"	126-139	136-150	146-167
5' 9"	129-142	139-153	149-170
5'10"	132-145	142-156	152-173
5'11"	135-148	145-159	155-176
6' 0"	138-151	148-162	158-179

Source of basic data: *1979 Build Study*, Society of Actuaries and Association of Life Insurance Medical Directors of America, 1980.

certain conclusions were reached that allowed the following recommendations:

• A women should be as close to her ideal weight as possible before conception. Thus, women who are significantly below ideal weight (by the standards published in 1983 by the Metropolitan Life Insurance Company, shown on this page) should gain weight before becoming pregnant. Women who are obese (120 percent or more of ideal weight) should lose weight before pregnancy.

• Although it is general practice for a woman to take a prenatal vitamin and iron preparation during pregnancy, this practice should begin as soon as a woman plans to become pregnant.

• Special attention to consuming adequate amounts of calcium should begin during the prepregnancy period. Specifically, adult women consuming less than 800 milligrams of calcium per day (provided by two servings of dairy foods) or adolescent females consuming less than 1,200 milligrams of calcium per day (three servings of dairy foods) should try to increase their intake to these levels before becoming pregnant.

• Any woman with a previous history of a child born with a birth defect (particularly neural tube defects like spina bifida) must supplement her diet with a daily multivitamin tablet, including the recommended dietary allowance for folic acid and zinc, as soon as she decides to become pregnant. For this treatment to be most beneficial, pregnancy should be delayed for at least one month after supplementation begins.

• During the prepregnancy period, the woman should discontinue smoking, drinking alcohol, taking megadoses of vitamins and minerals, taking drugs not essential to the mother's health, and consuming very large amounts of caffeine (more than three to five cups of strong coffee or the equivalent per day).

These conclusions are based on two major considerations. First, by the time pregnancy is actually diagnosed, the period of embryogenesis (when the embryo is actually forming) is almost over. Thus, any nutritional improvements designed to minimize the risk of early miscarriage or congenital malformation must have been instituted before a woman actually knows she is pregnant. Such measures as beginning vitamin and mineral supplements and discontinuing practices that may adversely affect the embryo are best done in the prepregnancy period. Second, certain practices, if accomplished during the prepregnancy period, will simplify the course of the pregnancy when it does occur. Thus, achieving as close to ideal weight as possible before becoming pregnant will make it easier to achieve proper weight gain during pregnancy. Beginning a diet that focuses on calcium and iron before pregnancy will make it easier to consume adequate amounts of these minerals while pregnant. The conference participants felt that these recommendations, given the information available, were safe, appropriate, and could have an important impact on the outcome of pregnancy for many women.

"Select" Beef

In 1987 the U.S. Department of Agriculture changed its name for a lean grade of beef from "good" to "select." This designation was first proposed by Public Voice for Food and Health Policy—a consumer group—and later endorsed by such organizations as the National Cattlemen's Association and the American Heart Association. The grading of beef by the government depends on its marbling, or the fat within the meat. About 12 billion pounds of beef are inspected and graded in the United States each year, receiving a "prime" rating for the highest percentage of fat and a "choice" rating for the intermediate percentage. Now the leanest grade of beef is called "select." (Under a different rating system, beef can be called "extra lean" if it contains less than 5 percent fat; "lean" or "low fat" if it contains less than 10 percent fat; and "light," "leaner," or "lower fat" if it contains less than 25 percent fat.)

The renaming of the lean grade as select is a rare case of wide agreement, among diverse industrial, governmental, and consumer groups such as the American Meat Institute, the Western States Meat Association, and the American Cancer Society. It is hoped that consumers will be more apt to buy beef labeled "select" than "good." Supermarkets are permitted to decide whether to use the revised labeling.

While beef that is higher in fat is generally considered more flavorful, the select grade has acceptable taste and is considered more healthful. To prevent select beef from becoming tough, it should be cooked for shorter periods of time than high-fat beef.

See also the feature articles FACTS ABOUT FAT, PROTECTION FROM FOOD POISONING, *and* WHAT ATHLETES EAT *and the* Spotlight on Health *articles* BREAKFAST CEREALS *and* THE DEBATE OVER FOOD IRRADIATION.

MYRON WINICK, M.D.

Obstetrics and Gynecology

Growing Use of Lasers in Gynecology • AIDS and Pregnant Women • Dalkon Shield Update • Pap Tests: How Accurate Are They? How Often Should They Be Done?

Advances in Laser Technology

The use of lasers in gynecology is expanding, with newer machines and better techniques being developed. Since they were first used in gynecological surgery in 1974, lasers have provided doctors with new methods of treatment for many common gynecological problems.

Lasers produce highly concentrated beams of light—far more intense than sunlight (lasers have been used to burn through metal and even diamonds). There are various types of lasers, each with distinctive properties applicable to different medical situations. For example, the carbon dioxide laser is extremely useful for gynecological surgery because this laser beam is strongly absorbed by water and most living tissues have a high water content. The beam's energy

is converted to heat that causes water to vaporize. The beam thus destroys any cells with which it comes in contact. The size of the beam can be controlled to allow it to function in a manner similar to a knife. By operating with a laser beam instead of a knife, surgeons can greatly reduce surgical pain and bleeding and perform operations more quickly; all this results in faster healing, shorter hospital stays, and more outpatient procedures.

The carbon dioxide laser has been used extensively to remove cervical lesions, particularly precancerous ones, as well as vaginal and vulvar lesions. These lesions are a common medical problem among young women.

More recently, advances in laser technology have made possible applications in other areas of gynecology. For example, neodymium-YAG lasers are starting to be used to remove scar tissue, abnormal membranes, or fibroids (benign tumors that can sometimes cause bleeding and interfere with pregnancy) from the endometrium (the lining of the uterus). The laser beam is directed through a hysteroscope, a flexible telescopic instrument inserted into the uterus via the vagina and cervix.

In a procedure also in its infancy, the laser (through the hysteroscope) is being used to remove the endometrium itself. This promising procedure could eventually negate the need for some of the hysterectomies that are currently performed in the United States each year. In a hysterectomy, the uterus is taken out. One of the reasons for this procedure is excessive uterine bleeding that does not respond to other treatment. With a laser, the surgeon can destroy the malfunctioning uterine lining without making any incision or removing the uterus.

Lasers are being used extensively to treat endometriosis, growth of endometrial tissue on the outside of the uterus or elsewhere in the pelvic cavity; the condition can cause pain and infertility. The tissue can now be eliminated using a laser beam passed through a laparoscope, a telescopic instrument inserted via a very small incision in the abdominal wall and used to examine the interior of the abdominal cavity. This procedure makes major surgery unnecessary. Used with a laparoscope, lasers can also be effective in removing fibroids from the outside wall of the uterus. Lasers have been employed as well to open blocked fallopian tubes, a cause of infertility, and to remove adhesions or scar tissue within the pelvic cavity, complications of infection (among other things) that can also cause infertility.

Prenatal Test Questioned

Recent research suggests that low levels of alpha-fetoprotein (AFP) in the blood of a pregnant woman may not be as predictive of chromosomal abnormalities in the fetus as was previously believed. The fetus secretes AFP into the amniotic fluid that surrounds it in the uterus; from there AFP enters the mother's bloodstream. A blood test for AFP was first developed after doctors discovered in the early 1970's that an elevated level of AFP in the amniotic fluid was associated with spina bifida (in which part of the baby's spinal column is exposed) and anencephaly (in which the baby is essentially born with no brain).

Then, in the early 1980's, an astute researcher noted that women who had babies with Down's syndrome had very low AFP levels. Down's syndrome is caused by a duplicate of chromosome 21, and those afflicted with the disorder are usually mentally retarded. Obstetricians began using the AFP blood test to screen for Down's and other chromosomal abnormalities—particularly in women under age 35, who do not routinely have amniocentesis or the more recent CVS (chorionic villus sampling), in both of which fetal cells are examined directly. (The risk of having a child with a chromosomal abnormality is generally smaller for younger women than the risk of miscarriage from amniocentesis or CVS.)

As a screening tool, the AFP blood test looked promising; it would supposedly earmark those women from a low-risk pool who were in danger of having a child with a chromosomal abnormality. Amniocentesis could than be done to confirm the problem. However, the accuracy of low AFP values in predicting such abnormalities is now widely questioned. Studies suggest that only 0.5 percent of all women with low AFP levels will have an infant with a chromosomal abnormality. This figure represents only one-third to one-fourth of the total number of women who have infants with chromosomal defects. And since amniocentesis leads to miscarriage in a very small percentage of cases, some doctors question whether it should be performed on a younger woman solely on the basis of a low-AFP test result. A woman who gets such a result should discuss with her doctor an appropriate course of action. (The reliability of excessively high AFP readings in predicting spina spifida and anencephaly has not been questioned.)

AIDS in Women

By early 1988, more than 57,000 Americans had been diagnosed as having AIDS (acquired immune deficiency syndrome). Women represented nearly 8 percent of those individuals, accounting for over 4,200 AIDS cases. A larger number of women in the United States have been infected with the virus that causes AIDS, known as HIV-I (for human immunodeficiency virus type one), but have no clinical signs of the disease. In them, the virus can be detected only by blood tests. Most of the female AIDS victims or carriers of the virus are in their childbearing years.

AIDS or HIV-I infection in pregnant women is particularly dangerous. The virus can be transmitted to the child, either while the fetus is in the womb or at birth, even if the woman shows no signs of disease. Up to 60 percent of infants born to women with AIDS or HIV-I infection will test positive for the virus. Currently, physicians estimate that the number of AIDS cases among newborns in the United States is doubling every 14 months and that in 1988, thousands of babies will be born infected with the virus.

Infants with AIDS frequently gain little weight and fail to thrive. They may develop toxoplasmosis (a parasitic infection) or become infected with the cytomegalovirus. The disease in very young children tends to be severe and to progress rapidly. A high percentage of infants with AIDS will die within one to two years of birth.

The effect of pregnancy on the woman herself is unpredictable. Some HIV-infected women do well. Others have a difficult pregnancy with numerous medical problems, including weight loss, malnutrition, anemia, toxoplasmosis, tuberculosis, pneumonia, and a worsening of herpesvirus infections, fungal infections, and warts. Some women will develop their first clinical symptoms of HIV-I infection while they are pregnant and go on to develop full-blown AIDS. Studies have found that the percentage of asymptomatic HIV-infected women who develop symptoms of AIDS within 30 months of giving birth is far higher than the percentage of HIV-I carriers in other risk groups (homosexual men, hemophiliacs, and intravenous drug users) who show symptoms six years after diagnosis of HIV-I infection.

Responsibility is the key to preventing infection with HIV-I. If a woman cannot be certain that her partner is free of infection, she should refrain from sex or insist on use of a form of protection such as a condom. Using a condom does not totally eliminate the risk of transmission of the virus, but it does markedly decrease that risk.

For American women, the main risk factors for acquiring the virus, besides sexual intercourse with an infected male, are intravenous drug abuse and transfusion of blood or blood products prior to April 1985 (when blood began to be tested for the presence of antibodies to HIV-I). In addition, a very small number of women have acquired the virus through artificial insemination.

Any woman contemplating pregnancy should consider being tested for infection with HIV-I, particularly if she falls into one of the high-risk groups. When administered and analyzed properly, current tests are believed to be 99 percent accurate in detecting antibodies to the virus, although antibodies may not develop until months after exposure to the virus has occurred.

There is no evidence at this time that HIV-infected pregnant women face an increased risk of miscarriage or of having a child who is malformed or has other congenital defects. However, because of the potentially devastating effects of the virus on both mother and child, a woman infected with HIV-I should consult with her doctor and seriously consider terminating the pregnancy. For the woman who completes the pregnancy, it is not totally clear whether the virus can be transmitted through breast milk. As a result, at present most doctors are discouraging these women from breastfeeding.

See also the feature article AIDS UPDATE.

Dalkon Shield Case

Thousands of women who claimed they were injured by using a type of intrauterine device called the Dalkon Shield may finally receive compensation from the IUD's manufacturer, the A. H. Robins Company. In February 1988, Robins—which had filed for bankruptcy 2½ years earlier because of the number of claims against it—accepted a takeover proposal from the American Home Products Corporation. As part of the plan, American Home agreed to set up a trust fund of some $2.5 billion to compensate women claiming injury from the Dalkon Shield. A federal judge approved the takeover plan when American Home agreed to make $100 million available for quick settlement of some of the claims. The plan still had to be approved by Robins shareholders and creditors—a group that includes the claimants.

The Dalkon Shield was inserted into millions of women in the United States from 1970 to 1974. The device was associated with an increased risk of pelvic infections, miscarriage, and sterility, and Robins took it off the market. Some women continued to use it, however, and in 1980, Robins advised doctors to remove it from those patients. Four years later the company offered to pay the costs of such removal. Eventually, Robins—asserting that it could not meet the claims brought against it by women who suffered serious side effects from the IUD—filed for protection under the U.S. bankruptcy code.

Questions About Pap Tests

Early in 1988, two prominent medical organizations jointly issued revised guidelines for how often women should have Pap tests, which detect cancer or precancerous lesions of the cervix. Meanwhile, some medical experts have criticized the way these tests are often performed. Many suggested that doctors collecting the cells to be studied and the laboratories that analyze them need to be more careful, in order to reduce the number of inaccurate results.

Criticism has mounted of laboratory procedures in handling Pap tests, the standard method for detection of cervical cancer in its early stages. Since lab technicians must personally evaluate each slide under a microscope, incorrect readings result when the staff is overworked or under pressure. Here, a lab scene.

Dubious results. In the half century since the Pap test came into use, the number of annual deaths in the United States from cancer of the uterus or cervix has declined dramatically. Thanks to the early detection afforded by the test, fewer than 10,000 American women a year die from these cancers. Nevertheless, even more malignancies could be detected in a very early, generally curable stage if test procedures were improved.

When a woman has a Pap test, a doctor scrapes cells from the opening of the cervix, where the cancer nearly always begins, and sends them to a lab for visual analysis by a technician. It has been estimated that current Pap tests fail to detect anywhere from 10 to 40 percent of abnormal cell samples—those containing cancerous or precancerous cells. The reasons generally cited for these "false negatives" are that doctors do not take an adequate cell sample for analysis and, especially, that overworked lab technicians miss too many detectable abnormalities. The American Society of Cytology recommends that lab technicians, for best results, read no more than 50 samples a day. But at some labs, technicians may read four times that number or more.

The high rates of false negatives are particularly disturbing because, while the number of deaths from cervical cancer has declined, the risk of getting such cancer has increased for many women. Factors that increase the risk include becoming sexually active at an early age, having multiple sex partners, having several children, and contracting infection with the human papilloma virus, which causes the genital warts that recent studies have linked with cervical cancer.

How often? In 1980 the American Cancer Society, which had previously urged annual Pap tests, began recommending that women who had two successive negative annual Paps need have subsequent tests only once every three years. Since cervical cancers grow very slowly, more frequent tests, the society claimed, saved few additional lives and so did not justify the enormous expense. However, many physicians and the American College of Obstetricians and Gynecologists continued to advocate that the tests be done annually. In January 1988 the two organizations issued new guidelines. A compromise between the groups' earlier positions, these guidelines now urge women to have annual tests for three years, starting at age 18 or when the woman becomes sexually active. If all three turn out negative, tests can be performed at longer intervals in low-risk women, at the discretion of the individual's doctor.

See also the Spotlight on Health articles THE MANY ROLES OF ESTROGEN *and* UNDERSTANDING MISCARRIAGES.

JOHANNA F. PERLMUTTER, M.D.

Pediatrics

New Ways to Prevent Meningitis • Circumcision Reconsidered • Vitamin E to Prevent Brain Hemorrhage • Correcting Crossed Eyes • Siamese Twins Separated • The Dramatic Rescue of Jessica McClure

Preventing Meningitis

Two studies reported in 1987 offered promising strategies for protecting very young children against bacterial meningitis, an infection of the lining of the brain and spinal cord. One study evaluated the effectiveness of a new meningitis vaccine, approved by the U.S. Food and Drug Administration late in 1987 and in Canada shortly thereafter. The second study tested the effectiveness in infants of antibodies (protective proteins) taken from the blood plasma of adults immunized against a bacterium that causes meningitis.

The most common cause of bacterial meningitis is an organism called *Haemophilus influenzae* type b (or *H. influenzae*), which in addition to causing meningitis, can produce severe infection of the throat, lungs, bloodstream, joints, and skin. Preventing diseases caused by *H. influenzae* has been a goal of researchers for many years.

New vaccine. Researchers from Helsinki, Finland, reported in September 1987 the results of an evaluation of a new, improved vaccine against *Haemophilus*. Like the previously licensed vaccine, the new vaccine (called Haemophilus b conjugate vaccine) works by stimulating the body's immune system to produce protective antibodies that attach to, and kill, the bacterium. The problem with the older vaccine (called Haemophilus b polysaccharide vaccine), which became available in the United States in 1985 and in Canada early in 1986, is that it doesn't protect children who are most vulnerable to infection—those under two years of age. While the polysaccharide vaccine is very effective in children two years of age and older, it is ineffective under 18 months of age and only questionably effective between 18 and 23 months of age. This is because the vaccine does not reliably stimulate the production of antibodies in the very young. Unfortunately, since three-fourths of all cases of serious *H. influenzae* disease occur in children less than two years old, it is clear that only a small proportion of *Haemophilus* infections can be prevented using the older product. The advantage of the new conjugate vaccine is that it induces a much more vigorous antibody response in toddlers and infants.

In the Finnish study, approximately 30,000 children were immunized with the conjugate vaccine at 3, 4, 6, and 14 months, and 30,000 children (the comparison group) were scheduled to receive the vaccine at 24 months of age. The researchers found that vaccinated children were far less likely to develop serious *H. influenzae* infections like meningitis than those who were not immunized during infancy, indicating that the new vaccine is effective in preventing *Haemophilus* disease in infants. Side effects of the vaccine were uncommon and generally mild, consisting of local soreness or low-grade fever.

Another approach. A study published in October 1987 used a different strategy to prevent *H. influenzae* infections in infancy. Instead of trying to stimulate antibody production by vaccination, the authors gave infants hyperimmune globulin, a substance that was made from the plasma of immunized adult donors and so already contained antibodies against *Haemophilus*. The study was carried out in Apache Indian infants, who are known to have a high risk of contracting *H. influenzae* disease. Approximately 700 infants were divided into two equal groups. One group received the hyperimmune globulin by injection at two, six, and ten months of age, and the other group received an injection of a placebo (an inactive substance) at the same ages. The investigators found that within the first 90 days after the initial injection, there were no serious infections in the immune globulin group, while there were several such infections in the placebo group. However, by the fourth month after the first injection, the initial differences between the two groups had disappeared. These results show that giving hyperimmune globulin to young infants can prevent *Haemophilus* infections for up to three months.

Debate Over Circumcision

The American Academy of Pediatrics has created a task force to reconsider its official position, adopted in 1971, that there is no medical justification for circumcision of newborn boys. The impetus for this reevaluation stems in part from recent reports suggesting that uncircumcised male infants have a higher risk of developing urinary tract and other infections than do circumcised males.

Circumcision is a procedure that takes about five minutes to perform; the infant's foreskin is cleansed, then carefully removed with a blade. Although many doctors choose not to give any type of anesthetic, others believe strongly that a local anesthetic should be used to reduce pain.

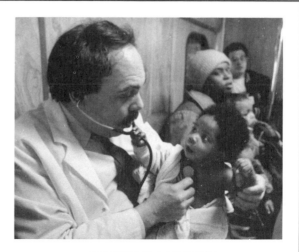

DOCTOR MOBILE

For many homeless mothers and children living in welfare hotels, the only available treatment for a nonemergency childhood health problem is to wait and hope it goes away. In November 1987, however, the homeless children of New York City were presented with an alternative: the mobile clinic of the New York Children's Health Project.

Financed largely by singer/composer Paul Simon, the clinic is affiliated with the New York Hospital-Cornell Medical Center and is operated by Dr. Irwin Redlener. The oversized van, equipped with a laboratory, two examining rooms, and a waiting room, parks outside 12 welfare hotels on a rotating basis.

Most of the children who visit the clinic suffer not from acute illnesses, but from chronic ailments, often prolonged or made worse by lack of treatment: ear infections, impetigo, anemia, asthma. Some suffer from malnutrition or lead poisoning or are infested with lice. Some need vaccinations, eyeglasses, or hearing aids.

Of the estimated 13,000 children now living in welfare hotels in New York City, Redlener and his staff had seen about 3,000 by early 1988. They intended to seek out the families who had not yet taken advantage of the medical van, perhaps by going door-to-door in the hotels. Concerned that homeless children are developing psychological and developmental problems because of their unstable home lives, Redlener also hoped to expand the service to include various types of counseling.

PEDIATRICS

Circumcision has been practiced for thousands of years and still remains a religious rite among some groups, such as Jews and Muslims. It gained popularity in the United States in the latter part of the 19th century, when doctors suggested that it would reduce the risk of infection and venereal disease. The procedure became so common that, according to physicians' estimates, by 1970 almost 90 percent of the newborn males in the United States were circumcised. After the 1971 American Academy of Pediatrics report concluded that there was no medical need for the surgery, the percentage of boys routinely circumcised declined. In 1986 only about 60 percent of male infants were circumcised.

The procedure has raised a hotly contested debate around the United States, with opponents claiming that because circumcision offers no proven medical benefit, it inflicts unnecessary pain and amounts to "child abuse." Proponents point to research showing that circumcision prevents urinary tract infections. For instance, in a study reported in 1987, a Texas pediatrician determined the prevalence of circumcision in a group of nearly 220,000 male infants born in U.S. Army hospitals around the world. Over a ten-year period, the percentage of boys circumcised steadily declined from 85 percent to 70.5 percent. That decline was paralleled by an increase in the number of urinary tract infections diagnosed in male infants. Most of those infections occurred in uncircumcised boys. These observations are consistent with the findings of other recent studies, all of which suggest that circumcision reduces a boy's chances of developing a urinary tract infection. Some proponents go even further, claiming that circumcised adults may actually be less prone to infection with the viruses that cause AIDS and herpes. These advocates suggest that viruses might more easily break through the tenderer skin of uncircumcised males.

The issue has also become a financial and legal one. The procedure may cost anywhere from $75 to $125. Many families must pay the fee themselves, since a growing number of insurance companies are refusing to pay for surgery they consider of uncertain value. In addition, several lawsuits have been filed. Some parents charge that doctors violated their child's constitutional rights by performing a procedure for which there is no medical justification, others that they were not properly advised by their doctors about the operation. Opponents of circumcision are urging state legislators to pass laws requiring that doctors explicitly advise parents of the pros and cons of the procedure.

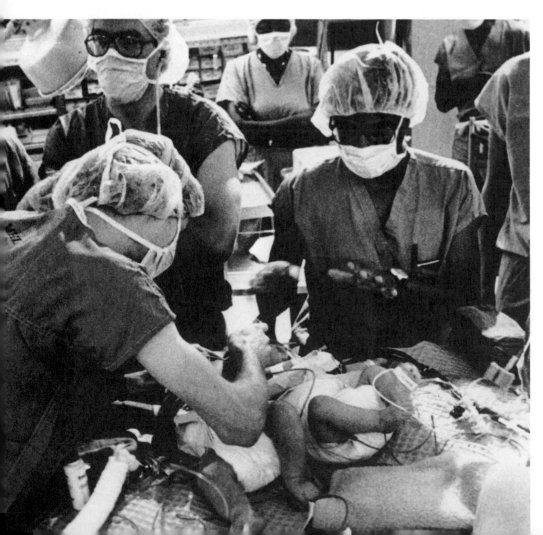

Doctors at the Johns Hopkins Hospital in Baltimore separate Benjamin and Patrick Binder, West German Siamese twins born attached at the back of the head. The backs of their skulls were later fitted with permanent titanium mesh plates over which bone should grow, creating a cosmetically acceptable appearance.

Vitamin E and Brain Hemorrhage

According to a recent study from Manchester, England, early treatment of premature infants with vitamin E may prevent a feared complication of prematurity: periventricular hemorrhage, or bleeding into the brain. Despite the many technological advances in the care of tiny newborns, periventricular hemorrhage remains a major cause of death and brain damage in these babies. This condition is especially frustrating because it usually occurs around three to four days of age, when some of the other problems of prematurity—such as lung disease and jaundice—are stable or beginning to improve.

In the Manchester study, some 230 newborns who were at least eight weeks premature were divided into two groups. The treatment group received daily shots of vitamin E during the first three days of life, while the control group received no treatment. Ultrasound examination revealed that periventricular hemorrhage was much less common in babies treated with vitamin E than in those who received no treatment, indicating that vitamin E may play an important role in preventing this serious complication of prematurity.

New Treatment for Crossed Eyes

According to a recent report, children with strabismus (cross-eye or walleye) can be treated successfully without surgery, using a special medication to paralyze and change the length of the eye muscles. Although imbalance of the eye muscles—the cause of crossed eyes—traditionally has been corrected by an operation, the promising new approach involves injecting individual eye muscles with a chemical known as botulinum toxin (the same substance that causes botulism). Once the eye is anesthetized, the toxin can be injected directly into the eye muscle. This paralyzes and lengthens the injected muscle and shortens the opposing muscle on the other side of the eye.

In 82 children treated with this technique, all but 1 improved. Because the procedure tended to undercorrect the malalignment, 85 percent of the children had to undergo a second injection of the chemical. No serious complications were observed, although occasionally other eye muscles were temporarily affected by the procedure.

Twins Successfully Separated

In a dramatic 22-hour operation performed in September 1987, doctors at the Johns Hopkins Hospital in Baltimore separated seven-month-old Siamese twins who were born joined at the head. The West German twins, Patrick and Benjamin Binder, had separate brains but shared a major vein inside the head, which

Jessica McClure, the tough little Texan who spent more than 58 hours trapped in a well, leaves the hospital with her parents. Doctors had to amputate one toe and graft skin on her forehead, but overall the 18-month-old emerged from her ordeal in remarkably good shape.

made the operation extremely risky. After several months of rehearsing—with rubber dolls joined at the head with Velcro—the 70-member medical team undertook the delicate procedure. To convert the shared vein into two separate veins, the doctors prepared the twins as if they were undergoing open heart surgery. The babies were hooked up to a heart-lung machine, and their body temperatures were lowered to 68 degrees Fahrenheit. The twins' hearts stopped beating at that temperature, and blood flow practically stopped. This allowed the doctors to cut the babies' shared vein and reconstruct new ones using previously removed pieces of pericardium (the outermost lining of the heart).

315

PUBLIC HEALTH

As part of the original operation, the doctors had planned to insert a protective titanium mesh plate in the back of each of the twins' heads where they had been separated. But because of profuse bleeding at that time, the doctors deferred the implants, leaving the twins with only soft tissue covering their brains. In February 1988 surgeons finally implanted the permanent plates. Bone will grow over the mesh plates, and doctors hope the twins will be left with cosmetically presentable skulls.

After their most recent operation, which doctors thought would be their final major surgery, Johns Hopkins officials reported the twins to be in stable condition.

Rescuing Jessica

An intensive rescue effort lasting over 58 hours came to a joyful conclusion in October 1987 as 18-month-old Jessica McClure was hoisted from an abandoned well in Midland, Texas. The ordeal began while the youngster was playing with friends in her aunt's backyard, when she apparently fell into the 8-inch-wide opening of a dry well, becoming trapped about 22 feet below. Rescuers responded quickly by drilling another, wider hole parallel to the well where the child was trapped. The plan was to drill a tunnel from the larger shaft to the dry well, creating an escape route for Jessica. To prevent complications—such as vomiting and choking—of possible internal injuries, no food or water was given. The only physical amenity the youngster received was warm air blown into the well.

Unfortunately, tunneling through the hard rock took much longer than expected. Worse still, even when rescuers reached Jessica, she was so firmly wedged that they couldn't free her. Luckily, with the aid of a special hydraulic drill, workers were eventually able to enlarge the channel enough to release the child and gently remove her to safety.

Incredibly, this resilient toddler emerged with no broken bones or serious injuries, other than a bruised forehead and damage to the right foot (caused by decreased blood flow to the foot, which was wedged in a crevice in the well). In November 1987, Jessica received skin grafts to repair her injured forehead and foot. Luckily, emergency surgery immediately after her release was able to save Jessica's foot, although her little toe was amputated.

See also the feature articles Do You Have a Gifted Child? *and* Raising an Adopted Child *and the Spotlight on Health articles* Children's Ear Infections, Curing Bed-wetting, Discussing Death With Children, Measles: A Preventable Disease, Tonsils, *and* What Is Autism?

RAYMOND B. KARASIC, M.D.

Public Health

Number of Homeless Up • Rocky Road to a Smokefree Society • Child Abuse: The Lisa Steinberg Case • Curbs on ATV's • Lyme Disease Update

Plight of the Homeless

One of the ugliest social and health problems in the United States is growing worse. Although estimates of the number of homeless people in the country vary widely, most authorities agree that the number has been increasing and that more and more of the homeless are young and female. Although most obvious in the cities, the problem has also invaded the suburbs.

Causes of the situation include escalating housing costs and cutbacks in federal financial support and housing programs. Many of the homeless are mentally ill, left to fend for themselves because of the inadequacies of community mental health systems. The extensive deinstitutionalization of patients in state psychiatric hospitals that began several years ago assumed that community treatment and support systems would be established, but these systems have withered from a lack of federal and state funding. (*See also the Health & Medical News article* Mental Health.) Economic dislocations, such as job phaseouts and business collapses, have helped create the so-called new poor—people with a capacity to be productive who have simply gotten caught in social forces they are powerless to control.

People who have to make do without a home may lose their self-respect and experience a sense of hopelessness; they may be deprived of rights that tend to be associated with one's place of residence (such as schooling for the children) and may fail to receive adequate nutrition and medical care. This means that the homeless tend to have many physical and mental health problems. Many of the homeless turn to alcohol; a study reported in 1987 found that in a year's period most of the 40 deaths recorded among the homeless in Atlanta were alcohol-related. Moreover, "shelters" established for the homeless often are ideal places for infections to spread. It was reported in mid-1987 that at least three tuberculosis outbreaks had been recorded in shelters for the homeless since 1984. Some recent studies suggest that the prevalence of TB among the homeless may be up to 300 times higher than among the general population.

Responsibility for Risks

Recent U.S. court cases regarding cigarettes and seat belts show how difficult and complex a job it is to develop public policy to promote healthful behavior.

Caveat smoker. For smokers, it seems, the ancient principle of "Let the buyer beware," or "caveat emptor," is far from dead. According to this dictum, in the absence of a warranty by the seller, it is up to the purchaser before buying to detect any problems a product may have. (The warranty may be implied— for example, one may expect that food sold for immediate use is fit for consumption.)

Scientists say that cigarette smoking is responsible for the majority of deaths in the United States from lung cancer and chronic obstructive lung disease, as well as for many heart attacks. Years ago, pressure from public health groups led to a federal law requiring a health warning on every package of cigarettes sold. It is not clear what effect the warning labels have had in reducing smoking levels, but they have provided tobacco companies with a powerful defense against lawsuits on behalf of smokers who developed such illness as lung cancer. In 1987, three lawsuits against tobacco companies for large damages were

A shocking case of child abuse was revealed in the death of six-year-old Lisa Steinberg (right) in New York City; her adoptive parents, former editor Hedda Nussbaum and lawyer Joel Steinberg (below), were charged with murder. For years the evidence of domestic violence in this home was glaring—neighbors and acquaintances alerted police and other city officials several times. But for some reason, puzzling in hindsight and unsettling to all, no public agency was able to intervene in time to avert tragedy.

top, New York Newsday Photo; bottom, William E. Sauro/New York Times

resolved in the companies' favor, on the grounds that the warnings adequately informed consumers about the hazards of cigarette smoking. In January the U.S. Supreme Court declined to review a 1986 federal appeals court ruling to this effect. August saw federal appeals courts decide two more cases in the companies' favor. Ironically, the successful achievement of one approach to the reduction of smoking (warning labels) now seemed to preclude using the legal liability route to the same end.

Many observers expected that a case in Mississippi would bring the tobacco companies' chain of victories to an end: the family of a smoker who had died of lung cancer alleged not only that cigarettes cause cancer but also that his cigarettes had been contaminated with cancer-causing chemicals and that he had become addicted to cigarettes before the label warnings were introduced. The lawsuit ended in a mistrial in January 1988, however.

Seat belt defense. The idea that a person who chooses to take risks must be willing to pay the price has also been applied by the courts to automobile accidents. At least in states where passengers are required by law to wear seat belts, full damages may not always be awarded in civil lawsuits for persons not wearing seat belts who are injured or killed in an accident, because they are considered to be "co-contributors" to their injuries or deaths. They might be able to collect only the amount of damages they probably would have received if they had been wearing seat belts. In January 1987 a Michigan driver was even acquitted of negligent homicide in the deaths of two crash victims because the two were not wearing seat belts as required by state law. The defense contended that even if the driver caused the accident he did not necessarily cause the deaths.

Passive Smoking

The growing movement to ban or restrict cigarette smoking raises another issue. It is one thing to say that a person who chooses to engage in a certain activity may be at least partly responsible for the harm that results from that choice. But what about people who do not choose to share in an activity but must still suffer at least some of its consequences? This point is raised by those opposed to passive smoking—that is, to having to inhale other people's smoke. In more and more instances, business and government are limiting areas where smoking is allowed. But such measures raise complex issues of the conflicting rights and freedoms of smokers and nonsmokers—issues that in the end must be decided by the courts and legislative bodies.

A warning shot was fired over the bow of aggressive public health boards in 1987. Early in the year the New York State Public Health Council adopted regulations banning smoking in most indoor public areas and restricting it in other indoor spaces, such as workplaces. After a nine-month legal battle, the state's highest court, the Court of Appeals, in November overturned the regulations. The court did not dispute the existence of mounting evidence about the dangers of passive smoking but said that only the Legislature could authorize such regulations. In most states the state board or commission of health has authority to do only technical rule making after lawmakers lay out basic guidelines. In New York the Court of Appeals ruled that the Legislature had not passed sufficient enabling legislation for the Public Health Council's action.

See also the feature article LUNG CANCER: PREVENTION AND TREATMENT.

Child Abuse

A late 1987 incident in New York City brought home the fact that child abuse is a problem that occurs in all social classes. Six-year-old Lisa (Elizabeth) Steinberg died of beatings she received in her adoptive family's apartment. The couple who were raising her—Joel Steinberg, a lawyer, and Hedda Nussbaum, a former writer and editor of children's books—were charged with murder. For the year as a whole, over 100 children reportedly died of abuse or neglect in the city.

The Steinberg case also illustrated that it may be difficult for people who suspect such a problem exists to successfully communicate this to authorities. Authorities may be slow to respond; when they do take action, they have to take into account the privacy rights of the individuals involved. Neighbors of the Steinberg-Nussbaum household said they had repeatedly reported incidents of domestic violence in the apartment. Once when police did come, they reportedly found that only Nussbaum had been beaten, and she declined to press charges. On another occasion a toll collector on the New York Thruway noticed a sobbing bruised child—Lisa—in Joel Steinberg's car and informed police; state troopers stopped the car but let it proceed after ascertaining that the girl, who said she had not been abused, was not kidnapped.

Curbs on ATV's

A settlement reached in March 1988 between the Consumer Product Safety Commission and the Justice Department and five manufacturers brought a partial victory to critics of the three-wheeled and four-wheeled off-road recreational vehicles called ATV's (for all-terrain vehicles). The immensely popular vehicles—more than 2 million are in use in the United States—

had long been criticized as dangerous. Since 1982, accidents involving the vehicles, most often when they flipped over on the rider, had caused thousands of serious injuries and the deaths of about 900 people, more than a third of them under 16 years of age. In the March 1988 agreement, which required approval by a federal district judge and superseded a similar agreement reached in December 1987, the manufacturers said they would stop selling three-wheeled ATV's, the type regarded as most dangerous. The ATV industry also agreed to mount an informational campaign to acquaint owners with the dangers presented by ATV's. New purchasers of ATV's, as well as those who had bought a vehicle in the preceding year, were to be offered hands-on training.

Some consumer advocates branded the agreement inadequate, since it did not require manufacturers to buy back ATV's from consumers. In mid-January 1988 a public interest law firm filed a lawsuit to gain refunds for owners of three-wheeled ATV's who return their vehicles.

Lyme Disease

Progress was reported on a practical rapid diagnostic test for the "new" illness known as Lyme disease. Were it not for AIDS, Lyme disease would be receiving much more public attention, for it can have serious, even fatal complications. First identified in Connecticut in 1975, it was initially thought to be limited to New England. By 1987, however, the disease had been reported in more than 30 U.S. states and on six continents. To some extent the growing number of cases around the world probably reflects better diagnosis and reporting, but most researchers are convinced that there has been a true increase in the disease's incidence. The corkscrew-shaped microscopic organism that causes the disease is carried by small deer ticks of the *Ixodes* family. Migrating birds and animals, and also human travelers, could account for its spread.

As often happens with so-called new diseases, the symptoms of Lyme disease had been recorded before (a report in Europe dates from almost a century ago), but they were not recognized as belonging to a distinct disease until a clustering of cases in Lyme, Conn., led investigators to describe it in detail. The first sign of the illness is usually a spreading, bulls-eye rash centered at the site of the tick bite. Weeks or months later, arthritis may follow, and sometimes heart and/ or nervous system abnormalities may develop.

At present no vaccine against the disease is available, but serious complications can be avoided if antibiotic treatment is begun early enough. For this reason, researchers have been looking for a practical diagnostic test capable of rapidly detecting the causative

bacterium in the bloodstream. The first clinical trials of such a test were expected to begin in 1988.

Flu Outbreak

Much of the United States was affected in the first months of 1988 by the latest strains of influenza to strike North America—the Shanghai flu and its variant, the Sichuan flu. Symptoms included fevers, a sore throat, and muscle aches.

The viruses that cause influenza undergo rapid change, rendering less effective the vaccines developed in previous years to combat then-prevalent strains. As a result, health authorities attempt to predict which strain will hit in the oncoming season and develop an appropriate vaccine. Officials thought North America would be struck by a strain called Leningrad flu, but the Shanghai-Sichuan flu caught them by surprise by striking instead.

JAMES F. JEKEL, M.D., M.P.H.

Respiratory System

Improving Oxygen Therapy • Risks of Marijuana Smoking • Sleep Apnea in Women • Better Ventilator Therapy

Oxygen for Lung Disease

New, more efficient devices and techniques have been developed to provide oxygen to patients with chronic obstructive pulmonary, or lung, disease. In such patients, air flow to the lungs is reduced as a result of illnesses like emphysema or chronic bronchitis. Long-term oxygen therapy is called for when blood tests determine that oxygen levels in the patient's blood are too low. The harmful effects of chronically low blood oxygen levels include depressed heart, brain, and kidney function—leading to increased risk of death.

Oxygen is usually administered through tubes or prongs sitting on the upper lip and extending into the nose, the so-called nasal cannula. Depending on the severity of lung disease, oxygen is prescribed either for certain periods, such as during sleep or exercise, or continuously throughout the day. The cannula is generally connected to a large oxygen tank, which is

PARADISE OVERGROWN

At one time, Tucson, Arizona, was regarded as an allergy sufferer's refuge, with thousands of snifflers migrating to the Southwest to breathe the dry, clean, pollen-free desert air. But as the city's population rose (by a factor of ten since the early 1940's), so did the pollen count—by a factor of 35.

Incredible as it may seem, the new residents, overcome by homesickness, began to import exactly what they had moved to avoid. Replacing native cactus and desert plants, they landscaped their lawns and yards with lush grass and shade trees to recreate the green environment they missed. Along with the greenery came a return of allergy sufferers' sneezes, watery eyes, and runny noses.

Today, Tucson and other large cities in the Southwest have more pollen in the air than many eastern and northern cities, and some Tucsonites are fighting to get their pollen-free air back. Recently, an ordinance was passed in Tucson banning the sale of Bermuda grass and mulberry and olive trees, all popular yard plants and heavy pollen producers. But this measure may have come too late. Bermuda grass is impossible to eradicate, mulberry trees live an average of 30 years, and olive trees can survive for 500 years.

Needless to say, allergists find it difficult to recommend that patients move to the Southwest for relief; they might do just as well to sit tight and carry a big handkerchief.

not portable; the system is therefore used primarily in the home. Also used almost exclusively in the home are less bulky machines called oxygen concentrators, which actually distill oxygen from room air for delivery to the patient. One type of oxygen system has good capability for home use as well as the ability to be portable: liquid oxygen systems include a large stationary reservoir usable at home that also can be tapped to fill smaller, portable tanks.

Oxygen therapy has a significant social and economic impact, especially when patients require oxy-

gen continuously. The bulky equipment makes daily activities more difficult, and some patients are so self-conscious about the highly visible nasal cannula that they go into a self-imposed isolation. Economically, the cost of oxygen can be staggering. In 1985 the U.S. medicare program spent about $530 million on home oxygen therapy. For the individual patient, monthly oxygen costs can be as high as $300 to $500.

The new oxygen systems seek to lower the cost of oxygen therapy by delivering oxygen more efficiently and thus reducing the amount consumed. By lowering the rate of oxygen consumption, they can also make it easier for people to use portable tanks, with their limited storage capacity, when away from home. In two of the new systems—the reservoir cannula and the demand pulse system—greater efficiency comes from delivering oxygen only when the patient inhales.

The standard nasal cannula provides oxygen throughout the patient's breathing cycle. The oxygen delivered while the patient exhales is wasted. In the reservoir cannula there are the usual nasal prongs, but the lower portion widens into a chamber (reservoir) where oxygen from the tank is stored during exhalation and then made available when the patient begins to inhale. Researchers at the University of Arkansas have demonstrated that excellent blood oxygen levels can be maintained, during both rest and exercise, with less oxygen consumption. Unfortunately, the mustache-shaped reservoir is bulky and somewhat unsightly. In the Arkansas study almost half the patients stopped using the reservoir cannula before the research was completed. (A possibly less unsightly alternative is the Oxymizer Pendant, in which the oxygen storage device hangs in front of the chest instead of sitting directly under the nose.)

The demand pulse system is more complex. Electronic devices sense when the patient inhales and deliver oxygen from the tank only at that time. Several demand systems are available, and the oxygen savings are considerable; however, there is a large initial cost for such sophisticated equipment.

A third new type of oxygen system delivers oxygen directly to the trachea, or windpipe, via a small plastic tube (transtracheal catheter) inserted into the windpipe. The rationale for this approach is that if oxygen is administered as close to the lungs as possible, less is wasted in the mouth and upper airways. Studies have demonstrated oxygen savings with this method while acceptable blood oxygen levels are maintained. Because the transtracheal catheter can be concealed by a shirt or scarf, preliminary studies suggested patient acceptance was high despite the fact that a minor surgical procedure is required to initially place the catheter. In a later study, however, half the patients either experienced complications necessitating the removal of the catheter or elected to have the catheter removed.

Risks of Marijuana Smoking

New studies clearly indicate that smoking marijuana regularly has harmful effects on the respiratory system and could potentially lead to serious lung disease. These findings are of particular concern because regular marijuana smoking is widespread in the United States; it is estimated to be practiced by 17 million American adults. Even though the popularity of marijuana has declined in recent years among adolescents and young adults, surveys indicate that 7 percent of people age 18 to 25 still use marijuana daily; more than one-half of these users smoke two or more joints a day. And according to a recent survey, marijuana smoking has become increasingly common among Americans age 26 to 49. Current smokers are also smoking a more potent preparation than previous users. "Street" marijuana now contains almost five-fold higher concentrations of 9-tetrahydrocannabinol (THC), the chemical that produces the marijuana "high," than were present several years ago.

Two recent studies evaluated lung symptoms and lung function (capacity and the ability to deliver oxygen to the bloodstream) in habitual heavy smokers of marijuana who were around 30 years old. These subjects were compared to smokers of both marijuana and tobacco, smokers of tobacco only, and nonsmokers. In one study, almost 150 heavy marijuana smokers were asked to complete a detailed respiratory symptom and drug use questionnaire and were given lung function tests. In this group, symptoms and abnormal test results were common. Chronic cough, sputum production, wheezing, and episodes of bronchitis were found in a quarter to half of the subjects. No differences in the prevalence of these symptoms and in lung test results were found between marijuana users and tobacco users, and no additive effect of marijuana and tobacco smoking was found.

In a further study the same researchers performed fiber-optic bronchoscopy in 29 of the subjects. (The bronchoscope, a flexible tube with light source inserted through the nose or mouth, allows the physician to see the inside of the patient's airways.) Compared to nonsmokers, marijuana smokers and tobacco smokers had airways markedly abnormal in appearance.

Sleep Apnea in Women

Sleep apnea—repeated brief cessation of breathing during a night's sleep—most commonly affects men and postmenopausal women. Two recent studies focused on why younger women are less susceptible to this problem and on what factors may put some women in this group at higher risk.

In sleep apnea, breathing usually ceases for about 10 seconds, but it can stop for up to a minute at a time (the patient then awakens and starts breathing again). These breathing interruptions lower oxygen levels in the blood, which can impair the functioning of the heart, brain, and lungs.

One immediate cause of apnea is blockage of the upper airway by the tongue. During sleep, pressures in the airways when one inhales tend to pull back the tongue. Normally, these pressures are resisted by activation of the tongue muscles to prevent the tongue's falling back and obstructing the airway. Physicians know alcohol consumption can worsen sleep apnea, and studies have shown that alcohol decreases the activity of the tongue muscles in all men and in about half of the women tested.

A recent study suggests that some premenopausal women's resistance to the effect of alcohol may be due to the female sex hormone progesterone. The investigators studied alcohol's effect in younger women during two stages of the menstrual cycle: the initial low-progesterone phase and the later high-progesterone phase. When their progesterone levels were high, the women were resistant to alcohol's apnea-inducing effect. These data point to hormonal influence in the low incidence of sleep apnea in premenopausal women.

Other research has attempted to identify risk factors for premenopausal women by studying such women who did develop sleep apnea. Researchers at the University of Virginia evaluated ten premenopausal women with this disorder. Two of them were found to have structural abnormalities of their upper airways, and the remaining eight were extremely overweight. The data suggest that protective mechanisms against sleep apnea before menopause can be negated by anatomic problems or extreme obesity.

Other Research on Sleep

A new study indicates that sleep disturbances other than sleep apnea are common in the general population. Researchers at the University of Arizona found that 41 percent of over 2,000 subjects studied had difficulty falling asleep or staying asleep, frequent nightmares, or excessive daytime sleepiness. These problems increased in frequency with advancing age. Earlier studies had shown that women generally report a higher incidence of sleep disorders than men. The Arizona study confirmed these results for people up to age 65. After that age, however, excessive daytime sleepiness was more frequent in men than in women. And patients with lung disease had a higher incidence of sleep disorders than subjects without lung disease.

Sleep disorders, including sleep apnea, are generally diagnosed by overnight sleep studies, which are designed to, among other things, count the number of breathing interruptions. More than five interruptions per hour of sleep is felt to justify a diagnosis of sleep apnea. However, according to recent research with sleep studies at the University of Pennsylvania, people over age 64 may have no significant adverse effects from five or more breathing interruptions per hour. These data suggest that it may be quite normal for older individuals to have more breathing interruptions. The reason for an age-associated increase in such incidents is not known.

Improving Ventilator Therapy

A new way to assist breathing during sleep has been found effective for some severely ill patients with chronic respiratory failure. Patients with diseases producing muscle weakness, such as some types of muscular dystrophy, or with nerve diseases like amyotrophic lateral sclerosis (Lou Gehrig's disease) may breathe less effectively at night, causing a worsening of such daytime symptoms as headache, impaired intellectual capacity, and drowsiness. These patients may be helped by overnight use of a mechanical ventilator, essentially a machine that breathes for the individual by delivering bursts of air to the lungs. Until now, use of a ventilator generally required a tracheostomy, a surgical opening into the windpipe through which a tube from the breathing machine was inserted. This "invasive" treatment was not acceptable to many patients with a known fatal illness.

Recently several noninvasive methods of providing nighttime ventilator assistance have been developed, and researchers in the United States and Australia have reported success in improving patients' symptoms by delivering air from the ventilator through a mask that covers the nose instead of through a surgical opening in the throat. Patients who used the nose mask at night were able to resume more normal daytime activities. Not all patients with chronic nerve or muscle disease are candidates for this form of ventilator therapy, and some might not accept it. But in selected patients, it may allow a better quality of life for the remaining time they have.

See also the feature article LUNG CANCER: PREVENTION AND TREATMENT *and the Spotlight on Health article* CAUSES AND TREATMENT OF ASTHMA.

SUSAN K. PINGLETON, M.D.

Skin

New Hope for Aging Skin • Healing With Cultured Normal Skin Cells • Cyclosporine and Psoriasis • Baldness Remedy Update

Acne Cream Removes Fine Wrinkles

Excitement continues to surround research into the chemical relatives of vitamin A, the retinoids. Perhaps the most spectacular recent development is the finding that they may help reverse some aging changes in the skin. Results so far appear to document that the prescription drug tretinoin, a retinoid sold under the brand name Retin-A (in Canada, StieVAA and Vitamin A Acid), can reverse many of the sun-induced changes in the skin that dermatologists call photoaging. A small but carefully done study released early in 1988 reported smoother, rosier skin, fading of freckles, thickening of the epidermis, and reduction of fine wrinkles. Coarse wrinkles were less affected, however. According to the scientist who developed the drug, Dr. Albert Kligman of the University of Pennsylvania, tretinoin cream has to be applied daily to reverse and prevent the formation of wrinkles, and its benefits will be lost unless it is used for years.

The "retinoid era" began with the release of tretinoin some two decades ago for direct application to the skin in the treatment of acne. Then research on retinoid applications shifted focus, moving away from such "topical" use of the drugs to their use as internal medicines. The oral medication isotretinoin (Accutane) was released for the treatment of acne, and etretinate (Tegison) became available for the treatment of severe psoriasis. In the United States the Food and Drug Administration approved the marketing of etretinate for this purpose in 1986; the drug had already gained approval in Canada.

The currently available vitamin A derivatives are highly effective drugs, but they possess significant side effects when used internally. Most disturbing is their capacity for producing birth defects. The search continues for new chemical variations of vitamin A that are effective but less toxic.

Another approach to solving the problem of side effects involves a shift of interest back to the direct application of the drugs to the skin. Isotretinoin, already established as an effective oral medication for severe acne, was reported in 1987 to also be effective as a topical treatment for acne. The only observed side effect was mild redness and scaling. In the case of tretinoin, nearly all those who received the drug topically in the photoaging study experienced skin irritation. The medication also makes the skin more vulnerable to sunburn. Tretinoin's long-term effects, of course, remain unknown. Also unknown are its effects on fetal growth, so it should not be used by pregnant women.

Cultured Cells Save Skin

A new approach to a rare skin disease promises to lead to treatments or cures for various other conditions. It involves a technique that had already been used to treat extensive burns. A small sample of normal skin cells is taken from the patient; they are cultivated in the laboratory and then transplanted

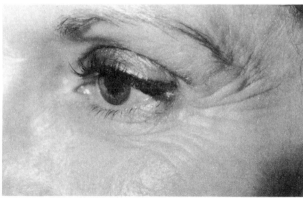
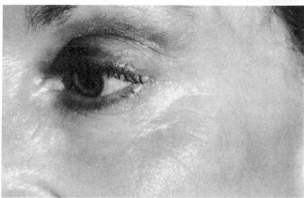

The drug tretinoin, long used to treat acne, became big news when it was found to reverse the effects of photoaging, skin changes caused by the sun. Photos show the fine lines on a 48-year-old woman before (top) and after (bottom) nine months of treatment with tretinoin cream; her wrinkles have been noticeably reduced.

back to the patient. Such skin grafts are called epidermal autographs. Recently, the first successful application of this technique to skin disease was reported, as dermatologists treated the rare hereditary disease epidermolysis bullosa with epidermal autographs.

Because of a structural defect in the skin, people with this disease are unable to tolerate minor friction, such as when the skin is rubbed. Daily bumps and bruises that would normally be insignificant can result in blisters or ulcers. When these blisters cover large areas, infections may invade through the damaged skin, eventually leading to death.

To produce an epidermal autograph, cells are taken from areas of the skin with no blisters and are grown in special "cultures." Strangely enough, when the cells are harvested from the culture and returned to the patient's ulcerated areas, they do something that the initial cells, because of their inherited structural defects, were unable to do. The grafted cells from the culture grow over the ulcer and heal the wound. Although scientists are not certain why the technique works, some suggest that certain immune-system cells disappear during the culturing process. It may be that the immune-system cells provoke the blistering reaction.

The use of epidermal autographs possesses great potential for the treatment of skin disease. In some diseases, such as epidermolysis bullosa, the cultivation of cells in a laboratory may be enough to cause spontaneous repair of an inherent defect. Even when a defect is not spontaneously eliminated, however, culturing the cells may offer the scientist a chance to take positive steps to repair the inherent defect before returning the cells to the patient. For example, cultured cells could be irradiated, treated with chemicals, or perhaps even altered genetically.

Because skin cells are so accessible to researchers, skin disease is an ideal initial target for this type of manipulation. Advances with the technique in dermatology are likely to be the forerunners of similar approaches to internal disease. As the specific genetic defects are identified for many inherited internal diseases, variations of the technique will offer the opportunity for cell repair. Like taking your car to the garage for repair, in the future we may be sending our cells to the laboratory for treatment.

Cyclosporine for Severe Psoriasis

New hope for psoriasis sufferers may come from a drug used mainly with organ transplants, cyclosporine. Through mechanisms that are as yet poorly understood, this drug alters the immune system, thereby helping to suppress the body's natural tendency to reject transplanted organs. By chance it was found that the drug might be beneficial against psoriasis. The first reports of cyclosporine's possible effectiveness against the skin disease came from a few organ transplant recipients who had psoriasis; the disease ceased to be a problem shortly after the transplant recipients began taking cyclosporine. It did not take long for dermatologists to try the drug on patients whose psoriasis did not respond to conventional treatments. Preliminary studies have reported that cyclosporine may be beneficial in treating many different forms of psoriasis.

Because cyclosporine can cause significant side effects, including severe kidney damage, it is unlikely to become a treatment for standard psoriasis. Its use will probably be restricted to severe, unresponsive psoriasis. In investigating how a drug that is known to alter the immune system also clears psoriasis, however, scientists are likely to gain new understanding of this puzzling disease. Up to now the majority of psoriasis research has focused on the end result of the disease—the abnormally rapid reproduction of skin cells that leads to thick scaling patches of skin. Cyclosporine's unexpected effectiveness in treating psoriasis is now focusing scientists' attention on the role the immune system plays in the disease. This change in direction of research promises to yield new treatments.

Baldness Remedy

The type of hair loss known as male pattern baldness is a widespread but poorly understood hereditary affliction of males and sometimes also females. Although not a threat to health, such balding can represent a severe assault on one's appearance and self-image. People rarely discuss the problem with their doctors, but the magnitude of their concern can easily be gauged by the myriad of lotions, potions, shampoos, and vitamins marketed as a cure. Despite a barrage of claims, the only product scientifically proved to affect the balding process is the prescription drug minoxidil. A topical form of the drug has been marketed in Canada for some time under the trade name Rogaine. In 1987 an advisory panel recommended that the U.S. Food and Drug Administration also approve Rogaine for use against male pattern baldness.

Multiple studies have been published documenting the efficacy of minoxidil in male pattern baldness. Although the results varied slightly, many people who used the drug for six months to a year experienced a decrease in hair loss. Up to a third of the individuals studied actually saw new hair growth.

Minoxidil was initially developed as a medication to be taken orally for high blood pressure. The drug dilates peripheral blood vessels in the body. Unfortunately, it has many side effects when used internally, including widespread hair growth on the body. However, it was soon discovered that applying a solution of minoxidil topically also stimulates hair growth. With topical application, the hair growth effect can be localized to desired areas, and the drug's other serious side effects avoided. The mechanism by which minoxidil encourages hair growth remains unclear, but it is believed that by dilating blood vessels, the drug enhances blood flow to the skin, and this may cause hair to grow.

The topical use of minoxidil is essentially free of significant side effects. Unfortunately, the new hair that is grown seems to disappear when the drug's use is discontinued. This means that people hoping to benefit from minoxidil's limited ability to stimulate hair growth should probably expect to use the drug indefinitely.

Minoxidil is far from a miracle cure for baldness, but research on how the drug works may lead to the development of new treatments for male pattern baldness. Serious studies have already begun on the drugs viprostol, diazoxide, and cyclosporine.

EDWARD E. BONDI, M.D.

Teeth and Gums

National Dental Survey • Diagnosing Gum Disease • Titanium Crowns • Reducing Decay With Xylitol

National Dental Survey

In the most comprehensive survey of adult dental health ever conducted, teams of dentists trained by the U.S. National Institute of Dental Research examined nearly 21,000 adults aged 18 to 103 during 1985 and early 1986. Overall, the news was good: most people had not lost their teeth, and although gum disease remains a problem, it is not as prevalent as in the past.

The examinations were conducted at approximately 800 business establishments and 200 senior citizen centers throughout the continental United States. The sample population was selected on the basis of race, residence, and income as a cross section of all employed adults and senior citizens who are not confined to institutions. The survey looked in detail at the number of missing teeth, the number of fillings and cavities on root surfaces and on the crowns (enamel) of the teeth, the prevalence of gingivitis (inflammation and destructive changes in the gums), and the amount of loss of supporting tissue in people with the more serious form of periodontal (gum) disease.

Only 4 percent of the employed adults surveyed (aged 18-64) had lost all of their teeth, and half had lost only one tooth at most. In the senior population, 41 percent had lost all their teeth; only 2 percent had all their teeth. This was still a considerable improvement, however, over the findings in a 1960-1962 survey in which 50 percent of the seniors were found to be toothless. The biggest improvement was in adults aged 55-64. Only 14.6 percent were toothless, compared with 36.3 percent of those aged 55-64 in 1960-1962.

The survey revealed that both employed adults and seniors continue to have decay of the enamel as they age. Comparison with surveys done in 1971-1974 indicates, however, that the number of decayed and filled teeth is lower through the age of 34 than in the past, although there is no decrease in decay in people above age 35.

For the first time, decay of the root surfaces was measured in a national survey. Prevalence of root decay was three times greater in the senior group than in the employed adults (57 percent versus 21 percent). This reflects the increased exposure of the root surfaces as a result of the recession of the gum line that accompanies aging and periodontal disease. Covered by cementum (a bone-like tissue) rather than enamel, these root surfaces are very vulnerable to decay. Only about half of the decay of the root surfaces had been filled, indicating a need for greater attention by dentists to research on root caries (decay) and increased emphasis on preventive strategies for older adults, such as fluoride, proper diet, and good oral hygiene.

The majority of adults surveyed showed signs of periodontal disease, with increasing prevalence and worsening of symptoms with age. To check for gingivitis, the gums were gently probed at 28 sites to see if bleeding occurred. In 43 percent of the working adults and 47 percent of the seniors, such bleeding was noted. For the more serious form of periodontal disease (periodontitis), a special probe was used to measure "loss of attachment," the amount of supporting tissue that had been destroyed by disease. Overall, the prevalence of periodontal disease was high: 77 percent of the working adults and 95 percent of the seniors had at least one site with attachment loss. However, the amount of loss was modest, averaging about 2 millimeters in the employed adults and 3.2 mm in the seniors. More severe destruction (4 mm or more) was found in 24 percent of employed adults and 68 percent of the older group. As with root caries, more attention in the future should be given to periodontal treatment and preventive approaches in the more vulnerable elderly population.

In general, the prevalence of gingivitis and periodontitis, and the level of disease, was found to be lower than in past surveys, reflecting better oral hygiene and more frequent dental visits. Many people, however, were not included in the survey (the unemployed, housewives), and their dental health status is unkown.

Diagnosing Gum Disease

Laboratory tests are now available for identifying specific kinds of mouth bacteria to aid the dentist in diagnosing, planning, and evaluating treatment in periodontal patients. Although there are hundreds of different species of bacteria in the mouth, and dozens of them reside in the spaces between the teeth and gums—the pockets that are the sites of tissue breakdown in periodontal disease—probably no more than ten or so are associated with destructive disease. A

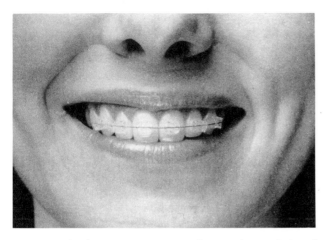

A new orthodontic system is replacing the traditional metal brackets with man-made sapphire. Called Starfire brackets, they are transparent and virtually invisible and will not stain or warp.

decade of research has established that three bacteria are particularly damaging: *Bacteroides intermedius, Bacteroides gingivalis,* and *Actinobacillus actinomycetemcomitans.* Their elimination by surgical, antibiotic, or mechanical treatment (for instance, dental cleanings) is the basis of modern therapy. Until recently, identifying and quantifying these bacteria has been primarily a research activity, but it is now possible for the practicing dentist to sample specific tissue sites and send the samples to a special diagnostic laboratory for analysis.

The first commercially available DNA probe for testing periodontal bacteria was recently approved by the American Dental Association. The test, which utilizes new molecular biology technologies, takes advantage of the fact that the genetic material DNA in bacteria is made up of two twisted, complementary strands that are unique for each species. In the diagnostic laboratory, single "control" strands of DNA prepared from a particular species are matched with the complementary strand of DNA from the sample sent in by the dentist. This sample is marked radioactively so that it can be easily detected if it combines with the control DNA.

One of the other test procedures under investigation for the diagnosis and treatment of periodontal disease involves identifying specific bacteria on the basis of their reaction with fluorescent antibodies, a reaction that the dentist can see with a special microscope in the office. Another identification method is based on presence of characteristic bacterial enzymes. It is hoped that a test kit for these enzymes can be developed for use by the dentist in the office, rather than sending the sample to a laboratory.

Researchers are also looking for ways of determining whether or not the disease at a particular site is in an active state—an important factor in determining the best treatment strategy. Specifically, they are examining samples of fluid from periodontal pockets for products (such as certain enzymes) derived from tissues undergoing destruction or from an influx of infection-fighting white blood cells. Studies have shown that such "markers" are strongly associated with progressive disease. It is becoming evident that dentists will no longer have to rely solely on X rays and periodontal probes for diagnosis but will turn increasingly to supplementary laboratory tests.

New Dental Technologies

Titanium tooth crowns. A breakthrough in the technique for casting titanium has been made by research metallurgists at the National Bureau of Standards in Washington, D.C. This has made it possible to use this lightweight and corrosion-resistant metal for fabricating precision-cast titanium crowns in place of the much more expensive gold-alloy crowns commonly used. A trial of these crowns is now under way at the dental research center at the bureau. Titanium is currently being used in a variety of surgical and oral implants (placed directly in bone), but this is the first time it will be studied with exposure to food, oral bacteria, saliva, and the action of chewing.

Laser surgery. A new portable carbon dioxide laser has been designed specifically for some forms of oral surgery. Widely used in medicine, laser surgery in dentistry has not been popular in large part because most carbon dioxide lasers have been large, heavy, and suited more to a hospital operating room than to a dental office. The new laser is well adapted to perform a variety of soft-tissue surgical procedures like removing tissue overgrowths, small lesions, and benign tumors. Because the laser seals blood vessels as it cuts or vaporizes the tissue, it allows the dental surgeon to operate in a bloodless environment and makes the procedure less traumatic physically and psychologically for the patient.

Reducing Decay With Xylitol

Chewing gums sweetened with sugar substitutes—such as sorbitol, mannitol, saccharin, and aspartame—are widely used in the United States because they do not promote tooth decay, a concern with products sweetened with sucrose (table sugar). Another sugar substitute—xylitol, a naturally occurring sugar alcohol—is widely used in Europe because studies done in the late 1970's in Finland indicated that it actually reduces the formation of tooth decay in children.

Recent studies done in Finland, Polynesia, Hungary,

and, most recently, Canada support the original observation. Chewing three sticks of xylitol-sweetened gum each day further reduced dental decay even in children who were receiving the benefits of various fluoride-containing products. Xylitol appears to have an additive effect beyond fluoride and is especially beneficial in children with high susceptibility to decay. So far, xylitol use in the United States is approved only for "special dietary conditions," but new safety studies are likely to persuade the U.S. Food and Drug Administration to broaden its approval.

See also the Spotlight on Health article ROOT CANAL.

IRWIN D. MANDEL, D.D.S.

World Health News

Brazilian Radiation Scare • Global Fight Against AIDS • Resurgent Yellow Fever • New Malaria Findings

Radiation Contamination in Brazil

The world's worst radiation accident of 1987 occurred in Goiânia, Brazil. Regional newspapers called the incident Goiâniabyl—referring to the 1986 explosion and fire at the Chernobyl nuclear power plant in the Soviet Union. The Brazilian accident was less severe than the Chernobyl disaster, which released radioactive dust that spread thousands of miles. But the incident in Goiânia pointed up the urgency of appropriate disposal of nuclear wastes.

Goiânia is a state capital, with a population of about a million. In September young scavengers broke into an abandoned medical laboratory and radiation therapy clinic and removed a heavy lead cylinder. They sold it to a junkyard dealer, who opened it up and found inside a powder that emitted a bluish glow. Gradually the powder, lethal radioactive cesium 137, made its way through Goiânia neighborhoods. Children played with the magically glowing substance, some rubbing it on their skin. At least one child ate it. Its true nature was not discovered until symptoms of radiation poisoning developed and the powder was brought to the attention of health officials.

About 250 people were found to be contaminated. At least four died. The canister reportedly held only 17 grams of cesium, but cleaning up the contamination cost the government millions of dollars and produced 1,000 drums of radioactive waste. As word of the contamination spread, so did fear of exposure to the radiation. Tens of thousands of people were tested for radioactivity. Businesses in the affected area lost clients and employees; some shut down.

The episode provided an object lesson in the disastrous consequences of failing to handle modern technology with the requisite caution. When the medical clinic had closed down, the operators failed to notify Brazil's National Commission on Nuclear Energy. For its part, the government had failed to make any follow-up inspections after the clinic was approved in 1982. Moreover, the government commission lacked a disaster plan, and the government's response to the disaster was delayed.

AIDS Epidemic

International meeting. AIDS is "a global problem that poses a serious threat to humanity," according to a conference held in London in January 1988. Sponsored by the World Health Organization and the British government, it was the first international meeting of health ministers and senior health officials to be devoted to AIDS; 146 countries were represented. The conference declared 1988 a "Year of Communication" on AIDS, and delegates resolved, "We are convinced that, by promoting responsible behavior and through international cooperation, we can and will begin now to slow the spread" of the disease. Meanwhile, the World Health Organization predicted that the number of AIDS cases worldwide would reach 300,000 in 1988.

Heterosexual transmission. AIDS spreads most commonly through virus-carrying blood or blood products (such as on contaminated needles shared by drug addicts) and through intimate sexual contact. Up to now, transmission through heterosexual contact has occurred more readily in developing countries than in developed nations, like the United States, which has the largest number of reported cases.

Haiti is one country where AIDS appears to be spreading through heterosexual activity. When the incidence of new cases in men and women is approximately equal, it is assumed that the AIDS virus is transmitted predominantly through heterosexual contact. (When, as in the United States, male homosexuality and/or sharing of contaminated drug needles are the primary routes, there are many more male than female cases.) As of March 31, 1987, Haiti had 851 officially reported AIDS cases; many experts suspected that the true number of cases was almost twice as large. Although both figures are far less than 1 percent of the population, in 1986 the proportion of cases involving heterosexual females had reached almost 40 percent, suggesting considerable heterosexual transmission.

Some of the other countries in Latin America, as well as some in Africa and even in Asia, are concerned over the special dangers of heterosexual spread. Transmission by heterosexual contact means broader segments of the population are at direct risk of exposure. In Asia the rates of AIDS are low, but most of the known AIDS cases involve prostitutes, who may have acquired their infection from servicemen and visitors from the United States and Western Europe.

Africa's tragic situation. Although it reports fewer cases of AIDS than does the United States (which has better diagnosis and reporting capabilities), Africa has been hard hit by the disease. As much as 10 percent of some population groups may be carrying the AIDS virus in cities in Central and East Africa—the continent's so-called AIDS belt. Overall, some 2 million Africans may be infected, according to the World Health Organization.

Many researchers regard prostitutes as major transmitters of the disease. Surveys in 1987 in the People's Republic of the Congo found the virus in 34 percent of prostitutes tested in Brazzaville and in 64 percent tested in Pointe Noire. While heterosexual contact is apparently the most common mode of transmission in Africa, blood transfusions (used to treat malaria-related anemia and other problems) may occupy second place in some areas where blood donations are not adequately screened for the AIDS virus. A study reported in early 1988 investigated children with malaria at a hospital in Zaire; it found that several children who had received transfusions were infected with the AIDS virus, while only one child who had not been given transfusions was so infected. The Zaire hospital subsequently began screening blood donations, but some other hospitals, partly for economic reasons, continued to use unscreened blood.

Reuse of unsterilized needles in some African healthcare facilities provides another means of transmission, and in some areas transmission from pregnant women to their unborn children is a serious problem.

AIDS paranoia. With fear of AIDS continuing to spread, some countries sought to protect themselves by taking measures aimed at foreigners, regarded as the source of the disease. In 1987, China began requiring foreigners (except diplomats) who wanted to stay for more than a year to be tested for the AIDS virus or produce evidence that they had been tested in their native country. Chinese returning from abroad were also to be tested. The Soviet Union began testing for AIDS all foreign visitors planning to stay more than three months. By themselves, such measures were likely to be of limited value, because the disease can be easily transferred to native prostitutes by short-term visitors.

Some foreigners voiced concern that the testing might itself be a threat to health. Sanitation at many Soviet and Chinese healthcare institutions was widely viewed as substandard, and nonsterile needles could transmit infections—including AIDS. In December 1987 the Canadian government warned its citizens not to receive acupuncture or other skin-penetrating therapy in China; it was thought that a Canadian woman who died of AIDS might have contracted the disease from infected acupuncture needles.

See also the feature article AIDS UPDATE.

Traditional Plagues

As health officials celebrated the tenth anniversary of the eradication of smallpox in 1987, they debated whether the remaining stocks of the smallpox virus should be destroyed. Meanwhile, efforts to control yellow fever were seeing setbacks, and new research was reported on malaria.

Smallpox virus controversy. The elimination of smallpox is one of the triumphs of public health. The last naturally transmitted case occurred in Somalia in 1977. Subsequently the World Health Organization declared the disease eradicated. As far as is known, reference stocks of smallpox virus have been preserved only in high-security laboratories in Atlanta and Moscow. Some experts have argued that these stocks should be destroyed to prevent possible accidents (two 1978 cases in England were caused by virus from a laboratory) or to guard against use of the virus for biological warfare. Others maintain that the reference samples should be kept for unforeseen future scientific uses or for use in research and vaccine development in case of accidental or intentional release of virus. If, however, a decision were made to destroy all the remaining virus stocks, verification of the destruction would pose a much greater problem than for nuclear arms.

Yellow fever in Nigeria. One of the great killers in history has been yellow fever, whose name refers to the jaundice produced when the virus destroys much of the liver. The disease is spread by a few varieties of mosquitoes. Public health control efforts over the past century have largely limited it to certain tropical rain forests. Fear has remained, however, that should the infection be reintroduced into urban areas, huge numbers of people might be involved before the epidemic could be stopped. Just such a scenario appears to be developing in Nigeria, where an epidemic that began in late 1986 has caused thousands of known deaths. The actual death toll is probably much higher than the confirmed fatalities. The Nigerian government, working with the World Health Organization, began a major vaccination campaign and a mosquito control effort.

A freak radiation accident occurred in southeastern Brazil when scavengers removed a canister of lethal cesium 137 from an abandoned medical laboratory. Children played with the glowing powder, exposing some 250 people to contamination; here residents are tested for radiation.

Malaria research. Malaria remains one of the most serious health problems in the Third World. In addition to its toll in human suffering, the substantial numbers of cases recorded each year—many ending in death—have severe economic consequences. The disease has had a resurgence in recent years. The mosquitoes bearing the malaria parasite have become increasingly resistant to insecticides, insecticide production has been cut back (for environmental reasons), and some strains of the malaria parasite have developed resistance to drugs such as chloroquine that previously were successful in treating the disease.

In 1987 researchers found that certain drugs, including several known as calcium channel blockers, reduced the resistant parasites' ability to expel the antimalaria medication rapidly. (This rapid-release capability was thought to explain the resistance to the medication.) The discovery raised the possibility that such drugs might prove an effective means of counteracting resistance to chloroquine. Questions of safety, however, remained. Calcium channel blockers can cause heart complications.

Efforts to develop a vaccine against malaria have produced new insight into the problems involved. Some potential vaccines are targeted against the sporozoite—the form of the parasite injected into the bloodstream by a mosquito bite. Researchers working with mice found that although vaccines made from parts of the sporozoite produced antisporozoite antibodies in the blood, the protection afforded by the antibodies was much less effective than that provided when sporozoites weakened by radiation were given as the vaccine. In the latter case the immune system's so-called cell-mediated defenses (including various white blood cells) came into play. For maximum effectiveness, an antisporozoite vaccine would apparently have to produce cell-mediated immunity as well as the "humoral" immunity represented by blood antibodies.

In March 1988 researchers reported on another type of vaccine, targeted against the merozoite the later parasite stage, which infects red blood cells and causes malaria symptoms. The new vaccine was tested in a small number of people in Colombia; it appeared to induce either partial or total protection from the disease in four out of five subjects.

See also the feature article A HISTORY OF EPIDEMICS.

Contaminated Cheese

A major outbreak of listeriosis food poisoning in Switzerland in 1987 served as yet another reminder that even people in developed countries, where such bacteria-caused illnesses seem to be under control, cannot let down their guard. The Swiss cantons of Vaud and Zürich halted the sale of soft-ripened vacherin Mont d'Or cheese on November 20, after the cheese was blamed for ten cases of listeriosis, including two deaths, in Vaud since the beginning of the preceding month. The Swiss vacherin Mont d'Or was withdrawn from the world market. The bacterium involved, *Listeria monocytogenes*, can cause flulike symptoms and meningitis; in a pregnant woman the infection can lead to a stillbirth. By the end of 1987, 111 cases of the disease had been reported in Switzerland since 1983, with 31 deaths.

See also the feature article PROTECTION FROM FOOD POISONING. JAMES F. JEKEL, M.D., M.P.H.

329

Contributors

Azrin, Michael A., M.D. Resident in Internal Medicine, Jewish Hospital of Washington University, St. Louis. CURING BED-WETTING (coauthor).

Azrin, Nathan H., Ph.D. Professor, Behavioral Sciences Center, Nova University, Fort Lauderdale, Fla.; Author, *Toilet Training in Less Than a Day*. CURING BED-WETTING (coauthor).

Becker, Brenda L. Editor and writer specializing in consumer health topics. THE DEBATE OVER FOOD IRRADIATION.

Begley, Sharon. Science Editor, *Newsweek*. CARING FOR AN ALZHEIMER'S PATIENT.

Besalel, Victoria A., Ph.D. Director, A and B Psychology Clinic, Fort Lauderdale, Fla. CURING BED-WETTING (coauthor).

Bondi, Edward E., M.D. Associate Professor, Department of Dermatology, University of Pennsylvania, Philadelphia. SKIN.

Callender, David L., M.D. Resident in Otolaryngology, Baylor College of Medicine, Houston. CHILDREN'S EAR INFECTIONS.

Carleton, Susan. Writer specializing in health and medicine. GIVING AND GETTING BLOOD; HOW TO SELECT A DOCTOR; WHAT ARE PLACEBOS?

Charash, Bruce D., M.D. Assistant Professor of Medicine, Division of Cardiology, New York Hospital-Cornell Medical Center, New York City. HEART AND CIRCULATORY SYSTEM (coauthor).

Chau, Teresa P., M.D. Geriatric Fellow, State University of New York, Buffalo; Veterans Administration Medical Center, Buffalo. AGING AND THE AGED (coauthor).

Cohen, Lynne. Contributing Editor, *Canadian Medical Association Journal*; Rockcliffe Park Correspondent, Ottawa *Citizen*. GOVERNMENT POLICIES AND PROGRAMS (CANADA).

Cowart, Virginia. Principal, Medical Information Service; Contributing Editor, *Physician and Sports Medicine*. MEDICAL TECHNOLOGY.

Csuka, M. E., M.D. Assistant Professor of Medicine, Medical College of Wisconsin, Milwaukee. ARTHRITIS AND RHEUMATISM.

Fisher, Jeffrey, M.D. Assistant Professor of Medicine, Division of Cardiology, New York Hospital-Cornell Medical Center, New York City. HEART AND CIRCULATORY SYSTEM (coauthor).

Forland, Marvin, M.D. Professor of Medicine, Associate Dean for Clinical Affairs, Department of Medicine, University of Texas Health Science Center at San Antonio. KIDNEYS AND URINARY SYSTEM.

Goodwin, Mary T. Chief Nutritionist, Montgomery County (Md.) Health Department. BREAKFAST CEREALS.

Hager, Mary. Correspondent, Washington Bureau Staff, *Newsweek*. HEALTH PERSONNEL AND FACILITIES.

Hartley, Marcia, M.S. Education Director, Infant Health and Development Program, The Children's Hospital, Boston. DISCUSSING DEATH WITH CHILDREN (coauthor).

Jekel, James F., M.D., M.P.H. Professor of Epidemiology and Public Health, Yale University School of Medicine. PUBLIC HEALTH; WORLD HEALTH NEWS.

Kales, Anthony, M.D. Professor and Chairman, Department of Psychiatry, Pennsylvania State University College of Medicine, Milton S. Hershey Medical Center. INSOMNIA.

Karasic, Raymond B., M.D. Assistant Professor of Pediatrics, University of Pittsburgh. MEASLES: A PREVENTABLE DISEASE; PEDIATRICS; TONSILS.

Katz, Paul R., M.D. Fellowship Coordinator, Division of Geriatrics, State University of New York at Buffalo; Medical Director, Nursing Home Care Unit, Buffalo Veterans Administration Medical Center. AGING AND THE AGED (coauthor).

Kimmelman, Charles P., M.D. Director of Resident Training, New York Eye and Ear Infirmary; Associate Professor of Otolaryngology, New York Medical College. EARS, NOSE, AND THROAT.

Krieger, Andrew W., D.D.S., M.P.H. Assistant Clinical Professor of Dentistry, School of Dental and Oral Surgery, Columbia University, New York City. ROOT CANAL.

Mandel, Irwin D., D.D.S. Professor of Dentistry, Director, Center for Clinical Research in Dentistry, School of Dental and Oral Surgery, Columbia University, New York City. TEETH AND GUMS.

Marshall, Merville C., Jr., M.D. Staff Physician, Department of Medicine, Long Island Jewish Medical Center; Assistant Professor of Medicine, State University of New York at Stony Brook. GLANDS AND METABOLISM.

Maugh, Thomas H., II, Ph.D. Science Writer, Los Angeles *Times*. GENETICS AND GENETIC ENGINEERING; MONOCLONAL ANTIBODIES: MEDICINE'S POWERFUL NEW TOOL; THE MANY ROLES OF ESTROGEN.

McLellan, A. Thomas, Ph.D. Director of Clinical Research, Psychiatry Service, Philadelphia Veterans Administration Medical Center; Associate Professor, Department of Psychiatry, University of Pennsylvania. DRUG ABUSE (coauthor).

Moreno, Jonathan D., Ph.D. Associate Professor of Philosophy, Health Care Sciences, Child Health and Development, George Washington University; Philosopher-in-Residence, Children's Hospital National Medical Center, Washington, D.C. BIOETHICS.

Moses, Hamilton, III, M.D. Associate Professor and Deputy Director, Department of Neurology, The Johns Hopkins Medical Institutions. BRAIN AND NERVOUS SYSTEM; PARKINSON'S DISEASE: NEW ADVANCES.

Murphy, Carol, M.S.W. Research Social Worker, Infant Health and Development Program, The Children's Hospital, Boston; Child and Family Therapist. DISCUSSING DEATH WITH CHILDREN (coauthor).

O'Brien, Charles P., M.D., Ph.D. Chief, Psychiatry Service, Philadelphia Veterans Administration Medical Center; Professor and Vice Chairman, Department of Psychiatry, University of Pennsylvania. DRUG ABUSE (coauthor).

Pelot, Daniel, M.D. Associate Clinical Professor, Division of Gastroenterology, Department of Medicine, University of California at Irvine. DEALING WITH HEARTBURN; DIGESTIVE SYSTEM.

Perlmutter, Johanna F., M.D. Assistant Professor, Department of Obstetrics and Gynecology, Harvard Medical School. OBSTETRICS AND GYNECOLOGY; UNDERSTANDING MISCARRIAGES.

Pingleton, Susan K., M.D. Professor of Medicine, Director, Clinical Investigations, Pulmonary Division, University of Kansas Medical Center, Kansas City.

CAUSES AND TREATMENT OF ASTHMA (coauthor); RESPIRATORY SYSTEM.

Powell, Bayard L., M.D. Assistant Professor of Medicine, Section of Hematology/Oncology, Bowman Gray School of Medicine, Wake Forest University, Winston-Salem, N.C. CANCER.

Puliafito, Carmen A., M.D. Assistant Professor of Ophthalmology, Harvard Medical School; Director of Laser Research Laboratory, Massachusetts Eye and Ear Infirmary. EYES; GLAUCOMA.

Rodman, Morton J., Ph.D. Professor of Pharmacology, Rutgers University, New Brunswick, N.J. MEDICATIONS AND DRUGS.

Rotherham, James A. Staff Director, U.S. House of Representatives Subcommittee on Domestic Marketing, Consumer Relations, and Nutrition. GOVERNMENT POLICIES AND PROGRAMS (UNITED STATES).

Schopler, Eric, Ph.D. Professor of Psychology and Psychiatry, Director, Division TEACCH, University of North Carolina; Editor, *Journal of Autism and Developmental Disorders*. WHAT IS AUTISM?

Spiegel, David, M.D. Associate Professor of Psychiatry and Behavioral Sciences, Director, Adult Psychiatric Outpatient Clinic, Stanford University School of Medicine. MENTAL HEALTH.

Temple, J. Donald, M.D. Assistant Professor of Medicine, Center for Blood Diseases, University of Miami Hospital and Clinics. BLOOD AND LYMPHATIC SYSTEM.

Thro, Ellen. Science writer specializing in environmental topics. ENVIRONMENT AND HEALTH.

Trenk, Barbara Scherr. Writer specializing in health issues. FACTS ABOUT HMO's; SUNGLASSES.

Winick, Myron, M.D. R. R. Williams Professor of Nutrition, Professor of Pediatrics, Director, Institute of Human Nutrition, Director, Center for Nutrition, Genetics and Human Development, College of Physicians and Surgeons, Columbia University, New York City. NUTRITION AND DIET.

Woody, George E., M.D. Chief, Substance Abuse Treatment Unit, Philadelphia Veterans Administration Medical Center; Clinical Professor, Department of Psychiatry, University of Pennsylvania. DRUG ABUSE (coauthor).

Yogman, Michael W., M.D. Director, Infant Health and Development Program, The Children's Hospital, Boston. DISCUSSING DEATH WITH CHILDREN (coauthor).

Zetterman, Rowen K., M.D. Chief, Section of Digestive Disease and Nutrition, University of Nebraska Medical Center; Associate Chief of Staff for Research, Veterans Administration Medical Center, Omaha. HEPATITIS.

Index

Page number in *italics* indicates the reference is to an illustration.

A

AA, *see* Alcoholics Anonymous
Abdenour, Mike, 80
Abortion
  adolescents, 136, 248–249
  Canada, 279–280
  fetal tissue donation, 247
  HIV virus, 311
  multiple fetuses, 247–248
  pills, 275–276
  U.S. government policies, 278–279
  see also Miscarriage (spontaneous abortion)
Abscess, dental, 226–227
Abuse
  elder, 241
  see also Child abuse and neglect
Accidents
  all-terrain vehicles, 318–319
  Amtrak/Conrail collision, 260
  Goiânia nuclear radiation, 327, *329*
  Jessica McClure well accident, *315*, 316
  seat belts, 318
Accutane, *see* Isotretinoin
ACE inhibitors, *see* Angiotensin-converting
    enzyme inhibitors
Acetaminophen
  alcoholics, 77
  measles, 202
  tonsillitis, 189
Acetazolamide
  glaucoma, 215
Acid rain, 265–266
Aclovate, *see* Alclometasone
Acne
  tretinoin, 322–323
Acquired immune deficiency syndrome, 152–
    165
  Canada, 281, 328
  circumcision, 314
  colony-stimulating factor, 257
  drug abusers, 259
  heterosexual contact, 259, 327–328
  incidence, 327
  kidney disease, 290
  medications and drugs, 279
  psychological factors, 11, 301
  transfusions, 195–196, 249
  U.S. government policies, 279
  vaccines, 271
  women, 310–311
  worldwide epidemic, 166, 168, 327–328
Acromegaly
  somatostatin, 275
ACS, *see* American Cancer Society
ACT, *see* Asthma Care Training
ACTH, *see* Adrenocorticotropin
Activase, *see* Tissue plasminogen activator (TPA)
Acupuncture
  AIDS, 328
  smoking, *120*
Adalat, *see* Nifedipine
Adenoids
  ear infections, 200
  surgery, 189
Adenovirus
  tonsillitis, 189
Adolescents
  abortion consent, 248–249
  death, understanding, 213
  pregnancy, 134–143
  smoking, 123
Adoption, 42–55

adolescents' babies, 137
  alcoholism, 72, *73*
  surrogate motherhood, 248
Adrenal glands
  Parkinson's disease, 192–194, 247
  stress reaction, 6
  tumors, 147–148
Adrenaline, *see* Epinephrine
Adrenocorticotropin
  multiple sclerosis, 252
  stress reaction, 6
Aerobic exercise
  after 50, 191
  biking, 93–94
  heart rate, 93, 191
Aerosol sprays
  asthma drugs, 204–205
  ozone damage, 268
AFDC, *see* Aid to Families With Dependent
    Children
Aflatoxin
  liver cancer, 258
AFP, *see* Alpha-fetoprotein
Africa
  AIDS, 155, 328
  onchocerciasis, 270
Agent orange
  cancer, 255
Aging and the aged, 240–242
  Alzheimer's disease, 228–230
  dementia, 251
  dental survey, 325
  exercise, 190–191
  insomnia, 176
  Parkinson's disease, 192–194
  skin, 323
  sleep disturbances, 322
  teeth and gums, 325
  see also Medicare
Agriculture, U.S. Department of
  beef labeling, 308–309
  food irradiation, 221
A. H. Robins Company
  Dalkon Shield, 311
AIDS, *see* Acquired immune deficiency
    syndrome
Aid to Families With Dependent Children
  adolescent pregnancies, 137, 140
  medicaid, 277
Air pollution
  acid rain, 265–266
  lung cancer, 119
  measurement, 266–267
  ozone, 267–268
  pollen, 320
  tobacco smoke, 318
Al-Anon, 79
Alateen, 79
Albuterol
  asthma, 204
Alclometasone
  skin disorders, 299
Alcohol
  gastrointestinal bleeding control, 257
Alcohol consumption
  breast cancer, 74, 254
  heart problems, 75–76
  homeless, 316
  hypertension, 75
  miscarriage, 77
  prepregnancy, 308
  sleep apnea, 321–322
  smoking, 74
  see also Alcoholism

**Alcohol, Drug Abuse, and Mental Health
    Administration**
  AIDS, 279
Alcoholic hepatitis, 72–73
Alcoholics Anonymous, 78–79
Alcoholism, 68–79
  Canada, 282
  methotrexate, 243
Aldactone, *see* Spironolactone
Aldosterone
  blood pressure, 146
Aldosterone antagonists
  hypertension, *150*
Alfenta, *see* Alfentanil
Alfentanil
  anesthesia, 299
Ali, Muhammad, 246
Allergies
  asthma, 204
  bites and stings, 39
  food, and bed-wetting, 234
  Tucson (Ariz.) pollen count, 320
All-terrain bicycle, *see* Mountain bike
All-terrain vehicles, 318–319
Alpha blockers
  hypertension, *150*, 151
Alpha-fetoprotein
  prenatal testing, 309–310
Alpha-tocopherol
  Parkinson's disease, 193
Alupent, *see* Metaproterenol
Alzheimer's disease
  caring for patients, 228–230
  dementia, 251
  genetics, 251
**Alzheimer's Disease and Related Disorders
    Association,** 230
AMA, *see* American Medical Association
Amantadine
  Parkinson's disease, 193
American Academy of Pediatrics
  children's diet, 304–305
  circumcision, 313
American Association of Blood Banks, 195, 196
American Board of Medical Specialists, 186
American Cancer Society
  cancer incidence and death rate, 253
  lung cancer, 114, 116, 117, 123
  mammography, 254
  Pap test, 312
American College of Physicians
  methotrexate, 243
American College of Sports Medicine
  exercise after 50, 190–191
American Heart Association
  low-fat diet, 113
  stress test, 190
  Type A behavior, 9
American Home Products Corporation
  Dalkon Shield, 311
American Lung Association
  asthma, 205
American Massage Therapy Association, 15
American Medical Association
  AIDS, 126
  directory, 186
  doctors' income and workload, 283–284
  food irradiation, 221
American Medical Directory, 186
American Psychiatric Association
  diagnostic criteria, 304
American Red Cross
  blood donations, 195
American Sign Language, 62–64

Immune therapy
  neurological disorders, 252
Immunization
  measles, 201, 202
  smallpox, 172–173
  yellow fever, 173
  see also Vaccines
Immunoglobulin
  measles, 202
Implants
  ear, 261–262
Independent practice association, *see* Individual practice association
Inderal, *see* Propranolol
Indians, American
  Apache Indians, *Haemophilus* infections in, 313
  Pima Indians, obesity in, 306
Indigestion, *see* Heartburn
Individual practice association (IPA), 232, 282
Infantile paralysis, *see* Polio
Infants
  AIDS, 310
  anencephalic organ transplants, 247
  cholesterol, 304–305
  ear infections, 198
  low-fat diet, 304–305
  meningitis, 312–313
  see also Newborn infants; Prematurity
Infection
  AIDS patients, 154, 301
  ear, 198–200, 201
  gram-negative, 296
  medications and drugs, 296–297
  miscarriage, 219
  tonsillitis, 188–189
  tooth, 226
Infectious hepatitis, *see* Hepatitis A
Infectious mononucleosis
  tonsillitis, 189
Infertility
  bioethics of new reproductive techniques, 248
  Dalkon Shield, 311
  hormonal treatments, 297
  in vitro fertilization, 247
  laser treatment, 309
Inflammation
  medications and drugs, 299
Influenza
  pandemic, 174
  Shanghai-Sichuan flu, 319
Inhalers
  asthma, 205
Inheritance, *see* Genetics
Insecticides, *see* Pesticides and herbicides
Insect repellents
  backpacking, 38
Insects
  food irradiation, 221–222
  see also specific insect
Insomnia, 176–177
Insulin
  diabetes, 225
Insurance, *see* Health insurance
Intal, *see* Cromolyn sodium
Intercourse
  miscarriage, 219–220
Interferon
  cancer, 224
  colds, 263
  leukemia, 256
  multiple sclerosis, 252
Interleukin-2
  cancer, 256, 298–299
Intermedics, Inc., 292
Intertach, 292
Intestines, *see* Digestive system
Intrauterine device
  Dalkon Shield, 311
Intravenous drug users, *see* Drug abuse
In vitro fertilization, 247

Involuntary smoking, *see* Secondhand smoke
IPA, *see* Individual practice association
Ipratropium bromide
  asthma, 205
Iron
  prepregnancy supplements, 308
Irradiation, *see* Food irradiation; Radiation
Isoetharine
  asthma, 204
Isoptin, *see* Verapamil
Isosorbide dinitrate
  congestive heart failure, 289
Isotretinoin
  acne, 323
IUD, *see* Intrauterine device
Ivermectin
  onchocerciasis, 270
IVF, *see* In vitro fertilization

J

Jeffreys, Alec, *273*
Jenner, Edward, 172
Jews
  circumcision, 314
  Gaucher's disease, 272
Jobes, Nancy Ellen
  right-to-die case, 245–246
Jogging
  after 50, 191
Joint Commission on Accreditation of Health Care Organizations, 186
Joints, *see* Arthritis

K

Kabikinase, *see* Streptokinase
Kaiser Permanente Medical Care Program, 231
Kaposi's sarcoma
  AIDS, 154
Karolinska Institute (Sweden), 193
Karr, Philip, 223
Kellogg, John H., 178
Kidneys, 290–291
  blood pressure regulation, 145–146
  cell cancer, 298–299
  glomerulonephritis, 189
  methotrexate, 243
  transplants, 225
Kidney stones
  children, 290
Kirk, H. David, 47
Kligman, Albert, 323
Koch, Edward
  homeless mentally ill, 303
Koch, Robert, 174
Köhler, Georges, 223
Koop, C. Everett
  AIDS, 165
  smoking, 117
Koplik's spots
  measles, 201

L

Labeling
  cigarettes, 317–318
  food, fat content of, 113
  food, irradiated, 221, 222
  meat, 308–309
LAK cells, *see* Lymphokine-activated killer cells
Lamprene, *see* Clofazimine
Language, *see* Communication
Laparoscopy
  endometriosis, 309

La Raza Medical Center (Mexico), 194
Large intestine, *see* Colon
Larynx
  lasers, 262
Lasers
  coronary arteries, 292–293
  dental surgery, 326
  glaucoma surgery, 215
  gynecology, 309
  larynx, 262
  nearsightedness surgery, 269
  scanning ophthalmoscope, 270
Lasix, *see* Furosemide
Late luteal phase dysphoric disorder, *see* Premenstrual syndrome
LAV (lymphadenopathy-associated virus), *see* HIV
Law
  abortion legislation, 248–249, 278–279, 279–280
  Canadian drug patent law, 280–281
  drug approval, 279
  handicapped children education act, 60
  Health Maintenance Organization Act, 231–232
  nontreatment of the dying, 246
  workplace drug testing efforts, 260
  see also Congress, U.S.; Government policies and programs, Canadian; Government policies and programs, U.S.
LDL's, *see* Lipoproteins
L-dopa
  Parkinson's disease, 192, 193
Legs
  artery obstruction, 292–293
Lendl, Ivan, 83
Leningrad flu, 319
Lens (glasses)
  color change, 293–294
  sunglasses, 206–207
  see also Contact lenses
Leprosy
  clofazimine, 297
LES, *see* Lower esophageal sphincter
Lesions
  gynecology, 309
Leucocytes, *see* White blood cells
Leucovorin
  AIDS, 157
Leukemia
  interleukin-2, 256
  pesticides, 255
  second primary cancer, 255
Leukocytes, *see* White blood cells
Levobunolol
  glaucoma, 215
Levodopa, *see* L-dopa
Levy, Ronald, 223, 224
Lexington School for the Deaf, 62
Librium, *see* Chlordiazepoxide
Life-sustaining treatment
  bioethics, 244–246
Light, *see* Ultraviolet light
Lightning
  protection, 36
Linoleic acid
  dietary recommendations, 108–109
Lipoproteins, *see* High-density lipoproteins; Low-density lipoproteins; Very-low-density lipoproteins
Listeriosis
  Swiss contaminated cheese, 329
Lithotripsy, *see* Shock wave therapy
Liver
  alcoholism, 72
  cancer, 74, 224, 258
  cholesterol, 105, 110, 288, 294
  cirrhosis, 72–73, 77, 237
  glycogen synthesis, 85
  hepatitis, 236–237
  hepatomegaly, 72
  lipoproteins, 106

Photo/Art Credits